News from Marion

Marion County, Ohio
1844-1861

Sharon Moore   **Heritage Books, Inc.**

Published 1995 by

HERITAGE BOOKS, INC.
1540E Pointer Ridge Place
Bowie, Maryland 20716
1-800-398-7709

ISBN 0-7884-0343-5

A Complete Catalog Listing Hundreds of Titles
On History, Genealogy, and Americana
Available Free Upon Request

Dedicated to my descendants:
Sandie, Chris, Ali, and Cory

Reading through the Marion, Ohio newspapers for clues to the Elliott ancestors, I wished there were an index to the papers. Then genealogists like me wouldn't need to wade through pages and pages of boring articles to find what they were looking for. But then I thought—what a shame that would be! To miss those little gems of long-ago reporting I ran across while researching.

The idea for this book was thus born. Why not take the newspapers and cut out all the political writings, news from far-off places, and repetitive advertising and put what was left into a book for all to read? Genealogists could access the data by means of a complete index and those interested in Marion history—or American culture—could browse through it or read it as a whole.

Reading the articles in chronological order presents readers with stories of Marion and its people. You will come to recognize families as its members marry, have adventures or scandals, and die. Stories unfold day by day as they did for those long ago readers in Marion and you begin to feel a part of that time and that place.

I've included in this book all the items from the paper that I believe might hold clues for genealogists, including all marriages and deaths. You will also find most every article in the newspapers mentioning residents of Marion County and events happening there. In addition, I have included items of national interest that helped shape the times and anything else that caught my fancy. There is a bit of the poetry, jokes, and moral lecturing to give a taste of what those newspapers were like in those days but I could not bring myself to include much of the political writings that made up the bulk of the paper. A few advertisements are included to add some color to the mix.

The excerpts in this book are edited to a minimum. The spelling and grammar are left as they are in the original, unless minor changes were made for readability. I have not purposely changed the spelling of any name. Even when I think the paper made a mistake, I kept what they had used, rather than make a false assumption.

Genealogists—be aware that this is a tertiary source! You have not only the misspellings and misunderstanding of the newspaper editors but any of the misreadings and typos of my own that I have labored so hard to avoid.

I hope you enjoy as much as I did, the colorful, optimistic writing of some editors and are amused by the carping, baiting tone of others. You'll find that most every ethnic and religious group is insulted—but we can't change the past to make it more in line with our present-day sensibilities. May you see how much we have changed and how far we have come—and find many other ways in which nothing at all has changed!

My thanks go to Vera, Autumn, and David Elliott for helping hoist heavy equipment up to the "genealogy room." I am grateful to my parents, Fred and Marguerite Moore, for instilling in me a sense of curiosity about the world. Special appreciation goes to my best friend and husband Roger Elliott, who inspires my creativity and indulges my whims.

Sharon Moore
Anaheim Hills, California   April 7, 1995

The chart below shows the changes of name, publisher, and editor of the Marion county Whig/Republican newspaper that took place from its first issue to the Civil War. The chart also shows the issues of the newspaper that are not included in this book. The *Marion Mirror*, the county's smaller Democratic newspaper, is not included in this book.

	Publisher	Editor
May 1844–May 1847 *Buckeye Eagle*	T.P. Wallace	S.A. Griswold
May 1847–May 1849 *Buckeye Eagle*	S.A. Griswold	S.A. Griswold
May 1849–May 1850 (Not included) *Buckeye Eagle*	D. J. Bean	
May 1850–Aug 1851 *Buckeye Eagle*	Wm. C. Trimble/Henry Haldeman	Henry Haldeman
Aug 1851–Jan 1853 *Marion Buckeye Eagle*	Wm. C. Trimble/Henry Haldeman	Henry Haldeman
Jan 1853–Jul 1854 *Buckeye Eagle*	Henry Haldeman	Henry Haldeman
Jul 1854–Sep 1854 (No paper issued)		
Sep 1854–Apr 1856 (Sep 1854–Dec 1854 not included) *Independent American*	James R. Appleton	James R. Appleton
Apr 1856–Apr 1857 *Marion Eagle*	Joseph W. Dumble	Joseph W. Dumble
Apr 1857–Jun 1857 *Marion County Republican*	Joseph W. Dumble	Joseph W. Dumble
Jun 1857–Sep 1857 *Marion County Republican*	Joseph W. & S.R. Dumble	Joseph W. Dumble
Sep 1857–Apr 1858 *Marion County Republican*	Dumble & Co. (W.P. Dumble)	W.P. Dumble
Apr 1858–Jan 1859 *Marion Republican*	Dumble & Co. (W.P. Dumble)	W.P. Dumble
Jan 1859–Apr 1859 *Marion Republican*	Dumble & Co. (S.R. & W.P. Dumble)	W.P. Dumble
Apr 1859–Sep 1859 *Marion County Republican*	Dumble & Co. (S.R. & W.P. Dumble)	W.P. Dumble
Sep 1859–Mar 1861 *Marion County Republican*	Dumble & Co. (W.P. Dumble)	W.P. Dumble

BUCKEYE EAGLE.

Prospectus

For publishing in Marion Ohio, a Weekly Whig Newspaper, to be entitled the

Buckeye Eagle.

The undersigned feels convinced that the establishment of a good Whig paper in the town of Marion, at the present crisis, will contribute materially to the advancement of the Whig cause in that section of the country.

The *Buckeye Eagle* will advocate with an earnest zeal, as in a becoming temper, the true Democratic Whig doctrine. The News of the Day will also receive a due share of attention. Agricultural articles will be introduced from time to time; and a Poetical and Miscellaneous department will usually be kept up, sufficient to afford entertainment for the general reader.

The *Buckeye Eagle* will be furnished to subscribers at Two Dollars per annum. Country Produce, of most kinds, will be received in payment of subscriptions, at the regular market price.

T.P. Wallace, Publisher.

Editorial Salutation

To those about to become readers of the *BUCKEYE EAGLE*.

I take this mode of coming before you, fellow citizens in compliance with what I believe to be your wishes, and in conformity with a well-established usage, for the purpose of making a brief exposition of the principles by which it is intended to characterize this journal, and of the course I have marked out for myself as its Editor, in the promulgation and maintenance of those principles.

The *Buckeye Eagle* will be in the main, political in its character—though by no means, at all times, exclusively so. But, more particularly, in times like the present, when the two great parties of the country are drawn up in formal array against each other will this paper partake much more largely of a political, than any other character.

The principles of this journal are to be identical with those of the great Democratic Whig party of the Union.

To the advocacy of Democratic Whig Principles in the columns of the *Buckeye Eagle*, I intend to devote my humble abilities. Whigs of Marion! give us but that support and encouragement which you are able to render, and which we confidently look for and we assure you that you shall have no reason of any remissness on our part (we speak now on behalf of both Editor and Publisher) in endeavoring to present you with an interesting and valuable paper.

S.A. Griswold

May 29, 1844

Receipts for the *EAGLE*

John Cullison	$2.00
Gardner Durfee	$2.00
H.W. Baker	$2.00
A.N. Baker	$2.00
Benjamin Moore	$1.00
Abel Renick	$1.00
Charles Smith	$2.00
John Q. Lakin	$1.00
Robert Lambett	$2.00
John Zuck	$2.00
John Dumble	$1.00
William Davids	$1.00
B.C. Thomas	$1.00
Elias Reily	$1.00
John Moore, Jr.	$1.00
C. Idleman	$1.00
D.T. Fuller	$1.00
William Everett	$1.00
Alson Norton	$1.00
Hiram Terrill	$1.00
John Seibert	$1.00
Joseph Boyd, Sen.	$1.00
C. Haldeman	$1.00
John F. Clark	$1.00
H. Gorton	$1.00
Sylvester Gooding	$1.00
A.J. Williams	$1.00
John B. Rush	$1.00
S. Scribner	$1.00
Joseph Mason	$1.00
M.W. Welsh	$2.00
Thomas Bay	$1.00
William Holmes, Jr.	$2.00

Jun 5, 1844

"Annexation"

Married—In this town on the 4th instant, Mr. John W. Dickinson to Miss Elizabeth Kerr, both of Iberia, Marion county.

Jun 12, 1844

Whig Rally!

The Marion County Clay Club will meet at the Court House in Marion on Saturday next at 2 o'clock P.M. The friends of our distinguished candidates, CLAY and FRELINGHUYSEN, together with all who are in favor of *Protection to American Industry* and a *Sound National Currency* and opposed to *Free Trade, Direct Taxation* and to the EXTENSION of slave territory and the SLAVE POWER by means of the Annexation of Texas to the United States are earnestly exhorted to give their attendance on this occasion.

Jun 19, 1844

"Annexation"

Married—On the 13th instant, Mr. William Cramer to Miss Hannah Tooly, all of Salt Rock township, Marion county.

Jun 26, 1844

"Annexation"

Married—On the 13th inst., Mr. Samuel Biggerstaff to Miss Mary M. Hain, all of Pleasant township, Marion county.

Died—At his residence in Morven township, in this county, from the kick of a horse, Mr. Abner Wing, aged near eighty years. He survived the injury but a few days, and appeared to be resigned to the inscrutable decree of Providence.

Mr. Wing was a native of Dutchess county, N.Y. He had been a resident of this State some twenty years, and of this county about fifteen years. Though far advanced in life he still retained his youthful vigor of body and intellect.

"All flesh is grass."

Jul 10, 1844

Great Popular Demonstration

The recent anniversary of American Independence was celebrated in this village by the Democratic Whigs of Marion and the adjoining counties in a manner worthy of the day and of the noble cause which it commemorates.

The day was as pleasant as heart could wish. A cloudless sky was over us—and a gentle breeze bore gracefully up the splendid American Flag and beautiful streamers attached to our stately ash pole, while it imparted vigor and animation to every breast.

Early on the forenoon the sturdy yeomanry of the surrounding country began to arrive; in most instances bringing their wives, their daughters and their sons. Soon our streets were alive with warm-hearted, enthusiastic Whigs.

The main procession was formed in front of the Court House, a little before noon and moved towards the beautiful grove upon the farm of our fellow citizen J.S. Copeland, adjoining town upon the north-east. The Marion Guards, a small but well-appointed volunteer company, were stationed at the head of the column, followed by the Bucyrus Band.

The procession extended, in very close and compact order, for about a quarter of a mile in length. On arriving at the grove, the vast company were ranged around a number of tables, occupying, in all, a space of near five hundred feet in length, and loaded to repletion with the substantial viands furnished by the generosity of the Whig farmers of the surrounding country, and the citizens of our village. These tables were entirely surrounded by the dense crowd to the depth of several feet.

After the repast was concluded, the assemblage encompassed the speakers' stand, and was called to order by the President of the Marion county Clay Club, Wm. Brown, Esq. The Declaration of Independence was read with appropriate emphasis and fine effect by Dr. Henry A. True of this place. The stand was then occupied by Alfred Kelley, Esq. of Columbus who held the undivided attention of the audience for the period of about an hour and a half, in a speech of extraordinary power. Judge Carey, of Crawford county was then called for and responded in an animated speech of considerable length.

The stand was next occupied by James Purdy, Esq. of Mansfield, who dwelt at some length upon the subject of the distribution of the proceeds of the public lands. At the conclusion of an able speech of some three quarters of an hour's duration, he resigned the stand to another speaker.

The Hon. Joshua Marion of Licking County next addressed the assemblage. His speech was eminently calculated to win the attention and to draw forth the plaudits of his hearers as well from the force and pertinency of the arguments employed, as from the racy intermixture of appropriate anecdote and apt and amusing illustration with which it was plentifully spiced.

Thomas W. Powell, Esq., was then called to the stand by many voices. He promptly came forward and for about fifty minutes entertained the people with decidedly the happiest effort we ever heard from him.

During the delivery of these five speeches, which occupied a period of several hours, the utmost order and decorum were observed by the large concourse and although they were for the most part obliged to stand, yet there were but very slight symptoms of fatigue manifested.

The exercises of the day were closed by the singing of a few choice Whig songs by the Marion Glee Club; after which the crowd dispersed in good order and apparently well pleased with the manner in which the day had passed off.

The number of persons present is generally estimated at about *three thousand*. We have been told that the number of Ladies present exceeded *eight hundred*, by actual count, and we are fully satisfied that they did not constitute much over *one fourth* of the whole number of people upon the ground.

Disturbances among the Mormons
Jo Smith, the Prophet killed

The feud existing between the Mormons residing at Nauvoo, Illinois and the inhabitants of the surrounding country has at last resulted in the violent death of the leader of the former. Jo Smith and his brother Hyrum, being charged with certain offenses had surrendered themselves to the authorities, and were lodged in jail at Carthage on the 26th ult. The jail was forced open by an armed mob, and the prophet and his brother assassinated, by being shot and stabbed. We have no room for particulars this week.

Jul 24, 1844

Married

On the 22d instant, John E. Davids, Esq. to Miss Charlotte Bain, all of Marion.

Aug 14, 1844

Anti-Slavery Meeting.

The Marion County Anti-Slavery Society will meet according to adjournment, at the house of Daniel Lynn, in Claridon township on Tuesday the 20th day of August next, at 10 o'clock A.M. Come friends—come foes—come one, come all.

Allen McNeal, Rec. Sec.

Sep 18, 1844

Married

On the 17th inst., Mr. Orren Patten to Miss Laura T. Priest, both of Marion.

Obituary.

Died—In this town, on the 15th inst., Oliver Marion, son of Frederick and Matilda Ashbaugh, aged 5 years.

The deceased came to his death from the kick of a horse, received while on a visit to his grand father's in the country. The injury sustained was in the region of the liver, and he survived it but a few hours. It was only on the 28th ult. that the bereaved parents followed to the grave Orrilla Mirium, an interesting daughter in the 7th year of her age.

How inscrutable are the ways of Providence.

Another Revolutionary Hero Gone!

Died—In Richland township, Marion county, Ohio, on the first day of September, Joseph Powell, aged 101 years, 9 months and 4 days.

The deceased was a soldier of the Revolution, having at an early period volunteered in the American service, and served a great portion of the war under Washington. He was in the battle of Bunker Hill, Brandywine, Monmouth and Stoney Point; and also in a skirmish which took place at or near Pittsburgh. With the exception of a slight wound, he passed unharmed through all those courses.

Peace to his ashes.

Sep 25, 1844

Married:

On the 17th inst., Mr. Isaac C. Olds of Indiana to Miss Mary Ann Reese, of this county.

Oct 23, 1844

Notice.

All those knowing themselves indebted for Grave Yard lots will please call and discharge the same, as soon as possible, as the money is much needed for Grave Yard purposes, and further indulgence cannot well be given. Accounts are in the hands of Orren Patten, Township Clerk.

Married,

On the 3d inst., William Daley of Big Island to Miss Mary Collins, of Grand Prairie twp, Marion co.

Oct 30, 1844

Obituary.

On the 21st inst., in Marion, Gardner Durfee, aged 37 years and 9 months. His surviving friends and community in general have lost an affectionate friend and worthy citizen.

Nov 20, 1844

Married:

On the 14th instant, Mr. William Everett to Miss Electe L. Lewis, all of this county.

Nov 27, 1844

Married,

On the 27th ult., Mr. Nehemiah Davis to Miss Mary Ann, daughter of Mr. Hugh V. Smith, all of Salt Rock township, Marion county.

On the 25th instant, William Robbins, Esq. to Miss Camelia Salmon, both of this place.

Dec 4, 1844

Hymenial.

Married—On the 28th ult., M.L. Plumb to Miss Mindwell Baker, all of Marion.

Jan 8, 1845

Married,

On November 24th, 1844, Thomas Elwell to Miss Nancy Cory, all of Grand township.

On the 1st, Mr. Joseph Higgins to Miss Helen Rubins, all of Grand township.

On the 31st ult., Mr. Hiram Mills to Miss Anna H. Lake.

Died:

On the 1st inst., in Grand township, Mrs. Ruth Brownlee, wife of James Brownlee, senr. and daughter of James and Deborah Sargeant, aged 39 years, 2 months and 2 days.

Jan 15, 1845

Married,

In Marion, January 9th, George W. Hull of Delaware county, and Miss Artamissa Scribner of Marion county.

Died:

Very suddenly, at his residence in Tully township, on the 2d inst., John Parcell, Esq., aged 45 years.

Mr. Parcell retired to bed in apparently his usual health and in a short time was found by his wife to be dying. He breathed but three times after his situation was discovered.

A kind husband, an affectionate father, and a valuable and correct member of society has passed suddenly away, leaving a large circle of afflicted friends to mourn his loss. The deceased served for many years as a Justice of the Peace, and well did the title apply to him. The neighborhood in which he resided will miss the kind and judicious arbitrator who has so long reconciled their little differences without any remuneration, save the satisfaction of promoting peace and good feeling.

Jan 22, 1845

☞ We received a communication last week on the subject of the death of Mrs. Mary Wilcox of Delaware county, which without a particular examination we agreed to publish in this week's paper. On looking over it more closely, we find that such is its length and in so unintelligible a manner is it put together, containing, withal, allusions altogether unnecessary in a notice of the kind, as in our opinion, to render it improper for publication. It is, therefore, omitted, and in its place we have copied a notice of the same event from the *South Bend (Ia.) Free Press*, (a paper edited by a son of the deceased,) which is brief and appropriate.

Died:

Of dropsy, in Waldo, Delaware county, Ohio, on the 15th ult., Mrs. Mary Wilcox, consort or Mr. Hira Wilcox, and mother of the editor of this paper, aged 57 years.

The deceased had been long afflicted, but her sufferings were borne with that meekness and submission which characterizes the true christian. She died in full confidence of receiving that glorious reward which awaits the righteous. Whilst we mourn the loss of a kind and affectionate mother, we feel that our loss is her gain. She requested her friends not to mourn for her, for she was about to make a happy exchange.—*South Bend (Ia.) Free Press*.

Jan 29, 1845

Married,

On the 20th inst., Thomas Davids to Miss Mary Ann Mounts both of Pleasant township.

On the 21st inst., Mr. Eber Baker, of this place, to Mrs. Susan Wilson, of Delaware.

Mar 5, 1845

"A Word to the Wise." &c.

We take the annexed extracts from an article in the *Sandusky Clarion*, commenting upon the proceedings of the Rail Road meeting held in this place a few weeks since. We are ignorant as to the justice or injustice of the charge made against our citizens, of apathy in reference to public improvements in former days. The *Clarion* remarks:

It thus appears that the Marion people are at length aroused to the necessity of doing something for themselves. We are glad to see it, and hope they may be successful in securing the benefits to be derived from judicious internal improvements. They have at length found that "calling upon Hercules," without "putting their shoulder to the wheel," will not make the cars move in their direction. They probably have counted too much upon the importance of their position.

It was thus, we suppose, when the Sandusky and Columbus turnpike was made. They supposed their town was of sufficient size to induce the company (poor and feeble as it was,) to make the road two or three miles longer for their accommodation; yet they would not take stock to aid the undertaking, and by so doing give themselves power in the location. *Consequently*, the road was not made through Marion, and consequently the company drew upon themselves the hostility of the citizens.

Marion will be compelled to "put its shoulders to the wheel" at last.

Mar 12, 1845

Rail Road

A meeting of the citizens of Marion County is requested at the Court House, on Wednesday the 26th day of March, inst., for the purpose of taking such measures as may be deemed necessary for insuring immediate action upon the great object of constructing a Rail Road under the charter now granted us from Columbus through this county. Delaware county is awake and acting manfully her part, let us not be behind her in our efforts.

All interested and the citizens of the county in general are urgently requested to attend.

Wm. L. Kendrick	E.F. Hardy
Wm. Brown	R. Patten
T.J. Anderson	David Epler
Thos. Search, Senr.	T.R. Fisher
H.N. Wheeler	John Seibert
Thomas M. Sloan	P. Bunker

Jas. H. Godman	B.R. Durfee
John Bartram	J.J. Williams
Nathan Peters	Enos Irey
John C. Godman	Henry Hain
Wm. Bain	George Rowe
S.S. Bennett	Henry Peters
G.H. Busby	J. Selman
J.D. Butler	J.R. Knapp

Apr 23, 1845

Married,

On the 21st inst., J.W. Boyd to Miss J.M. Davids, both of Pleasant township.

Apr 30, 1845

Weather, &c.

The unusual and long-continued drought which prevailed in this region, for several weeks previous to Wednesday last, was on that day brought to a termination by a copious and refreshing fall of rain. Since that time we have been favored with frequent and plentiful showers, which have imparted to vegetation of all kinds, the most cheering and enlivening appearances, and have doubtless been productive of incalculable benefit to the growing crops.

We are informed that the wheat looks unusually promising in many places in the neighboring country, while in spots it has been severely injured by the drought. We are also told that a good deal of corn has already been planted, which is remarkably early for that operation in this part of the country.

May 14, 1845

Blackbirds and Corn.

The farmers tell us that they never knew the blackbirds to be so destructive to the young corn, as they are this season. The corn came up finely—the frost first nipped the blade, and now these black rascals are digging it up by the roots. Many farmers are obliged to re-plant quite extensively, from this cause alone.

A remedy which would be effectual in putting a stop to the depredations of this pestilent little thief on our large prairie fields, would be an inestimable public blessing.

May 21, 1845

Died:

On Thursday the 15th inst., Joseph Ross, only son of John and Lydia A. Wildbahn, aged five years and two months.

❖

On Monday the 19th inst., Aurelia Virginia, youngest daughter of John and Lydia Wildbahn, aged two years and eight months.

 Dust and wind! oh, for a big rain!

Married,

On Tuesday 13th inst., at Locust Grove, Mr. Geo. B. Smith, of Delaware to Miss Juliette T., daughter of Dr. C.H. Wetmore

May 28, 1845

The Weather— Drought—Frost— Gloomy Prospect.

The drought still continues and is unprecedented within our recollection, at this season of the year. On Thursday last, there fell what would have seemed a copious rain in ordinary times—but such was the parched condition of the earth, that its only perceptible effect was to enliven somewhat the appearance of vegetation for a few hours. A cold dry wind immediately after set in from the north, and on Friday, Saturday, and Sunday nights severe frosts occurred, which cut down, for the *third* time, a large portion of the corn and other tender vegetation which had ventured to appear above ground.

We took a stroll into the country, a day or two since, and then for the first time realized the extent of the injury, which the combined forces of drought and frost have inflicted upon the farmers' prospects. A speedy favorable change in the weather only, can save the farming interest from immense loss, and avert absolute privation in numerous instances.

Jun 4, 1845

The Weather—Again.

Since the publication of our last paper we were visited by a heavy shower of rain but while the good people of this region were felicitating themselves and returning thanks for the welcome visitation, a chilly north-easter set in, and on Thursday night every thing green that was not out of the reach of frost, was again laid out, as cold as a wedge.

The frost of that night was said by many to have been the severest of the month, and its effects were truly lamentable to behold. In some sections, even a great portion of the *wheat* is said to be irrecoverably injured, while the oats and corn are generally killed to the ground, and whether they will spring up *again* or not it is difficult for us to say.

Up to Tuesday morning (the time of writing this,) there had been no more rain, and from appearances it could hardly be told that there had been any for six weeks.

Married,

On the 31st ult., Mr. Cornelius Devore to Mrs. Anna Gaffield.

Died:

In this village, yesterday morning, the 3d instant, of scarlet fever, Platt Ralston Spencer, third son of Ozias and Lydia Bowen, aged about two years and seven months.

Jun 11, 1845

Don't Crow Too Soon!

About 10 o'clock, yesterday morning, it commenced raining, with every appearance of a steady and long continued outpouring of the so much wished for element. Some imprudent individuals unthinkingly began bragging in the public streets that "now, there was no doubt but we were really going to have a fine rain"—our wife had got the best barrel snugly placed under the spout, for the purpose of catching 'a little rain water'—and we, foolishly enough, had just digged our pen into the ink, to commence an editorial under the head of "*Joyful tidings!—Rain at last!*" Of course the rain ceased at once, and the lazy clouds passed on, mocking the wishes of us earth-enslaved unfortunates.

Now, if you want to have it rain, *for certain*, don't go to fixing up your contrivances for 'catching water,' every time you see a cloud; but continue to insist that it is not going to rain, until it has poured down incessantly for the space of eleven hours, fifty-nine minutes and a half. By that time you will be 'out of the woods,' and we'll give you leave to crow as loud and as long as you please.

N.B. While placing this in type, it is 'coming down' right merrily, but we don't believe there is going to be 'much of a shower.'

Married,

On Tuesday 3d inst., Mr. Thos. J. Sprague to Miss Anna Welchhonse, all of Marion county.

Jun 18, 1845

Died:

On the 9th inst., after an illness of 36 hours, James Mortimer, son of James H. and Ann S. Godman, aged 8 years and 10 months.

Married,

On the 12th inst., John J. Williams, Esq., to Miss Amanda S. Wilson, all of Marion.

Jun 25, 1845

Breach of Promise.

A case of this kind was tried in the Court of Common Pleas in this place last week. The parties were Mr. John Auginbaugh and Miss Louisa Fenzell, recently of Grand township, we believe. After a patient hearing, the jury returned a verdict of $1,850 in favor of Miss Fenzell, the plaintiff. The case was somewhat interesting, but we are unable to give its details.

☞ A man, by the name of Pigman, was convicted in this place last week, for passing counterfeit money. He has not yet received his sentence.

Married,

On Thursday, the 9th inst., Evan Gillespie to Miss Catherine Drake, all of Marion county.

Jul 2, 1845

☞ We are informed that in a few instances, the farmers of this county have commenced harvesting their wheat. The general opinion now seems to be that in this region the early sowed wheat will be light, while that sowed late will afford about an average yield.

Cheap Postage.

This is the first number of the *Eagle* that goes our under the new Post Office Law, and consequently when sent a distance of thirty miles or less, will be free of postage.

We publish the names of the post offices which come on the free list.

Marion County.
Big Island
Caledonia
Cardington
Cochranton
Grand
Iberia
Letimbreville
Little Scioto
Merritt's
Mount Gilead
New Winchester
Smith's Mill
Underwood's

Crawford County.
Broken Sword
Bucyrus
Chatfield
Loss Creek
Osceota
Olentangy
Poplar

Delaware County.
Alum Creek
Berkshire
Bennington
Delaware
Galena
Little Mill Creek
Norton
Patterson
Prospect
Radnor
Scioto Bridge
Unison
Westfield
Williamsville

Wyandot County.
Bowsherville
Little Sandusky
Tymochtee
Upper Sandusky
Wyandot

Hardin County.
Dudley
Kenton (probably)
Pleasant Dale

Richland County.
Gallion
Ontario

Knox County.
Chesterville
Harvest

Jul 23, 1845

Weather, &c.

The greater portion of the last two weeks has been about as hot weather as has been experienced within our recollection, and during that time this region has been favored with frequent heavy rains. The rapid growth of the corn crop within a number of days past, has been entirely unprecedented, and the late meadows have been materially benefited by the recent rains.

Died,

On the 12th inst., Eveline, youngest daughter of George H. and Eliza Busby, aged 10 years, 4 months and 11 days.

Jul 30, 1845

Died,

On the 19th instant, near Caledonia, of Inflammation of the Brain, Mary, wife of John Frederick, Jun. The deceased has left a husband and five small children to Mourn her loss.

☞ Jacob F. Hoffman, who settled in Ohio about ten years ago, will learn something to his advantage by writing to his brother, John Hoffman, Pavillion, Gennessee county, New York. Editors in Ohio are requested to notice.

Aug 6, 1845

See Here:

Will some of our subscribers bring us a few "roasting ears"?—Also, some new potatoes?—Likewise, a quantity of almost any other good garden "truck"? Not too much at a time, however. Our garden turned out very badly this season, the principal product being a choice lot of dog-fennel, with a few scattering tufts of weeds that we don't know the names of.

Died,

At Iberia, Marion county, O., on the morning of the 24th of July, 1845, after an illness of about five weeks, Mrs. Jane L. Shunk, wife of William Shunk, in the 29th year of her age.

The deceased was a daughter of Archibald Brownlee, late of Washington county, Pa. Her death was occasioned by one of the most sudden and fatal of all nervous afflictions, Palsy, which left her speechless for the last ten days of her life. She left behind a fond husband and two small children, with numerous relatives and friends by whom she was beloved and respected.

Quit That!

Persons in the habit of borrowing newspapers from the Mansion House and never returning them are requested to discontinue the practice. If you want papers to read, subscribe for them. I take papers for the benefit of the traveling public and others who may call at my house, but not to be taken away by every one who can lay hands on them.

Those having papers belonging to the Mansion House, will confer a favor by returning them. Fair play, Gentlemen is all that is asked.

A. Seitz

Aug 13, 1845

Married,

On Tuesday the 19th inst., Mr. Thomas L. Whisler, to Miss Mariah Stiverson, all of Marion county.

Aug 27, 1845

Manly Exercises.

A school is now open in this place, under the direction of Mr. J.A. Dumm, for instruction in the broad sword and small sword exercises, pugilism, and every other branch of the Art of Self-Defense. Those desiring instructions, will seldom have a better opportunity, as we know Mr. Dumm to be a competent teacher. He may be found at the American House.

Sep 17, 1845

Married,

In this town, on the 11th inst., John Holderman to Miss Harriet A. Davis, both of Grand Prairie township.

Also on the same day, James E. Williams to Miss Margaret Shaw, both of Marion township.

Sept 24, 1845

Heavy Robbery.—A gentleman, named E.C. Davidson, of Marion, Ohio, while at the Holiday Street Theatre on Friday, had a pocket book taken from his pocket, containing about $7,000.

Mr. D. is a drover and had recently sold a drove of cattle in Lancaster and the adjoining counties of Pennsylvania and had extended his trip to Baltimore to take the cars for the West, which he designed to have done on Saturday morning, and therefore, rather than deposit his money, thought he had secured it by placing it in an inner pocket of his coat. He did not miss the pocket book until he was about to retire to rest at the United States Hotel. This, though a heavy loss, Mr. D. is fortunately able to bear; it affords another warning, however, to persons not to carry money with them to such a place.—*Baltimore Sun.*

Oct 1, 1845

Died,

At Upper Sandusky, on the 16th of September, 1845, Matilda O.M. Griswold, infant daughter of Victor M. and Caroline M. Griswold, aged fourteen months.

Civil War!—Difficulties with the Mormons.

The citizens of Hancock county, Illinois, (in which Nauvoo is situated,) have taken up arms against the Mormons, with the avowed determination of driving them from its limits.

The immediate cause of the outbreak seems to have been this: An anti-Mormon meeting was held in a school house which was fired upon by a party of persons, supposed to be Mormons. No one was hurt though the door was riddled with balls. The old settlers flew to arms in all directions and at the last advises were ranging through the country, chasing the Mormons from their farms, and burning their barns and dwellings.

We think it highly probable that the Mormons have been quite as much 'sinned against,' as 'sinning.'

Oct 8, 1845

Married,

On the 5th inst., Philip Lobrich to Miss Catharine Lucas.

Oct 15, 1845

Concert of Mons. and Mad. Canderbeck.

A musical entertainment was given by these distinguished artists at the Court House on Monday evening. A large and highly respectable audience were in attendance and if the rapturous applause which broke out at the close of each piece was any evidence of their gratification, their delight was heartfelt. Mons. Canderbeck is a violinist of deserved celebrity. His lady, as an harpiste, is unequaled by any that we ever heard, and the notes of liquid melody that dropped from her fingers will vibrate upon our senses for many a day.

Nov 5, 1845

Married,

On the 30th ult., at Mt. Gilead, Dr. Silas M. Mouser, to Miss Mary Jane House.

Dec 3, 1845

The Weather.—Winter.

After an Autumn for which we do not believe the very 'oldest inhabitant' of this region can instance a parallel, for its average mildness, dryness, and pleasantness, old Winter is at length upon us, and in the very guise, too, in which we always desire to greet him. On the evening of the 26th of November, at the close of a beautiful Indian Summer day, the wind set in from the north, bringing with it a respectable snow storm. The roads in every direction being about as solid as marble and as smooth as a floor, it required but little snow to put them on order for the use of runners, which, early on the following morning, began to be put in requisition.

A day or two afterwards, there was another slight fall of snow; and on Monday morning, we were favored with about two inches more which has made the sleighing really fine, and set everybody agog in earnest for a *ride*. Such a tinkering up of old "jumpers," and such a manufacturing of new—such a searching in unknown places for the long forgotten sleigh-bells—such a demand for crockery crates, dry goods boxes, and every description of horse-flesh, hasn't been known in these diggings since—since *the last snow*, any how.

The boys have addicted themselves to hand-sleds, of which it is not uncommon to see some half dozen attached by means of ropes to the tail of a big wagon or sled loaded with 10 ½ boys to the square yard making 'a going of it' up or down the street with a prodigious rush!

And then, those glorious moonlight sleigh-rides are coming into vogue among the boys and girls 'of a larger growth'—who speed away to some neighboring village, where with light and merry hearts (and lighter heels perchance) they for a few brief hours innocently chase dull care away.

'Tis a blood-stirring, healthful sport, and we like to see it. We say, then, propel yourselves, lads and lasses, whilst you possess the stimulus of hilarious juvenility, for when you become aged and venerable—you know the rest.

Dec 21, 1845

Married,

In the city of Columbus, on the 15th inst., Mr. R.A. Knapp, editor of the *Marion Democratic Mirror* to Miss Caroline Overdier, of the former place.

☞ The *Nauvoo Neighbor* says that the Mormons have nearly two thousand five hundred wagons completed for their journey to the Pacific next spring. Many strangers are visiting Hancock county and Nauvoo for the purpose of purchasing property and they are invited to do it.

Jan 7, 1846

Information Wanted.

Jacob Siler, a German, who is insane, left the residence of the subscriber on Sunday the 4th last. He had on an old brown overcoat, blue cassinett pantaloons, coarse shoes, (considerably worn,) and a cloth cap trimmed with fur. He was seen on Monday evening about a mile and a half east of the turnpike on the Mansfield road, and was then going east.

Any person who will give information to the subscriber where he is, will confer an essential favor. If put on the right direction and told to go home, he would most probably return.

Jos. Kagg.

Married,

On the 4th inst., Joseph Neel to Miss Ellenor Gillespie, all of this county.

Jan 14, 1846

Agricultural Exports, Trade, and Statistics of Marion County.

Wheat sold	220,000 bu.
Flax seed (and oil)	1,850 bu.
Grass seeds	2,500 bu.
Butter	123,000 lbs.
Wool (from 97,000 sheep) (not all sold)	250,000 lbs.
Pot and pearl ashes, from 29 Asheries	425 tons

Imports.

Merchandise by 36 merchants and traders	2,300,000 lbs.
N.Y. salt	4500 bbls.
Hogs driven out of the county	13,000
Beef cattle	7,000
Horses & Mules, taken eastward	450
Flouring & grist mills	30
Saw mills	47
Carding machines and Mulling mills	22
Oil mills	2

Marion county in her manufactures, trade, and agricultural tonnage, must necessarily fall short of equaling some of her sister counties, whose much greater surface, older settlements, and long established facilities of river and canal transportation have greatly contributed to their present condition.

Marion county is amongst the smallest counties in Ohio; and but twenty-five years have elapsed since the first acre of its soil was sold by the General Government. Our chief market for our surplus produce has been at the Lake, seventy miles distant over a road not exceeded in badness (in wet season) by any road of equal length in Ohio. Thus situated, is it surprising that our energies and resources have, thus far, been but slightly developed? Although rapidly increasing in population and wealth, yet, when it is considered that less than one tenth of our most productive soils have yet received the plow, our agricultural productions must necessarily fall vastly short of what they are destined to be in a very few years, could we fortunately avail ourselves of Rail Road or Canal transportation.

Your committee.

Married,

In this township on the 8th instant, Mr. Martin Miller, Jr. to Miss Mahala Gunn.

Feb 4, 1846

Died,

In Marion, O., January 9th, 1846, Ann Eliza, daughter of James H. and Ann S. Godman, aged 1 year and 3 days.

Feb 13, 1846

Something New!!

There will be a meeting of the friends of Temperance—and enemies too are desired to come, if such can be found—at the Presbyterian Church, on Thursday evening, 19th inst. A general attendance is solicited. Several addresses may be expected.

Married,

On Wednesday, the 11th inst., Mr. Frisby W. Yoe, of Kenton, Hardin county, Ohio to Miss Mary Walker of Pleasant township, Marion county.

Married,

On Thursday evening, 19th inst., William Noble to Miss Barbara Cope—all of Pleasant township, Marion county.

I.O.O.F.—A Lodge of the Independent Order of Odd Fellows was instituted in this town, on Wednesday evening, the 4th inst. We understand that it takes the title of "Kosciusko Lodge."

☞ The weather, for the past week, has been unexceptionable. The snow has entirely disappeared. without the assistance of rain; the sky having been almost uninterruptedly clear, for about ten days. The birds are singing and the breezes breathe of the "sweet south," and of Spring. This state of affairs is rather out of time and season. We'll catch weather of another sort before the first of May—see if we don't.

☞ A dreadful epidemic has broken out in this vicinity within a few days and rages to an uncommon extent. The malady is known by the name of "Spring Fever." Although generally believed to be beyond the reach of medicine, yet no case has, up to this writing, proved fatal.

☞ Our 'corporosity' has for a few days past, monopolized rather more than its share of attention in the streets. Reason why:—we've been wearing our new trousers!

Fire!

On Saturday last, this village was visited by the most destructive fire which has occurred in it for many years. Between 5 and 6 o'clock, P.M., a dense column of smoke was seen issuing from the roof of the tannery belonging to our respected fellow-citizen, Joseph J. Williams, Esq.

The alarm was immediately given, and the mass of the male population of the town were soon on the ground surrounding the building. But from the location of the fire, rendering it peculiarly difficult of access, and the head-way it had already gained, it was speedily discovered that it would be impossible to save the building, and the attention of the crowd was turned towards saving such of the implements, stock, and removable property as were most convenient to be laid hold of. So rapid, however, was the progress of the destructive element, that very little was saved besides the books, the lightest of the tools, and about fifteen dollars worth of finished leather and some twenty, out of eighty cords of bark. There was an immense lot of dry hides hanging upon poles in the upper part of the building, which was totally consumed. The building itself is burned to the ground. The total loss of property will not fall much below $1000, and only $150 of which are covered by insurance.

The fire is believed to have originated in the upper loft of the building and to have been communicated from the stove chimney. It must have been smoldering for a considerable time before it was discovered. The stable of Mr. Benj. Williams, situated within a few feet of the burning building, although repeatedly on fire, was, by the strenuous and persevering exertions of the citizens, saved from material injury.

At this fire, our citizens had an opportunity of observing what a beneficial use could have been made of *one small engine*, had such an article been on hand. Water was plenty, and hands were plenty—but something was needed to throw the former a little further than the unaided hand of man could throw it.

Marion has heretofore enjoyed a remarkable exemption from disasters by fire. It may not be so hereafter. Will this late hint be lost upon our property owners?

Back Again.—At the term of the Court of Common Pleas which closed its session yesterday, Pigman, who was convicted last fall, of passing counterfeit money and sent for a four years' term to the Penitentiary, whence he was remanded back here for another trial—was re-convicted and again sentenced to imprisonment in the Penitentiary—this time for three years.

Distressing Casualty.

A melancholy accident occurred in Pleasant township, in this county, on the morning of the 16th inst., by which the wife of Mr. William Lugenbeel lost her life. The manner of her death, as it was related to us, was as follows:

Mr. Lugenbeel and another man were engaged in cutting down a large tree, when Mrs. L. approached to call them to breakfast. They warned her that the tree was about to fall, and she retired to what they all considered a safe distance. But the tree in its descent struck another, which, being dead and decayed, broke off, and fell; and this one, in its fall, reached to where the lady was standing. It struck her on the head and shoulders, breaking her skull and crushing in the bones of the shoulder. She breathed but a short time afterwards.

Apr 1, 1846

 We're in a rage. Someone has taken our umbrella from the office. Who the ____ has got it?

Married,

On Thursday evening, March 26, Mr. John M. Christian, Principal of the Marion Academy, to Miss Paulina E. Busby, daughter of G.H. Busby, Esq., all of Marion, Ohio.

❖

On the 19th ult., Mr. Hezakiah Johnson to Miss Louisa Fickle; all of this county.

❖

On the 21st ult., Mr. Archibald McFarland to Miss Margaret Carr, all of Marion county, Ohio.

Apr 8, 1846

Married,

On Tuesday evening, March 31st, Nirum C. Rundle to Miss Minerva Brown, all of this place.

❖

In Tiffin, Seneca Co., on the 2d inst., Mr. Hiram Pratt of Melmore to Miss Frances Sina Kelley, of the former place.

Apr 15, 1846

Married,

At London, Ohio, on Thursday last, George W. Sprung, Esq., formerly of this town and Editor of the *London Sentinel* to Miss Lydia C. Jones, all of that place.

Apr 22, 1846

 To cure the tooth-ache, plunge your feet in cold water. Strange, but true.

Married,

On the 16th inst., Mr. John Hess to Miss Elizabeth Malone, all of this county.

The Season.

Vegetation is coming forward as rapidly as it can, considering the extreme dryness of the weather. Plum trees, in some instances, are in full bloom, and the peach and cherry, generally, are beginning to show their blossoms.

Apr 29, 1846

Rose-Bush Stolen!

One with many branches—about 2 to 2½ feet high—wood part quite red, was stolen from near my house a few days since. I will give two dollars reward for the conviction (before a justice of the peace) of the person (man, woman or child) that stole it.

J.S. Copeland.

May 13, 1846

Died,

At his residence in Salt Rock township, Marion county, Ohio, on the 30th of April, Mr. Abraham Neff, aged 59 years, 3 months and 8 days. He was a good neighbor and a worthy citizen, and departed this life at peace with himself and all mankind.

The Mormons.

We learn from the *Nauvoo Eagle* that all the Mormon publications have been discontinued. The archives and trappings of the church have been removed and are now on their way to California. The Church has ceased to exist, the "Twelve" have gone, and with them the acting spirit of Mormonism.

May 20, 1846

Married,

On Thursday, 14th inst., Thomas Walters to Miss Mary Cunningham, all of this township.

May 27, 1846

Change of Editors.

Our contemporary, the *Democratic Mirror* of this place, has just changed proprietors. The last number contained the valedictory of the late editor, Mr. R.A. Knapp, whom our good wishes accompany in his retirement. It is announced that the paper will hereafter be under the editorial management of Mr. John B. Dumble, a young gentleman of this town, who is a good practical printer and probably otherwise well qualified for the task he is about to undertake.

We wish him every success, excepting that implied in the political ascendancy of his party.

Jun 3, 1846

Requisition for Troops.

The War Department has made requisitions upon all the States, to furnish their proportion of men to make up the force of 50,000 authorized by act of Congress for the purpose of carrying out war with Mexico.

Volunteers from Marion County.

Wednesday last, the day of the Brigade muster in this place, witnessed the largest turn out of men we ever saw in Marion. The number of recruits enlisted was 19, which has since been increased to about 30. Most of them are quite young men.

Jun 10, 1846

Movements of Ohio Troops.

At the latest date from Camp Washington, (the general rendezvous of the Ohio Volunteers, near Cincinnati) about a thousand troops had arrived there. Before that time, the greater part of the quota furnished by Ohio is on its march to that point.

The volunteers of this Division are encamped at Marysville, Union county; about 50 in number, as we are informed. Capt. Armstrong, one of the volunteers from this county, returned here on Monday last, to endeavor to obtain more recruits. We have not heard what success he has met with. The object is to form a complete company, and we believe that recruiting officers have been dispatched to the other counties of the Division with the same object.

For the Buckeye Eagle

Mr. Editor:—Will you allow me a small space in your paper to say to the "nice young men" who have recently been distinguishing themselves by the acute tricks of drawing linch-pins out of buggies, removing signs, and displacing and secreting various articles of property, that a clue to their identity is in the possession of more than one of our citizens, and that a repetition of these pranks may not be altogether safe. They may experience a species of *Lynch*-ing not quite so funny as that they have been engaged in.

I would caution them against nourishing the idea that the respectability of their connections will prevent an exposure, if the performances of Saturday night last are repeated. It is a pretty state of things when the limbs and lives of our fellow citizens are to be endangered to furnish sport for worthless loafers, *genteel* or otherwise.—That serious accidents have not already occurred is almost miraculous. Two buggies each ran a wheel off, the day after the above mentioned midnight antics, one of then breaking an axle-tree. Again I say to these nocturnal prowlers, beware—there are more eyes upon you than you are aware of.

ARGUS

Jun 17, 1846

Married,

On the 11th inst., Thomas Search, jr., to Miss Matilda C. Sharpless, all of Marion.

Independence Day!

Is there going to be any Fourth of July in these diggings? It used to come along not far from this time of the year. We should like to see an old-fashioned fourth of July once more, with its orations, dinners, toasts, &c. It is one of the worst signs of times that Americans are beginning to be unmindful of that memorable anniversary.

Afflicting Accident.—Mr. James Hattan, of Zanesville, a peddler, who has make frequent visits to this place, met with a sad calamity on the 3d inst. His horses took fright while he was rolling up the curtains of his vehicle, and ran—in the act of dragging them up by the lines, he was thrown under the wheels, which passed over both his legs, breaking one of them in a shocking manner.

Worst of all, his little daughter, who was in the wagon, was so severely injured by its upsetting, that she survived but an hour or two.

The Requisition Filled.

The complement of troops called for in Ohio was made up some days since. A great many more had volunteered than were needed, numbers of whom were on their way to the various places of rendezvous. Some of those who are rejected will thus be put to considerable inconvenience and expense, which we think should be defrayed by the General Government.

Jul 8, 1846

Married,

On Thursday morning July 2d at the residence of H.A. True, M.D., Mr. Richard H. Johnson of Lima O., to Miss Sarah H., daughter of James Reed, formerly of New York City.

On Thursday, 2d inst., Theodore A. Cross to Miss Beulah C. Mason, all of Big Island township.

The Fourth,

Was celebrated by the citizens of this place, each one pretty much in his own way. There was a general closing of stores and shops, and about as much regard evinced for the memorable anniversary as could be expected, in the absence of any concerted public celebration.

Quite a numerous party of young ladies and gentlemen devoted the day to a horseback excursion to a beautiful spot on the bank of the Scioto, some seven miles distant from this place. The cavalcade, on leaving town, presented a somewhat novel, but very gay and enlivening appearance. So many pretty ladies on horseback, in their long graceful riding skirts, their saucy looking caps with plumes waving in the breeze, and other *et ceteras* not necessary to mention, were not an ugly sight to look at, by considerable, and upwards. Had the gentlemen been but clad in suits of ancient armor, the whole might have been taken for a troop of "courtly knights and ladyes fair," of the days of chivalry, journeying—no matter whither. Having arrived at the spot selected for the purpose, a collation was partaken of, in the *pic nic* style.

We learn that the affair passed off in the most pleasant and agreeable manner, with no accidents but such as served to heighten the fun and enjoyment of the occasion.

Jul 15, 1846

Married,

On Thursday the 9th inst., Mr. Ebenezer Peters to Miss Elizabeth A. Raichley, all of this town.

Jul 22, 1846

 A report was brought to this place last night, of the death of C.J. McNulty, which is said to have taken place somewhere on his passage down the Mississippi River, with the Ohio Volunteers.

Married,

On Tuesday evening, the 21st inst., Mr. T.P. Wallace, publisher of the *Buckeye Eagle*, to Miss Jane E., daughter of Maj. Gen. H. Busby.

Jul 29, 1846

Married,

On Sunday, the 26th inst., in Marlborough township, Delaware county, Joseph Scheble, of Marion to Miss Malinda Foreman of the above place.

[With the above notice, there came a generous *loaf* of CAKE, of the richest quality, and tastefully ornamented. Our "b'hoys," and myself, while engaged in stowing away the cake, could not refrain from expressing the wish that such a wedding might take place every day! All hands unite in wishing our young friend and his fair bride a happy and prosperous journey through life. Amen.]

Death of C.J. McNulty

This well-known individual finished his earthly career on the 12th inst., at Memphis, Tennessee, after a short and violent illness. His remains were to have been buried at Helena, Arkansas, with military honors.

Aug 5, 1846

Married,

In Marion, on Thursday, July 31st, James McCully to Miss Sarah J. Merritt, all of Scott township.

On the 2d inst., Allen Ball to Miss Forrilla Terrill, both of Salt Rock township.

Aug 12, 1846

Married,

On the 1st inst., Christopher Van-Fleet to Miss Charlotte Payne, all of Marion county.

On the evening of the 9th of August, John Rice to Miss Rachael Davis, all of Iberia, O.

Aug 12, 1846

Interesting Letter.
Correspondence of the *Buckeye Eagle*.

Albany, N.Y.
July 27, 1846

Mr. Griswold:—We left Marion as you know on Monday last. A light shower the day previous made the ride quite pleasant until nearly noon, when we were much annoyed

New Spring and Summer Goods at Reed's!!

by dust all the way to the Lake. The extraordinary crops of Grass, Oats and Wheat continued their unsurpassed abundance the whole distance to the Lake.

A very pleasant ride of thirty hours took us across the Lake to Buffalo; this city continues to increase more rapidly than any I have witnessed elsewhere, unless it is Cincinnati.

Took cars to Niagara Falls and viewed the "wonders of Creation," which to my mind eye were not much more wonderful than our crops of Wheat! Wheat!! Wheat!!! We saw several Indian Squaws seated in the ground under shady trees, at the Falls, busily employed in making fancy articles of cloth and beads; small straw baskets, moccasins, cushions, &c., &c. There are several "Indian Stores," "Curiosity Shops," "Indian Museums," "Indian Collections and Manufactures," &c., &c.

Nearly every visitor had numerous specimens of "Indian art" to take as presents to his friends; about nine-tenths of which I guess were imported from Germany and France, for I am sure that all the Indians on the Seneca and Oneida Reservations would not make one-fourth of what is here sold.

On reaching Rochester next day we found Apples, Pears and Peaches in perfection and abundant. From Rochester to this place they appear to have plenty of rain and crops showed a healthy appearance. The canal boats going east were numerous and heavily laden with Flour, Wheat, Wool, Corn, Oats, Pork, Ashes, &c., &c. Those going west were very light and many entirely empty; the number of Dutch emigrants going west, which we met, were, I think about 2000 in one hundred miles.

After I have passed through New England, visited Boston and seen what them "'fernal Yankees" are doing, I may possibly write you again.

J.S.C.

Aug 26, 1846

Correspondence of the *Buckeye Eagle*

Easton, Mass.
August 10, 1846

Mr. Wallace:—I have now traveled 300 or 400 miles in "Old Massachusetts." The great number of old people one meets here is truly astonishing. I think that on about one-third of the grave stones are inscribed ages of 70 to 95 years.

A friend placed in my hands a small volume, printed in 1835, entitled, "A History of the Copelands, complied from Town and Family Records." They are remarkable for their longevity—and I take the following extracts: "Lawrence Copeland and Lydia Townsend were joined in marriage by Rev. Mr. Kibben of Boston, Oct. 12, 1651. Lawrence Copeland died at the age of one hundred and ten years." They had nine children.

Jumping 50 years ahead I take the following: Jonathan Copeland (my great Grandfather) married Betsy Snell in 1705; they had 11 children, who died at the following ages: Jonathan, 90 years; Jonathan jr., 92; Joseph, 77; Elijah, 80; Daniel 86; Ebenezer, 87; Keziah, 86; Hannah, 85; Catherine 95. The others I did not find. Several hundreds of their descendents are now living, scattered in several States.

J.S.C.

Died,

On the 12th inst., in Upper Sandusky, Mrs. Elizabeth D., consort of Elisha B. Wise.

Sep 2, 1846

Married,

In St. Peter's Church, Delaware, on the 27th ult., George W. Campbell, Esq. of Sandusky City, to Miss Elizabeth W., only daughter of William Little, Esq. of the former place.

In this place, on the 1st inst., Mr. Franklin L. Reed to Miss Harriet A. Bennett.

On the 20th ult., Hampton Wood to Miss Susannah Marsh, all of Marion county.

On the 27th ult., Mr. James Wood, to Miss Ruth Bay; all of Marion county.

Sep 9, 1846

Died,

At her residence in Mt. Gilead, on the 19th inst., Mrs. Petnanda E. McWright, wife of A. McWright, M.D., in the 28th year of her age.

By the death of Mrs. McWright, a husband has lost a fond and endearing companion, an only daughter has lost a kind and affectionate Mother, and community an amiable and intelligent friend.

Sep 16, 1846

Mad Dogs!

There was quite an excitement in this town last week, on the subject of mad dogs. A public meeting was held, at which it was resolved that there had been and were mad dogs in the town and vicinity, and that all dogs found running at large during the next thirty days should be slain.

The regular report of the proceedings we find it utterly impossible to publish for want of room. The excitement has about died away, and the dogs are again running at large uninjured—so that there is probably little need of the publication of those proceedings, even were it practicable.

Married,

On Thursday the 10th inst., at the residence of William Taylor, Esq., Mr. Charles Porter, of Marietta, O. to Miss Emily O. McAtee of Salt Rock, Marion Co., O.

[Along with the above notice, we were furnished with something wherewith to *drink the healths* of the happy parties—'twere best, perhaps, not to mention *what*, for fear of raising an excitement among the temperance folks. At any rate, all of "us" *did* drink "health, long life, prosperity and happiness" to the newly wedded pair—such of us as had conscientious scruples, taking the "pure cold water" for it, while what was left of the *wine* (there! by dad it's out!) was laid aside for cases of *sickness*. We here repeat the expression of our good wishes.

P.S. There was a case of serious indisposition in our office a day or two since. The patient is now doing well, but we are out of "medicine." (!)]

In Marion county, September 10th, 1846, Mr. Hiram Owens to Miss Satina Sprague, both of Montgomery township.

Sep 20, 1846

Died,

In the hospital at Matamoras, Mexico, on the 22d day of August, 1846, of the measles, Mr. John Orr Wallace, of Comp. C. 3d Reg't Ohio Volunteers, aged about 23 years.

The deceased was a native of the State of Vermont, where his parents, several brothers and sisters, and numerous relatives still reside. He was living in this place at the time he enlisted in the services of the United States against Mexico, and had previously for some time been a resident of the town of Bucyrus.

It will afford some consolation to his friends to know that the soothing attendance and ministrations of friendship were not wanting during the melancholy scenes that preceded the close of his existence. Mr. Albert Brown, a brother volunteer, also of this place, was his assiduous and careful attendant throughout his illness and took an active part in procuring a proper performance of the last sad offices to his earthly remains.

Thus has closed the earthly career of a noble spirit. Talented—educated—in the height of young manhood's most ardent hopes and aspirations—he has been cut off, another victim to the accursed lust of dominion which has seized upon our government.

Vaccination.

Dr. Applebaugh has just received from Columbus fresh Vaccine matter. Persons wishing to have themselves or children vaccinated, will pleas call on him.

Oct 7, 1846

Married,

On the 30th ult., James P. Gray to Miss Nancy F., daughter of George King, Esq., all of Salt Rock twp.

On the 1st inst., M.P. Bean to Miss Ursula L., daughter of David Epler, Esq., of this place.

Oct 14, 1846

Married,

On the 4th inst., Mr. Edward Cooper to Miss Emeline Miller, all of Scott township.

On the 11th inst., in Marion township, Mr. Michael Redman to Miss Martha Justice.

Oct 21, 1846

Our Paper

Has for some weeks back been occupied chiefly by political matter and advertisements. Hereafter, our space for general reading matter will be much increased and we intend to fill it with the most entertaining and useful variety in our power to command. More subscribers wanted.

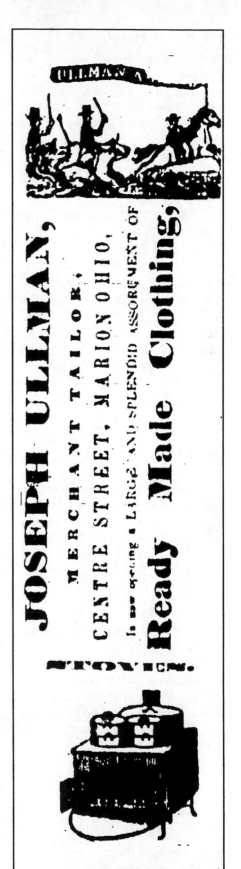

Died,

At his residence in Pleasant township, on the 5th inst., Jacob Idleman, in the 61st year of his age. The deceased was an old and highly respected resident of this county, and has left a large circle of connexions and friends to mourn his loss.

❖

Very suddenly, in Marion, on the 11th inst., Mr. John G. Clark, aged 47 years and 6 months.

This dispensation of an All-wise Providence has robbed a wife of a kind husband, a family of an affectionate father, and the community of a very worthy citizen. Peace to his ashes.

❖

On the 11th inst., in Marion twp., at the residence of N.M. Leatherberry, his son-in-law, John Fries, father of the Hon. John Fries, the present Representative in Congress from the 47th district in this State, and a worthy and much respected citizen, in the 64th year of his age.

❖

In Big Island township, on Friday morning October 2d, Mr. Peter Vanhouten, aged 62 years, 4 months and 24 days.

By a long life of benevolence and honesty, Mr. Vanhouten had endeared himself to all who knew him and his death will be a severe loss to the community.

Oct 28, 1846

Married,

In Columbus, on the 19th inst., W.A. Turney of this place to Miss Catharine E. Williams of Columbus.

Nov 4, 1846

Married,

On the 27th of October, John B. Dumble, editor of the *Marion Democratic Mirror* to Caroline E., daughter of Alexander Elliott, of Mt. Vernon, O.

❖

On Monday, the 2d inst., Mr. James Cran to Miss Electa Southwick, all of Marion township.

Nov 11, 1846

 Notices of patent medicines which appear in this paper are not editorial.

Nov 13, 1846

Died,

At the residence of his parents, in Pleasant township, on the 12th November, Jenkins J. Davids, aged 28 years, 2 months and 13 days.

The deceased although young in years departed this life with calm resignation without a murmur.

Nov 25, 1846

Married,

On the 22d inst., Moses Larcomb to Miss Antha Messenger.

Dec 2, 1846

Married,

On the 29th ult., Jacob Ulsh to Miss Elizabeth Gruber.

Dec 9, 1846

 We are requested to give notice that Rev. Samuel Allen, (formerly a resident of this town) will preach at the M.E. Church in this place, on Sunday next, at 11 o'clock. A.M.

 Persons hooking wood from our office pile, are requested to take that which is not cut for the stove. It may be well, also, to avoid such sticks as are charged with gunpowder.

Married,

On the 3d inst., Mr. Thomas A. Robinson to Miss Eliza Dickason.

Jan 6, 1846

Great Rains and Floods.

The Old Year wept itself out, and the New Year wept itself in—and such a copious outpouring of waters it was never our lot to see. From three o'clock P.M. on the 31st ult., to three P.M. on the 1st inst., not less than seven to eight inches of rain fell, as indicated by the quantity contained in vessels placed where they could receive none but that which came directly from the heavens.

The consequence has been the most disastrous freshets in the streams of this region, that have ever been known. Old residents inform us that they have never seen so much of the country covered with water.

Most of the bridges and mill-dams of which we have yet heard within twenty-five miles are swept away. The grist mill known as 'Idleman's mill,' on the Olentangy, between

Waldo and Norton, is said to be gone and the saw-mill dam, and two bridges across the same stream at Delaware have also been carried off. In every direction we hear of fences, hay and grain stores, and in some instances, hogs and cattle being swept away or submerged.

These rains and floods may be regarded as the grand finale of the Great Drought of 1845–'46.

Died,

At his residence in Pleasant township, on the 18th inst., Joseph Boyd, Sen., in the 81st year of his age.

Jan 13, 1847

The Floods.

Although the first accounts of the recent unprecedented floods were somewhat exaggerated, yet the reality has been sufficiently disastrous. The region in which the greatest rise of waters occurred appears to have included the Muskingum, Scioto, Miami and Whitewater vallies.

The streams of these vallies, with the exception of the Muskingum, reached a height much greater than ever before known. The damage down along the course of the streams, great and small, can never, of course, be fully ascertained. There is scarcely one of them, however insignificant usually, that did not, during the late overflow, sweep away or seriously injure more or less of the property of various found along its banks.

The report of the carrying away of 'Idleman's mill,' on the Olentangy, we are informed was incorrect.

Married,

On the 31st ult, Mr. George Merriman to Miss Maria J. Bowes, all of Mersailles, O.

Jan 20, 1847

Strange Discovery.

Dr. Morton, a dentist of Boston, has invented an apparatus for the inhalation of a vapor by which corporeal sensibility is suspended—so that the most difficult surgical operations may be performed without the patient being conscious of any disagreeable sensations. Experiments have been performed which satisfactorily demonstrated the adaptedness of the invention to that object. A strange discovery, truly, but not quite equal to Mesmerism.

Feb 3, 1847

Married,

On Thursday evening, the 29th ult., Mr. William Stevenson, Esq., of Marion county to Miss Caroline Piel, of the vicinity of Mersailles, Wyandot, O.

Died,

In this place on the morning of the 26th ult., Ella Imogene, only daughter of P. and R.H. Bunker, of Marion O., in her twentieth month.

Feb 10, 1847

Died,

In this town on the 1st inst., Ellen Mary, daughter of Benjamin H. and Nancy L. Williams, aged three years and one month.

Married,

On the 4th inst., James Walker to Miss Elizabeth Steverson, all of Marion county.

On the same day, in this town, James L. Priest to Miss Abigail M. Brown, all of Marion township.

Feb 17, 1847

Ireland.
Great Distress—Fever, Starvation—Deaths from Want!

Most appalling are the accounts of destitution from all parts of the country. The *Dublin Evening Post* says: "Even in the metropolis many thousands of the poorer classes are in utter destitution." Another journal says: "It is remarked as one of the strongest evidences of intense suffering, that emigration is still in progress from Sligo, even at this inclement season."

The *Mayo Constitution* publishes the reports of no fewer than eight inquests held on one day on the bodies of poor people, all of whom, according to the evidence and verdicts, perished for the want of the common necessaries of life." Another paper reports forty-seven deaths by starvation.

The Famine in Ireland.—A Loud Call upon Philanthropic!

If there has been a time during the present age when the people of all civilized nations who are blest with an abundance or even a sufficiency of the good things of this life, were called on by every dictate of humanity to contribute liberally to the relief of a suffering member of the Great Family of Nations, we think that now is that time. Old Ireland, which, while furnishing the world with the brightest examples of every endowment that adorns human nature, has endured more grievous afflictions than have fallen to the lot of any other people in modern times, has now added to the catalogue of her miseries, the appalling one of FAMINE.

In such a case as this, America—the most highly favored of nations in all respects, and at this time in the possession and enjoyment of an unusually bountiful portion of the products of her ever generous soil—is in a peculiar manner designated as the fountain whence the streams of relief are to flow.

Citizens of Marion, what say you? Shall we not forthwith devise some means by which our mite may find its way to some nook of that dearth-stricken land, and mayhap rescue some of our fellow-beings from a horrid death by starvation?

A public meeting appears to us to offer the most feasible means of rendering efficient any plan that may be adopted to effect the object to which we have been inviting attention.

Feb 24, 1847

Married,

On the 17th inst., John Snyder to Miss Catherine A. Vanorsdoll, near Mersailles, Wyandot co., O.

❖

In this town, on the 21st inst., Mr. Christopher C. Gooding to Miss Harriet Wilson.

Church for Sale or Rent!

The Lot and Building, (the Methodist Old Church.) An excellent Shop for Carriage and Wagon Maker, or Cabinet and Carpenter's Shop—large and well lighted—good dry stand, high and dry lot.

J.S. Copeland.

Also wanted, two good farm hands, of steady and industrious habits, of which I will pay cash. Those fond of running to groggeries, dancing John, drinking Whiskey and huzzahing for Folks, need not apply.

J.S.C.

Mar 3, 1847

Married,

On the 10th ult., Charles Hahn to Miss Sarah Newson, near Mt. Gilead, Marion county, O.

Relief for Ireland.

We regret to say that at present there appears to be little probability that any concerted public move in this matter will be made by our citizens. Most of those with whom we have conversed on the subject, seem disposed to regard the accounts which have reached this country in relation to the famine in Ireland as partaking too largely of the nature of "humbug," to call for their extending the hand of relief.

Without doubt, however, there are many in this community who, with us, entertain a very different opinion and who would be glad of an opportunity of contributing according to their means, to the great work of humanity which is now arousing the active sympathies of the benevolent throughout the civilized world.

For the information of such, we will state that at a great Relief Meeting recently held in the city of Columbus, an Executive Committee was appointed, whose duty it is to receive and take charge of all moneys, provisions, &c, that may be sent them and to forward them to the place of their destination.

Mar 10, 1847

Married,

On the 4th day of February, 1847 Nathan Nichols to Miss O. Buffington, all of Marion county, Ohio.

Died,

In Marion on the 21st ult., Ellmore C., son of H.W. and Elizabeth Baker, aged 12 months and 14 days.

Mar 17, 1847

 Santa Anna has issued a Proclamation to his troops in which he says their motto is—CONQUER or DIE! This may be set down to the account of Mexican bombast.

Married,

On the 10th inst., Elisha B. Wise and Sophronia S. McBee, all of Marion township.

Died,

In Marion, on the 11th inst., Henry Ellis, only son of Horace W. and Elizabeth Baker, aged 2 years, 8 months and 3 days.

Mar 31, 1847

Died,

On the morning of the 25th March, 1847, Margaret Ellen Shunk, daughter of John and Rebecca Shunk, aged 2 years and 4 months.

Apr 7, 1847

Married,

On the 25th ult., Mr. Milton Morrall, of Salt Rock township to Miss Eleanor Shoots, of Grand Prairie township.

Apr 14, 1847

Married,

On the 4th inst., Mr. Alexander A. Purvis to Miss Polly Slyter, all of Morven township, Marion co., O.

Apr 21, 1847

Married,

On the 21st Feb., Mr. John Burtsfield to Miss Nancy J. Vanmeter.

On the 5th inst., Mr. Morvin Lerch to Miss Elizabeth Buckingham.

May 5, 1847

Married,

On the 2d inst., Mr. Elijah L. Ferris to Miss Christena Kennedy, both of Mersailles, Wyandot co., O.

May 12, 1847

PUBLISHER'S VALEDICTORY.

With the preset number, the third volume of the *Buckeye Eagle* closes, and the connection of the undersigned with it as Publisher ceases. Mr. Griswold, who has had the exclusive management of the editorial department of the paper from its commencement, now takes charge of the entire establishment, and the *Eagle* will in future be published under His sole management and control.

I embrace this as a fitting occasion to return my heartfelt thanks to those who have so generously afforded me "aid and comfort," in the prosecution of the enterprise of publishing a Whig newspaper in this place.

With sincere wishes for the health and prosperity of the patrons of the *Eagle*, as well as of the *Eagle* itself, and hoping that they may continue to afford each other sustenance, pleasure and instruction, I here resign the affairs of the establishment into the hands of my successor.

Respectfully,
T.P. Wallace.

May 19, 1847

To the Patrons of the *Buckeye Eagle*.

By the announcement made last week, you were made aware that the undersigned was to assume the entire control of this paper with the publication of the present number.

The grand secret of the excellence of a newspaper lies in the support which is given to it. As a general rule, a paper will always possess and exhibit a degree of merit corresponding to the liberality of the support which it receives.

There is a very mistaken idea generally prevailing among newspaper subscribers, relative to the profits of this business. Four or five hundred subscribers, at two dollars each, seem to many of them amply sufficient to enable the Publisher to *coin money*, almost; but we can assure them most positively, that five hundred paying subscribers to the *Eagle* would not begin to justify the carrying it on, in the absence of the income derived from job-work and advertising.

The word advertising, reminds me of another matter: The large space in the *Eagle* occupied by advertisements has been the cause of a good deal of complaint. It is true, this is an objection which has some weight— but consider, friends, what would you have the poor Publisher to do?

In the first place, he cannot get along without the revenue which he derives from this source. In the second, he cannot be so rude and uncourteous as to reject the favors of his advertising friends, and shut his columns against them. Would you rather be entirely without a paper published in your county, than to have it occasionally rather overladen with your merchants' and mechanics' notices; notices in relation to public matters and local enterprises of all sorts; those relative to settlements of estates; relative to public sales of property by legal officers of private individuals; the various kinds of legal notices of your lawyers, &c, &c, all of which are of great importance to some?

However, I intend to give the patrons of the *Eagle* as little ground for complaint on this score as possible. The advertisements will be compressed into the smallest space compatible with justice to the advertisers; and in the portion of the paper allotted to ordinary reading matter, I shall use a greater proportion of small type than heretofore. My aim shall be to make the *Eagle* deserve the support of the citizens of this county, whether it receive it or not.

I look confidently to the friends of the Whig cause, and to those who desire to see the *Eagle* continue to flourish and prosper, with increasing vigor and capacity for usefulness, for substantial encouragement and assistance in my endeavors.

Respectfully,
S.A. Griswold

Painful Occurrence.

On Friday morning last, the field-piece which has for some months been kept in this place being about to be removed, it was proposed to fire a few rounds before it was taken away. Accordingly, a small company of our citizens took the cannon a short distance east of town, and after firing five rounds, the piece went off while Mr. William H. Wallace of this place, was in the act of ramming the charge for the sixth.

By this sad mishap, Mr. Wallace received a most severe injury and his escape from instant destruction seems almost miraculous. His right hand was partially blown away, and so awfully shattered as to render it necessary to amputate the limb above the wrist. From the estimation in which the young man is held in this community, the event ex-

cited a general and profound feeling of sorrow; and he has the warmest sympathies of all who know him, in view of the misfortune with which he has been visited.

Married,

On the 27th ult., A.D. Matthews to Miss Jane E. Roberts, all of this county.

On the 10th inst., in Richwood, Union county, Rev. John Burgess of the North Ohio Conference to Miss Sarah E. Gray, of Marion county, Ohio.

Died,

On the 5th inst., at the residence of her son-in-law, O.R. Stone, Esq., Mrs. Hannah Leffingwell, aged 86 years.

The deceased was born in the state of Rhode Island and emigrated to Ohio sixteen years ago. During her residence in this place, she had endeared herself to all who knew her, and her death is regretted by those who have been the recipients of her favors.

May 26, 1847

Married,

On the 13th inst., Mr. Adam Harsh to Miss Mary Dunbar, all of Pleasant township, Marion county.

Jun 9, 1847

Coroner's Inquest.

An inquest was held over the bodies of two young men supposed to be about twenty-one years of age, near Groveport in this county; they had only been at the Grove a few days, employed by A.M. Burgis in a brick yard as laborers.

Their clothing was chiefly country made linsy or jeans, they were about an ordinary size, freckled, with rather sandy hair. They told Mr. Burgis they came from Marion county, and in a memorandum book found in their pocket book, the names of Adam Wolf and Benjamin Nichols were found, also on a pocket Testament in their clothes the name of Adam Wolf was found.

It was supposed they had went in to bathe, and not being acquainted with the water, they got in where they could not swim.

For any further information required by the friends of the deceased address the undersigned or W.H. Rarey at Groveport.

H. Howard, Coroner
Columbus, June 3d, 1847

General Intelligence

It is singular what wrong view men have of the rate of pay. A clergyman will receive his $1,500 and $2,000 and the Judge his $3,000 and the book keeper his $1,000 per annum, while the mechanic who works twice as hard as any of them is thought to be extravagantly paid if he gets $500 per annum.

Died,

At Worthington Ohio, on Monday morning 31st of May, ult., Ruth Griswold, relict of Ezra Griswold, formerly of Simsbury, Hartford county, Connecticut, in the 80th year of her age.

The family of the deceased immigrated to Ohio in the fall of 1803, arriving at Worthington, then a dense forest, on the 29th day of October, and *occupying the first cabin ever inhabited by a white family in that town.*

She continued to reside in that pleasant village to the time of her death, venerated and beloved by her friends and relatives and highly respected by all her acquaintances.

Jun 30, 1847

Died,

In this town, on the 19th inst., Lydia, consort of Hon. Ozias Bowen, and youngest daughter of Eber Baker, Esq., aged 30 years, 10 months, and 2 days.

Married,

On the 24th inst., Noah Gillespie to Miss Emeline C. Owens, of Montgomery township.

Advantages of Bathing.

Let me remind my readers of the importance of washing off the impurities which the circulation of the blood is continually depositing upon the human surface, since all this pernicious filth is subject, if left there, to be taken up again by the absorbents, to the manifest prejudice of health and life. This is the grand cause of the various and fatal diseases of summer, its mildest effect being, the debility which renders that season so uncomfortable.

Apart from the benefit to health, the physical enjoyment of a bath should tempt its constant use.

Jul 7, 1847

Married,

On Thursday 17th ult., at the residence of Aviah James, William T. Toben, of Rappahannock county, Va., to Miss Susannah James, formerly of Muskingum county.

Jul 14, 1847

Married,

In the city of Philadelphia, on the 16th ult., Dr. Wm. R. Applebaugh, of this place and Maria W. , daughter of the late Rev. Samuel Hanse, of the former place.

On the 4th inst., Hugh C. McGaven of Mersailles, to Miss Martha J. Sinderman, of Sandusky Plains.

On the 11th inst., Adam Shrock to Miss Martha Blocksom, both of Marion county.

Jul 21, 1847

Married,

On Thursday the 13th ult., Mr. George Barnet to Miss Hannah E. Dutton, both of this place.

Died,

At the residence of her mother in Delaware, on Wednesday evening the 14th inst., after a protracted illness, Mrs. Mary M. McKibbin, consort of James McKibbin, and last surviving daughter of Thomas Butler deceased, in the 27th year of her age.

Dying of consumption, she lingered for months with too little of life to bind her affections to it; and without a murmur or complaint bore those afflictions which were just enough to prepare her for that rest which the world cannot give.

Aug 4, 1847

Obituary.

Andrew Kerner of Marion county, Ohio departed this life in peace, July 27th 1847, being 47 years of age. He obtained regeneration by faith in Christ at an Indian Camp meeting at Upper Sandusky about twenty-three years ago. A few days afterwards he was received into the Methodist Episcopal Church in the vicinity of his residence, in which he continued an exemplary member until his death.

His life was terminated by Bilious Fever. He left a pious consort, five children, and numerous relations and friends to mourn his departure.

Aug 18, 1847

Died,

On the 10th instant, in St. Mary's, Mercer county, O., Dr. Wm. J. Mouser, formerly of this place.

The Lightning Line.

The Magnetic Telegraph being now in full operation to Columbus, it is a possible thing to receive intelligence at this place from New York city in twelve hours! or only the time required to convey it from Columbus hither by the ordinary modes. Had we a daily mail from Columbus to this place, we, here in Marion, would always be in possession of the important events of the day before yesterday, and many of those of yesterday, in the principal Atlantic cities. It is difficult to realize that such is the fact, yet it is no less wonderful than true. This is indeed an age of wonders.

Sep 1, 1847

Died,

In Claridon township, On Sunday, August 5th, Susannah R., consort of Jos. M. Strawbridge, in the 34th year of her age.

In this township, on Sunday the 29th ult., Martha, consort of John Anderson, formerly of Fairfield county in this State, in the 39th year of her age.

Sep 15, 1847

Died,

In Marion Ohio, on the 7th instant, Margaret, consort of Thomas Henderson, in the 46th year of her age.

Sep 22, 1847

Died,

At his residence near Mt. Gilead, on the 13th instant, of bilious fever, after an illness of five days,

William Loren, in the 54th year of his age. The deceased was a native of Washington county, Pa.—emigrated to Ohio and settled at Mt. Gilead in 1834.

He was a worthy, enterprising and highly respected citizen, and has left a wife, several children, and a large circle of friends to mourn his loss.

At his residence in Marion township, on the 8th instant, Samuel McPherrin, Sen., aged 71 years, 6 months, and 19 days.

In this township, on the 13th instant, Solomon Uncapher, in the 48th year of his age.

Sep 29, 1847

William H. Wallace.

Mr. Wilson has held the office of County Treasurer some fourteen years, was first elected by Whigs, and has always been supported by many of the best Whigs of the county. But can he reasonably ask any further support at their hands? We respectfully urge that he cannot.

Through the aid of his office, in a great degree, he has secured a competence of this world's goods, and there is not the slightest impropriety in his making way for the young man whose name heads this paragraph; one who is equally honest and capable, whose pecuniary resources are quite limited, and whom a sad misfortune has disabled from earning a livelihood by manual labor, which we know he would be only too glad to be able to do, and the ability to do which, were he again in possession of it, he would not exchange for all the offices the people of the county could bestow upon him.

It depends upon the Whigs whether a political opponent, who has been enriched by a long continuance in the office, shall still hold it, or a good Whig, to whom misfortune and narrow circumstances would render it a peculiar and essential benefit, while the interests of the public would be as strictly guarded and taken care of as under the present arrangement of affairs.

We entreat those Whigs who may have it in contemplation to vote for Mr. Wilson as an act of personal friendship, or for any other reason, to weigh the whole circumstances before they do so, and answer to their consciences the question: "Is it your duty as a Whig and as a man, to take this step?" We have no fears of the result.

Married,

On the 23d inst., in Marlborough Township, Delaware Co., Mr. Isaac Stratton to Miss Rachel Houseworth, all of said township.

Oct 6, 1847

Died,

On Tuesday, the 28th of September, at her residence in this place, Mrs. Sarah Ann Lumbert, consort of Robert F. Lumbert, and daughter of Benjamin and Margaret Herbert.

The deceased was born in Wales in the year 1820, and emigrated with her parents to the United States in 1824, and settled in Radnor Township, Delaware county, Ohio. She was united in marriage with Robert F. Lumbert on the 20th day of December, 1842.

When some 16 or 17 years of age she professed religion and united with the Baptist church, of which her parents were members, and some four or five years since she united by letter with the Methodist Episcopal church, of which she remained an acceptable member.

After suffering with Bilious intermitting fever for some ten days, she died in peace, leaving her husband and an infant babe about 15 months old, with many relatives and friends to mourn their loss.

On Wednesday, she was removed to Delhi, Radnor township, Delaware County, where a funeral discourse was pronounced and she was entombed beside a sister who had deceased some time before her. May her husband and friends follow her pious example.

Rail Road.

We fear that our leading Capitalists are not sufficiently impressed with the importance of exertion at this time, in favor of the location of the contemplated Rail Road. A few years hence and Marion will be a place that "was, but is not," if the route selected passes us by on the other side. Marion now has degenerated into a three times week empty coach, and one must see that no distant day will see us deserted by stages, travelers, and a great portion of the trade we now posses, unless prompt action be had. Now is the time. The chance once neglected is gone forever!

Oct 13, 1847

The Election.

Unwelcome as the task is, we have to announce this morning that the Whigs have met with a Waterloo defeat in this county. The locos have elected their entire ticket by majorities ranging from 150 to 300 and upward.

Married,

In this town on Tuesday evening, the 12th inst., B.F. Clark to Miss Tabitha D. Williams, all of this place.

Oct 27, 1847

Married,

In this town on Tuesday the 26th inst., Mr. William Heese to Miss Caroline Grassley.

Nov 10, 1847

Married,

In Delaware on Thursday evening, 4th inst., Mr. Chauncey Hills to Miss Margaret C., daughter of Hon. H. Williams, all of that place.

Died,

In this place on the 30th ult., Mrs. Laura Patten, consort of Orren Patten, Esq., in the 25th year of her age.

A long residence in Marion had endeared her to all—to the young and old, the grave and gay, she was equally dear.

Nov 17, 1847

Married,

On the 4th inst., Mr. Jacob Lee to Miss Tabitha Jane Thompson, both of Salt rock township.

On the evening of the 10th inst., A.P. Lockwood to Miss Amanda S. Sloan, both of this place.

Died,

In this place on the 16th instant, Hon. Joseph J. Williams, aged 33 years, 5 months, and 17 days. The funeral will take place tomorrow (Thursday) at 10 o'clock A.M.

Judge Williams was one of our worthiest and most respected citizens. After a protracted and distressing illness, he died in the full triumph of faith, leaving an inconsolable widow and an interesting family of young children to mourn their bereavement.

Nov 24, 1847

For the *Buckeye Eagle:*
Marion County Bible Society.

At a meeting of the Board of Managers of the Marion County Bible Society, auxiliary to the American Bible Society, held in Marion October 6th, 1847, the undersigned were appointed a committee to address the citizens of the County, on the subject of immediately making suitable efforts to supply all the destitute families and youth of the county, with the word of God.

It is the object of the American Bible Society to give a wider circulation to the Holy Scriptures and the only copies to be circulated are of the version now in common use. It is proposed to furnish every family in which there is not found a whole Bible with one, and every youth under sixteen years of age, who can read, with at least a New Testament. This will be done by making a donation in part or in whole, of a Bible to every family in which there is not a whole Bible, and in which there is no member who is able and willing to purchase one for its use.

Such are the facilities of the American Bible Society for publishing that they can furnish Bibles and Testaments cheaper than any other book establishment in the United States.

In order to accomplish this desirable object, the County Society has ordered some four hundred dollars worth of Bibles and Testaments, which will be in the depository in Marion within a dew days. The County Society has also appointed a County agent, Rev. Wm. K. Brice, whose duty it is, by organizing auxiliary societies in every Township in the County, to endeavor to raise funds sufficient to supply the destitute families and youth of their respective Townships and to explore the entire County by visiting every family supplying their Biblical wants, by sale or donation, as he best can.

It would, perhaps astonish every citizen of the County, to know the number of families there are, in which there is neither a Bible nor a Testament, and whose members are either unable or unwilling to purchase one. The ladies of Marion have formed a society, auxiliary to

the Marion County Bible Society and have undertaken to visit all the families of the town of Marion, and to supply their Biblical wants.

H. Whiteman
H.A. True
B. Wall

Married,

On the _____ inst., James Bolton to Miss Emily Jane Shriner, all of Marion county.

In Letimbreville, on the 18th inst., Mr. John Swigart to Miss Dorliska S. Price.

Dec 1, 1847

Public Notice.

There will be a petition presented to the Legislature of Ohio at their next session, asking for so much of Marion county to be attached to Delaware county, as lies south of a line drawn east from the northeast corner of Union county and west of the course of the west line of the seventeenth range United States Military Survey in Delaware county.

Died,

In Upper Sandusky, on the 14th ult., after a short illness, Mr. John Hamlin, in the 54th year of his age.

Human Skeleton Found.

On the 21st of last month a large portion of the bones of a human skeleton was found in the woods, in Richland township, in this county, out 10 miles from Marion, by Jonas Dipard, Daniel Sult, and Samuel Mansur. They were induced to make search for these bones, from the fact of Mansur having picked up the skull, in the vicinity where they were found, while out hunting a few days previous.

Along with the bones was found a gun, a cane, and several other articles, (among then two pint flasks,) identified as having belonged to one Alexander Hughey, an old man, a pauper, who resided in that neighborhood about a year since.

He started out with his gun, &c., the day previous to the first of January last, and not returning, it was supposed he had gone to a sister's who resides in Fairfield county, (as he had frequently talked of doing.) so that no apprehensions for his safety were felt and no search made.

He was a man of intemperate habits, and there can scarcely be a doubt that the bones now found are his. The poor wretch evidently perished from exposure to the severity of the season, assisted doubtless by the contents of the flasks found with his remains.

The bones were collected and buried by the individuals who found them.

Dec 22, 1847

Pardon.

Notice is hereby given, that a petition will be presented to his Excellency the Governor of the State of Ohio for the free pardon of Nathaniel Pigman, a convict in the Penitentiary of this State, from the county of Marion, Ohio, after the expiration of 30 days.

Jan 5, 1848

Married,

On the 26th ult., Mr. Joel M. Evans to Miss Susan Hain, all of Pleasant township, Marion county.

On the 30th ult., James Burnison to Mrs. Rachael Courts, all of Marion county.

On the 2d inst., Mr. William O. Barnett to Miss Hannah Smith, all of this town.

"Chicken Pox," "Varioloid," &c.

There are a few cases in town of a disease about which there seems to be a great contrariety of opinions. We have heard one physician express decidedly the opinion that it is Varioloid, (a modification of small-pox to which persons who have been vaccinated are liable,) while others say it is only Chicken pox. "When Doctors disagree," it is not for us to decide—but we are altogether incredulous as to the complaint's being in any degree akin to the small-pox. Whatever it be, it has been quite harmless (to life) in this place, as yet.

Highly Important!

There are a number of persons with whom the subscriber has had dealings from one to six years previous to the 15th of last April. All those he wishes to see immediately, as he has important information to communicate to them.

T.B. Fisher

Jan 12, 1848

Married,

In Green Camp township, of the 6th instant, Mr. William N. Fish to Miss Jane Humphrey.

Died,

In this town on Tuesday this 11th instant, Margaret Elizabeth, daughter of Henry and Amy Warner, aged six years.

Jan 19, 1848

Married,

On the_____ instant, Mr. Jacob Jones to Miss Ann Clay both of Marion township.

Jan 26, 1848

Health of Marion,

We regret that it is our duty to state that our town is not yet free from the disease of which we spoke in our paper of the 5th inst. Within ten days past, several new cases have occurred in different parts of the town, and the utmost caution is requisite to prevent its spreading further. The greatest number of cases up to this time have been comparatively mild, and but one death has occurred out of perhaps twenty cases in town.

Died,

On the 17th inst., Katharine, daughter of William and Magdlene Davids in the 16th year of her age.

Married,

On the evening of Wednesday the 19th instant, Mr. E.P. Copeland of Carey, Wyandot county to Miss O.P.H. Norton, daughter of Dr. Alson Norton, of Big Island.

Feb 2, 1848

Married,

On the 23d instant, Dr. Jacob Booth, of Letimbreville to Miss Barbara R. Thomas of Marion.

Feb 16, 1848

Died,

On Friday the 11th inst., at the residence of his father, Judge Samuel Irey, in Claridon Township, Marion county, Ohio, Mr. Charles Hamilton Irey, aged 18 years and eight months.

The deceased was a dutiful son, an affectionate brother and an agreeable companion. His moral habits were good; his deportment honorable; and he was already an ornament to society.

A funeral discourse was delivered on last Sabbath by the Rev. H. Whiteman to a very large, attentive and deeply affected congregation, after which his remains were followed by a very large procession to Caledonia, where his body was entombed.

Married,

On the 10th instant, Jacob Young to Miss Mariah W. Graham.

Feb 23, 1848

"Cold Plague."

A disease has made its appearance in the vicinity of our town, (proving fatal in two or three cases, thus far,) which we suppose to be identical with that which is raging in some parts of the State by the name of "Cold Plague," and in others by that of "Spotted Fever."

One of our most experienced Physicians informs us that it is the same in character with a malignant epidemic which prevailed in Western New York, in the winter of 1812–13; and has furnished us a statement of the symptoms of one of the cases under his charge, the substance of which we publish:

The patient was first attacked with a severe chill, followed by fever, violent pain in the head and stomach, nausea, vomiting, and coldness of the extremities. At intervals there was a tremor or shaking of the whole body, though unaccompanied by any complaint of chilliness. Livid spots appeared upon one of the legs, which were painful, and the color of which occasionally changed to a scarlet red. Delirium supervened a few hours after the attack, after which it was impossible to get the patient to swallow any liquid. The tongue appeared almost natural for the first 24 hours, after which it assumed rather a dark brown color. There appeared to be some inflammation and swelling of the throat; the tonsils and uvulae were also affected.

The same medical gentleman informs us that the most efficacious mode of treatment of this disease is to bring on reaction, which can only be done by inducing copious perspiration. The most prompt and energetic means at hand for that purpose, would be at once resorted to in case of an attack, where medical aid cannot immediately be procured. The disease is said not to be contagious.

Morrow County.

A report was brought to town yesterdays, that the bill to erect the county of Morrow has passed the Senate on Monday, and became a law. Some twenty odd rounds of artillery were heard yesterday forenoon, in the direction of Mt. Gilead, which gives a color of plausibility to the report. We trust it may prove true.

Mar 1, 1848

$125 REWARD!

Mr. Editor: On the night of the 3d of February, 1848, the Barn of James McKibbin in Washington township, about 4½ miles north of Gilead, and about 5 miles south of Iberia, was fired by an incendiary, and entirely consumed. Damage about $500.

The citizens of Iberia and vicinity offer a reward of one hundred and twenty-five dollars to any person or persons who will give such information as will lead to the detention and conviction of the persons or persons guilty of the incendiarism.

JUSTICE.

The Treaty of Peace.

The vague and contradictory rumors in relation to a treaty of peace with Mexico, which have been rife throughout the county for several days past, have at last assumed the form and impress of authenticity. The terms of the Treaty as we dimly understand them, are, the establishment of the Rio Grande as the boundary between the United States and Mexico, and the cession by Mexico of the Provinces of New Mexico and Upper California to the U. States, and the payment by the United States to Mexico of a compensation therefore, say Fifteen Millions of Dollars.

Mar 22, 1848

Married,

In Allegheny City, Pa., on Wednesday, 15th instant, Maj. W.M. Hardy to Miss Kate, daughter of Lewis Peterson, Esq.

❖

In this town, on Wednesday, the 15th instant, Hon. Olias Bowen of Marion, Ohio to Miss Eliza M. McIntire.

❖

On Wednesday, the 15th instant, William Conkright to Miss Rachel Mounts, all of Pleasant township, Marion county.

A Promising Artist.

We visited with a friend, a few days since, the room of Mr. V.M. Griswold, a young and promising artist in our city. Mr. G. is a self-taught, intelligent, modest young gentleman, and we predict for him, when he shall have studied more and gathered the assistance of experience, a wide-spread fame.

A landscape which he had nearly completed, attracted our deep and long attention. We have seen no better points in the very best pieces, by our very best artists; yet the picture was not faultless, by any means. Several other pieces and a portrait

we saw in the room, which are remarkable, considering that the young artist is from the interior of our State, and has never had the advantages of comparison and instruction.

We hope our citizens who delight to patronize promising and worthy yon men, will call at Mr. G.'s room.

Peace!

The Ratification of the Treaty of Peace with Mexico affords some grounds for believing that our country is about to be delivered from the miserable plight into which she was wickedly forced and has been kept for two years.

Died,

In this place, March 10th, 1848, Luella Helen, infant daughter of Rodney and Princess Spalding, aged seven months and ten days.

Suicide.

Mr. Daniel Eustice, of this township, committed suicide in our Jail, on last Wednesday, by hanging himself with a bed cord. He had been insane for several weeks and was placed in jail for safe keeping, until he could be received into the lunatic asylum at Columbus. His body was warm when discovered, but was cut down too late to save life. We understand he had a wife living in Penn'a. Of the cause of his insanity we have not been advised.—*Mirror.*

 Nor have we. We only know that the deceased was a very intemperate man, up to the time or nearly so, of the attack of insanity during which he put an end to his own existence.—Ed. *Eagle.*

Mar 29, 1848

Died,

On Friday the 24th inst., at the residence of her son Benjamin Kerns, of this county, Mrs. Sarah Kerns, relict of Benjamin Kerns, of Ross county, Ohio, in the 60th year of her age.

Apr 5, 1848

 The fare for passengers on the Mad River and Lake Erie Railroad, from Cincinnati to Sandusky City, is $7.

Died,

In this town on the 31st of March, 1848, Joseph T. Hardy, in the 81st year of his age.

Apr 12, 1848

Married,

On the 2d inst. Mr. Willard Rosa to Miss Elizabeth Jones, all of Pleasant township Marion county.

Apr 19, 1848

 The N Y Sun predicts that the next news from Ireland will tell of insurrections never to cease or abate until her freedom is attained.

May 10, 1848

Died,

On the 27th ult., in Pleasant Township, Mary Louisa, daughter of John D. and Susanna Robison, aged one year, ten months, and thirteen days.

May 17, 1848

Married,

On the 4th, Mr. John Huggins and Miss Mariah Maiz of Marion County.

May 31, 1848

Married,

On the 24th in Marion, Mr. James B. Robinson of Kenton and Miss Helen May Staulding of Marion.

Fire Engine.

The Town Council of Marion here within a few days procured a handsome and powerful Fire Engine. A Company has been formed and organized. We are informed that an Engine House and suitable cisterns are to be constructed as speedily as possible. A good move for Marion.

Jun 7, 1848

Died,

In Portsmouth on the 19th, George Griswold Burr, son of Rev. E. and H.G. Burr.

Jun 14, 1848

Married,

On the 11th instant, Mr. Daniel F. Freeman and Miss Nancy Biggerstaff, all of Pleasant township.

Died,

Ellen Mary Thew, only daughter of Joseph and Mary S. Thew, aged 3 years, 8 months.

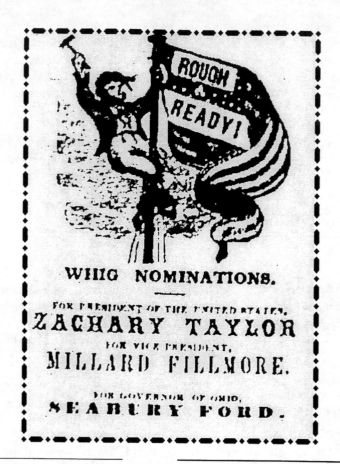

WHIG NOMINATIONS.

FOR PRESIDENT OF THE UNITED STATES.

ZACHARY TAYLOR

FOR VICE PRESIDENT,

MILLARD FILLMORE.

FOR GOVERNOR OF OHIO,

SEABURY FORD.

Absquatulated.

On the 11th instant, a light gray four-year old mare strayed from the pasture of the subscriber in Marion and has not been heard of since. Any person furnishing information of the said animal will be liberally rewarded.

T.B. Fisher

Jun 28, 1848

Lost.

The subscriber has lost the first volume of Bell's Anatomy. Neighbors will you be so kind as to examine your books and if you find said volume, please return it to the office.

T.B. Fisher

Jul 12, 1848

Shocking Affair.

A most melancholy tragedy was enacted in Grand Prairie Twp, some four miles north of this place, on Monday last, the actors were young boys, one of whom, aged about six years, came to an untimely and violent death by the hands of one of the others.

The particulars of this most lamentable occurrence, as we have heard from different individuals, vary somewhat; but as near as we have been able to gather, the facts are, that two or three lads of a family named McWherter, went to the house of a neighbor named Leach, whose family were mostly absent from home. Alva Leach, the deceased, however, was there when the other boys came up. One of the McWherter lads, about eight or ten years old, then attempted to take down a gun which was hanging up somewhere on the premises; when the Leach boy told him not to do it, as the gun was loaded. The other declared his determination to get it down, at all hazards; threatening, at the same time, to shoot the boy who remonstrated against his attempt. He succeeded in getting down the gun, which he immediately cocked, presented it at Alva, and fired, shooting him directly through the head. The latter fell and expired instantly, with scarcely a struggle. He was buried yesterday.

These particulars may not be entirely accurate; but they are as nearly so as our information has enabled us to give, and they are probably, in the main, not far from correct. The principal discrepancies in the accounts we have heard, are with regard to the ages of the boys—some placing them as high as 8 and 14 years.

Such a deed, in one so young, seems almost too unnatural for belief; and its consequences, we should think, must overwhelm both the families concerned, with anguish indescribable.

___

Milk-Sickness

Within a few weeks we have heard of several deaths in different parts of this county, from the above disease. In the family of Mr. A. Cope, residing six miles south of this place, seven persons were attacked with it, three of whom have died, and some of the others are said to be still in a precarious situation, though on the mend. We have been informed that some 10 or 12 years since in the same neighborhood, eight person, of a family of ten, died of this disease, within a period of about a week.

Married,

On the 2nd, Mr. William Kraner and Miss Elizabeth Romoser, all of Pleasant Twp.

On the 2nd, Mr. Samuel Ulsh and Miss California, daughter of James Likens of Scott Twp.

___

Jul 26, 1848

Suicide.

A man who has been confined in Jail in this place for some time past, committed suicide on Friday evening last, by opening his jugular vein with a spring lancet. When discovered, at about dusk, he was quite dead.

The act appears to have been perpetuated after the most cool and deliberate preparation. The deceased (who we understand was a physician) sent out, on the afternoon of his death, and procured a lancet and a small looking glass. Having attached the glass to the wall of his cell by means of a pen knife, and placed an empty barrel in a convenient position to rest his elbow upon, he appears to have seated himself before the glass, and applied the lancet to the side of his neck with such precision and skill as to produce an effusion of blood which doubtless caused his death in a very few minutes. Several letters, which he had addressed to his friends and relatives were found in the cell.

Among them were one to his wife (residing in the county of Richland, we are told) and one to the sheriff of this county. In the latter (which we read and which was exceedingly well written) he briefly alluded to the reasons which led him to commit the rash deed and requested that Editor should refrain from publishing his name. We have therefore omitted to mention it, although aware that it must become generally known nevertheless.

This makes the second case of suicide which has occurred in our Jail within six months past.

___

Aug 2, 1848

Died,

In this town on Saturday, July 29, Corilla P., youngest daughter of Edward and Ann Sharpless, aged 2 years, 4 months and 24 days.

___

Correction.

In giving an account of the recent case of suicide in our jail, in our last paper, our information led us to make the erroneous statement that the deceased sent out and procured the lancet with which he effected his purpose, on the day of his death.

Sheriff Epler informs us that, unknown to him, the deceased had the lancet in his possession from the time he entered the jail.

___

Aug 9, 1848

Married,

July 31st in the M. E. Church in Middleton, Mr. Robert F. Lumbert to Miss Margaret Adams.

___

Aug 16, 1848

Married,

July 30th, Mr. Anches Kraner to Miss Margaret Dutt, all of Marion.

Died,

On July 24th at this place, Emeline C., daughter of Joseph and Laura Ann Sosey, age 18 months 17 days.

Sep 6, 1848

Married,

On Sept. 3, Mr. William T. Payne to Miss Mary Jane Bartram.

Sep 13, 1848

Married,

On the 10th in Marion Twp, Mr. James M. Ford to Miss Mary Travis.

Sep 27, 1848

Married,

On the 16th, Joseph Crab of Madison County and Miss Jane Helwick.

On the 16th, Mr. G.H. Shefts and Miss Nancy McKelvy.

On the 25th, Mr. Sanford J. Ackerman and Miss Christene Bunnel.

Died,

At his residence in this town, on the 21st of September, 1848, Thomas Walters, aged 30 years and 10 months.

The deceased was a native of Wales, whence he emigrated to this country in 1840 and resided in Marion for nearly six years. He was universally esteemed in this community as one of its most industrious and useful citizens and his death has caused a vacancy not easily to be filled. He had been a remarkably healthy man during his life, and his last illness was of only about a week's duration. He has left a widow and one child, together with a large circle of relatives and friends to mourn their loss.

Oct 11, 1848

Died,

In this place on the 25th day of September, after only about 3 days illness, Marietta E., daughter of Edward and Ann Sharpless, aged 4 years, 7 months and 22 days.

Whether the relatives of the deceased were to long enjoy her society, had almost always been to some a matter of serious doubt in consequences of the ill health which was her unhappy lot, the principal part of her life. But for a length of time previous to her last illness, her health improved, by which their doubts were removed, and they led to look upon her as promising them many years of pleasure. But in an hour when Death was least expected, his footsteps were heard, and next, his chilling hand was seen to nip this little flower from nature's garden.

But to the consolation of surviving friends, One Stronger Than Death, was to claim and then to transplant it to the more congenial soil of Paradise there to bloom in immortal beauty and bless with its fragrance the family of heaven.

Married,

On Oct. 9th, Mr. James R. Beebe to Miss Mary E. Scott.

Oct 18, 1848

Married,

On the 12th inst. in Denmark, Morrow County, Paul Sharpless to Miss Amanda R. Coffy, both of Marion.

At the same time and place, A.H. Brown and Miss Ann Elder also of Marion.

Oct 25, 1848

Died,

In this place on the 20th inst., Elizabeth, daughter of David and Mary Jameson, aged two years, one month, and four days.

Important.

All persons indebted to A.P. Lockwood are requested to call and pay immediately, as the subscriber is determined to close up his credit business before the 1st of December, 1848. All persons will govern themselves accordingly.

A.P. Lockwood

Nov 1, 1848

Married,

On the 26th, Mr. Otho W. Willett of Marion to Miss Mary E. Wells, formerly of Palmyra, N.Y.

On the 26th, Mr. Elder D. Lindsey, formerly of Hollidaysburgh, Pa., and Miss Keziah J. Randall of Marion.

On the 26th, Mr. James Havens and Miss Bellona Brown, all of Marion.

Nov 15, 1848

Subscribers Wanted.

Now is the time to subscribe for the paper. We intend hereafter to make the *Eagle* more interesting and hope to receive a large accession of new subscribers.

Married,

On the 4th, Mr. Valentine Coleman and Miss Elizabeth Whiteman, both of Waldo Twp.

Nov 22, 1848

Married,

Mr. Timothy T. Thew and Miss Harriet Dutton, both of Marion.

Nov 29, 1848

Married,

On the 2nd., Mr. John Ush to Miss Eliza Baker, all of Marion.

Nov. 12th, Mr. John Petty and Miss Phebe Wynn, all of Green Camp Twp.

Nov 15th, Elisha D. Sprague to Miss Catherine Waples of Marion.

Nov 23rd, Stephen Morris to Miss Mary Jane Stepman, all of Marion.

Dec 13, 1848

Married,

On the 3rd inst., Alonzo Carpenter to Miss Dorcas Johnson, all of Pleasant Twp.

Died,

On December 7th in this place, Ursula L., consort of M.P. Bean, editor of the *Bucyrus Forum*, and daughter of David Epler, at age 20.

Dec 20, 1848

☞ Who's going to California?

Married,

On the 5th, Mr. George W. Prettyman and Miss Nancy Spangler, both of Marion.

On the 13th inst., Mr. J. Barnhart to Miss Susan E. Holmes, all of this place.

Dec 27, 1848

Something Extraordinary.

During the past week the section of county hereabout was visited by a storm of mingled sleet and rain of unusual severity and duration. The atmospheric temperature being at or below freezing point, everything on which the rain and sleet chanced to fall became encountered with a thick coating of ice.

The consequence has been the destruction of a great many fruit trees in the orchards of our farmers, and the unrooting and breaking down of thousands of trees in our woodlands. We have been informed by persons living a few miles from town in various directions that saplings of forty feet in height were bent to the ground with their load in all parts of the forest; and that on Sunday morning the egash of the falling limbs from the heavy timber, and frequently of the largest trees themselves, kept up an almost incessant roar. A man had better been somewhere else than in the woods at such a time.

Ho! For Gold-ifornia.

The Gold fever is rising to a high pitch, in this goodly village. Several of our citizens contemplate taking an excursion to the auriferous region of the Sierra Nevada, as soon as the necessary preliminary arrangements can be completed.

Either a Hoax or a Most Awful Mistake.

A story is going the rounds of the papers of this state, and no doubt will reach the furthest village of the Union, of a horrible murder, and to have been recently perpetrated in this county, and by a citizen of this town. From a number of versions of the affair in different newspapers before us, we select the most detailed and romantic, which we find in the *Ohio Statesman*, and is as follows:

"Horrible and Extraordinary Murder.

"The Cleveland papers give an account of the most extraordinary murder of a citizen of that place by the name of Johnson. The murder occurred in Marion County, and under the following horrid circumstances, as detailed by the *Plain Dealer*, from a telegraphic dispatch to that place; "He was in the employ of Hilliard and Smith buying cattle, and was at the time in Marion county in this state. He had put up at a tavern in Marion where he had intended to make headquarters for a time—had explained to the landlord his business, and as usual the next day went into the country around to look for cattle. The landlord knowing that he had considerable money about his person, sought him when about twelve miles from his tavern and alone in a place, shot him, robbed him, dragged his body some distance and placed it between two logs and covered the same with brush.

"Johnson feigned death until the landlord left, when soon after a teamster was passing by he made himself heard to say, "Put me in your wagon and drive to the tavern fast as possible." The teamster did so, taking him to the same tavern where he put up. On arriving, the landlord came out to take the horses, when Johnson raised his head and said, "That is the man that shot me! He has two thousand dollars of my money!" And in ten minutes after, Johnson was dead.

"The landlord, overwhelmed at the evidence of his guilt, gave himself up, confessed the murder, and is now in jail.

"Truth is indeed stranger than fiction.—That Johnson in his dying extremity should insist upon being carried twelve miles in a lumber wagon to convict his murderer, is not considered at all remarkable by those who knew him. He was a man of great probity of character, undaunted courage—had been a cattle buyer for many years, and handled an immense amount of money. He

understood well the dangers of his calling, went armed and had some experience in the stratagems of robbers. It must have been a shrewd villain who found him off his guard; and to be circumvented he yielded up his last breath to bring his murderer to justice.

"Johnson leaves a devoted wife and an interesting family in this city to mourn his death."

Now, either the name of the county is misprinted in the accounts, or there has been played off a most unmitigated and villainous hoax, the author of which richly merits a sound horsewhipping. Nothing of the kind narrated in the above article or anything approaching it in the slightest degree, has occurred in this town or county. The Mr. Johnson spoken of, has frequently been here, in his avocation of cattle buyer, but, as we are informed, he has not been in the neighborhood some two or three months past.

The papers which have circulated the account of this supposed murder, will of course make the proper correction.

Married,

In Marion on the 25th, Mr. Charles Wood to Miss Eliza Jane Patterson, all of this place.

Jan 3, 1849

Married,

Near Marion on the 26th, Thomas Silverthorn and Miss Ellen Clark.

On the same day near Claridon, Mr. Richard Lawrence and Miss Sarah Wilson.

On the 27th, Mr. George N. Mears and Miss Sarah Jane Johnson, all of Marion County.

Jan 17, 1849

Died,

In Middletown on Dec 26th, Rachel Bridge, wife of Dr. Bridge, aged 25 years, 1 month and 13 days.

Jan 31, 1849

Married,

On the 24th, Mr. D.F. Cosner to Mary P. Pixley, of Marion county.

On the 30th, Dr. James H. Carpenter of Boydston's Mills, Indiana to Minerva J. Anderson, daughter of John Anderson of Marion County.

Feb 7, 1849

California Items.

There is yet no diminution of the gold excitement all over the country. Almost every town of any size in the Union will be represented in El Dorado. We still think Marion county will turn out a respectable delegation, although croakers declare the whole thing will fizzle out.

Married,

On the 4th, Mr. Jacob G. Redd to Miss Elmira Sanford, both of Marion County.

On the 14th, Mr. John Nicholson to Miss Henrietta Sanford, all of Marion County.

On the 31st ult., Thomas Manby to Miss Sarah Jane Thompson, all of Marion County.

Feb 14, 1849

Attention!

We want those indebted to this office for job work and advertising to come forward and square up immediately, in some shape or another. Those indebted on subscription to the *Eagle* for a year or more are also earnestly solicited to call and pay up or settle in some form.

Nothing but the most urgent necessity could draw from us a notice of this character, and we trust those indebted will realize that we really need what is due us and act in the premises as justice shall dictate.

Married,

On the 8th, Mr. Benjamin Baker to Miss Elizabeth Ulsh, both of Marion County.

On the 8th, Lewis Smith to Miss Alcinda Simms, all of this place.

Feb 28, 1849

Died,

At Big Island on the 6th inst., Dr. Alson Norton aged 56 years and 2 months.

Dr. Norton was one of the pioneers in this county. When he emigrated to this county there were but two families living in Big Island township and the early settlers bear in grateful remembrance his numerous attentions at the bedside of the sick. During a period of 28 years has he stood ready as a minute-man at responding to the call of the sick and distressed. He appeared to be one of Nature's physicians, possessing in a remarkable degree that peculiar "genial tact," that peculiar faculty of finding means to the end, so essential to the successful practice of medicine. This combined with great prudence, and a kind and benevolent disposition made him justly popular as a physician and respected as a citizen. There is probably no man living in the county to whom the citizens owe a greater debt of gratitude nor one whose loss would be more severely felt.

Melancholy Accident.

A young man named Edward Kopler, in the employ of C.B. Mann of this town, as an ostler, came to his death yesterday, from the kick of a horse in the stable of his employer. He lived about half an hour after receiving the injury. He was a German, and his parents, we are informed, reside a few miles south of this place.

Married,

On the 2nd inst., Allen D. Baker to Miss Lydia Ann Vanosten, both of Marion.

Mar 7, 1849

To the Patrons of the *Buckeye Eagle.*

As the connection of the present editor with this paper will cease at the expiration of the current volume, it may not be amiss at the present time to submit to our readers a few remarks which are suggested by the contemplated change in the proprietorship of the establishment.

Nine numbers more will complete the fifth volume of the *Eagle*, and the fifth year of our connection with it as Editor. We have nothing to say of our past course in conducting the paper—the fact of its having been sustained in a flourishing condition up to the present time we may be permitted to take as evidence that our labors have been in a good degree satisfactory to those who desire to have a Whig paper permanently established and kept up in this place. And although our connection with this paper will not, probably, prove to have been profitable to us in a pecuniary point of view, (owing, in part, to a radical and, we fear, incurable deficiency in our personal organization with regard to the management of financial and business matters,) yet we shall not be able to sever it without a feeling of regret; and, whether digging in the mines of California, or toiling for a bare livelihood somewhere else, we shall ever recur with pleasing recollections to our sojourn among the good people of Marion county.

Mr. D.J. Bean, a young man of whom from a short acquaintance we have formed a most favorable opinion as to his qualification for sustaining and improving the character of the paper, has become proprietor of the office and will enter upon his duties with the commencement of the next volume. He is a first rate practical printer, a sound Whig, and no doubt capable of conducting a paper with credit and ability.

We will say, in conclusion, that the approaching retirement of the present editor renders it extremely desirable that all accounts should be immediately settled, up to the close of the present volume. As we shall probably leave this neighborhood in the course of a few weeks, we shall be under the necessity of leaving our affairs in such a condition as will secure the most speedy possible settlement of all accounts which we hold against individuals.

Married,

On the 4th, H.H. Scribner to Miss Rachael Rush, all of Marion county.

Mar 14, 1849

Gambling

Mr. Editor—Sir: It is a prevailing sentiment that this vice is on the ascendant. I am most creditably informed, not long since, that many of the boys in this region, who have not yet attained to their teens, have cards in their pockets, and as they have opportunity, try their hands at the game.

Now sir, I believe, as a community we are highly culpable on this subject; and probably none are more at fault here than the professed and acknowledged ministers of the gospel and officers of justice. Have they labored to form a correct public sentiment on this subject? Have they instructed and warned the youth against this most ruinous practice? Have they sought to save the young

from the first approaches to the card table and polluting influence of example?

In this world of progression, things are first seen in their incipient stages. So of the different forms or modes of gambling of which card playing is the most common. It is first the card player, then the gambler. Men begin to play for diversion, or what they are pleased to call pastime. Few, if any, have gambling in view, when for the first time they take their seat at the card table. And in how many cases has the first attempt determined the destiny and sealed the ruin of the precious young man forever. Little does the thoughtless and inexperienced youth think that card playing will lead to gambling–gambling to drinking, swearing, lying, stealing, robbery, and often to murder.

Jonas Hartzell

Mar 21, 1849

Died,

On the 16th of March in this place, Mary Ann Patten, daughter of Richard and Susan Patten, aged 14 years, 9 months and 16 days.

Mar 28, 1849

Married,

On the 25th of this month, Mr. Emery Brewer and Miss Cynthia Lapham, all of this county.

Died

Near Marion on the 18th, Mary C., daughter of John and Assenath Patten, aged 2 years, 3 months and 24 days.

Apr 4, 1849

Township Election.

The vote given at the election held in Marion township on Monday last, stand as follows:

For Trustees	
John Zuck	338
John Ballentine	338
John Anderson	343

Clerk	
Orren Patten	364

Treasurer	
O.R. Stone	310

Justice of the Peace	
Joseph Beckman	14
John R. Knapp, Sr.	145
S.A. Griswold	200

Assessor	
Marcus Williams	83
Samuel Scribner	122
William M. Baker	154

Constables	
James L. Wilson	79
Wallace Haxter	275
John Moore	176
Joshua S. Batch	79
Alexander C. Runyan	31

For Subscription	367
No Subscription	2

The returns from several townships indicate that the majority in the county in favor of Railroad Subscription has been very large.

For California.

A company of our citizens left this place yesterday, and took up the line of march for the gold regions of California. It consists of Messrs. John Dumble, H. VanHouten, G.W. Bowers, J. Brady, John Smith, and ____ Cooper. Messrs Bowers and Brady preceded the rest of the company some days, for the purpose of purchasing team and provisions. They take their wagons from this place to Cincinnati, and thence proceed by water to Independence or St. Joseph, Mo. They are and will be provided with almost every conceivable requisite for the long and toilsome journey and carry with them the warmest wishes of all our citizens for their abundant success and safe return to their homes.

A company of six or seven, with one wagon, headed by Arthur Lapham, Esq., left Big Island township on the 26th ult., for California—and Gen. Rowe's company of about the same number, we understand will take their departure for the same destination, on Tuesday next.

Married

On the 1st inst., Samuel Berry to Miss Julian Bounds, all of Marion co.

Apr 11, 1849

NOTICE

Is hereby given that my wife, Phebe refuses to live with me, therefore I forbid all persons trusting her on my account as I am determined to pay no debts of her contracting after this date.

Samuel Terpany

Gone!

The California company raised in this place by our enterprising fellow citizen Gen. George Rowe, left town yesterday morning for their destinations at the gold diggings. The names of those composing the company, as far as we have been able to ascertain them are as follows: Gen. Geo. Rowe, Wm. Fisher, ____ Rowe, Samuel Keese, John Summerlot, A.W. Madison, Benj. R. Topping, Chas. Maynard, John Chambers, David Zuck, ____ Rogers, ____ Bunn. We think there were one or two others whose names we have not learned.

This company is comprised of the right kind of stock for an expedition of such a character, being mostly vigorous active whole-souled young men.

Our warmest wishes for their safety, entire success and unbounded enjoyment of the pleasures which may attend the trip and that they may escape its worst hardships, attend them as they go. We hope to greet them in future years amply rewarded for all the toils they have undergone.

Married,

On the 1st inst., Mr. John Berry and Miss Elizabeth Martin, all of Marion co.

On the 29th ult., Mr. Jacob Nichols of Marion county to Miss Elizabeth Hite of Wyandot county.

On the 29th ult., Elias Riley to Miss Susan Emily Fish, all of Marion co.

Keep a Bright Look Out!

On the 15th inst. or thereabouts it is expected the big California steam balloon will sail from New York City on its flight to the Land of Gold. The intention being to reach California in five days, the machine will probably pass over this region somewhere near noon of the day on which it takes it flight—that is, if it gets a reasonably early start in the morning.

Our town lies nearly in what will be the line of its flight, and it can doubtless be readily seen if the day be fair, should it pass within 50 miles of us. Therefore, keep your peepers peeled everybody!

Died,

April 5th at this place, Charles Carroll Warber, son of Henry and Amy Warber, aged 3 months, 4 days.

Apr 25, 1849

Interesting Event.

We want all those interested to take particular notice that the present volume of the *Buckeye Eagle* will close, and our connections with it will cease, on this day two weeks hence—and that we are most outrageously in want of money!

Cold Weather.

For ten days past, this region has been treated to about all the varieties of winter weather, probably left out by mistake in the month of January. Freezy, blowy, snowy, thawy, and then freezy again, has been the order of the day, until the prospect of fruit of most kinds must be well nigh annihilated.

May 2, 1849

Married,

In Paris, Monroe county, Mo., on April 11th, Mr. James M. Bean, Printer, formerly of Circleville, Ohio to Miss Frances V. Konkle of the former place.

On Apr 26th, Stephen B. Allen to Miss Elizabeth McWherter, both of Marion county.

Died,

In Marion, on the 26th ult., Rebecca, daughter of Adam and Julia Ann Sears, aged 5 years, 10 months and 3 days.

Near Marion on the 27th ult., Mary Ann Skinner daughter of Henry and Mary Ann Skinner aged 2 years, 11 months and 9 days.

May 9, 1849

Married,

On the 5th inst., Mr. Calvin W. Knapp and Miss Emily Gilmer.

R.   PATTEN

The following Medicines, Paints and Dye-Stuffs, are the principal articles on hand:

Asphaltum	Fowler's Solution Arsenic	Oil Bergamot
Aloes	Fenugreek	Oil Senaca
Antimon, Wine	Fustic	Oil Camomile
Arrow Root	Felix Elixer of Life	Oil Lemon
Arsenic Alba	Godfrey's Cordial	Oil Peneroyal
Angustura	Glauber Salts	Oil Sassafras
Acid Sulphuric	Glue	Oil Orange
Aqua Fortis	Gentian	Oil Spearmint
Aether Sulphuric	Guiacum Cost.	Oil Tanzy
Acid Tartaric	Gum Gamboge	Oil Wintergr'n
Alcohol	Gum Camphor	Potash Sulphate
Alum	Gum Guiacum	Prussian Blue
Annatto	Gum Foelida	Pirk Root
Ague Pills	Gum Shellac	Putty
Antimony Pulv.	Gum Arabic	Precipitate red
Adhesive Plaster	Gum King	" white
Baberry Bark	Gum Scammony	Perigoric
Blue Vitriol	Gum Opium	Pills Gregory's
Burgandy Pitch	Gum Galbanum	Pills Harlich's
British Oil	Gum Sandirac	Pills Felix's
Barbadoes Tar	Gum Tragacant	Pills Molton's
Batemans Drops	Gum Myrrh	Pills Hooper's
Benzoin	Gum Amonia	Pills Katz's
Balm Columbo	Gum Copal	Pumice Stone
Balsam Fur	Hays Linament	Prussic Acid
Balsam Cherry	Hyve Syrup	Piperine
Balsam Honey	Ivory Black	Princess Pine
Balsam Copavia	Ipecac	Phosphorus
Balsam Life	Indelible Ink	Piera
Balsam Peru	Iron Rust	Quinine Sul.
Bears Oil	Indigo	Quassia (Sick Head
Bl'k Snake Root	Jallup Pulv.	ache remedy)
Blue Pill Mass	Lamott's Cough Drops	Quicksilver
Black Lead	Liquorice Root	Rad Rhei
Bay Rum	Liquorice Ball	Red Sanders
Borax refined	Litherage	Rotten Stone
Calomel	Lead White	Rochell Salts
Cantharides	Lead Red	Red Tartar
Chalk prepared	Laudanum	Squills
Chalk white	Logwood	Soda Sub. Carb.
Chalk red	Lip Salve	Sugar Lead
Cologne	Lampblack	Sarsaparilla
Camomile Flowers	Lemon Acid	Salt Petre
Cloves	Lemon Syrup	Sweet Oil
Castor Oil	Lancets	Sermaurabo
Columbo	Lunar Caustic	Senna
Carb. of Iron	Madder	Sulphur
Corrosive sub.	Mace	Sal. Tartar
Corks Viol	Macassar Oil	Snake Root
Corks Bottle	Manna Flake	Spts. Lavender
Cinnamon Bark	Magnesia Cal.	Spirits Turpentine
Conserve of Roses	Magnesia Carb.	Sealing wax red
Cascarilla	Muriatic Acid	" " black
Copel Varnish	Morphine Sul.	Spanish White
Cream Tartar	Milliner's Glue	Starch
Canella Alba	Mustard ground	Sponges
Castor Russia	Murcurial Ointment	Saleratus
Court Plaster	Mesrum Cort.	Saffron English
Chinese Vermillion	Nutmegs	Syrup Buckthorn
Chromic Yellow	Nitric Acid	Syrup Sarsaparilla
Chromic Green	Nitre Dulcis	Sands' Sarsaparilla
Curcuma	Nux Vomica	Sulphate d Morphine
Camwood	Nut Galls	Sal Soda
Copperas	Nic Wood	Salamoniac
Castile Sapo	Oxalic Acid	Snuff
Cooper's Isinglass	Orange Peel	Terri d Senna
Castor Oil Candy	Opodildoc	Tartar Emetic
Cobalt	Oil Vitriol	Tamarinds
Candies	Oil Savin	Tonic Extract
Digitalis	Oil Anise	Turbenthina
Dragons' Blood	Oil Cinnamon	Tinctures
Drop. Lake	Oil Harlem	Turkey Umber
Duncan's Expectorant	Oil Peppermint	Uva Ursi
Eye Water	Oil Spruce	Valerian Red
Emetic Tartar	Oil Juniper	Verdigis
Epsom Salts	Oil Almonds	V. Turpentine
Emory	Oil Lavender	V. Red
Emp. Adhesive	Oil Spike	Viols assorted
Emp. Diachylon's	Oil Stone	Vermifuge
Emp. Strengthening	Oil Wormseed	Vitriol Elixer
Emp. Robrand's	Oil Cloves	Whiton's Rhumatic
Epispastic	Oil Amber	Drop
Essences	Oil Origanum	Wafers

May 17, 1850

Marriage.

On the 15th inst., Mr. William C. Trimble, one of the Publishers of the *Buckeye Eagle* to Miss Loretta M. Haldeman, Daughter of the Editor.

Attachment.

At my instance an attachment was this day issued by S.A.Griswold, a Justice of the Peace of Marion township, Marion county, Ohio, against the property and effects of Adam Sherman, an absconding debtor.

Joseph Underwood.

May 24, 1850

☞ Our exchanges bring favorable reports of the wheat crop throughout the State. It is thought to be out of all danger except the rust. Nothing can be more cheering to the farmer nor tend more to invigorate the commercial and mechanical departments of life, and may not the printer too begin to look cheerful for of course they will remember him amid the general prosperity, sufficiently at least to send in old arrearages.

To Those Concerned.

Any and all communications intended for insertion in the *Buckeye Eagle* in future must be free from low vituperations and gross personalities.

He that cannot write something to inform the mind or improve the judgement either in science, morals or politics, should not attempt to write for the press.

As a further reason, First we wish not to publish anything that would offend the chaste ear of the fairer portion of our readers.

Secondly, we wish to make our paper a source of useful intelligence.

Thirdly, we think if two or three or more of our citizens get their belligerent feelings so much excited, that they can no longer contain them, and must give vent to them, to their own disgrace and the injury of their neighbors, they had better turn out in the street and puff off and be done with it, and their folly will be sooner forgot than if made a subject of newspaper record.

Fire in Marion.

The blacksmith shop of Messrs. Clark & Jones, caught fire on Monday the 20th, in the roof, by the sparks finding access through the lath where the plastering was off under the roof.

The fire company were on hand and tendered prompt and efficient service.

The fire was extinguished without doing much damage.

Jun 7, 1850

Married,

In Marion on the 27th inst., Mr. Philip Henkle to Miss Christiana Kastner.

Died,

On the 12th of May in Middleton, Marion county, Allen Artherton, formerly of Sunbury, Ohio, aged 26 years.

Jun 14, 1850

The B'hoys.

Certain young men and half grown boys, that are being pretty well known of late, are tendering themselves quite notorious, as disturbances of the peace and quiet of our generally, very orderly place.

For several evenings, they have been visiting the church, (where the German Methodists have been holding a protracted meeting, for some two weeks,) whence we understand they are guilty of every kind of low and obscene action. Actions that would be a disgrace to an untutored savage.

On Tuesday evening we learn they locked the door and carried off the key, making it necessary for someone to crawl out of the window in order to devise some means of opening the door; whence he was met by a flourish of dirks, as we are told, and curses too horrible to repeat.

We would only say to those same young gentlemen if they are seeking notoriety, they are in a fair way to obtain it. Respect for their friends, and a hope that they will take a timely warning and mend their ways—induces us to withhold their names for the present.

Married,

On the 9th inst., Thomas W. Smith to Miss Sarah Ann Strawser, both of Montgomery township, Marion county.

Jun 21, 1850

A Beautiful Sight.

A few evenings ago we visited the old stone church, where we had the pleasure of beholding one of the most beautiful sights our eyes have feasted on for some time. From one to two hundred of the youth of our Town of every age and sex, assembled to tune the melodies of their innocent voices, and the affections of their hearts to the praise of God.

We could not but admire the order and harmony with which the whole exorcises passed off; every little group with their respective teachers at their head, seemed but intent to add to the general interest by close attention too and active participation in every-thing that was passing.

How much more appropriate thought we, these exorcises than those of some of our misguided youth who prowl round our streets at night (when honest men are sunk in repose,) committing deeds of mischievous villainy for which their cheeks would burn with shame if the light of day shone upon them.

Jul 5, 1850

Taking the Census.

Our friend J. Wildbahn is or will soon be calling upon the good people of this county, to record a list of their substance, as well as the number of members comprising each family.

We trust his talk will be made pleasant and easy, by the promptness with which the necessary questions proposed to each person, thus be answered.

Jul 12, 1850

Married,

On the 4th inst., Mr. Solomon Pitman to Miss Jane M. Parcel, all of Marion county.

Jul 26, 1850

Census of 1850.

We are indebted to the politeness of our friend Wildbahn, the deputy Marshall for this district for taking the census for the following statistical items:

Number of families in Marion, 225.
Number of inhabitants, 1350.
Value of real estate owned in the town of Marion, 556,543 dollars.
Value of live stock—horses, mules, oxen, cows, sheep, swine &c, owned in the town of Marion, 28,053 dollars.

California Letter.

Sacramento City
April 30, 1850.

Mr. B.J.C.—Sir: It is with pleasure that I inform you that I am well and hope you are in the enjoyment of as good health as I am. My health is very good indeed, my weight is now 204 lbs., nearly 24 lbs. more than I ever weighed before. I am now living on the American fork seven miles from Sacramento City. It is a most delightful place at this time. The plains are as beautiful as a garden of flowers, and the air is as pure as the purest that blows on the earth, the hare that inhabits them are the finest that can be produced. And the wild Geese! There is scarcely a day that we do not bring one or two of them down as our prey. We have plenty of game of all sorts, and above all such Salmon! The most delightful! I think they are the finest fish that I have ever eat; some weighing from ten to forty pounds. Trout, too, and other fish are very abundant. We have also vegetables of almost every kind at this season of the year.

I am working at my trade here and have been ever since I come to this country. I have not mined any yet, but intend to go to the mountains in about two weeks to try my luck. I think that I can make what money I want this season, if I keep my health, and if I do I shall be back this fall.

I have been working up here ever since the high waters in February, which overflowed Sacramento City. And a great high water it was; the whole city was overflowed. The loss of property was immense. A great many buildings were ruined, and it played smash with the tents, of which there were a great many in the city. I was working in the city at the time, making sash. It stopped my calculations.

There were not many lives lost. I heard of three that were drowned, one of them was a colored man that was drunk and fell out of the boat. The rise of the waters was very rapid; about ten feet in one day and part of a night. My loss was between two and three hundred dollars, and twelve days time. Since then I have been getting 12 dollars a day at my trade. Board rates here from eighteen to twenty dollars per week, other things in proportion.

There has been some very rich discoveries made in the mines lately. I am going over to Trinity River in a week or two with a friend of mine who was there last season. He worked five weeks before rainy season commenced, and in that time dug six thousand dollars. I shall get me about two or three mules to pack over there. The distance, from here, is about 400 miles. I could get an ounce per day for working in the city this summer and should take it, but I fear it is going to be very sickly; I therefore prefer going to the mountains to preserve my health.

I would merely state to you, Benjamin, if you have any notion of coming to California, don't come the overland route by any means; I have had a trial of it and that satisfies me. David Zuck, myself, and four more of the boys left the team near Goose Lake, 400 miles from the valley, with five and a half pounds of hard bread apiece to travel through on. We reached Losson's settlement in nine days, having traveled nearly 45 miles per day. I got work in Sacramento City at ten dollars per day; worked five days and was taken down with the fever, the effects of starvation in the mountains.

Yours, with respect, &c,
John Sumerkott.

Aug 2, 1850

Died,

On the 26th inst., Ella Margaret, daughter of Ebenezer and Elizabeth L. Peters, of Marion, aged 8 months and 18 days.

Of apoplexy in this place on the 29th ult., Mrs. Elizabeth Rowe, mother of George Rowe, Esq., now in California.

Concert by the Blind.

The blind! There is something interesting in everything associated with the mental and moral improvement of this class of persons.

We were on Tuesday night permitted to listen to, and witness the vocal and instrumental performance of the three young men, that are now traveling with Mr. Machold, teacher of Music in the Blind Asylum. The performance was excellent.

Married,

On the 29th inst., Philip McClasky, a true son of "Erin," to Miss Julia Ann McWherter, all of this county.

Aug 9, 1850

Married,

At C.B. Mann's on the 6th inst., Mr. Abraham Beaver to Miss Charlotte May, both of Grand Prairie township, Marion county.

On August 1, 1850, William M. Chesney to Miss Rachel Merriman, oldest daughter of Charles Merriman, Esq., all of Marseilles, Wyandot county.

Died,

In Bucyrus on the 3rd inst., William Cooper, aged 79 years, 7 months and 3 days.

Aug 16, 1850

Married,

On the 6th inst., William McCoy to Miss Sarah E. Bowdish, all of Marion township.

On the 14th inst., Mr. James P. Grey to Miss Merica Miller, all of Marion county.

Sep 6, 1850

Died,

At the American House, in this place, of Cholera morbus, Sept 5th, William Hull, junior partner of the Law firm of Bunker & Hull, a young man of bright promise and high hopes.

The profession has but few young men of greater promise or more strict integrity to lose; ambitious, honest, and honorable. The friends he was daily serving by his consistent course, were a sufficient guaranty of his worth.

Married,

On the 22nd day of August, 1850, Mr. Joseph Rollston of Marion to Miss Elizabeth A. Bolton of Claridon township.

On the 3rd inst., Mr. Corydon Allen to Miss Lucinda Grapes, all of Marion.

Sep 13, 1850

☞ It is circulated pretty generally we understand, that there is Cholera in Marion. We are happy to have it to say there has not been a single case of it as yet.

Died,

In Kenton, on the 30th ult., Corilla A., wife of G.T. Copeland, and only daughter of H. & P.H. Peters, aged 20 years, 3 months and 20 days.

Attachment.

At my instance an attachment was this day issued by John Wiley, a Justice of the Peace of Claridon township, Marion county Ohio, against the property and effects of George Easterday, an absconding debtor.

Adam Sherman.

Sep 20, 1850

From the Gold Diggings.

Sacramento City, California
July 20th, 1850

Dear Sir:

Nicholas Kepner, Adam Epley, John W. Miller, Henry R. Whitsel, and myself, arrived here this morning, all in reasonably good health, after a long and tedious journey. We will start for the Uba or feather river mines to morrow morning. We came the Carson river route: it is said to be the best road; but the best is bad, we suffered very much and lost our waggon and the most of our horses. We got in with Jims, Wesley's horse and our clothes on our backs and pretty well strapped I can tell you.

Isaac Ulsh and Benjamin Baker stopped in Hangtown to go to mining. The miners make from four to six Dollars per day there in the dry diggings. Dilingham and Isaiah Pearce, Henry F. Pearce and Red, we left on the other side of the desert. I am very uneasy about them, they would not, or Dilingham would not cross on the night, we crossed in the night and liked to have perished and it was a great deal worse in the day time. We heard that Henry Pearce had got across and was packing water back to some one of the men that had gave out. We did not learn which one it was.

The prospect for gold they say is as good as ever but it is hard to procure. It is lottery I tell you. I suppose that John Merchant and others are waiting with great anxiety to hear from us and what advice we will give them about coming. All we have to say is never come the overland route for all the gold in California; as for myself I intend to scratch hard for a raise, but as soon as I make a decent raise I am bound for home. We never will be recompensated for what we have endured if we get piles upon piles of money it will never pay the damage done to our constitutions.

You will please let this letter suffice for all our friends and families for a hearing. We send our respects to all our friends, and Henry R. Whitsel and myself particularly send our love to our wives and little children.

The only thing that troubles us now is that we received no letter from our families. Why it is that we received no letter at Sacramento we cannot tell.

This letter you must excuse, for, if I had the head of a Washington on my shoulders I could not compose a letter at this time, but as soon as we locate in the mines we will write you a more satisfactory letter. Direct your letters to Vernon Post Office, no more at present.

Yours,

Aron Manahan
Nicholas Kepner
Henry R. Whitsel
Adam Epley
John W. Miller

Married,

On the 6th inst., Mr. James McWilliams to Miss Mary Ann Bushey, all of Marion county.

In Waterloo, N.Y. on the 5th inst., Mr. M.M. Camp of Marion to Miss Maria Johnson of the former place.

Sep 27, 1850

Married,

On the 12th inst., Mr. Vincent D. Pettet of Pitt township, Wyandot county to Miss Jane T. Hughes of Marion county.

Died,

In Marion, September 24th, William Albert, son of William H. and Sarah M. Miller, aged 15 months and 9 days.

Oct 11, 1850

Died,

On the 24th ult., Herman P., son of W. & J.D. Williams, aged 5 months and 5 days.

In Marion on the 4th inst., Dr. R.H. Cochran, aged 25 years, 5 months and 10 days.

Married,

On the first inst., Adolphus F. Wilson and Miss Violet Chambers, both of Gilboa, Putnam county.

Oct 18, 1850

Married,

On the 13th inst., Mr. Oscar Baker, of Marion to Miss Jane Powell of Green Camp township, Marion county.

On the 12th inst., Mr. Frederick Hinaman to Miss Abagail Mouser, both of Marion.

On the 17th inst., Mr. Lafayette Lesnet to Miss Ethelinda Hoddy, all of this place.

Died,

On the 12th inst., Mrs. Hannah Search, wife of Thomas Search and mother of Jas. H. Godman, Esq., of this place, after an illness of some eight days. She was born in Loudon county, Virginia, Dec. 28, 1782. Removed to Ohio in the Fall of 1811. Ohio was then an unbroken wilderness, and she and her family encountered many hardships, privations and trials, such as are usually incident to new countries. All of which the deceased bore with equanimity and fortitude.

She joined the Meth. E. Church in 1808 or 9 of which she continued a most exemplary and useful member to the day of her death. Few have so universally enjoyed the confidence of all around her and no one ever left a brighter example of piety and virtue as a legacy to her family and friends. She leaves two sons, a number of grand-children and a large circle of friends to lament her loss.

Oct 25, 1850

LOOK OUT.

Runaway from the subscribers on the morning of the 24th inst., an over grown boy, named Isaac B. Clark, an apprentice to the printing business. This is to forewarn all persons from trusting or harboring him on our account as we shall pay no debts of his contracting.

Haldeman & Trimble.

Wanted.

The subscribers wish to get a boy, from 14 to 16 years of age to learn the printing business. One that can come well recommended for steady moral habits will meet with a good situation.

Haldeman & Trimble.

Married,

In this town on the 19th inst., Mr. Henry Granger to Miss Angeline Sutly, both of Marion.

Died,

October 10th, 1850, of Whooping-cough, Henry, son of Isaac and Mariah Haldeman, aged 3 months and 21 days.

Nov 1, 1850

California Letter.

Placerville, Upper California
August 13th, 1850

I reached the "land of gold" the 23rd of July and should have written you sooner but wanted to wait until I could tell you I was well. My health is now good as ever it was. I was very much fatigued when I arrived, by traveling and going with scant rations, for I did not have as much good victuals as I would have relished for the last four or five hundred miles and was obliged to walk nearly the whole of that distance. This is the first hardship I ever knew.

I promised you a description of the trip. The first three hundred miles to Fort Kearney was very pleasant but as soon as we left that point trouble commenced; one of our horses gave out and we were obliged to leave the train and travel alone in the wilderness. We proceeded in this way without difficulty three or four days when we fell in with a train from Michigan; we had been with them but a day or two when our second horse gave out, and we then had but three mules to depend on, and fifteen hundred miles to travel. We left the train and tried it alone once more.

In a day or two we were overtaken by Miller and the rest of the Marion boys, and stayed with them until within six hundred miles of this place where we commenced packing. We left them and Dillingham with good teams and wagons, the latter thought we were very foolish for leaving our wagons. I thought then of home. But it went much better than I expected. We would have saved time by packing sooner, but we got in eight or ten days before the rest of the boys. They all left their wagons and packed at last. Dillingham left all his horses on the road within two hundred miles of here.

You can imagine the suffering and loss of property on the road. I don't suppose that one tenth of the wagons or half the horses ever crosses the Sierra mountains. Just as a specimen of the loss we counted seventy-five wagons left on the last sixteen miles of the desert and they are strewed from the top of the Sierra Nevada mountains back for at least one thousand miles, but not quite as thick.

An emigrant who came in a week ago, and said that on the last eight miles of the desert there were a hundred and twenty-seven horses and 165 mules and two dozen oxen dead, in and by the roadside. Where I crossed in forty miles it now takes sixty; the road I come in is blocked up by dead horses and the stench is so great it is impassible. Oh! The sufferings in that spot. Several men have perished there. No one that does not witness or experience the sufferings across the plains can have any idea of the feelings of the emigrant in this adventure. The suffering is more than California can ever repay.

There were more lives lost on the road by being drowned, than in any other way, I believe that the Humbolt and Green Rivers shortened the lives of many. Provisions are high and plenty.

Flour is 18 to 20 cents per pound
Pork 30 cents
Cheese $1.25
Butter from $1 to $1.25
Salt 50 cents
Sugar 60 cents
Coffee 75 cents to $1
Beef 25 to 35 cents
Tea $1 to $1.25

Molasses $4.00 per gallon and other things in proportion. Common coarse boots $12 to $16 per pair, other clothing is reasonable. Board by the week $18. Miners can board themselves very well at $7 per week. Barley is selling at 25 cents per pound and hay at 20 cents per pound. I do not pretend to say that hay is worth it, for you see that would be $400 per ton. Sole leather $1 per pound.

I do not like California at all—extract the gold from the soil and it would have no attraction for me. It is very hilly and stony. A horse would soon starve to death if permitted to run at large. The grass and woods where there are any on the hills, are as dry as ever they were in February at home. We had some winter in June. It snowed the fourteenth, fifteenth, sixteenth, and seventeenth of June until the snow was six inches deep on the mountain and froze ice ½ of an inch thick. I have not been out of sight of snow any month this year. We traveled over it five miles in July. The days is quite warm here now and the nights cold.

My advice to my friends if they wish it about coming to California, is to be content with what they have and stay at home. Still I am not discouraged and am I glad I came. I think any one with health and perseverance may do well.

There is as much gold as I expected, but it is harder to procure. Hundreds have already become discouraged and borrowed money and started home. Some have started to work their passage back without any money at all. There is but little satisfaction to be taken here on the Sabbath. They have action in the street, preaching on one side of it and open gambling on the other side; it seems very strange to attend church and see no females present. We can work for weeks here and see neither women nor children, but cords of men.

Yours &c,

E.H. Clark

_____

Married,

On the 29th inst., Samuel Terpany to Miss Samantha Randall, all of this place.

_____

Nov 8, 1850

Married,

At the American House on the 31st inst., Richard C. Layton and Miss Mary Dunham, both of Claridon township, Marion county.

On the 1st inst., Joseph A. Drake of Grand Prairie township to Miss Sarah Fickle of Marion township, Marion county.

_____

Nov 15, 1850

A CARD.

The Ladies of the Methodist Sewing Society will prepare a supper, on Wednesday evening, 20th inst., at the Odd Fellows Hall. A number of useful and fancy articles will be offered for sale. The proceeds are to aid in the purchase of a Bell for the Methodist Episcopal Church. Doors to open precisely at 6 o'clock. Supper 6½ o'clock. A general attendance is respectfully solicited.

Admittance, $1.00 per couple. Single tickets 50 cents. Oysters extra.

Married,

On the 3rd inst., Mr. Samuel H. King to Miss Jane Thomhson, both of Marion.

On the 3rd inst., Isaac Davis to Miss Phariby Walker, both of Marion.

On the 24th of October, Mr. Dewit C. Britton to Miss Sally Vanausten, both of Marion.

Nov 22, 1850

California Letter.

Nevada City, Sept 22, 1850

Dear father:

I improved the present occasion in writing to you, ardently hoping that you enjoy the blessings of good health. My health has been by a kind providence preserved to this time. I reached California after a most tiresome and laborious journey of ninety days. Space will not permit me to give you a full and detailed account of the entire journey. I will have to content myself therefore, with a brief sketch of it. We left St. Joseph, Mo. April 20th, the weather was fair though rather cool, but on that account for our

Horses; the road was good to Ft. Larime, which is nearly 700 miles from the United States boundary.

In the Bear River valley, we met with many Indians but they were all well disposed.

From the point where we struck Humbolt River to the sink of the river, the distance is about 300 miles. When we reached this river our hardships actually commenced.

We were obliged to swim for many rods very often, and cut what grass we could with our pocket knives for our famishing animals. As a matter of course, animals fell by the wayside in great numbers. Our horses ran down so low that we were obliged to leave our wagon about half way down the Humbolt. Pearce's mess left their wagon about the same time. Pearce came on then with his father. Many, very many were obliged to leave all they had save all they could carry on their backs. This soon produced misery and want, such as I trust never again to see. We were compelled to live on half allowances for two hundred and forty-five miles, but considered ourselves well off compared with others.

From the sink of Humbolt River to Carson River the distance is forty-eight miles over a dreary desert. In this distance there is neither a drop of water or spear of grass. The number of fallen animals in this distance was immense. It was in this strip that we had to leave our gray horse. After traveling up Carson River valley for some forty miles we were obliged to exchange our Charley horse for twenty-five pounds of flour; he was run down so low that he could travel no farther.

The road along Carson River was good, and the valley abounds with excellent grass. The river we followed to the Sierra Nevada mountains. These mountains are the most stupendous of any in North America. They are will timbered with several species of pine, the tallest and straightest trees I ever saw. The ascent of these mountains is in places very difficult, but the descent is very gradual. The tops are capped with perpetual snow. There are but a few months of the year that they can be crossed near this point. From the summit the road winds in various directions on the chain of mountains, up hill and down, sometimes passing over large masses of rocks until descended in a pleasant valley.

The distance from the point where we struck Carson river in Weberville, (the first settlement in California we reached) is 260 miles. We left Isaac Ulsh and Benjamin Baker at Weberville and came on to the Yuba, where we commenced mining. Not being satisfied with the prospects at the Yuba, we came to Little Deer Creek, where we have remained ever since.

Mining, as has often been remarked, is like a lottery business, it is not him that performs the greatest amount of labor, that makes the most, but rather him that strikes a rich spot, for the gold is by no means equally distributed through the earth; the best of the diggings have been worked out and the number of people that are here seeking after gold is immense and still arriving by the hundred, both by water and by land. Hundreds as soon as they land and look about them, return again without even trying it.

Hundreds would return if they had means to do so. There is a very moderate calculation, 20 men here to where there might be one. The emigration to these shores has been carried to an extreme from all parts of the earth and of every hue and shade may be seen. God only knows is to become of them all. It is true there is gold plenty here yet, but it is mostly deposited in such small quantities that renders it nearly impossible to collect it at the present rate of living.

The climate in this country is most delightful—the sky is cloudless from April till September. The rainy season is nearly at hand. We have had a few showers during the past week already, which is nearly a month sooner than last season. The morals of this country I am sorry to say are very deficient. I saw today a man preaching the gospel to about ten hearers, while more than twenty under the sound of his voice were busily engaged in washing gold, their noise with toms and cradles and shovels nearly drowned his voice. Gambling is carried to a greater extent here than anywhere in christendom. It is surprising to see men, after risking health and life itself, endure a painful separation from kindred and friends and then after being successful enough, give it up to men that would cut their throats to get it.

I feel tolerable well satisfied so far. You will hear from me soon again. Write as soon as possible. Direct your letter to Sacramento City, Upper California. Mister Enoch Clark and William Coffy are here and are well and in good spirits. Darkness compels me to close. Please give my best respect to all enquiring friends. I remain your obedient son,

John W. Milker

Nov 29, 1850

Attention!

Flour, pork, beef, wood, potatoes, oats, corn and cash taken on subscription at this office. Come along friends let us be having some of them.

Married,

On the 26th inst., Mr. Edward J. Cadwalader of Delaware county to Miss Martha Scribner of Marion county.

Dec 6, 1850

Married,

In Marion on the 25th ult., Mr. Sylvester Austin to Miss Elizabeth Culbertson.

Dec 13, 1850

Married.

On the 15th inst., Mr. Alexander Comstock to Miss Catharine Berger, both of Marion.

Dec 20, 1850

Died.

On the 6th inst., Col. Samuel Bowdish aged 62 years.

Col. Bowdish was one of the early settlers of this county, and was genuinely known as one of our most energetic and enterprising farmers and stock dealers. Nearly two years since he was attacked with an affection of the brain, which gradually undermined his mental facilities.

Among the last acts of his life, before his mind failed him, was the making of a liberal donation to the Presbyterian Church in this town, of which he had long been a prominent member. He leaves an amiable widow and a large circle of friends to mourn his loss.

Dec 27, 1850

New England in Ohio.

A day or two ago we had the pleasure of seeing upon our streets what we think might redily pass in some places for a New England sleighing party—a large sled drawn by four horses, a commodious box sufficiently large to stow away a dozen or twenty young gleeites—all snugly seated in the bottom with their heads just perched above its sides sufficiently to catch the refreshing breezes of the Plains, enough to impart to their noses the beautiful tint of the cherry, while ever anon their joyful voices and the gleeful laugh gave indication of real enjoyment.

It is seldom that we see such scenes in Marion. Good sleighing snows here are like "angel visits, few and far between."

For the past few days the streets have been lined with sleds and sleighs.

Married

On the 19th inst., Mr. Samuel Smith to Miss Nancy Jane Baker, both of Marion.

Jan 3, 1851

The Wife.

If you wish to be happy and have peace in the family, never reprove your husband in company—even if that reproof be ever so slight. If he be irritated speak no angry word. Indifference sometimes will produce unhappy consequences. Always feel an interest in what your husband undertakes, and if he is perplexed or discouraged, assist him by your smiles and happy words.

If the wife is careful how she conducts, speaks and looks, a thousand happy hearts would cheer and brighten our existence, where now there is nothing but clouds of gloom, sorrow, and discontent. The wife, above all others, should strive to please her husband, and to make home attractive.

Married.

On the 1st inst., Mr. Watrman H. Higgins to Miss Rachel Bratton, all of Marion.

On the 1st inst., Mr. Alfred A. Reed, of little Sandusky, and Miss Sarah Bartram, of Marion.

Absconded.

On the 27th of December last a boy named Zepheriah Reed left my residence. All persons are hereby notified not to trust or harbor him on my account as I will pay no debts of his contracting.

C.W. Cherry

Died.

Of Consumption, on the 28th day of December, near Marion, Mr. Samuel Reed, in the 46th year of his age.

The deceased was a native of Washington county, Pa. In youth he had indulged the hope of an interest in the Savior, but did not see his way clear to make a profession of religion until some months since, when he united with the Presbyterian Church of this place. Naturally unassuming and retiring, possessing rather a taciturn cast of mind; his worth was best appreciated by those who were intimate with him. Though a great sufferer, grace enabled him to bear his trials with exemplary patience and resignation. As the hour of his departure approached, he was calm and tranquil. He knew in whom he had believed.

Jan 16, 1851

Married.

On the 9th inst., Mr. William W. Brady of Big Island township and Miss Lefy A. Cook of Salt Rock township.

List of Letters.

☞Remaining in the Post Office at Marion Ohio, on the first day of January, 1851.

New Year. 1851. AULT & GORTON.

HAVING turned over a new leaf, for 1851, we wish it to be distinctly understood by all that are indebted to us, by note or book account, to call and pay up without delay, as we intend to collect all our outstanding dues by the first of April next.
Those interested will govern themselves accordingly.

AULT & GORTON.

A
Alexander J S 2
Arthur Harriet
Ames O
Albrecht Rev

B
Buck J
Bender T
Baines R
Baldwin T
Breman W
Beesley J
Blackford John R
Brady David
Bell Hiram
Bacon Perry C
Bossler Marcus
Burnison Samuel
Blocksom Samuel

C
Clark Juliet C
Cleveland Kingsley
Carey J W
Christy A
Carney C
Calvert James
Culbertson John
Chard Jas
Concklin Ann Miss
Cramner Aeg Mr

D
Dennis T
Dodge J
Davidson James
Daebart John
Drake D B

F
Fellows J
Fletcher J
Fletcher John

G
Gillis Samuel
Gillit John M
Gumpf George
Godman Joseph or William
Griswold Martin
Gregory J

H
Haldeman J
Hamler Samuel

Hain Samuel
Haines Leah
Heartman Samuel
Hanby E

I

Idle Fredrie

J

Jurey Abner
Jurey John 2
Jones Mrs A M

L

Laughry John
Likens James
Littleton Almira
Larue Wm
Little Leonard

M

Meliger Isaac
Milliser Jacob
Miller John
Miner Wm Esq
McClosky Julia Ann
Morral John

N

Nimiller Henry
Neff Geo F
Noble Barbary

P

Pool J D Esq
Peters S Mr
Peters Edward Esq

R

Ruple Jane Mrs
Rammonar _____
Ryne Patrick
Russell Joseph B
Richey Widow
Reynolds William
Ripley Thomas
Rowan T M Mr

S

Snyder Christian J
Sherman Mary Mrs
Straw Mr Esq
Sutherland R Esq
Sligerman M Esq
Schooner Maglier Mrs
Stephens Henry R
Smith Robert 2
Snyder Jacob P
Stafford Esquire Mr

T

Turner J N Esq 3

Tunis Josiah

U

Uhl Wm J

V

Vanderwerker & Barker

W

Wilson Lambert
Welsh E R
Welch S D 2
Wood G B Dr
Welsh M W
Woodsum James (California)

Y

Yerk J S

German.

Deubart Heinrich
Wilkan Heinrich
Christian Johannes

Persons calling for any of the above letters will please say "advertised."
S.A. Griswold P.M.

☞ There is a report in circulation, that our worthy friend and fellow townsman, Horace W. Baker, who went to California last spring, is dead. We hope it is not so, but fear it is too true. Mr. Baker was an excellent man, and we regret his loss to this community.

Jan 30, 1851

To the Citizens of Marion.

Fellow Citizens:

Plank Roads are being constructed North and South of us, while we remain isolated from the Improvements that are absolutely necessary, nay inevitable if we go along with the age we live in. We seem to have all our energies absorbed in the Railroad. The Railroad is good enough for purpose it was contemplated; Railroads are the great iron bands that unite large cities. But the Railroad will not convey the farm-

ers to our stores, nor will it bring the local business to every man's door; while the Plank Road is every man's road, inasmuch as every man that has a wagon can enjoy its benefits.

Married.

On the 23d inst., Mr. Benjamin W. Cramer, of Richland Twp and Mrs. Mary Graves of Marion.

Feb 6, 1851

California Items.

Through the politeness of a lady in this place, we have been permitted to read a letter from her husband in California; which, by the way, don't give much encouragement to new adventurers for the region of Gold. He states that Mr. John McCan, who formerly resided in this place and left a year ago for California had his back broke by a bank caving in upon him. There was hopes of his recovery, but not much.

Married.

Married on the 16th of January, Mr. Samuel Powell and Miss Tamsey Andrew, both of Marion.

On the 30th ult., Mr. John Cullison of Claridon and Miss Lavina Brady of Marion.

Mar 6, 1851

Married.

On the 4th inst., Mr. Peter J. Henry to Miss Sarah Smith, both of Marion.

"The Insult from the Pulpit."

Having been several times spoken to in the course of the past week in relation to our denial of the charge make in the *Mirror* of week before last, and feeling satisfied that a good deal of misapprehension exists in the public mind in relation to the whole matter, we have obtained, from friend Wildbahn, a statement in substance, of what passed between the parties at his house on Monday after the meeting, which we think will throw some light on the matter.

Mr. Haldeman,

In answer to your enquiry, as to what conversation took place, between Elder Quigley and Miss C., at my house, on Monday morning after the last Quarterly meeting in this place, I would say, that according to the best of my recollections it was in substance as follows:

Miss C. called at my house about 8 o'clock on Monday morning, and accosted the Elder as follows:

Well, Mr. Quigley, I suppose you don't know me?

Elder. *No I don't.*

Miss C. I am the person you scandalized at church on Saturday evening, by charging me with *laughing three times in your face.*

The Elder's reply was, *I don't know that I did—I don't know you.*

Miss C. remarked—yes you did, for you looked at me at the time.

The Elder said—*well miss if you are the person that laughed three times* in my face, you are the person I rebuked.

Miss C. From the fact of your looking at me at the time, I thought you meant me and community has fastened it upon me.

Elder. *I am sorry indeed* if you are innocent that community should be so unkind as to charge you with the offence. But if you are the person that did *laugh* so as to call forth my reproff you would do well to just confess it, and if you did not—make no confession—no, never!

The Elder then asked Miss C. whether the bonnet and shawl she was then wearing, was the one she wore on the previous Saturday evening. Her reply was, *they were the same.* The Elder then said, well Miss, the person I reproved I think had none of that inside trimming in her bonnet, that I see you have now, and I think she had not so full a face as you have. I always make it a rule when any person *laughs three times* in my face during a sermon, to rebuke them.

Miss C. then remarked that all she done was to answer a Miss _____, who sat behind her and enquired if she would not make room for her as she had a very uncomfortable seat where she was. I merely answered her question and smiled and done nothing more.

The Elder remarked that the mere act of *asking or answering a question* was not out of place in church, and that he never paid any attention to it.

John Wildbahn

The above statement the reader sees, is over the signature of a man of undoubted veracity. Has any one the temerity to gainsay it? We presume not. What does it prove then? Simply that "the charge" preferred against Elder Quigley in the *Mirror* of week before last was faire. Does anyone ask what charge?—We answer the charge in the *Mirror*, that the head and front of offending, that called forth a sharp rebuke from the Elder the last quarterly meeting in this place, "was simply

one lady asking another to make room on another seat as the one where she was, was uncomfortably crowded."

P. S. Some one, however, may say, the above is a mere evasion of the Elder, to screen himself from public opinion. Such a charge would involve a new issue from the one in question heretofore. It would not only be then, that the Elder had spoken harshly to a lady without a sufficient reason, but that he is not a man of his word and has spoken falsely to evade responsibility—is any one prepared to make that issue?

Mar 13, 1851

 The chivalry in Marion are quite southern in their feelings lately—perhaps its because the weather has been so warm. No blood has been spilt however, nor lives lost, nor cabbage heads busted nor crout spoiled.

Mar 20, 1851

Married.

On the 20th inst., Mr. H.M. Ault and Miss Mary C. Gorton, both of Marion.

❖

At the Hotel of C.B. Mann in Marion, on the 18th inst., Mr. John Petri to Miss Magdalina Stecher, all of this county.

❖

On the 6th inst., Mathew Lingral, of Union county, to Miss Martha Essex, of Marion county.

Census Statistics.

According to the last Census, the white population of Ohio is 1,957,65—the colored population 23,495, total population of the State, 1,980,960.

Marion county has 12,536 for a white population, and 18 of a colored population.

Marion township	W	C
has a population of	980	
Marion town	1,290	17
Scott township	717	
Claridon	1,342	
Richland	1,229	
Pleasant	1,198	
Grand Prairie	474	
Tully	735	1
Big Island	600	
Montgomery	643	
Grand	336	
Salt Rock	347	
Waldo	1,008	
Prospect	848	
Green Camp	383	
Bowling Green	406	

Mar 27, 1851

Married.

In Tiffin City, on the 20th inst., Mr. John W. Bartram, of this place to Miss Adaline Kelly, of the former place.

Apr 3, 1851

California Letter.

Dry Creek, Eldorado Co., Cal.
Feb 1, 1851

Dear Brother,

I take this method to inform you that yours of the 22nd of November came to hand, and I assure you that it afforded no small degree of pleasure to receive a letter from house and friends, and to hear that you are all enjoying good health.

Although it afforded me much pleasure to hear from you, it also afforded some pain to hear from the unfortunate, which causes me to sympathize in their behalf. No doubt but you, according to the news that generally goes back to the States, expect to hear something favorable of the mines, and of our great success in mining, but I am sorry to inform you that I cannot write anything favorable, either of the mines or of my own success in them. The emigration has been so great that the mines have been over-run and there has been a general failure. Miners are making, at the present, from three to ten dollars per day in the dry diggings.

It is supposed that the coming season will be the best for mining on the rivers that there has been since the discovery of the gold as there has been very little rain so far and the streams are as low as they were last summer. This has been the most pleasant winter that I have ever witnessed. We have cool nights and considerable frost, but the days are nearly as warm as ours in harvest.

This kind of weather in the States would prove very unhealthy but this is not the case here. At the present time the health is extremely good.

I have been mining since my arrival in California but with poor success. I design going to teaming in the course of a few weeks, considering that better than mining. According to the state of things I do not expect to make much of a future, but I think I shall be able to return with something of a pile at least. It is my intention to return in the course of a year. It is true that I sometimes feel lonesome when I think of those that I have left behind, but I look forward to the day when I will be permitted to enjoy their sweet society so far. Although lonesome at times I have plenty of company, yet I sometimes think that it is not altogether the right stripe. The Marion boys are all living within a few miles of each other and meet once a week. I will have you to judge of the merry times we have when we meet together, each to try his hand at that at which he is most experienced.

You undoubtedly think as I did when in the States that Californians were deprived of every comfort of life. It is true that we are deprived of the blessing of society to a great degree. Yet we have all that heart can wish (except female society) in the line of living.

This California expedition is designed to qualify the old bachelor for his retired and useless life. No doubt but you would like very much to have a view of us performing in the line of cookery and washerwoman. Although we consider that we get along very well keeping bachelor's hall, yet we believe we would get along far better if we were permitted to enjoy the society of the better half of society.

If there are any that design coming to California next season, tell them they must endure months of toil and hardships in crossing the plains, and must climb mountains of snow that are almost impassible, and keep watch at the same time for Indians and the grisly bear that frequently spring upon the traveler, and that they will be very fortunate if some of their cumber are not left in the plains, their flesh to be torn in pieces by wild beasts and their bones left to bleach on the sandy waste of the far west. Not also, that after enduring all those trials and difficulties and no more than one out of ten will be able to return with a fortune.

Nothing more at present. Present my respects to all enquiring friends. I remain yours until death,

John W. Miller

P.S. The Marion boys are all in good health. J.W.M.

Apr 10, 1851

Married.

On the 3d inst., Mr. Robert Carr, to Miss Elizabeth Redding.

At the same time and place, Mr. Nathan Burns to Miss Elizabeth Carr, all of Big Island township.

Died.

In California, on the 5th day of last Jan., Philander Gorton, formerly of this place—son of Col. Gorton. He leaves a wife and 6 small children to mourn the loss of an affectionate father and kind husband. Mr. Gorton spent his early years in and near Marion and will he remembered by those who knew him as a kind hearted boy and an excellent man. A few years after he was married he removed from this place to Noble county, Ind., where he resided until he started for California, one year ago last Oct., and where his family still resides.

The particulars of his disease and death we have not been able to learn farther than that he had but little apprehension that his disease was unto death, and confidently hoped to get well. He sunk suddenly and expired.

Revival

We learn by a letter form the Rev. L. B. Gurley, that they have had a revival at Wooster station. About forty entered the covenant of grace. We would inform our friend that a revival is now in progress in Marion, that bids fair, from present indications, to exceed even that of Wooster.

May 15, 1851

Money Sweetens Labor

This number closes the publication of the laws. To many of our readers no doubt they have been dry and uninteresting, but they were messages containing the knowledge of duties we are required to perform daily, they are also the safe guards of our rights. This is also the first number of a new volume.

We have edited and have been associated in the publication of the *Eagle* 16 months. During which time we have spared no pains to make it an efficient Whig paper. Many of our subscribers have shown their appreciation of our labors by paying us up, and some even paying in advance; but, others act as if our furnishing them the paper was a matter of course and such a thing as pay entirely out of the question. NOW WE WANT MONEY and MUST HAVE IT.

Will our friends that are one and two years in arrears please call and pay up and commence anew. A word to the wise is sufficient.

 It is thoughty that it will take 8 years to complete the Washington Monument.

Fruit Prospects.

We have had a late backward Spring, and some very severe late frost, which we have no doubt, has done up the fruit business in our county for the season.

The weather has also been very dry, too much so, for vegetation to flourish, even though it has been warm. The wheat crop however has been rather benefited by it than otherwise, as it would have been too forward, say some of our farmer friends, if the weather had been warm and the earth moistened by occasional showers. The grass has been some injured, though we trust not very seriously as the few warm days and refreshing showers we have had the last week past makes it look quite green and promising.

May 22, 1851

Married.

On the 22d inst., Parkinson B. Thew and Miss Matilda Dutton, both of Marion.

On the 15th inst., in Mt. Gilead, Mr. Dubois St. John of Cardington and Miss Matilda Kingman of Lincoln.

On the 15th inst., Mr. Johnson Lidgard to Mrs. Ann Hatfield, all of Claridon township, Marion county.

Jun 5, 1851

☞ We learn from some of our Agricultural friends that the yellow weevil is working pretty strongly on some fields of wheat.

Jun 12, 1851

Died

On the 11th ult., Mrs. Rachel, consort of John Haldeman of Salinesville, Columbiana county, Ohio. She leaves a large family of children and an affectionate husband to deplore her loss.

Jun 19, 1851

Vote of Marion County

License to sell intoxicating liquors *yes* has generally prevailed throughout the county except in the Township of Marion and Claridon. Marion voted a majority of 54 License *no.* Claridon 71.

Jun 26, 1851

Arrest of a Horse Thief.

The scoundrel that stole Mr. Hind's horse a few weeks ago has been ferreted out and is now in a fair way to reap the reward of his doings. It seems he rode the creature to wood county, as we are informed and there traded it for some cattle, which he subsequently sold for cash.

Learning that hand-bills describing the creature had arrived in the county, he became apprehensive of detection, and went and stole the creature a second time, took it some distance in the woods, tied it to a tree with a chain he borrowed of a neighbor for the purpose and, with a axe beat out its brains hoping thereby, we suppose to escape detection, left the axe, chain &c, with the dead creature and fled for his residence in this county.

The chain and the axe gave a clue to the villain—the hand bills to his residence. A warrant was immediately placed in the hands of the sheriff of Wood County, who pursued him to this place and took him on last Saturday. He proved to be a neighbor's son, of Mr. Hind's. His parents are wealthy and respectable; nor did his circumstances require him to steal horses for a living. We pity his friends, but, we hope that he will not fail to receive the full penalty of the law, consequent upon his offence.

Mr. Hind's will probably get paid for his creature, we hope so.

Jul 3, 1851

Advice to Young Men.

Live temperately—go to church—attend to your affairs—love all the pretty girls—marry one of them—live like a man, and die like a christian.

The New Costume.

This new mode of creating attractions in the appearance of the fair ones, made its debut in our streets during the passing week. On the 4th we understand it is to be all the go, with the Ladies, and of course with the gentlemen too, as they always approve what the Ladies like.

A Daily Mail

The advantages of a daily mail, to a commercial town like Marion, are too obvious to require any argument to convince the citizens they ought to have one. The only question that arises on the mind of any one, perhaps, is how we shall go to work to get it. That part of the subject, however, belongs to the sovereign citizens, and we refrain from any remarks upon it; but with their leave we would suggest that a meeting upon the subject by the citizens of the place, might lead to the suggestion of proper means or mode by which to obtain it.

Fourth of July Celebration

There seems to be no preparation for celebrating the 4th, but at Newson's Spring Garden. That, we understand, is to be the great event of attraction for the day, for both young and old. A dinner will be prepared for those who wish to partake—a revolving swing is in operation for the accommodation of those who wish that kind of recreation. And others who prefer it can promenade in the garden, admire its walks, its flowers, its arbors, together with its varieties of flourishing and thrifty vegetation; and critics if they please the taste and skill of the gardener in the arrangement of the whole or if peradventure their industrious feelings should be overtaxed, they can lounge under the shade of some beautiful apple tree in the neighborhood and make love to some fair one, or talk over the scenes and events of by gone days, and if that dont suit them they can close their eyes to all that's interesting about them, and snooze away the day as many a loafer has done before them, for remember, it is Independence day.

Returned Californian.

We take pleasure in announcing the return of our old friend and fellow Townsman, John Dumble, who left here near three years ago with a number of others in search of the Elephant upon the coast of the Pacific. He has returned, and we doubt not, has seen the *Hannimal* to his hearts content.

We have not ascertained whether he brought with him a Pocket full of rocks, as the saying is, or not; but, we have no doubt he feels sufficiently gratified, that he has been permitted life and health to return at all, even, though he may not have been permitted to accumulate any of that, the love of which, is declared in the BOOK of books, to be the root of all evil.

The Turkish Costume.

We have but little objection to the introduction of new fashions amongst the ladies particularly if such fashions are productive of greater health; but we regret, that the inventive genius of our fair friends is so far exhausted as to be obliged to borrow their changes of fashions from countries where the lights of Science, Religion and Civilization are but partially developed.

We think that it speaks but poorly for the fair daughters of enlightened and republican Americans. America! where the mind is left free to combat with the errors and evils of the past, and suggest or adopt such improvements as the nature of the case may require. We would certainly think in such a county, its fair inhabitants could find but little apology for adapting the costume and fashions of countries as yet but partially enlightened.

Married.

On the 3d inst., Mr. Edwin R. Bowe to Miss Ann Wells, both of Grand Prairie Township, Marion County Ohio.

On the 19th ult., Mr. Harman Berry to Miss Almira McWherter both of Marion Co., O.

Jul 10, 1851

Thunder Storm.

On yesterday, we had the heaviest thunder storm of the season. The rain poured down in torrents, accompanied with heavy wind and some hail. The farmers labor, in taking their Wheat, Grass and Corn, will be very much increased by it as it undoubtedly beat most of them to the ground.

 The Elephant is in town but it is very coy.

Married.

On the 3d inst., Mr. John Wahn of Upper Sandusky to Miss Mariah Barnett of Marion.

On the 7th inst., Mr. William Critzer of Marion, to Miss Helena Storner of Upper Sandusky, Wyandot county.

Jul 17, 1851

Died,

On the 9th of July after a short illness, Henry L., only son of F.C. and Mary Ruhermund, aged 1 year, 5 months and 14 days.

The New Costume.

The new costume has made its appearance in Marion. A couple of young ladies promenaded the streets on the evening of the 4th in Bloomer style.—*Bucyrus Forum*

 We have hardly room to mention the death of Dr. J.C. Norton, who died of a short illness on the 16th last. His loss to his family is irreparable.

Incidents and Sketches.

The flux is prevailing to some extent in town and also in the country, and numerous deaths are incurring from it. Three deaths occurred in one family some four or five miles South West of town, last week. Two cases of Cholera are reported to have occurred some three miles South of town, one man and his mother by the name of Rupely, the man recently from St. L.—the case of the mother resulted in death, the man is likely to recover.

The weather has been very warm for the past few days and we look for an increase in the prevailing disease.

❖

A colored man was imprisoned upon the charge of attempting to murder his wife a few days ago. His trial will come off at the next term of the Court of Common pleas for this county, which will be about the first of October next.

❖

The little room left in the grave yard, is rapidly filling these sickly times—wonder if the town council wont anon think it necessary to be making some further provisions for burying the dead.

Query.

Do the modern advocates of women's rights claim that women are oppressed by having to change their maiden names for that of their husband when they get married? And if they do, is it not as reasonable a claim as many others they make?

Jul 24, 1851

Death of Levi H. Randall

It is our painful duty this week to record the death of Levi H. Randall an old and esteemed citizen. He died, as will be seen by his Obituary notice in another column, which we copy from the *Monmouth Atlas*, published in Warren County Ill., on the 10th inst. of Cholera. He left home on the 1st of the present month, arrived there on the 5th, and on the 10th was a corpse.

Mr. Randall settled in Marion at an early day, and has been favorably known to the citizens as a steady, upright, industrious, straight forward business man. He leaves a large family to mourn his loss and an extensive circle of friends and acquaintances that will feel in his death, the loss of one most highly esteemed amongst them.

He went west for the purpose, as we are informed, of taking under his care, the Orphan children of a deceased sister-in-law and widowr'd brother, but was not permitted to consummate his errand of mercy.

 Those wishing an opportunity to judge of the fitness of the Bloomers dress for lady's wear, can be gratified by calling at J.S. Reed's & Co's, where the thing is on exhibition without cost.

Died

In this town, on the 12th inst., Laura Elizabeth, daughter of W.M. and Kate Hardy, aged one year and 10 months.

In Monmouth, on Tuesday, the 10th of July of Cholera, Mr. Levi H. Randall, aged 44 years, ten months and 21 days. Mr. R. was a resident of Marion Ohio, from which place he started on the first day of the present month and arrived in Monmouth on Saturday evening last. He was attacked with a slight diarrhea on the evening of the 8th, which continued until the next day about noon, at which time the disease assumed a more serious stage, and he died on the next day about 2 o'clock P. M. He has left a large family to mourn his sudden death.

On the 19th inst., Mrs. Mary Uncapher, aged 71 years, 4 months and three days.

On the 21st inst., Mary, daughter of Thomas & Ann Robinson, aged 21 years and a few days.

 The negro, broke jail this week, or rather slipped out when the door was unlocked, while Sheriff went to get a basin of water for another chap to wash, who had been Jug'd through the night for getting drunk.

He has been retaken however, after a few miles brisk travel, sufficient to get his blood to circulating freely, and give him a good appetite.

Local matters.

We understand that an impression is afloat that there is cholera in Marion. We can assure our country friends that such is not the fact, there have been two or three cases reported from the county, as we remarked last week, but we are gratified to have it to say, there is as yet no indication of its spreading any farther.

The flux is still prevailing and some are dying with it, and in some parts of the country especially, if our information is correct, the bills of mortality are heavy comparatively speaking, and in proportion to the population far exceeds those of town.

Mrs. Swisheim on Woman's Rights Conventions.

The following remarks from the pen of that distinguished lady, are well timed and show her to have a correct notion of what constitutes a woman's true position and legitimate rights:

"The physical right to be taken care of is one of woman's rights that we will never yield. Our physical weakness will be our strongest argument for claiming all legal, intellectual and moral powers of defense. In an intellectual and moral war, we ask no quarter on account of womanhood; but of every man we claim physical protection just because he is a man and we are a woman. As to meeting in convention to discuss woman's right to engage in any occupation for which she has capacity, it is sheer nonsense. There is no law to prevent women following almost any business, and why do they not take their right to work at any thing they please!

"There is no use claiming rights for those who do not want to use them, and those who do should just take them."

Jul 31, 1851

Married

On the 16th inst., Mr. Amos C. Cooper to Miss Ruth Thurlow, both of Big Island, Marion county Ohio.

On the 22d inst., Nelson C. Mitchel of Marion to Miss Mary Jane Martin of Claridon.

At the Mansion House in Marion on the 27th inst., Mr. E. T. Hull, M. D. of Olive Green to Miss Martha P. Stout of Waldo.

A SERMON

Occasioned by the death of John C. Norton, M. D. of Marion, Ohio, preached on Sunday the 27th day of July, by Rev. George B. Sturges.

Doctor John C. Norton was born on the 8th day of May 1814, at Berlin, Connecticut.

His Father, Stephen Norton, was a respectable farmer and both his parents were connected with the Presbyterian Church. At an early age, however, he went to live with his uncle, Professor Charles Hooker of Yale College, New Haven, and while there he attended the Episcopal Church. He graduated from the medical department of Yale College A. D. 1836. In the fall of 1836 he came to Ohio and commenced the practice of medicine in connection with his late uncle, Doctor Alson Norton of Big Island Township in this county.

In A. D. 1838 Dr. Norton was married to Olive, the eldest daughter of Col. Hezekiah and Alfe Gorton of Marion, and he settled in the town of Marion A. D. 1839; where by his talent and industry he earned a good reputation and obtained an extensive patronage as a physician; and continued in the practice of his profession to the time of his death. But little more than two years after their marriage his wife died; she was a patient cheerful sufferer and calmly "fell asleep in Jesus." He had then no children, and after remaining a widower about two years, he was married to a younger sister of his first wife, whom he has now left after more than nine years of affectionate union, with three children to mourn his absence.

Medical Notice of the Late John C. Norton M.D.

This was a case of dysentery, continuing about three weeks. The first five or six days he pursued his business, although obliged to resort to the constant use of opiates. For four or five days more, after taking to his bed, he prescribed for himself chiefly, availing himself of the suggestions of casual visitors.

In summing up and digesting the whole case, we would observe that although the symptoms may have been aggravated temporarily by what we cannot but regard as injurious treatment, yet that there was a peculiar torpor of the sympathetic nervous system, observed and felt by our late friend, which rendered his case critical, not to say hopeless from the very commencement, which marked the extent of the disease, so that we were deceived by delusive hopes of amendment, and which in some measure justified or extenuated on his own well known theory, a part of the treatment which he himself adopted.

Samuel Grafton M. D.

Henry A. True, M. D.

Aug 7, 1851

☞ A large tea spoonful of mustard mixed in a tumbler of warm water and swallowed will throw any poison from the stomach.

Married,

In the city of Indianapolis, on the 20th of July, J.W. Bain of this place to Miss Julia Hall of the former place.

Well done for John. Who'd a thought it?

Died,

On the 23d ult., Princess M., only daughter of Niram and Minerva Rundle, aged 2 years and eight days.

Aug 14, 1851

Died.

Pauline, daughter of F.G. & Elizabeth McWilliams, aged 10 months and 14 days.

Aug 21, 1851

Middletown

We paid a little visit to the little village of Middletown this week and felt gratified to see that notwithstanding some disadvantages of location, through the enterprise of the citizens, the place is improving.

A large stream mill is in course of erection and almost completed. This, when finished, if rightly constructed, will be a valuable improvement to the surrounding country and must enhance the prosperity of the place.

We are sorry the place is cursed with a stillhouse. Our opinion is, that in ten years, it will damage the place more than the cost of its construction and that the citizens would make money in the operation if they would indemnify the owners and then set fire to the concern and burn it to ashes.

We don't make these remarks out of any personal ill feelings towards anyone, but from conscious conviction that stillhouses have always had a tendency to cause a declination in the moral and physical well being of society around them.

Sep 4, 1851

Fire

A fire broke out last night about 10 o'clock, in the barn of William Bain; which on account of the hay and combustable in it, although apparently discovered early after it was communicated, was entirely beyond control, until it had consumed the building and also the barn of Dr. Holloway adjoining it.

The live stock and buggies were all saved, except one cow and perhaps a couple of pigs.

The citizens were promptly on the ground and labored with untiring diligence to keep the fire from spreading which they fortunately succeeded in doing. If however, there had been any wind, the fire must have spread, and in such case, its bounds cannot easily be imagined.

The fire is supposed to have been the work of an incendiary.

Sep 11, 1851

Marion Markets.

Flour per bbl. $3.50
Cabbage per head 2 cts
Corn per bushel 31 cents
Oats 16
Butter from 3 to 10 cents
Eggs from 5 to 6 cents

☞Edwin Forrest and a doggery keeper named Sinclair had a fight in the Open at Castle Garden a short time since.

Neither was badly hurt, but the affair was emidently disgraceful to all parties concerned.

Serious Accident.

On yesterday Mr. William Sloan was thrown from a Buggy, attached to a couple of runaway horses and severely hurt, but it is hoped not dangerously. The circumstances as related to us, are these, he and his father hitched a young colt and what they supposed to be a study old horse to a buggy, for the purpose of training the colt. As soon as they were fairly seated in the

buggy, the old horse started to run away. The hub of the buggy caught a board and tore it off. The board fell across the horses backs and across the lines, which so alarmed them that they became entirely unmanageable.

In running up the ally from Mr. Sloans Stable towards East Street, the board caught near the corner of Mr. Charles Smith's shop upon the ground at one end; the other end flew back and struck William Sloan on or near the eye and the old gentleman about the neck or shoulders, instantly dislodging him from the buggy, and leaving the young man still in it without the lines or any means of checking the alarmed animals. They ran some fifty yards farther when he was also thrown out as above stated and severely injured.

Accident.

Yesterday was fruitful in accidents. Last night Sheriff Mann was thrown form his buggy with a little boy and a gentleman by the name of Myers. Mr. Mann was considerably hurt, we understand, Mr. Myers slightly and the boy not at all. The horse was not found until the morning.

Sep 25, 1851

Married.

On the 18th inst., Mr. Chancy D. Palmerton to Miss Sarah Jane Hoxtor.

On the evening of the 24th inst., Mr. Dexter S. Bates of Big Island and Miss Mary Jane Graves of Marion.

Oct 2, 1851

☞We understand the horse races at Leatherberry's on yesterday, was the scene of a good many bloody noses.

Rather a poor school for the young, to hear it.

Oct 16, 1851

Something New Again.

We are requested to say, that a colored man, an emancipated Slave by the name of S.D. Depps, who comes well recommended, will preach in the United Brethren Church this evening, by early candle light. Last evening he preached 2½ miles south of town.

Those wishing to have an opportunity of judging of African talent will find it a favorable opportunity.

Map of Marion County.

By an advertisement in our paper of this week it will be seen that the complete map of our county is about being published.

We have long desired such a map and many of our friends have doubtless felt the want of it; and we are prepared to find that from the care used in getting it up, we are likely to have a good one. We learn that the information obtained from the extensive Rail Road Surveys, has been added to that formerly acquired.

Certainly every owner of a tract of land should possess a copy, and the low price of 50 cents at which it is to be issued, should ensure a large subscription.

Sad Calamity.

We understand that Mr. Dillingham of Pleasant township had his leg badly broken on yesterday. He was helping roll a saw log, and by some means, it rolled upon his leg and mashed and broke it terribly.

Oct 23, 1851

Afflictive Dispensation.

Died suddenly after a short illness Mrs. Bunker, consort of Peleg Bunker Esq. of this place.

Oct 30, 1851

Not Bad.

"Which travels faster, heat or cold?"

"Heat, you dunce, can't any one catch cold?"

☞There was a mad dog shot in the south end of town near the residence of Mr. Walter Williams on last Sabbath.

Nov 20, 1851

Died.

In Marion Nov 2d, Laura, daughter of Simon and Susan Huggins, aged 3 years and 18 days.

Nov 27, 1851

Death's Work

Died within a few days past, Mrs. O.R. Stone and A.S. Rundle. Mrs. Stone was a large woman weighing over 200 pounds; and died suddenly without any waste of flesh. Her coffin was 2 feet in the clear across the breast and the sides about 16 inches high. The corpse filled it pretty fairly. The bottom of the coffin was made of 1½ or 2 inch plank. The corpse was borne upon a bier, by four sturdy men, to the home of all, and seemed to be no trifling burden. She was one of the oldest citizens of the place. She has left no family to mourn her loss save a kind husband.

A.S. Rundle was a young man in his teens, mild and amiable, apparently in his disposition and pious in his walk and conversation.

Dec 4, 1851

☞ Let no one hereafter, blame any old bachelor in the state of O. for not marrying, since according to the late Census, it appears there are not ladies enough in the state to furnish each a wife by over 52,000. Not so strange at last that a love sick swain of the Buck-eye state should now and then be found to wander from the land of his birth; to find a mate.

Dec 11, 1851

Died.

On the 6th inst. after an illness of 2 days with croupe, John Jenkins, son of John E. and Charlott Davids aged 2 years, 1 month and 12 days.

Jan 1, 1852

Married

On the 24th inst., Mr. C.W. Brown of Upper Sandusky and Miss Sarah J. Randall of Marion.

On the 25th inst., Mr. Frederick Hoxter and Miss Mary Ann Mills both of Grand Prairie township.

On the 23d inst. Mr. J.S. Wheaton of Marion and Miss Eliza Ann Case of Delaware County.

Jan 8, 1852

Married,

On the 1st, George W. Rose of Mt. Blanchard, Hancock Co., to Miss Araminta Southwick, of Big Island township.

On the 1st, John Ulsh and Jemima Cunningham.

Jan 29, 1852

Married,

On the 22d, Julius Bennett to Miss Mary E. Conklin.

Died,

At Caledonia on the 12th, Helen Adeline, third and youngest child of Dr. James M. and Sarah J. Biggs of dropsy of the brain, aged 4 years and 2 months.

Feb 5, 1852

Died,

On Wednesday morning, the 4th, at his residence in this place, William Miley, Sr, aged nearly 46 years.

NOTICE.

The public are hereby cautioned against taking an assignment of a promissory note executed by me to John Dumble and payable to said Dumble on order, two years from date, dated November 15, 1851, bearing eight per cent interest, for one hundred and fifteen dollars. Said note was recently in the hands of Jeremiah B. Wheaton to whom I paid fifty dollars and he now refuses to endorse the same. I shall pay no more than the balance of said note deducting the fifty dollars and corresponding interest, unless compelled by law.

Samuel Saiter

Feb 12, 1852

Married,

On the 3rd inst., Mr. Samuel Law to Mrs. Jeffery, all of Marion.

On the 5th inst., Rodney Spalding to Miss Margaret Moyer, all of this place.

On the 3d inst., at Van Buren, Ohio, Dr. S.W. Holmes to Miss Sarah E., daughter of D. Ensminger, all of Hancock County, O.

Died

On the 7th ult., after an illness of 29 days, Doctor I., son of Benjamin S. & Rebecca Ann Welsh, in the 4th year of his age.

Feb 19, 1852

Missellaneous Items.

Pius IX is 59 years old, the King of Wurtemberg 70, the King of Belgium 61, the King of Prussia 46, the Czar 55, the King of Sweden 52, the King of Denmark 43, Louis Napoleon 43, King Bomba 41, the King of Bavaria 40, the King of Holland 34, Queen Victoria 32, Donna Marie 32, the King of Hanover 22, the King of Sardinia 31, the Sultan 28, the Emperor of Austria 21, the Queen of Spain 21, the Count de Paris 13.

Afflicting Dispensation.

Mr. Isaac Wood, an aged gentleman and respectable citizen farmer of the western part of this county was frozen to death on Wednesday or Thursday night of last week. Mr. Wood had been to Sandusky during the day and having as we are informed, drank a little too freely, fell from his horse on his way home, and thus lost his life. Mr. Wood has left a wife and large family of children, mostly men and women grown, and highly respected with whom we deeply sympathize in their sad bereavement.

Mar 4, 1852

Isaac Wood's Death.

We learn from the friends of the deceased, that his death did not result from drinking too freely as we were at first informed, but from a fit. He has for a few years past been subject to fits occasionally, and from all the indications when he was found, he was attacked with one of them, on the referred too in our paper of the 19th ult., and being a lone became so stupefied with cold before it subsided, that he was helpless! All know the lamentable result.

Mar 11, 1852

Married,

On the 4th inst., William H. Whan to Miss Louisa Barnett, all of Marion.

☞ There will be Services in the English Language on the Lutheran Church on Sunday evening Preashing by the Rev. Henry S. Lassar and subject! The holy sacrament of Baptism.

☞ The above was handed to our "devil" by some one, we don't know who as he refused to give his name. We publish it verbatim punctuation spelling and all, not feeling any liberty to change when the person sending refuses to give his name.

☞ A young man by the name of Moore was thrown from his horse (a colt) this week a short distance from town and pretty badly hurt. We understand however that his bruises are not likely to prove dangerous.

Mar 18, 1852

☞ Another Temperance meeting came off on Tuesday evening, in the Court House. We were not well and consequently not present but we rejoice to learn, the meeting was well attended, and passed off with uniform good feeling. We understand that addresses were delivered by the Hon. J.J. Williams, Peleg Bunker, Esq., Hon. T.B. Fisher, and a little to our surprise, the Hon. Geo. Patterson.

Mar 25, 1852

Examination of the Marion Union School

The first examination of the school took place on Wednesday, Thursday and Friday of last week.

This is called an age of progress, art and science have filled the earth with wonders, every thing they touch or that is brought under their almost magic influence, is suddenly changed to something more beautiful or more useful. Our Union School commenced about five months ago under very unfavorable circumstances. The commencement was looked upon more as an experiment than a reality; and by many as a very doubtful experiment. We will not stop at present to name the many grounds upon which those doubts were attempted to be based. Suffice it to say that five months experience has been sufficient to satisfy the most skeptical, that the progressive spirit of the age is on nothing more beautifully illustrated and no other thing more emphatically demonstrates its practical working for the good of mankind and especially of the young and rising generation upon whom all the hope of the future hangs than in the conception and adoption of the Union school system.

It was the first examination of the pupils of the first union school ever taught in Marion and it full and clearly demonstrated the superiority of the Union school system over any other system heretofore tried.

The branches taught in the primary department were spelling, reading, mental arithmetic and geography or at least these were the branches which the scholars were examined.

The secondary department exercises were continued by some dozen or 20 little boys and girls declaiming and speaking dialogues compiled for the occasion, nearly all of which performed their part well, some as a matter of course excelling.

No one examining this school can fail to be satisfied in every respect in imparting a thorough education to those placed under its fostering care.

☞ We have been informed there is to be a meeting of young men in the Court House on Saturday evening for the purpose of forming a temperance society. We hope it is so, it will do them good and no harm and help to make men of a few we might name, who have never troubled themselves much, heretofore with manliness, should they join it.

☞ There have been several mad dogs killed in town within the last two or three weeks.

Spirit Rappers.

A few of them have made their appearance in Marion, but they are thus far only the Small fry of the Gang; and have consequently attacked but little attention thus far; and their frauds have been easily detected.

Dr. C.A. Bodeman.

No doubt many were inquiring who the writer of "service on the Lutheran Church" was, since the little notice which appeared in our paper of week before last, stating that the preacher Mr. Lassar did not write it. Dr. C.A. Bodeman, however, has relieved all such from the necessity of our further inquiry on the subject by assuming the authorship and in an article which he had published last week, abusing our own dear self.

There are two distinct charges.

1st. That we changed the spelling and punctuation of the little notice above referred to.

2d. That we changed it out of ill will to the Lutheran Church, etc.

We don't know how the Dr. arrived at this conclusion as we have never made any such a declaration and as he infers it from the fact that we are not a member of that church, which we think a very unusual tolerance. This is a free country, a country where every man is allowed to worship at the church according to the dictates of his own conscious. It will be readily seen from these few remarks that the Dr. has no grounds to engage us with hating the Lutheran Church because we don't happen to adopt their articles of faith.

HOGS! HOGS!!

Cash will be paid by the subscriber for 200 head of STOCK HOGS— no Hog to weigh less than 80 lbs. gross—to be delivered by the 10th of July next.

T.M. Sloan.

Married,

On the 23d of March, Mr. J. Riley Clark to Miss Eve Elizabeth Free.

❖

On the 25th, Mr. Wm. Biggerstaff to Miss Samantha Berger.

❖

On the same day, Mr. Robert M. Davis to Miss Sarah Mount.

❖

On the 25th, Mr. John Bolander to Miss Ann McNeal.

❖

On the 28th, Mr. John Davis to Miss Sarah Myers.

❖

On the 31 ult., Isaac Young and Miss Isabella Baker, all of this place.

Married,

On the 8th inst., Wm. A. Butler to Miss Martha McKelvy, all of Marion County.

Died,

In Marion the 13th inst., Franklin W., infant son of Edmon and Lydia Thompson, aged 16 months.

Married,

On the 22d inst., Mr. John F. Hopkins and Miss Lydia Bates, both of Marion county.

❖

On the 25th inst., Mr. John Culberson to Miss Rebecca Ann Clark.

❖

On the same day, Mr. Jacob Baker, Jr., to Miss Marcy Lyone, all of Marion county.

❖

On the 24th inst., Mr. D.W. Elliott, to Mrs. Mary Hoover, all of Marion.

Died,

In Marion on the 26th inst., R.O. Clark aged 16 years and 10 months.

Married,

On the 29th ult., L.F. Ellis and Miss Eliza A. Pixley, all of this place.

Justice.

We hereby solemnly swear that we have carefully examined the manuscript copy of the notice which appeared in the *Buckeye Eagle* of the 11th of March; and find that the manuscript and published notice are word for word, punctuation and all exactly alike, except that in the manuscript there is a small dot over the letter o, in the word on, where it says 'on the Lutheran Church' which is not in the published notice, and in spelling of Lasar there is but one s, in the manuscript, and two in the printed copy; neither can we see any indication of change upon the face of the manuscript since it passed from the hands of the writer, nor is it our opinion that it has undergone any.

John Wildbahn.

B.H. Williams.

Sworn to and subscribed before me this 6th day of May 1852.

John E. Davis, N.P.

Married,

At Albany, N.Y. on the 6th inst., Mr. J.H. Mills of this place to Miss Maria C. Mesick of Albany.

Died,

On the 6th inst. in this place, of puerperal fever, Mrs. L.M. Trimble, consort of Wm. C. Trimble, junior publisher of the *Buckeye Eagle* in the 16th year of her age. She leaves a loving husband and an infant child and many friends to mourn her early loss. Mrs. Trimble was a highly esteemed member of the M. E. Church and though she was called away in the bloom of youth, her few days on earth were made out for her purity and christian like disposition.

She was a kind and affectionate friend, an obedient daughter and a loving wife. Her mind was a storehouse of preciousness—few of her age and opportunities can boast a mind so well stored with everything that tends to enrich it with the beautiful and useful. Had she lived, and continued with the same assiduity, to improve her mind, she would undoubtedly some day have occupied

a highly respectable standing among the higher galaxy of American female writers.

The following lines of her own composition she repeated to her husband a few hours before her death:

Love her, husband, while you may,
Cherish the sweet face, but to-day.
Kiss once more that brow so fair
Smooth the dark curls of her hair
And know death is drawing nigh
She is passing to the sky.

For she has felt death draw a pace,
And almost felt his cold embrace,
His shade has been cast o'er her heart
She knows full well that you must part.
That when the buds of springtime bloom
Their blossoms will be on her tomb.

After a short but painful illness, Samuel Grafton, M. D., in the 43rd year of his age.

Tribute of Justice

We learn various reports are in circulation through community, that Mrs. Trimble, came to her death in consequence of malpractice on the part of the attending physician, Dr. Sweney. Perhaps the person or persons who are the authors of these reports know them to be true, but of them, it is more than we know; and we being fully impressed with the belief, that Dr. Sweney, is a gentleman in the proper sense of the term and that he is fully qualified both by theory and practice to attend to the various duties of his profession; and also having made particular enquiry of Dr. Fisher, one of the best physicians in obstetrical cases, in the place, who was called in as council several days before her death. Our candid convictions are, that her case

was treated with skill and judgement; and that it was one of those cases in which the best of medical aid fails to save life.

Henry Haldeman.

W. C. Trimble.

Jun 3, 1852

Married,

On the 27th, Benjamin S. Camp and Phebe Court, all of Pleasant township.

Jun 10, 1852

Married

On the 6th inst., Adam Hain to Miss Ann Fosher, all of Marion county.

Jun 24, 1852

☞ There is to be a balloon ascension in Marion, on the 5th of July coming. The scene will no doubt be a grand one.

Jul 1, 1852

Struck by Lightning.

During the Thunder Storm on Wednesday afternoon, the lightning struck a small willow tree in the Hon. G. H. Busby's yard, which stood a few feet from the corner of his stable and literally tore it to pieces. The stable was not touched.

Some 2 or 3 rods distant, however, stood a locust in the same yard which was also struck. Near the bottom was a chain attached to the tree by a staple for the purpose of chaining a dog. This chain, McPherson's little boy had hold of, and was in the act of tying his dog when the lightning struck the tree. He received so severe a shock that he fell senseless, and for a short time seemed dead and animation was only restored by inflating his lungs and other appropriate means timely used. For a while his recovery was thought doubtful but this morning he is quite smart and there is but little doubt that he will entirely recover.

Married,

On the 20th, John Wyle of Michigan to Miss Mary Jane Cushman of Marion County.

Jul 8, 1852

☞ The balloon ascension on Monday evening was rather a fizzle.

Jul 15, 1852

Died

On the 6th inst., at the residence of her son, John Gaberson in Claridon township, Mrs. Rosanna Garberson in her 66th year. During the last 30 years she has been a professor of Religion.

Jul 22, 1852

Married,

On the 15th, Ebenezer Davis of Marion and Miss Ann E. Conklin of Waldo.

Died

Near Wyandot, July 18th, after a protracted illness, Henry P., son of B.S. and Rebecca Ann Welsh, in his 10th year.

Jul 29, 1852

Ladies Supper.

The young ladies supper on last Thursday night was a splendid affair, and no wonder, since it was gotten up by the fair. Ye love sick swains who want a wife that can cook a good supper, just come to Marion and you will find the girls where can do it. No doubt some envious little souls will say their mammies done it, but we know the daughters done some of it, for we saw them with their gloves off and sleeves rolled up working for dear life, and we guess they did the whole—a Yankee you know is allowed to guess and why not a Dutchman be allowed the same privilege.

Fatal accident on the C. C. & C. Railroad.

We learn from a passenger that two women had taken passage at Columbus upon the Northern train in a second class car, but unfortunately got into a first class car, the conductor finding them there ordered them into the other car, while the train was in rapid motion. They attempted to obey, and one of them succeeded, the other one fell through between the coupling of the cars, and was instantly killed, her body being literally cut into ribbons.

Aug 5, 1852

RUNAWAY

From the residence of the subscriber in Marion, on the morning of the 13th inst., Jacob Siler, a crazy man. He is about five feet, 8 or 10 inches high, heavy set, black hair, black beard, and can talk both dutch and english, but uses the dutch more fluently; he seldom, however, has much to say. Any person finding him will be suitably rewarded by sending him back to me.

Joseph Caig.

New things in Marion.

Daily arrival of the cars.

The lowering the grade of the streets and repaving them.

Paving side walks upon a uniform grade.

The old Market House fitted up by Dr. Galley and made to appear fair.

An ordinance passed by the council establishing market three times a week.

A whig and locofoco combination to promote and perfect the above new things.

Aug 12, 1852

Died

On the 29th ult. at West Campton, New Hampshire, Mr. B.F. Clark of this place, aged 36 years and 9 months. Mr. Clark has been afflicted with Consumption for some time and during the latter part of winter and spring was confined to his room.

Having revived a little strength he ventured on a Northern tour to Quebec for the improvement of his health and was on his return through New Hampshire as far as West Campton when he was taken worse and in a few days ended his earthly pilgrimage.

He leaves a wife and two children to mourn his early loss.

P.T. Barnum's Grand Colossal Museum & Menargerie.

The largest travelling EXHIBITION in the World, being a combination of all the most popular and unexceptionable amusements of the age—enlarged and improved for the season of 1852. The real, genuine, original **General Tom Thumb** is attached to this exhibition, and will appear in all his performances.

To Those having friends in California.

Thompson & Hitchcock have not sufficient confidence in Gregory & Co's Nevada Express to accept for a small amount, a three days draft. The hard working miners should not risk their earnings in the 'Express.' The draft protested was sent to our old friend John Uncapher, by his son George, now in California.

Married

On the 5th inst., David Sorrick to Rebeca Jane Stroble, all of Marion.

Aug 19, 1852

Glad to see them.

On Tuesday morning we had the first arrival of passengers cars.

Many of the citizens collected to see the strange & interesting but not unexpected visitors, amongst them was our neighbor of the *Mirror* grinning one of his hardest grins, but the Locomotive paid no attention to him, a bit more than if he had not grinned.

WATCH! WATCH!

WATCH THAT DASTARDLY CALUMNY, that Gen. Scott is a catholic, on the day of election, for wily Locofocos will surely be skulking round the polls like a wolf round a sheep cote seeking some one off their guard upon whom to make an impression with this vile slander, and get him to give the old Hero the pass if not to vote for Gen. Pierce. WE REPEAT IT, WATCH THEM.

☞ A horse thief was caught in this place on yesterday morning.

Carnival

The show last week called in together an immense crowd—from three to five thousand people—we never saw so many people in Marion at one time since we have been a resident of the place—and all appeared gay and happy, but our neighbor up street, he looked the very personage of some evil genius; his usual facile grin, had entirely disappeared, and a dark cloud thunder and lighting like aspect had assumed its stead, we felt at a loss to account for it, for Knapp will usually almost grin the green ones into the belief that he's an honest man; we felt perplexed, but finally however we recognized it as a public day and that he might perhaps be noting dummy, and making a little raise.

Hymenial

Married—On the 12th inst., Mr. George Davis to Miss Sarah Orr, all of Caledonia, Marion County.

☞ Attend to your door fastenings; black legs, cut-throats and burglars are on the increase in our town of late; both in impudence and numbers.

Aug 26, 1852

☞ The funeral of Mr. Adolphus H. Wilson, formerly of this place will be preached at the Episcopal Church next Sabbath at eleven o'clock.

Hymenial.

On the 22d inst., Mr. George W. Lind and Miss Mary Ann Miley.

Obituary.

Died—On the afternoon of the 9th inst., Mr. Adolphus H. Wilson, at Gilboa, Putnam Co., in the 24th year of his age.

The deceased was suddenly seized by Cholera, and lived only a few hours—leaving a kind and affectionate wife, mother, sisters and a large circle of friends to mourn. The deceased was a young man of exceedingly fair promise and usefulness—as a moral and upright man and good citizen.

Sep 2, 1852

Excitement

At the wild hunt two Deer were killed, two wolfs were seen, one snapped at. Two white men and one young nigger drunk—and yet the town remains healthy.

Hymenial

Married—On the 2nd inst., Dr. R.L. Sweney to Miss Elizabeth, eldest daughter of Col. W.W. Concklin, all of this place.

On the 16th ultimo, Mr. Jacob Huttler and Miss Margaret Dietz, both of Marion County, O.

On the 27th ult., Mr. Frederick Eavley and Maria Gottshal, both of Marion Co., O.

On the 26th ult., Ernst Werner and Miss Frederica Himmelreich, both of Marion Co., Ohio.

Sep 16, 1852

Fire

On Thursday night last about 8 or 9 o'clock the stable of Wallser Hoxter was set on fire by some incendiary and burnt to the ground. The citizens gathered in large numbers but it was impossible to save it.

Sep 30, 1852

Hymenial.

Married—On the 28th inst., Mr. Henry C. Godman to Miss Catherine L. Copeland, all of this place.

On the 28th inst., Harvey Wilmeth to Julia A. Monday, all of Marion.

Obituary

Died, on the 18th inst., near this place, Mr. Champ C. Hord, aged about 20 years.

Oct 7, 1852

Hymenial.

Married—On the 7th, William Dildine to Miss Sarah Jane Jones, all of Marion Co.

Oct 14, 1852

Obituary.

Died—On yesterday morning the 13th about four o'clock, Martin V.H. James, Son of Isaac E. & Betsy James of this place, aged 17 years, eight months and seven days.

Hymenial.

Married—On the 28th ult., Mr. George Foreman to Miss Margaret L. Johnson, all of Middletown, Marion Co.

Married—On the 3d inst., Mr. Samuel Bolander to Miss Belinda McNeal, all of Marion Co.

Oct 21, 1852

Notice.

Dr. Fisher will address the Citizens of Marion & Claridon townships at Holverstot's school House on Monday night next on the subject of Galphinism.

Obituary.

Died on the 12th of Oct., Mrs. Mary P. Terry, daughter of Eld. J. Mason in the 35th year of her age. She was a pious and worthy member of the Regular Baptist Church. She was perfectly resigned to her death and said she was going home to a better world.

Hymenial.

Married—In Pleasant Township on the 14th last, Doctor Tyler to Miss Mary Jane Davids.

Oct 28, 1852

Hymenial.

Married on the 18th, Mr. Benjamin Sharpless and Miss Isabella Thompson, all of Salt Rock township.

Nov 4, 1852

Hymenial.

Married—On Sunday, Oct 31st., Mr. Wilson Warner to Miss Harriet F. Arthur.

Married—On the 2nd inst., at McCutchenville, Mr. O.R. Stone of this place to Mrs. Amanda Taylor of McCutchenville, Wyandot Co., O.

Married on Thursday evening Nov 4, 1852, Mr. Lyman Spaulding to Miss Orrel E. I. Anderson, all of Marion O.

Nov 18, 1852

Hymenial

Married—On the 11th inst., Mr. Henry Concklin to Miss Phebe Jane Beede, both of Marion county.

Nov 25, 1852

Obituary

On Wednesday, Nov 17, Charles W. Concklin, aged 34 years.

Dec 2, 1852

Justice's Election

To the voters of Marion Township I offer myself as a candidate for Justice of the Peace at the election to be held in Marion township on the 3d of next month. Should I be elected, I shall probably in a few months be in a situation to give my undivided attention to the duties of that office.
S.A. Griswold.

Hymenial.

Married—On Friday evening, Nov 30th, at the residence of Mr. M. Woods, Mr. R. Noble Patterson to Miss E. Janny Fulkerson, all of this place.

Dec 9, 1852

A child burned to death

The following chilling circumstance took place a couple of weeks since in this place.

An infant child of C.W. and Theresa Cherry was left by the latter in the cradle with no one in the house save another child, a little larger, while she went out upon some errands. After she left the house, it seems the larger child took the small one, only between 8 and 9 months old, out of the cradle and set it on the floor. She had also got on a chair and taken a dress from a line over the stove, and laid it on the stove, where from the heat of the stove the dress took fire and part of it fell on the floor in a blaze; the little child appears to have crawled to the place of burning dress when its own caught fire.

When the mother came in, the little fellow had crawled under the table with its clothes all in a flame. The whole one side of its body was so badly burned that death ensued in a few days.

Jan 6, 1853

Hymenial.

Married on December 29th, Thomas Monday of this place to Miss Jane Amanda Fauke of Little Sandusky, Wyandot Co., O.

Jan 13, 1853

Hymenial.

Married on the 4th inst., Mr. Noah Smith to Miss Lavina Richy, all of Marion County.

Dissolution.

The partnership heretofore existing between Henry Haldeman and William C. Trimble, under the firm of Haldeman and Trimble is this day dissolved by the mutual consent of parties.

The books and accounts will be found in the hands of H. Haldeman who is authorized to settle the same.

Jan 20, 1853

Hymenial.

Married—On the 18th int., Mr. John B. Andrews and Elizabeth Ann Essex.

Jan 27, 1853

Plank Road to Kenton.

A friend of ours in the Western part of the county writes us there is considerable feeling on the subject of a plank road from Marion to Kenton. Our opinion is if the friends of the project were to make a move in the matter they will meet with a favorable response from Marion. It is worthy of note however that the citizens of Marion have heavy investments in the Bellefontaine and Indiana Railroad and that they have exerted themselves in the utmost of their ability to perfect and finish up that important enterprise.

☞ The Marion Froth mill, alias, the Editor of the democratic *Mirror*, was in full blast last week emitting a large amount of black viscid froth raising a severe stench—consult your health every body and hold your noses until the stench passes.

☞ Cold enough at last.

Feb 10, 1853

We heartily coincide with our friend Dr. Bridge, that a plank road from Delaware to Kenton, through Middletown, in the absence of a plank road from Middletown to Marion would work a serious injury to both Middletown and Marion; and we hope that the necessary steps will be taken to prevent it.

Feb 17, 1853

☞ The weather is fine.

☞ The Swiss Bell Ringers have paid our town a visit this week; and demonstrated some of the improvement in musical science in a manner very creditable to themselves as well as highly gratifying to the citizens that heard them.

Feb 24, 1853

☞ knapp says we choked a boy we had in our employ until the marks of our fingers were visible upon his neck more than a week afterwards. *This is false and knapp knew it when he uttered it.* We gave a boy in our employ a moderate shaking by the collar, because he was so much like our neighbor knapp—impudent and unworthy

of trust and would lie to conceal his defections. WE MADE NO MARKS ON HIS NECK BY "CHOKING" HIM NOR DID WE CHOKE HIM AT ALL.

Mar 3, 1853

Hymenial.

Married—On the 1st inst., Mr. John Rumbaugh to Miss Eliza J. Richardson, both of Caledonia, Marion County, O.

Anti Horse Thief Society.

The citizens of Marion County are respectfully requested to meet at the County Home in Marion at 4 o'clock P.M. on Friday the 11th day of March inst. for the purpose of taking measures to form an ANTI-HORSE THIEF SOCIETY. A general attendence of the citizens of the County is requested at the appointed hour.

Mar 10, 1853

The Graveyard.

We learn from good authority that there is a most disgraceful course of conduct carried on in relation to the Marion Graveyard. Several locks have been furnished in order that the sexton might keep it locked, and all of them have been broken off by some one, and the gate thrown open, and hogs and cows, &c., permitted to run it, and desecrate the graves as though they had ceased to be sacred in the memory of any one.

We hope this matter will be seen to and the sacrilegious SCOUNDREL ferreted out and brought to justice.

☞ Marion county is a very small county, the population being only about 13 or 14,000; and yet the business of the county Clerk we are credibly informed, amounts to about $1,600 per year, *in this small county of Marion*, and yet the legislature is afraid some of the poor Clerks of the Court in the State, dont get fees enough, and under certain contingencies are trying to provide more. This looks a little bare faced.

Mar 17, 1853

Severe Accident

A young Mr. Bowdish, son of Elijah Bowdish residing two miles north of Marion had a leg broken a few days ago while felling a tree on his father's farm some distance from the house. One or two others were with him at work that had left to go to dinner while the young man remained to finish the tree he was at before going. The tree lodged upon another and while making an effort to get down it started, and his position was such that he could not get entirely out of its way as it fell. It struck his leg in its descent and broke it and caught the toe of the boot on his other foot and held him fast for a time; but by a considerable of an effort he succeeded finally in extricating himself. He was about an hour there alone before any of the family found out his situation. Dr. R.C. Bowdish was called to set the broken limb and we understand the patient is doing quite well.

☞ A splendid assortment of mourning and second mourning ladies dress goods, to be found at the One Price Cash Store.

J. Ault & Co.

Obituary.

Died—On Tuesday, March 1st 1853, Samuel F. Fish, son of Samuel and Hannah Fish of Marion county Ohio, aged 25 years, 10 months and 23 days.

This dispensation of an All Wise providence has taken away a loving and beloved son and a kind brother. One whom we dearly love is not with us now. A little while ago, and he was with the young and happy; but alas! the bloom has faded from his cheek; he sickened and died. What were our feelings when we looked upon his pale face for the last time, and followed his beloved form to the cold and silent tomb! And Oh! When we heard the earth fall upon his bosom, how did our hearts bleed: and then to turn home without him, and from that day to behold the vacant seat and with tearful eyes gaze again and again upon some memento of the departed one.

Mar 24, 1853

☞ knapp's falsehoods about our "Choking a boy" are too fully apparent by the decision of the Committee who investigated the matter, who, as the result of such investigation, declared,—"Charges not sustained," to need any reply from us.

Obituary.

Departed this life on the 19th inst., at the residence of her parents, Mary Florence, only daughter of Charles and Abby Smith, aged 1 year and 9 days.

Mar 31, 1853

Mrs. Jones.

The celebrated Physiological Lecturer, Mrs. Jones, has arrived in town agreeable to previous notice and will lecture in the Presbyterian Church this evening. Mrs. Jones is highly spoken of by the press as a lecturer where-ever she has been, and we feel assured the Ladies of Marion will enjoy a rich entertainment by attending her lectures.

 Matthew Stull was brought before his Honor, Judge Hurd, on yesterday on complaint to keep the peace.

The evidence showed him to be a peaceable man when sober, but abusive and quarrelsome when drunk. He was required to enter into a bond of $100 to be of good behavior to the citizens of the State generally, and particularly his own wife and family, for the period of one year, which he failed to do, and was committed to jail. He is a poor man and can't give bail. He stands committed until he does—and in the meantime his family must be deprived of the benefits of his labor—their only means of livelihood. They must suffer, no matter what nor how much, and the county must pay for keeping him.

Just such cases may occur every day, our jails and poor houses may be filled to overflowing, the people may groan from the very oppressiveness of their taxes, and we are told there is no help for us. We enquire for the cause of the frequency of these complaints, and in very derision they tell us—whiskey. Is there no remedy?

Obituary

February 12—At the residence of her son-in-law—Isaac Haldeman—Marion, O., Sarah Miller, in the sixty-fifth year of her age.

She was the daughter of Doctor Elijah Herrick. She was born in Connecticut and was educated and received her early moral training in the rigid school of Puritanism. At the age of fifteen she attended a Methodist camp meeting; was deeply convicted of sin; and was powerfully committed to God. As she often related it, "All things became suddenly new—entirely changed." Her reward is on high.

❖

Died—Near Birlington, Iowa, March 20th, Mrs. Jane, wife of Asa Davis. For a number of years she resided in Marion and Hardin counties Ohio; but recently in Iowa.

Apr 7, 1853

Hymenial,

On the 30th ult., Mr. Lewis Gunn to Miss Sarah Stoneberger, all of Marion county.

Apr 21, 1853

Mr. Editor:

I have noticed for some time past certain persons pulling the bills of the merchants and tradesmen, put up at convenient places through town. It will be well for them if they will suffer themselves to be admonished that there is a law which makes it a punishable offense to tear down bills & if the practice is persevered in, the offenders, whether found to be men or boys will be brought to justice.

Vigilance

Hymenial.

Married—On the 7th inst., George King to Miss Margaret Parnhart, all of Marion county, Ohio.

❖

Married—On the 14th inst., Mr. Abram Bare of Putnam county to Miss Mary Bechtel of Marion County.

❖

Married—On the 14th inst., Mr. Archibald Hopkins to Miss Cordelia Higgins, both of Big Island.

❖

Married—On the 3d inst., Mr. Calvin Berry to Miss Eliza J. Sullivan, both of Green Camp.

 Our readers will be grateful to learn that on yesterday the Bellefontaine and Indiana Railroad was opened ready for the Cars, from Marion to Bellefontaine. The balance of the road, from Laramie Creek to Union, will be ready for the Cars by the first of June, providing the Company succeed in getting in the balance of iron in time.

Apr 28, 1853

 There will be a fine crop of peaches this season in Marion county if not destroyed by late frosts.

May 5, 1853

Hymenial.

Married—On the 26th ult., James Reed to Miss Martha Anderson.

❖

On the 27th ult., Mr. George Lawrence to Miss Martha A. Smith.

❖

On the 1st inst., Mr. Henry Kelly to Miss Angeline Payne.

❖

Married—On April 8th, Samuel A. McNeal to Miss Elizabeth Morison, all of Marion township.

❖

Married—On the 3d inst., Dr. M.B. Cochran of Delaware Co, to Miss Mary E. Gooding of this place.

May 12, 1853

HYMENIAL.

Married—On the 26th ultimo, Mr. John Cunningham to Miss Martha A. Short, all of this place.

❖

Married—On the 3d inst., Mr. John Bain, Jr. to Miss Eliza Scribner, both of Montgomery township.

❖

Married—On the 5th inst., David Reed to Miss Sarah Underwood, all of Claridon township.

Phrenology has been thought to have grown so stale and common place, that any attempt to afford an entertainment upon that subject, in the form of public lectures to a promiscuous and an intelligent audience, seemed rather characteristic of premature insanity than of sound mind. This is an age however, of mental as well as physical wonders and the lectures of Dr. Wagner commenced on last Tuesday evening evince that their is enough of the new and wonderful, when properly divested of its old clothes and dressed out in bran spanker new suit, even in the heretofore considered stale subject of Phrenology, to afford a rich intellectual entertainment.

Dr. Wagner is quite original in his style and address and speaks with great ease and fluency—his lectures are listened to with attentive interest. The Dr. has his lecture room fitted up with an unusual large collection of profiles, upon which in the course of his lectures, he points out the analogy between the development of the head and the character of the persons they are intended to represent.

On tomorrow (Friday) evening he proposes a lecture to gentlemen only on the subject of "masculinity." Dr. Wagner has generally been highly complimented for the ability with which he has treated this subject wherever he has lectured.

May 19, 1853

HYMENIAL.

On the 11th, Peleg Bunker, Esq. and Miss Lizzie Amburg were married at the residence of A. Amburg in Harrisbourg, Ohio.

❖

Married—On the 12th inst., Mr. Charles F. Miller of Marion and Miss Hannah Bunker of Galion.

May 26, 1853

HYMENIAL

Married—On the 22nd inst., Edward D. Hatch and A.L. Goodell, all of Grand township, Marion co.

Jun 2 1852

Obituary

Died—June 1, of disease of the lungs, Mrs. Sophronia Reed in the 64th year of her age.

Jun 9, 1853

Obituary.

Died—On Thursday morning the 2d inst. in this place, of Typhoid fever, Miss Phebe D. Hardy, daughter of John and Sarah G. Hardy, aged 16 years, 4 months and 6 days.

Some villain or villains stole a horse on the night of the 7th inst. from the pasture of Robert Douce living in Claridon township. The cowardly scoundrel left a note written with a pencil, warning them not to follow him as he was armed and would be dangerous if attempted to be taken. We venture that a resolute of two years old would take him if he was to overtake him—his threats show him a coward as well as a knave, his cowardly heart showed him he would be taken if they followed him hence the note for to scare them from pursuit—give the scoundrel a warm chase—a barking dog never bites.

Jun 16, 1853

 We learn from Mr. J.W. Bain that he has sold a spot of ground lying between the Delaware & Marysville roads to the firm of Bain and Williams for the purpose of converting it into a park. This will be a very desirable improvement and will make the "Hill" as it is now called quite a shire of attraction to the citizens of town.

Jun 23, 1853

Items from the Census returns.

The number of Deaths in Ohio during the census year was 28,949 or as one to every 66 ²/₃ inhabitants.

The Dutch reform church has 324 churches in the United States and $4,006,730 in value in church property.

The Episcopalian church has 1430 churches and $11,319,470.

The Free Church has 361 churches and $253,235.

The Friends church 715 churches and $1,710,367.

The German reform church has 327 churches and $965,680.

The Jews have 31 churches and $391,600.

The Lutheran church 1205 churches and $2,882,886

The Mennonites have 110 churches and $94,245.

The Methodist church has 12,484 churches and $14,730,571.

The Moravian church has 331 churches and $443,347.

The Presbyterian church has 4591 churches and $14,447,889.

The Roman catholic church has 4269 churches and $9,808,658.

The Swedenbargians 15 churches and $104,100.

The Tunker church has 52 churches and $46,025.

The Union church has 619 churches and $690,065.

The Unitarian church 244 churches and $3,278,122.

The Universalist church has 494 churches and $1,367,015.

Minor sects have 334 churches and $746,080.

Total number of churches in the United States, 36,221.

Jul 28, 1853

NOTICE.

Whereas my wife Phebe Jane has left my bed and board without just cause or provocation, I hereby forewarn all persons from trusting or harboring her on my account, as I will pay no debts of her contracting.

Henry Conklin

Aug 4, 1853

Mechanical Enterprise.

Marion has got its growth yet by some, consequently we have a great number of that worthy class of men called carpenters—capable of doing as good a job of work as can be done in the State—if any one doubts it let him come to Marion and examine their work and we pledge ourself he will give in that we are right. Our town is also well supplied with shoemakers whose work and industrious habits would do honor to the profession in any country.

The blacksmiths of the place are a hardy, industrious, honorable class of men, and capable of doing any job of work in their line that may be called for with as must taste, genius, and durability as done in any other part of the State—we were going to say of the world—but for fear that some one of the knowing ones would say we were not acquainted with all the Blacksmiths in the world—well we should not have cared much after all, since we would have had some trouble to show that we were wrong before he could require us to prove our affirmatives; and his chances to fail would be at least nine to one.

Saddlers.—The town is well supplied with this class of workmen; our worthy friend Walter Williams leads the business—he has constantly a good supply on hand in his line at a reasonable price.

Stone Cutters.—The Mr. Culbertsons attend to this branch of business and we believe are able to keep pace with the demands of the place.

Masons.—This department could give employment to a few more good workmen.

Wagon Markers.—The department is conducted by a couple of very worthy men.

Plastering.—This department is also pretty well filled with the best of workmen. Elder Lindsey is rather the most prominent workman at present.

Marble Factory.—An extensive Marble factory is carried on one door west of the Depot house by Mr. Conley, where the best quality of tomb stone, and of every variety can be had on the shortest notice.

Painting.—There are several gentlemen engaged exclusively in this business; many of their jobs manifest a large amount of skill and taste.

Taylors.—There are any quantity of them in town—all clever, good-natured fellows.

A few Queries.

Since Knapp has been pleased in his last paper to make some base insinuations in relation to ourself which he knows to be false as his own false heart, we propose to him the following questions which he can answer in his next paper if he chooses:

Were you (J.R. Knapp) driven out of Bucyrus for attempting to filch from the county treasury the hard earned dimes of the "dear people"?

Did Dabney Jackson Bean charge you correctly when he intimated that you were a little too intimate with the "Boxers" a few years ago?

Can a man give himself as much to drunkenness and gambling as you are reported to do and at the same time retain any respect for truth?

Did you ever ape the "dumb" man and beg a few coppers to bear your expenses at any other time than when you attended the State fair at Columbus two years ago?

Do you whip your wife, and if you do is it because you want a companion in your disgrace that you labor so hard to fix that kind of a base slander upon us?

Aug 11, 1853

HYMENIAL

Married—On the 4th inst., Augustus Madison and Miss Mary A. Van Kirk, all of this place.

❖

In Claridon, on the 4th inst., Mr. Robert Smith and Miss Mary Dickinson all of Claridon twp.

❖

On the 2d inst., Mr. Christopher Martin and Miss Catherine Grapes, all of this place.

Aug 18, 1853

Sudden Death

Mrs. Peters, consort of Capt. E. Peters, died very suddenly of an attack of Cholera Morbus on Tuesday morning—less than 12 hours sick.

 Weather rather cool to day.

 On Friday and Saturday of last week the Mercury rose to 95 Farenheite; on Tuesday of this week it ran up to ninety two. This we call hot weather for the latitude of 40½ degrees.

 A Miss Little was buried on Tuesday. She had been sick for some time of flux and was very much emaciated when she died.

Aug 25, 1853

Mr. Editor:—Your paper of last week contained a brief notice of the sudden death of Mrs. Kate Elvira wife of Capt. Eben. Peters. This truly estimable Lady was taken away in the midst of life and usefulness, being about thirty-six years of age. She was as universally esteemed as known. Affable and interesting in her manners; kind and sympathizing in her disposition; happy in herself and salutary in her influence; consistent and earnest in her piety; affectionate, prudent, faithful and assiduous in her conjugal and maternal relations, she is everywhere greatly missed and mourned.

HYMENIAL

Married—At the Empire Saloon, in Marion, on the 18th day of August, 1853, Mr. John A Copler to Miss Hannah Lichtenberger, all of Marion county, Ohio.

❖

And at the same time and place, Mr. Jacob Hadsly to Miss Christina Coffier, all of Marion county.

10 Dollars Reward.

I will give the above reward to any person who will arrest George Smith, and restore a gun stolen by him. Said George Smith is about 5 feet four inches high, and about 20 years, without beard, swarthy complexion, with dark eyes, had on when he left yellow pants, white linen coat and Buckeye hat with a broad black ribbon. Any person catching can deliver him to me at the county jail. My place of residence is two miles east of Middletown, Marion county.

Levi Marlow

Sep 8, 1853

Married

In Iowa City, Iowa, August 25th, 1853, Mr. Rufus Clark formerly of Marion O. and Miss Caroline E. Staly, formerly of Wyandotte county Ohio, but now a resident of Johnson county Iowa.

Sep 15, 1853

Married

On the 15th last, Mr. J.M. Strowbridge of Caladonia to Mrs. Sarah Williams, of Marion twp.

Sep 22, 1853

A Fatal Blow

While the Democratic convention was in session in our Court House, on Saturday the 3d inst., it is said that a Mr. Jacobee of Richland township, threw a *brick bat,* which (accidently) hit Billy Patterson on the head—the blow was unexpected, the recipient was able to speak for some minutes after, tho his brain was evidently on fire, and probably 'cracked,' but faint hopes of his recovery was entertained from the first—he continued to sink gradually until the following Wednesday about noon, when he died (politically,) dropping off in the midst of a tremendous shower of rain, thunder and wind.

Mr. Jacobee is a worthy farmer, a heavy tax payer of excellent character and is able to give bonds for his appearance or good behavior in any amount, as it was no doubt a premeditated accident. Alas for poor Billy—he was killed whilst advocating the "cardinal principles of the democratic party"—Plunders or four dollars per day (for member of the legislature) with waiters and roast beef.

Oct 6, 1853

HYMENIAL

On the 29th ult., Charles Berry and Miss Prudence Huffman, all of Pleasant Township, Marion County O.

Oct 13, 1853

Fairs—Marion County Fair.

The citizens of the county are generally aware that on the 6 and 7 inst. was held the Marion county Agricultural fair, about half a mile west of town. A large number of the citizens of the county were present, "more" it was remarked by an old citizen "than the county contained 20 years ago."

A number of fine cattle were on the ground—some exceedingly fine. There were also a fine collection of China poultry on the ground of different varieties. There was an auction of poultry on the evening of the second day. The prices paid however were so low that the sale was stopt after selling a few pair. Shanghais sold from $3 to $6 per pair or thereabout.

There was quite a large assortment of fruit, particularly apples, on exhibition—some very fine specimens of apples. There were also a number of articles, the products of the garden and the field exhibited.

The ladies department was not very well filled. Though the few articles exhibited, showed skill and taste in the manufactures, and were worthy, generally of high commendation.

HYMENIAL

Married—On the 6th inst., David Zuck to Miss Elizabeth Jump, all of Claridon Twp, Marion co.

Poetical lines were composed by Shelby Jump, and read at the marriage of his daughter.

Oct 20, 1853

HYMENIAL

Married on the 6th inst., Mr. William Moore and Miss Eley Morris all of Marion County.

Married—On the 18th of Oct. inst., Barney Shaffer and Miss Amanda Riley all of Marion twp, Marion county.

Married—On the 1st day of Oct. inst., Elder Asa Pierce of Knox County Ohio and Catherine Myers of Morrow County O.

Killed.

An old gentleman living two miles north of the city, on the farm of Mr. Noble, was killed on Tuesday, whilst on his way to visit at Kinnear's Hotel in Clinton township. From the circumstances, as far as we have been able to learn them, it appears that he, in company with several others, having procured a wagon to convey them to the Hotel was going along at a rather brisk trot, when the wagon running into

a mud-hole. He was precipitated backward to the ground breaking his neck and killing him instantly.

Splendid New Building

Judge Bennet has put up the finest building in Marion. It is 125 ft. in length and three stories high. Lower and 2d stories are 11½ ft and third story 15½ feet between joice; five rooms on the ground, suitable for stores, with a cellar under each. The second story is divided into rooms suitable for offices or any other purposes for which upper rooms are generally used.

The third story was put on by Messrs Fisher & Reed, and designed for a Town Hall—a thing very much needed in this place. In size it is well suited to such a purpose being 76 by 33 ft in the clear. The building is yet in an unfinished state, but in rapid progress of completion. When completed it will be an honor, and we think also, a source of profit to the builder.

Oct 27, 1853

OBITUARY

Died—Sept. 15th, of Yellow Fever, James Holloway, aged 31 years. The deceased was a son of Dr. Geo. Holloway of this place and well known in the community. He died at Mills Point 36 miles below the mouth of the Ohio and was buried at Cairo Ill.

The deceased was on his way home to visit his aged parents, full of life and hope for the future, and joy at the anticipated meeting, when the cold hand of death was laid upon him.

The county is becoming quite a fruit county, and as many farmers are very much interested in the improvement of their orchards we publish for their benefit the following catalogue of nursery trees for sale by Joseph Morris of Richland township Marion co. Mr. Morris has been engaged in the nursery business a number of years—fruit trees got of him may be relied on to be what they are represented to be.

In making this selection of fruit, my object has been to procure the best varieties, rather than to increase my list to an immoderate length. I do not intend that worthless fruit shall be imposed on any purchaser, knowingly, as fidelity on my part may be expected. I have about five acres in Nursery, and perhaps fifteen thousand trees of a suitable size for transplanting this Fall.

❖

CATALOGUE.

APPLES.

SUMMER QUEEN.—Medium size, yellow and red striped, flesh slightly red, shape conical, ripe in 8th month.

BOUGH APPLE.—Large sweet, pale yellow, ripe in 8th month.

EARLY PENOCK.—Large red and yellow striped, shape conical, fine sub acid flavor, very fine for cooking, ripe a little past mid summer.

WHITE JUNE EATING.—Valued for its early maturity, very good for cooking and eating.

SPICE SWEETING.—Quite large, yellow, very delicious in flavor, and quite sweet, ripe latter part of summer.

STRAWBERRY APPLE.—Medium size, a little tart, very fine for cooking and eating, ripe in 9th month.

FALL PIPPIN.—Large, yellowish green, slightly acid, very good a fall variety.

MOUNT PLEASANT SWEETING.—Large white, very pleasant, ripe the fore part of 9th month.

PUMPKIN SWEET.—Large white, very good for baking and drying, a fall variety.

POMEROY.—Good size, sweet, a very good apple for fall use.

RAMBO.—Red, medium, first rate fruit, well known.

ENGLISH RAMBO.—Large, red and yellow stripes, deep cavities at each end, very good.

TULPEHOCKEN.—Large, smooth, green apple, very good, a fall and winter variety.

BELLEFLOWER.—Large, yellow, a little acid, a fall and winter variety, much esteemed.

BELMONT GATE.—Rather large roundish, color pale yellow, crisp with a mild sub acid flavor.

RHODE ISLAND GREENING.—Large, becomes yellow when very ripe, of excellent flavor, and keeps until spring.

WHITE RAMBO.—Large, a fall and winter variety very fine for eating or cooking.

LOWRY QUEEN.—Rather large, red and greed striped, a winter fruit, very good.

WESTFIELD SEEK NO FURTHER.—Medium or rather large, none perhaps better for winter use.

BETLEHEMITE.—Medium size, mostly red, none better for eating or cooking, keeps through winter.

SHREVE APPLE.—Large redish green, as good perhaps as the best, and keeps until spring.

LOP SIDE.—Large red, very good and keeps until late in the spring.

ROMANITE.—Small red, round shaped, very productive, pleasant flavored, late keeping variety.

SWAAR.—Yellow, rounding, second size, first quality fall and winter.

MONSTEROUS PIPPIN.—Very large, conical and ribbed, pleasant acid, fall and winter.

ROMAN STEM.—Medium size, green, often a little russet, very good, keeps well through winter.

NORTHERN SPY.—Large, roundish, slightly conical, handsomely striped with red, flavor mild and agreeable, winter fruit.

SPITZENBERG ESOPUS.—Rather large, slightly conical, surface a high rich red, flesh yellow, firm and spicy, keeps trough winter.

RED GILLIFLOWER.—Large, flatish, conical, sometimes strongly ribbed, flesh fine grained, with a fine and agreeable flavor, winter.

GERMAN GREENING.—Good size, smooth surface, very good for eating or cooking, winter variety.

TALMON SWEETING.—Yellow medium or rather large, excellent for sweet cider and apple butter.

RAWLES JENNET.—Medium or rather large size; mostly red, mild and agreeable flavor; very good keepers.

GOLDEN RUSSET.—Medium size, mild and substantial flavor, very fine for winter use.

NEWTON PIPPIN.—Large green, an excellent keeper, variety very good.

PUTNUM RUSSET.—Large and rich fruit, first quality, good keeper.

POUND PIPPIN.—Quite large and tolerable rich, early winter.

WHITMORE SWEETING.—Medium size, white, very good for fall use.

I have obtained from reliable sources many other kinds not published here.

— — —

The above trees are invariably sold at ten dollars per hundred at the nursery, except when large quantities are sold.

HYMENIAL

Married—On the 20th inst., Mr. J.W. Bartram of this place and Miss Lucy Ann Vanfliet of Hardin co.

Nov 3, 1853

Carelessness—Censurable

During the past season a half dozen or more teams have run away on the streets of Marion. Now we will venture to say, that a due degree of care would have prevented every one of them. If the owners had tied their teams securely when they stopped, before leaving them they would have saved the loss that has frequently occurred to themselves, and the annoyance accruing to the citizens generally.

There is an ordinance requiring owners of teams, to not leave them on the streets without tying them under a penalty, the amount of which we do not recollect. This ordinance we think ought to be rigidly enforced. It is true there has fortunately been no person injured as yet by these runaways, but no one can tell but the very next one that occurs some person old or young may be killed thereby. Let the authorities enforce the ordinance without fear, favor or delay.

OBITUARY

Died—On the 31st inst., at the residence of T.J. Anderson, in this place, Thomas Johnson, after a painful illness of seven days. His disease was inflammation of the lungs.

He was born in western Pennsylvania in the year 1780, and emigrated with his parents to Jefferson co. when in his twentieth year.

Nov 10, 1853

Fatal Accident

On last Thursday, a Mr. Griffith in the employ of Messrs. Kinnear and company at the Marion Steam Sawmill, was killed by a small stick of wood accidentally caught by the big saw when in rapid motion and buried against his head, literally knocking his brains out.

Nov 24, 1853

Electric Lamp.

Considerable interest has been excited in scientific circles in London by the invention of a lamp, the light of which is produced by Electricity. An electro magnet is placed within the base of the lamp, connected outside with a battery. The electric fluid being made to pass between two points of the charcoal, called electrodes, a light of wonderful brilliancy is produced.

Dr. Watson, an electrician of great ability, has finally overcome all difficulties hither to encountered in regulating the electrode and battery currents. He has produced a lamp which regulates itself in these respects and a company has been formed to manufacture them for public use. They claim economy in their use but we are doubtful on that score.

An Outrage.

We have scarcely known an act of boyish wantonness or inconsideration that shocked us more than the following: The friends of Phebe Hardy had her likeness in miniature size set in the face of her Tomb-Stone.—It was beautiful.—On last week we were shown that likeness ruined—the glass covering smashed to pieces and the likeness completely spoiled—the act of a wicked or inconsiderate boy.

Such destruction and sacrilegious wantonness should not be allowed to go unpunished.

HYMENIAL

Married—On Thursday Nov. 17th 1853, Samuel Beerbower and Miss Nancy J. Huggins, all of Marion O.

Dec 1, 1853

Thanksgiving Day.

This legal festival day was observed by our citizens in an appropriate and commendable spirit. The stores and shops and business departments of the place were generally closed until after two o'clock. The churches met in Union at the Brethren church and held communion together giving thanks to God for his mercies during the past year and invoking his continued blessings during the year to come.

Died—In the town of Minerva, Stark Co., O. on the 23 of Nov. of Inflammatory fever, Levi Olmsted, son of Dr. L. & M.A. Haldeman, aged about two years.

Dec 8, 1853

HYMENIAL

Married—On Wednesday, Nov. 30, 1853, Mr. Benjamin F. Lee to Miss Narcissa Sapington, both of Marion township, Ohio.

Dec 15, 1853

HYMENIAL

On the 7th inst., Mr. Eli Porter to Miss Roxy McNeal all of Marion County O.

Dec 22, 1853

Man Killed by the Cars

On last Saturday one of the brakesmen on a freight train, had one leg and arm cut off by falling on the track between two of the cars. The cars were just leaving Caledonia and as is usual for the brakesman he attempted to board the cars after they were in motion, by passing up the iron ladder at the end of one of them. The round upon which his feet were placed, gave way, bringing his whole weight upon the one which he held on to by his hands, that also yielded, and he fell.

The accident occurred in the morning he lingered until evening before he died. We have the above intelligence from a young friend of ours conversant with the facts.

Jan 5, 1854

HYMENIAL

On the 29th ult., John W. Miller and Miss Olive Cunningham.

On the 1st inst., Mr. W.P. Thew and Mrs. Charlotte Washburn, all of Claridon Twp, Marion co. O.

On the 1st inst. at the Holt House in Tiffin, Dr. A.B. Haltbill of Little Sandusky and Mrs. Elizabeth B. Conklin of Marion.

Jan 12, 1854

Died.

In this village on the 3rd inst., after a short illness, William L. Kendrick, Esq., aged 36 years.

The deceased has resided in this place a long time and was universally respected for his urbanity of manners, kind disposition and strict integrity as a man and a public officer. He was Clerk of the court for several years, in which position he established a character for business which gave him a productive position in society.

Married.

On the 2d of Dec., Mr. Jacob Harshberger and Miss M.E. Short, all of Marion Ohio.

Jan 19, 1854

OBITUARY

Died on Thursday morning the 6th of liver complaint, Mr. Henry Saylor, aged 71 years.

Jan 26, 1854

HYMENIAL

On the 28th, 1853, Mr. Wm. R. Hughes of Jefferson, Cambria co. Pa., to Miss Racheal S. Ritner, of Allegheny county, Maryland.

Mr. Hughes formerly resided near this place and we have no doubt his many acquaintances here join us in wishing him and his fair bride the most unbounded joy.

OBITUARY

Died—On the 17th inst., Austin Wright Engineer on the B. & I. R. Road.

Far away from home and kindred, death placed its icy fingers upon his brow and claimed him as its victim.

Feb 2, 1854

The Ordinance

On yesterday the ordinance passed by the town council for the suppression of liquor traffick, took effect. Mr. Search we understand has relieved himself of his bar and his liquor some days ago and like a *good citizen* comes square up to the requirements of the Ordinance.

Every such man should have the countenance and favor of community. The man that refuses to obey law and the law of the community in which he resides is unworthy of the title of *good citizen*. All laws will be acquiesced in by all *good citizens* until others and better ones, if they are needed, can be obtained.

Small Pox

There is a case of Small pox in town north of the R.R. on main st. It is recommended by the town authorities to block its progress by vaccination. We hope this recommendation will be universally responded to. Every one should do all in his power to keep this fearful disease from spreading.

We have given its precise location that our country friends may know in what part of the town they are safe from its contagion.

OBITUARY

In this village, on the 16th inst., after a short illness, Mr. Emery Patten, aged about 24 years.

❖

Died a few days ago, an infant child of Mr. W.F. Paxton of this place.

Feb 9, 1854

 Some of knapp's friends, it would seem, have been telling him that the clerk of the court of Marion county should be a man of some dignity, and above being the author of such a tissue of low, abusive slang as constantly fills his paper. The idea of being a man of dignity turned john's head all topsy, it was something that had never entered his noddle before; his previous aspirations never having risen above those of an accomplished blackguard. After turning it over & over he appears to have resolved to give the thing a trial and accordingly he came out square in his paper telling us, that from henceforth he was going to be a man of dignity, alas for the frailties of poor human nature, in his very next paper we found him at his old dirty business again—sorry john dont succeed better in his attempts to "REFORM."

We always appreciate evidence of friendly feeling and good wishes in whatever form presented, though sometimes, from press of business, we may neglect to make the proper acknowledgement at the proper time.

Some two or three weeks ago we received a present of some beautiful grafts from Esq. Taverner, for which we hope the Esq. will not think us too late to return him our hearty thanks.

Sleighing is fine and some of our citizens are enjoying it as if they thought it quire a treat. This is the first sleighing snow we have had this winter worthy the name; and the first really cold weather; the mercury sunk from two to five degrees below zero Tues. night—varying in different Thermometers, owing we suppose to the different positions they occupied.

Feb 16, 1854

Fatal Accident

On last Friday Mrs. Woodcock, a lady living a short distance from town, was killed by the falling of tree while on her way home from town and in sight of her own residence.

Circumstances—Three men were cutting down a large hickory tree in the commons, in J.W. Bain's addition to the town of Marion, close by the route upon which she passed coming to town, and upon which she attempted to return; and had got the tree just ready to fall as she got that far on her way home. The tree was cut so as to fall to the south, a cut nearly in the direction of her home and across the track that she would naturally pass—when the choppers saw her they motioned to her to keep back; but she seemed to misapprehend their meaning, and pressed forward the more rapidly—determined if possible to save her, one of them ran to catch her, but the motive of the effort seemed to be misapprehended too, and she ran from him, apparently alarmed, making a circuit off from the tree for a short distance and them back again to her track which she reached just at the point of danger and just in time for one of the limbs of the falling tree to hit her on the head.

She seemed not to be conscious of any danger, only such as she appeared to apprehend from the men engaged in chopping down the tree and who tried to interpose their friendly offices for her safety, until she had fairly reached the fatal spot, when, says an eye witness, she gave two screams. Her skull was broken, one of her legs broken in two or three places, and one of her arms broken we believe and her person otherwise bruised.

Death was instantaneous. She leaves a husband and a somewhat helpless family to mourn her loss.

Feb 23, 1854

Wanted

Immediately, twenty Boys and Young Men for the devout purpose of standing at the Methodist Church door to stare persons out of countenance, especially ladies, as they pass into the Church.

A portion of these must be the sons of members of the church—the balance we will take from any quarter, providing they possess the requisite qualifications. The qualifications required are as follow, viz:—A good stock of impudence—a fair proportion of vulgarity and conceit—a thorough acquaintance with *slang phraseology*—a capacity to make indecent remark upon the appearance of a lady as she passes, loud enough for her to hear, and if a blush is brought upon her face, one should be able to laugh loud and heartily over the matter. It will be necessary for you to remain there during the whole service, talking and laughing in a rude and boisterous manner, so as to disturb the congregations that worship below as much as possible, and attract the attention of passers by.

As a reward for these especial services you will be properly *appreciated* by all decent and sober minded persons; and they will no doubt indulge the encouraging hope that you will in due time realize their most sanguine expectations of your becoming nuisance of the first stamp.

☞ We learn from the attending Physician that there are three new cases of Varioloid in the same house where the others occurred in the north end of town.

OBITUARY

Died—On Thursday, 16th inst., Clara M., youngest daughter of Hon. John J. and Amanda A. Williams, aged 4 years, 1 month and 12 days.

Feb 30, 1854

HYMENIAL

Married—On the 15th inst, W.C. Trimble and Miss Kate Gurley.

We copy the above from the Zanesville Gazette. Mr. Trimble was formerly a resident of this place and our partner in the publication of this paper. He approven himself here a worthy man. We wish him and his happy bride a life of prosperity and bliss.

Mar 9, 1854

Fatal Accident

On last Tuesday a young man drowned in the employ of Mr. Clark, as hostler, rode a horse to the Stone Quary south of the graveyard, which is now filled with water, for the purpose as we learn of washing his legs—the horse became refractory while in the water and threw him off and either kicked, or struck him with its fore feet; and before assistance could get to him and extend him any aid he was drowned. It is not certain, however but the bruises given him by the creature would have killed him, even if he could have been take from the water immediately. Two distinct prints of the creatures feet were visible on his body and breast.

OBITUARY

William H., son of I.H. and G.J. Cunningham, aged 2 years, 6 months and 15 days.

Apr 6, 1854

Obituary.

Died—On the 15th day of March, 1854, Frank May Cummings, aged 11 months & 12 days.

Married—On the 30th inst., at the house of N.G. Hord, Esq., Mr. Peter McNab and Miss Hannah Bowden.

Apr 13, 1854

Wanted.

A girl to do housework, inquire at this Office.

Apr 20, 1854

Catholic Influences to High Places.

It is said by those who profess to know that Roger H. Tuney, Chief Justice of the United States Supreme Court, and the Hon. James Campbell, Postmaster General, are Catholics. We recollect that many persons voted for Frank Pierce on the ground that he was opposed to the Catholics, and that locos urged them to vote for him on the ground that he was a better Protestant than General Scott.

Didn't these men know better or didn't they care to deceive their neighbors. It makes but little difference which, however, as in either case they are unworthy of confidence any longer. Everybody can, with these facts before them, better understand why the Pope who'd have the temerity to write a letter of recommendation with his Nuncio recommending him to the favor of the President.

☞ Dr. Booth died on Tuesday. The Dr. was a worthy citizen and a good Physician—his early death is a matter of deep regret.

Married.

Married—On the 11th of April, 1854, Mr. Robt. Ewings to Miss Rosilla Russell, all of Bowling-green twp, Marion Co. O.

On the same day, George Elling, of Detroit, Mich to Miss Catherine Klineknicht of Marion, Ohio.

On the 19th, C.W. Woodard to Miss Rebecca Ann Adams, both of Harden Co.

On April 5, Martin Lee of Salt Rock twp to Miss Anna M. Tehl of Wyandot Co.

Also, Milton Clark of Pickaway Co. to Miss Sarah Ann Lee of Salt Rock, Marion Co.

Also, A. D. Brady of Big Island Twp to MIss Harriet C. King of Salt Rock.

Obituary.

Departed this life, on the 11th of April, Mr. Jacob Holverstot aged about 60 years, of Marion Co. Ohio.

Died—On the 12th last, Phebe Lucretia, daughter of David C. & Margaret R. Moore, aged 1 year, 3 months 3 days.

Also, Francis S. Asbury, son of Hugh I. & Elsa B. Moore, aged about 1 year 4 months.

Apr 27, 1854

☞ We are happy to learn from some of our exchanges that the fruit has not been seriously injured by the late cold weather—we also hear from the farmers of this County that it has make a fortunate escape in the county.

Married.

On Apr. 20, William F. Miller and Miss Hannah M. Monday of Marion Ohio.

Married on March the 30th, John Kraner and Sarah Wild.

April 2nd, Philip Metzger and Catherine Dietsch.

April 2nd, Jacob Bering and Philipine Metzger.

April 9th, John Keller and Christina Curfies.

April 17th, Christian Lehner & Ernestine Augenstein.

April 29th, John Mergenhaler & Mary Schultz.

Obituary.

On Tuesday the 18th inst., after a lingering and painful illness, Dr. D.J. Booth, aged 41 years, 3 months and six days.

May 4, 1854

Marriage Notices.

We have not made up our mind to charge for marriage notices for the reason that we think the man that is possessed of soul enough to appreciate the value of a good wife would not have the assurance to ask the printer to publish his valuable acquisition for nothing; and he who has not, is properly a subject of pity and commiseration—a class of men for whom we always feel bound to do something.

May 11, 1854

Marion County Cattle. Roughness of County & People.

The writer of the following indicated that he is a graduate of the school of ignoramuses for no other school ever taught that the lands of Marion County were rough. And as to the people of the county it is not likely he has ever seen a dozen of them, unless it is a few cattle drovers whom he has treated so much in accordance with his own peculiar meanness that they were obliged to treat him a little roughly in self deference.

We advise him to take a few lessons in some other school before he undertakes again to deal in Geography of the Country and character of the people. We copy the choice morceau from the *Ohio Cultivator*, where it stood credited to the *N. Y. Tribune* of the 25 ult.

The remarks upon it by the editors of the *Cultivator* we append below.

"In the yard—70 Ohio Cattle from Marion county some of which are as rough as some of the land and people of that county and sell for 9 and 10 cts. The best bullock in the yard is a fat old slug, 10 cwt, and sold for $95. This is the poorest drove of Ohio cattle in market for some time. They are, we are sorry to say, fair representatives of the majority of cattle in that and other western States; coarse hair hides, big heads and legs, heavy bones, light hind quarters, coarse grained flesh, and but little sallow.

We pray the owners to keep such beeves at home we do not want them here."

Solon is very much mistaken in the men and capabilities of Marion; neither are the lands or people so rough as he insinuates.—Ed. *O. Cul.*

May 11, 1854

Married.

On Tuesday Evening, H.B. Durfee of Bellfountain, O. and Miss Lucretia Busby of Marion, O.

May 18, 1854

Married,

On the 8th inst., Mr. Madison Robinson to Miss Elizabeth Thomas, all of Marion, Ohio.

Obituary.

On the 5th inst. at the residence of Mr. Silas Idleman in Pleasant Twp from an injury received by a fall from a horse, Michael Vincent aged about 15 years.

Jun 1, 1854

Enigma

I am composed of 17 Letters.

My 9, 4, 6, 11, 6, & 16 is an important part of a Lady's outfit.

My 9, 4, 8, & 6 is an indispensable part of the human body.

My 9, 6, 12, & 15 is a savage beast common in the forests of N. America.

My 3, 6, 10, 13, 5, & 17 is to be found in every part of the habitable Globe.

My 2, 8, 11, 6, 9, 10, 5, 17, & 1 is the name of an unfortunate Queen of England.

My 3, 6, 14, 15 is a delicious fruit.

My whole is the name of a distinguished man of the 19th Century.

Answer to Enigma of last week—Christopher Columbus.

Publishing the Laws

The Locofoco Auditor and probate judge have commenced publishing the laws in this county in their own party paper, but withheld them from the whig press thus far. We have taken some little pains to post ourself as to the reasons which govern them in such a course, and shall at our leisure lay them before our readers. They will constitute an interesting item in the history of progressive Locofocism.

Jun 8, 1854

☞ The man who has advertised himself as reformed inebriate three or four times within the last four years has a breath still fetid with liquor as strong as any old whiskey barrel we ever smelt. Can it be possible that the smell of the crathur sticks so long after a man reformed or did the fellow tell a "chronic lie" when he published he had reformed?

For particulars in this case, ask our neighbor over the way.

The musical performance of Mr. Woodruff and Kleinguenther in Apollo Hall a few evenings ago was pronounced by our best musicians as a master effort. It is true it was not as interesting to the general theater as a less scienced effort has sometimes proven to be, but the practiced ear in musical symphonies was carried away with delight.

Answer to Enigma of June 1st.

Napoleon Bonaparte.

We received the above answer from C.C.W. & also from J.W.M. Esq. and the process by which the answer was obtained accompanied the answer.

George B. Durfee also handed in the same answer, but gave no showing of how he obtained it, we presume however that he obtained it by a solution of the enigma, though it would be much more satisfactory to have the solution accompany the answer.

Jun 15, 1854

☞ On last Saturday, Mr. Baker counted 107 horses hitched before the different business houses of the place.—A goodly number of customers for one day, is thereby indicated we should think.

Married,

On the 13th inst., Mr. D.D. Sutton and Miss Anna McMann, all of this place.

Jun 22, 1854

Public Worship.

The question of Slavery in its moral and social bearings will be made the subject of one or two sermons in the Presbyterian Church—the first will be delivered next sabbath. The public are invited to attend.

Jun 29, 1854

Highly Commendable

The Merchants of Marion have all agreed to close their stores on the Fourth of July.

Married.

On the 27th, Mr. Saml. R. Ballentine and Miss Letitia M. Heisler, both of Canaan, Morrow Co., O.

Obituary.

Died—On the 25th inst. after a short illness, Maryann McWilliams wife of James McWilliams, aged 22 years, 4 months 14 days.

She leaves a husband, two small children and a large circle of friends to mourn her loss.

Died—On Friday morning, June 30th, at the residence of Mrs. Holmes, Mr. Charles Holmes, aged 26 years, 9 months and 4 days.

Jul 6, 1854

Fourth of July— Freeride—Incidents

Middletown Celebration of the 4th &c.

On the morning of the 4th our feeling that circumstances justified our acceptance of the liberal offer of one of the gentlemanly officers of the B. & I. Railroad Co. to deadhead us to Indianapolis and back, we let the cars pass, but not without many good wishes that the happy company aboard would enjoy the ride.

Afterwards we preferred a free ride on I. Haldeman's lumber wagon, to Berwick and from thence to be furnished with a charger to Middletown. One bare board laid from axle to axle, furnished seats for nearly ½ of a dozen men and boys of us. It being several years since we traveled the same road, we could not help viewing the various improvements that have taken place since, with a good deal of interest. The farm of Mr. W. Riley formerly owned by ____ and which then presented a dilapidated and decaying appearance, is now adorned with a neat farmhouse, paled yard and everything around exhibiting a thriving aspect.

A little further we crossed the track of the Franklin and Warren R.R. and kept sight of it until we arrived at Berwick. At several points, a good deal has been done upon it and the grading is in an advanced state. At Berwick, the village of hazel brush and lofty trees, we placed ourself astride one of the noble chargers that had aided in drawing us thus far, and took the way to Middletown.

We had passed but a short distance on our way before we met two men in a buggy, one a cattle buyer and the other an inspector of liquors with a brief inquiry of the distance to Haldeman's mill and a query as to whether we were not lost, they passed on. When near to Middletown we met groups of people who had the appearance of having had a thorough drenching. Among them were a number of ladies in white dresses, in a predicament. Arrived at the village we found it crowded with people, carriages, farm wagons and horses. Flags were streaming from many of the wagons and suspended in various parts of the town. The sabbath school of the place and many others from the surrounding country had met there for the purpose of a grand sabbath school 4th of July celebration. The sons of Temperance had also met in large numbers to join in the festivities of the day, and to add to the general of the occasion a large concourse of the parents of the children and citizens of the surrounding country were present. Some estimates set the number of old and young present at 3000. The heavy shower of rain interfered a little with the enjoyment of the closing scenes of the occasion. But notwithstanding, the exercises closed with apparently results. We were not present during the exercises and can not there fore enter upon a detail of the order of procedure &c.

After spending some three hours in the place, we again found ourselves on our way home; safely arrived at Berwick, we had the exquisite pleasure of assisting to load the wehickkle, upon which we were to conclude our free ride, with lumber. Snugly seated upon it, we were conveyed to Marion again at the rate of 2 miles per hour where we arrived after dark. Notwithstanding the rapidity of our return, no accident occurred.

Union Sabbath School Celebration of the 4th at Middletown.

By invitation of the above school, the schools from Norton, Waldo, Pleasant and Thompson met in concert to celebrate the ever glorious 4th of July.

Fully one thousand persons united in the festivities of the day.

The Middletown Union Sabbath School was organized on the 4th of April 1854. The property of the school may be pretty correctly estimated by the average daily attendance which has been 70, and the amount of verses committed and recited in the school, which amount to 3439. One scholar committed 633.

Married,

July 4th, Jacob Young and Miss Agnes J. Kennedy, all of the vicinity of Letimberville, Marion Co., O.

July 13, 1854

☞ Is the mayor of the town of Marion in favor of the new liquor law? We have been told that he has expressed a decided opposition to it; he has also said that he is in favor of the execution of the law. It is also said that he was asked to issue a warrant of arrest for a drunken man and refused to do it, saying, "wait until he gets sober and I will then see about it." It is also said that he is a pretty regular visitor to places where liquor is retailed, and that it has been frequently smelled upon his breath after having been there, and some have been so uncharitable as to express the belief, that there was even greater evidence of his having partaken

than the smell of his breath. Now we cant vouch for any of these things, only the smell of the breath, our olfactories could tell a little tale about that, if they were allowed a tongue for a few moments.

We have but little to say about the mayor and should not have had anything, probably, at this time, if he had not requested us to say that he was in for executing the liquor law. Upon inquiry we found his actions and his words did not agree or at least his reputed actions—we thought therefore we would not do injustice to the mayor, and the public at the same time, unless we told both sides of the story, as we have heard it from reliable men.

"Actions sometimes speak louder than words!"

☞ It may be some of our readers may think that we are too plain in our remarks upon the subject of Intemperance and the subjects of intemperance. The fact is we are out of patience with the course of the friends of Temperance. We have had meeting after meeting, and passed resolutions pledging our united and constant efforts to put down the RUM HOLES of our town, and what has it all amounted to? Nothing. We have a law, though defective, still if properly carried out, would effect much good, but we have not the men in our place (with one Honorable exception) who will take the time or trouble to commence a prosecution under it—not we fear if our town was as thickly crowded with drunkards and rum shops as corn shocks and pigeons in a field in the month of December.

We have therefore determined to take our own course upon the subject. We shall give so far as we can reliable information about the subjects of intemperance and expose every mothers son of them. If we smell the vile stuff upon any man's breath we shall say so, we care not who he is; for the man who will drink only occasionally, at this day of light upon the subject, is on the high road to drunkenness and worthy to be held up before the public as a prospective drunkard. There are quite a number of them in our place and amongst our most respectable citizens—sustaining respectable relations in life, with whom we are associated daily that drink freely, their breath and bloated appearance and occasional unsteady walk betray them. Their neighbors know they are for all intents and purposes drunkards now—yes gentlemen we have our eyes upon you, we talk about you, all your neighbors talk about you, and yet you think you are not known; but you are mistaken.

Now we give you fair warning that we shall expose you. Some of you have pretence to be friends of temperance and the friends of the temperance law, but it is all hypocrisy, we have no confidence in a word you say.

Married

On the 27 ult., In Iroquois Co. Ill, John A. May of Grand Prairie Twp. O. and Miss Sarah Ann Nellans of the former place.

Jul 20, 1854

Married.

On the 23rd inst., Mr. Wm. Mitchell of Fredericktown, Knox Co., O. and Miss Kate Holler of this place.

Cholera.

This full scourge of mankind has for the first time make its appearance in this usually healthy town.

There has as yet been but two or three cases, and these amongst the foreign population.

We intend our country friends to be kept posted of the true state of things in relation to it, to the utmost of our ability to give them. We hope there will be no more here—those that have been were probably chargeable to some indiscretion on the part of the victims. People can not be too careful in their diet and other regimen of house.

Since writing the above, two cases of death have occurred. But if Cholera, they should be termed liquor cholera instead of asiatic. The free use of liquor was evidently the cause of the disease which terminated so suddenly their existence.

☞ Dr. Hodeman is to all appearances near his last and more than likely be dead before the paper coming in the hands of even our town readers. His wife died a day or two ago.

The number of cases of cholera up to this date Thursday morning as near as we can learn is about eight.

Later—He is dead.

Dec 30, 1854

Died, near Marion, on the 22d inst., Mrs. Ann Seymour, wife of Mr. Geo. Seymour, aged 33 years.

☞ The *American* is now printed at our office in Marion. Those who have withheld their patronage because it was printed elsewhere have now been accommodated, by a considerable sacrifice on our part. We hope they will now fall in.

Married.

On the 24th inst., at the residence of O. Days, Mr. Robert Hopkins jr. to Miss Martha J. Day, all of Big Island Twp.

Notice.

The undersigned have been duly appointed Administrators of the estate of Henry Haldeman, late of Marion co, deceased.

Isaac Haldeman
Harriet Haldeman

Jan 6, 1855

Married,

December 31st, Robert Mehhefey to Mary Henriett White, both of Marion Co.

Jan 13, 1855

☞ We learn that on the evening of the 3d inst., Rodolphus Little, son of Lyman Little, deceased, a boy about 15 years of age, wandered into the woods with his dog, hunting. Not returning the following day, his friends became alarmed, and enquiries were made, when a neighbor remarked that on the night previous he had seen a light in the woods not far from his house. They proceeded immediately to the spot and there found the remains of the unlucky child.

It appeared that the boy had set fire to a large hollow tree and laid down to rest. It appeared that the tree had burned down and fell upon him while he no doubt was asleep on the ground. It fell upon his lower extremeties which were consumed to ashes, his right arm was consumed to the elbow and the left badly burnmed. His clothes were consumed, except the collar about his neck.

No dount he was killed instantly by the fall of the tree as his eyes appeared to have never been opened from the time they were closed in natural sleep, says our medical informant.

Feb 2, 1855

☞ We have received the following report, with request to publish, which we do without vouching for the correctness, as we were not present.

Official Report.

By John Smith
Justice Court, Marion county, O.
Jan. 29, 1855

Present, John Moore, Justice, O.J. Johnson, constable, John Smith, reporter, Attorneys, and citizens generally.

State of Ohio vs. Wm. C. Johnson, M.D. Charge, retailing liquor contrary to law. Plea, 1st, Not guilty of sale; 2nd, Said sale for medicinal purposes.

[Here the Reporter must pause to record the fact, for the benefit of hereafter, that the defendant Mr. Johnson, who bore the charge with great dignity and serenity, is a physician, who claims to practice medicine, is a person about 50 years of age, six feet four and a half inches in altitude perpendicular, with a full open countenance of much benignity of expression; wears a cloak after the Roman fashion. Has resided 21 years in Marion, where he is generally and favorably known to the community among whom he has practiced medicine with great success, as all his patients have either got well or departed in peace.

Of late he has retired from active service, and established an infirmary where the sick, especially those afflicted with chronic complaints, more particularly of the Bowels, come for relief, and where they are permitted to prescribe for themselves of such medicines and in such quantities as may meet the immediate necessities of their cases.]

Witnesses for the State were called and stood up in a row. Chris. Martin was called as a witness, but not answering, was reported 'hid' by the constable when service of subpoena was attempted. Before being sworn Mr. Barker stated his unwillingness to testify, whereupon he was fined $5, which he requested the defendant to pay; the defendant refusing, he expressed his readiness to give evidence and was sworn.

Dr. M.C. Reed testified: Was formerly in partnership with defendant; had sold liquor and drank some; had seen Dr. Johnson sell, but always for medicinal purposes; had seen him prescribe brandy, whiskey, and gin, to crowds of five or six who were sick at a time, and sometimes to the same person 3 or 4 times a day. Some persons took their liquor mixed with drugs, witness generally took his clear, thought it frequently good for health.

James Barker: had drunk several times at Dr. Johnson's; had treated and been treated; generally had felt unwell when he drank.

Christopher Raichley: had drank often at Dr. Johnson's; how often he did not feel bound to tell, as it was his own business; was always sick when he got liquor, got sick pretty often; selected what medicine he wanted, and several times felt insulted because the doctor would not him have more.

John Kraner jr: had drunk at Johnsons, always as a medicine when sick, had sometimes taken a number of doses in one evening.

George Lynn: had no recollection of drinking at Johnsons, but thought it likely he might have done so as he was quite sickly.

Hosea Patten: had drunk at Dr. Johnsons several times. Was not accustomed to get sick; got his liquor because he wanted it.

Defendant offered no evidence.

Argument:

Peleg Bunker opened for the State. He thought the guilt of the defendant a clear proposition, and could not see what medicine could save him. Judge J. Bartram, for the defendant, said that he considered Dr. Johnson considerable of a man. He was a man of age, a physician of high standing was six feet and more, high. We have had the cholera in our midst, which was a very bad complaint, and had terrified a great many into hard drinking. These men were not to blame, who drank the liquor, and why were they, who sold it? Dr. Johnson was a man of bowels, and had a heart to accommodate. If no body would sell liquor, those who wanted it would suffer. Liquor sellers did not suppose they were violating any law; he had thought it was unconstitutional. Dr. Johnson was not to blame; if those who bought his liquor were; they said they were sick; the Dr. could not tell whether they were or not as he did not feel their pulses. Would any man be so unconsciable as to deny a sick man liquor? He closed his remarks, by appealing to the well known age, character, and standing of Dr. Johnson. (The defendant here manifested signs of emotion, the first which he exhibited during the trial.)

Mr. Hume closed on behalf of the state. He thought Dr. Johnson's standing made his example more dangerous, in the violation of the law.

Justice Moore, in reading his decision, remarked that it was a truth known of all men, that no one did anything for no purpose, and upon the strength of this principle as applied to the fact of this case, he must hand the defendant over to the Probate Court in bonds of $300, or in default commit him to jail.

The bonds were given according to law.

☞ On Sabbath last we attended the dedication services of the new M. E. Church of Marion. The house was crowded and the best of order prevailed. Bishop Ames delivered an excellent discourse on the nature, uses and application of faith in all the pursuits of life, both temporal and spiritual. His remarks were truly philosophical and intelligible to every mind, religious or irreligious; and calculate to do good. He is a pleasant speaker, and, no doubt, a good man—a real American. Long may he live.

The new house of worship is beautiful, neat, and commodious; an honor to the people of Marion.

Married, In Claridon Township January 30th, Mr. James M. Harvey to Miss Catherine Owen, all of Marion County.

On the 6th, Mr. Truman H. Roberts of Montgomery Township to Ruby S. Fish of pleasant Township, both of Marion County.

Feb 9, 1855

The *American* in Court

In the absence of the "old man," we mean the principal proprietor and editor of the paper, who has gone to Indiana on a visit to his family, we, the junior department, take the responsibility of saying a word or two explanatory of the circumstances which place us in a position where honest men do not like to be found, to wit, in law.

As peace-loving and law-abiding men, having come to Marion for the purpose of making an honest living, by industriously attending to our own business, and conducting a newspaper in a fair, dignified and honorable manner, it is but right to say that the situation of litigants in court is none of our own seeking, nor have we done ought, which we had supposed would place us, therein. The facts as they are which bred the lawsuit now pending against us run about after fashion.

Last week, certain trials growing out of the liquor law, were being prosecuted in the village which we did not attend; a report of one of which purporting to have been prepared by one "John Smith" was sent in with request to publish. Not knowing as to the correctness of the report but presuming it to be all right we concluded to comply with the request taking the precaution however to state in an editorial notice at the head of the article that we were not present at the trial and could not vouch for the statements it contained. In a free country where our courts open are to all, and their proceedings common property for observation and criticism we could see no harm in proceedings in this instance. The report was accordingly published.

On Friday forenoon last, two gentlemen (for which we took them to be) stepped into the office in rather an unceremonious manner. The first was a somewhat tall bony man with a sanguine nose and continence whose strong rather firy complexion inflamed with rage most probably gave his whole appearance a decidedly dangerous aspect. The other was a large heavy set man who bore with him a fully developed and rosy countenance but which at this time was clothed with no very benevolent expression; both of them appeared to be considerably excited and in no very pleasant humor.

The first announced the fact that his name was "Barker" and the second we understood to be John R. Knapp jr. editor of the *Democratic Mirror*. The two proceeded to demand of our senior proprietor if he published this paper and had published *that* report (meaning we took it the report of Dr. Johnson's trial;) being answered in the affirmative they then peremptoily demanded the original manuscript of the report with a revelation of who "John Smith" was.

Our senior gave them distinctly to understand that he considered their demand both unreasonable and ungentlemanly; that he would think himself guilty of the greatest impudence to use the mildest term if he was to go in to Mr. Knapp's office and demand his private papers and correspondence. If there was anything overdrawn in the report the coloring matter was probably put on for a joke and the better way would be to treat it as such; if they did not feel disposed to take it in that light he was not to be terrified into a breach of confidence towards his correspondence. He has published the article and stood responsible for so doing.

The two remarked that they did not like to be joked in *that* place as they were rather tender *there,* took their leave with severe threats of prosecution. Not long after we were waited upon by the sheriff with a summons notifying us that we were sued by James H. Barker in an action of "libel" for $1000 damages.

If any one stands in a bad light in this matter, and is likely to stand in worse, it is Mr. Barker, as it can lead to nothing but a public exposure of the truth against him. The ground work of the trouble is here, as we understand it.

One of our citizens, accused of violating the liquor law was arrested and several of those most strongly suspected of frequenting his bar were subponaed as witnesses against him, among the rest, Mr. Barker (Recorder of the County) and Mr. Knapp (late clerk of the court and editor of the *Mirror*) The proceedings were so rich that "John Smith" who is strongly suspected of being something of a wag, could not resist the temptation of reporting. Good citizens tell us that John has succeeded in obtaining quite a faithful picture of the thing.

Mr. Barker's suing will only serve for to make him ridiculous by showing how deep the anger has gone into him and how hard he takes it when every body else is laughing and will make them laugh the louder at the poor man's expense.

Feb 16, 1855

Mr. Independent:

We have been having more fun of late. Every-now-and-then I fall into a crowd who are discussing the question of "who is John Smith," and have joined in several interesting debates on the point myself.

My last report made quite a fluttering on some quarters. Mr. Recorder Barker does not like it at all. He says I was wrong in saying he was guilty of a contempt. He and John R. Knapp, jr. have commenced suit for libel. Knapp is to prosecute the case, we understand, for half of the

proceeds. When they get judgement, let me know the amount, and it will be promptly footed, as I am responsible for the amount of any judgement against you.

Yours "by times"

John Smith

Feb 23, 1855

Married

On last evening, James McWilliams to Miss Martha Graham.

❖

On the 13th February, James F. Burnham of Delaware, O., to Miss Catherine Stailey of Marion co., O.

Sudden Death—On last Tuesday night, the wife of Dr. Barnhart, of this place, was suddenly taken ill and died in a short time.

Mar 2, 1855

 Died in this vicinity on the 21st of February of a short illness, Mrs. Susan E. Barnhart, daughter of the late Samuel and Eliza W. Homes. Aged 21 years, 7 months and 2 days.

Mar 9, 1855

Married.

Mr. T.I. Magruder of this place to Miss Elizabeth Fribley of Tuscararas county, O. on the 17th of Feb. '55.

Mar 16, 1855

Suicide.

We learn that a man was found dead near Galion, by the side of the C.C. & C. Railroad track, just north of town, on Sunday last.—He was found hanging on a fence, by a small cord, his feet touching the ground. His name is unknown. He had in his pocket a string of beads, a cross, and a through ticket from Buffalo to Cincinnati. From his appearance he was supposed to be a German or Frenchman.—*Dem. Mirror.*

Small Pox.

We have heard that rumors are in circulation in various parts of the County to the effect that the Small Pox is raging violently in this place and would say for the benefit of all having occasion to visit Marion, that it is an exaggerated report and that there is not the least danger to be apprehended.

We have been assured by a respectable Physician that there has been, so far, only one case of the virulent disease, and that in a retired locality, and it is his opinion that its progress is arrested.

Mar 23, 1855

APPEAL To our Friends!

It is now six months since we commenced the publication in this county, with no subscription list. Being entire strangers in this community, and finding the former publications of the county in bad repute, we deemed it necessary to introduce the *American* by a six month's interview, before we should attempt to urge our claims for support upon the intelligent and independent people of Marion county.

It is now acknowledged by all who have become acquainted with the *Independent,* that it is wisely and ably conducted—that it is an honor to the county—a champion of freedom — and a real benefit to its readers. Then have we not a right to expect of you the small pittance which would save us from ruin, and yourselves from the disgrace which must attach to the failure of the enterprise?? We think we have; and we make this appeal to your honor, believing it will not be in vain.

Married—At Waldo on the 1st inst., Mr. James D. Armstrong to Miss Susan C. Eleatt.

Also, in the same, Mr. Marshall W. Moses of Delaware to Mrs. Nancy Stailey of Waldo.

Died—In Lewistown Pa. on the 12th inst., Dr. Wm. R. Applebaugh, late of this place, aged 37 years.

Mar 30, 1855

☞ Court has been in session for two weeks past and adjourns we understand today. The case of J.H. Barker against ourselves, for Libel, has been discontinued, as we learn.

Apr 6, 1855

Melancholy Accident—On Thursday the 29th ult., a young man named William Fuller, at the R. R. Depot in this place, attempted to couple together some cars that were being pushed by men, and was caught between them and crushed so severely as to cause an internal injury, which resulted in death after lingering in the most excruciating pain for twenty-four hours.

Apr 13, 1855

Marion County Court of Common Pleas

Mary Law }
   vs. }
Samuel Law }

Samuel Law is notified that said Mary Law, on the 9th day of April 1855, filed in the Court of Common Pleas for the County of Marion, Ohio, her petition for divorce. Setting forth that she was married to said Samuel Law, on the 2d day of February, 1852. That to induce her to marry the said Samuel, the said Samuel represented to her that he was a good mechanic, a man of steady habits, capable of taking care of, and providing for said Mary. That said Mary found said Samuel to be a man of grossly intemperate habits, wholly unfit for a husband. And the said Mary charges the said Samuel Law, with having been an habitual drunkard for more than three years last past—with gross neglect of duty and with fraudulently contracting marriage with her. That depositions will be taken by petitioner at the office of the Judge of Probate in the county of Ashland, Ohio on the 4th of June next to be used on the hearing of said petition.

And that plaintiff prays to be divorced from said Samuel, to be restored to the name of Mary Jeffery, for alimony and other relief.

By Bunker & Godman
Attorney's

Fire.

On Sunday morning last a fire broke out in the new frame building on Center street owned by N.M. Runyan; the building with almost its entire contents were consumed. For a time it seemed almost certain that the entire block west of the fire would be consumed. Still, by the great efforts of some few of our citizens and the excellent management of the engine and fire department, the fire was mainly kept in the building where it originated.

Notwithstanding the fire and Hose company worked well, we thought they lacked discipline and a great want of confidence in their own duties. Every man seemed to be a foreman; there was a total want of organization. This is, we think, not strange, when we consider the kind of Town Council and Mayor we have had heretofore, who it seemed were engaged for the last six months or more, resolving money into the pockets of the Town Marshall and others for services, alleged to have been performed for the corporation until the Treasury is bankrupt, leaving nothing to purchase the proper number of Engines or Hose &c., so that the property of our citizens might be protected, and our fire department shown the proper encouragement. We think that under the circumstances the fire company on the above occasion did remarkably well and should be encouraged.

Apr 20, 1855

Hints on Dress.

Large plaids are most becoming to tall persons. The effect of stripes is to increase the hight of the person.

Brown collors are very becoming to persons of "sandy" complexion. Generally speaking, however, these colors are more worn by elderly persons and those of mature age.

As a general thing, colored shoes for ladies are anything but elegant; even for the gayest party, white or black satin is decidedly preferable.

Fancy colors are more becoming to persons of a sanguine temperament and florid complexion. To ladies with light complexions, fair hair and rosy cheeks, the various shades of blue are quite becoming; where the countenance is pale, buff or white should be preferred.

John Smith—This notable personage, who has for some time past been *cutting* many of our citizens, has at last received his desserts, having been found guilty of manslaughter and sentenced to seven years in the penitentiary.

A CARD.

Since the burning of my store house has been the means of causing all kinds of story's to be put afloat by the active imaginations and combined passions of hatred, malice, and envy, centered in individuals who by the disappointments of life have had their minds soured in such a degree, that their own presents to themselves is almost unbearable— as to the origin of the fire and what was the cause? Some of which I cannot in justice to myself, and others let pass without a passing notice, and all of which I pronounce unmitigated falsehoods gotten up and put in circulation by the malicious, willful, lying propensities of THINGS who call themselves MEN, and I am sorry to say scoundrels, all of which I stand ready to prove to be false.

I cannot let this opportunity pass without returning the sincere thanks and gratitude of myself and family

to whole hearted men and boys (who are boys only in years) who so gallantly risked their lives and limbs in saving my property.

Your fellow Citizen,
N.M. Runyan

Married,

At the residence of Capt. Vincent, near the Buckeye, Calaveras county, California, on the 15th inst., Matthew Armstrong of Waldo, Marion co, Ohio, to Miss Mary Higgins of Chicago, Illinois.

☞ During the past week, the weather has been bright, beautiful and Springlike, such as we have long wished to see. Old Sol was out in his brightest and fairest colors, and so were the ladies. It seems that the more pleasant the weather, the prettier the ladies look.

Apr 27, 1855

Cholera—If you don't want the cholera to return to Marion this summer, go to work without delay, and clean our your back alleys, your yards, and your stables, and quit throwing your slop and dish-water about the door-yard. Unless these precautions are taken, we shall be much mistaken if the cholera does not visit us this season. We hope that our town authorities will take measures on this subject.

May 4, 1855

Married,

On the 2d inst., Dr. H.H. Harding of Iowa to Miss Emily Kilbourn of Marion.

May 18, 1855

Married

May 16th, Doctor J. Watson, of Marion to Miss Ellie Mills of the vicinity of Caledonia, O.

Jun 1, 1855

Married,

On Tuesday 29th inst., Solomon D. Epley to Miss Abba Sloan, both of this place.

Jun 8, 1855

Correction

In our last issue a marriage notice was published which proves to have been a fabrication. Our printer being totally unacquainted with the parties, the fraud was not detected until too late.

In future all marriage notices when not handed in by the officiating clergyman, or the parties, must be accompanied by a certificate or other equivalent; as there are certain men, and ladies, too, who would have us publish nothing but what we "know" in the legal sense of the term.

Jun 15, 1855

Five men were instantly killed by the falling in of a portion of the tunnel under Walnut Hills on Wednesday morning last. They were removing the props preparatory to arching when without the least notice, a portion of it fell and crushed these men to death instantly.

A Wife Wanted.

In giving publicity to the following, I do not wish it to be understood that I do so merely to be noticed by your fair readers. I do so for the purpose of relieving myself of a discontented feeling which occasionally fastens itself upon my mind, arising from the want of a congenial companion through life. In other respects I have but little to cause discontent—my prospects being fair, my health could not be better, and I do not want for kind friends.

If it were possible that I could meet with a lady of affectionate disposition, kind, amiable and of sweet temper and unsullied purity—could I become acquainted with such an one, I do not doubt but that I should soon learn to look in the more sunny pictures of the "great book of life."

As to myself, am five feet seven inches in height, black hair, dark eyes, and fair complexion, have seen the snows of twenty-two or three winters, am engaged in a profitable business and sober and industrious character untarnished.

For further information address Henry C. Willis, Marion, Marion county, O.

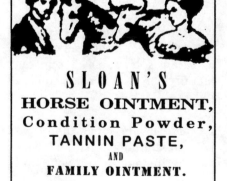
Married,

On the 5th inst., by Rev. I. Covert, Mr. D'Estaing S. Covert of Cincinnati to Eunice L., daughter of Col. W.W. Concklin, of Marion.

Jun 22, 1855

Fourth of July

We are requested to state that a public meeting will be held at the Court House on tomorrow at 7 o'clock P.M. to take into consideration the propriety of making some arrangements for a due observance of the memorable Fourth. All those interested are invited to attend, and we hope the result may be the getting up of a good old-fashioned celebration once more.

Marion Fire Company.

We understand the Marion Fire Company have in contemplation a public parade, in uniform, with their machine, (which is said to have been recently put in tip-top order,) on the Fourth. The recent efforts of this Company to increase and perfect the efficiency of its organization and the apparatus belonging thereto, are worthy of all praise, and we trust they may be handsomely backed by the citizens in all their undertakings calculated to promote that object.

Jun 29, 1855

Republican Meeting.

The independent voters of Marion county who are opposed to the political dishonesty of party demagogues and cliques—who are in favor of restoring the time-honored *Missouri Compromise*, so wantonly destroyed, and of resisting the encroachments of the slave power—who participated in the glorious Republican victory of last fall, and who desire to annihilate the last vestiges of *Old Hunkerism*, are invited to meet at the Court House in Marion, on

Wednesday, July 4th,

to appoint delegates to represent Marion county in the Republican convention to be held in Columbus on the 13th day of July, for the purpose of nominating a Republican State Ticket.

Married.

At the residence of Mrs. Harriet Jones, June 16, 1855, Mr. Noble R. Taverner late of San Francisco, California to Miss Becca M. Jones of Waldo, Marion Co. O.

❖

On the 22nd inst., John Tweddle of Denmark Ohio to Miss Mary Ann Sexton of this place.

Jul 6, 1855

Married.

On the 17th of June, John Yauger of Hayden Co to Miss Lucinda A. Mason of Wyandot Co, O.

❖

Isaiah Lowe to Miss Mary Maria Sprague, of Marion County, all of Ohio.

Jul 13, 1855

A Companion Wanted.

Having enjoyed single blessedness long enough I have resolved on matrimony soon as convenient. I shall merely state that I am a resi-

dent of Marion, am a mechanic by reputation, am five feet eight inches high, have brown hair, blue eyes, of respectable parentage, healthy, neither chew tobacco, drink liquor, nor use profane language and am said to be rather handsome.

Required—A plain sensible woman, possessing large benevolence, a kind sensitive heart, social, and an amiable disposition, a Christian, and move among refined society, the friend of the oppressed. If good looking, none be worse. She may be a Vegetarian and a Water Cure if she prefers, possessing energy and independence enough to say and do what she feels to be right on all subjects. Experience in household affairs. As to age, twenty-six would be preferred. For further information address T.W. Adinman, Marion, Marion Co, Ohio.

Married.

On July 10th, John Dumble to Mrs. Hannah Vantreese, all of Marion Co, O.

❖

On the 5th inst., Mr. Daniel Lowe to Miss Clarissa J. Swordon, all of Marion Co., O.

Aug 3, 1855

 An address in reference to the death of Mr. Monroe Hoddy, late of this place will be delivered by Rev. I.N. Shepherd, in the Methodist E. Church, Sabbath next, at 4 o'clock, P.M.

Aug 10, 1855

 Improvement marks our steps. Old buildings are undergoing thorough repairs—new ones are receiving the 'extra touches' which give them a citified appearance; and indeed, all 'old things are becoming new.' Hurrah for Marion and her enterprising denizens.

Died

August 6th, Waterman Higgins, Age 28 years, he was a worthy member of the Free Will Baptist church, bore his afflictions with christian fortitude, and "died the death of the Righteous." He leaves a wife, two children, and other relatives to mourn their loss.

Aug 17, 1855

Politics and Religion.

A class of politicians of the present day, represented in a considerable portion of the Democratic press, seems to be horrified at the idea of church members making themselves active in politics. All such as are suspected of Know Nothingism receive "particular fits."

Now, why is this? Does the atmosphere of the church unfit a man for the performance of the duties he owes the State? We deny all such doctrine. We are not inclined to advocate the union of Church and State, but see no reason why the same individual may at the same time be an active member of both. There may undoubtedly be too much of either, and too little. A government may run into superstition or it may sink into atheism. Which extreme is the most to be feared we pretend not to say. Certain is it, that if we had our choice and rested under the necessity of exercising it, it would not be cast for the rule of anti-religious scoffers.

☞ Vegetables are scarce, in fact there has been none of any account in market this Summer. Our farmers surely raise Potatoes, Cabbage, &c., in abundance. Why not bring them to market; they will find a ready sale for everything in the vegetable line, and at good prices.

Married.

On the 14th inst., Mr. A.P. Johnson of Marion Ohio to Miss M.E. Boyd at Spring Hill near Dayton, Montgomery County Ohio.

Aug 24, 1855

A Barber-ous Affair.

Mr. Editor:—The upper part of town was thrown into a convulsion of excitement a few days ago, by an "affair" which took of itself in that quarter. The Grand Worm of the Sag Nichts has been on the ground ever since, picking up items, which he will soon have ready to peddle. I was on hand as usual, and have concluded to give you the facts, so that you may have the unadulterated truth.

Hans, the German barber, was quietly seated on his own door-step, the other morning, enjoying a social smoke with himself and his long German pipe, preparatory to the day's work, when Bill, the black barber came along with his dog. Now whether the dog trespassed on Hans' property or growled, or showed his teeth, or bit, or threatened Hans, or behaved in any way towards Hans other than as a civil dog should do, or whether Hans

was the aggressive party, we leave to the affidavits of eye witnesses to settle hereafter as a matter of history.

Certain is it that Hans arose from his seat and threw a stone at Bill's dog, which taking effect about the ear, caused the animal to strike up a sudden waltz accompanied with certain musical discords, which probably neither the round nor the figure note singing man would recognize as belonging to his system. Bill, seeing his dog thus assaulted came to the rescue, by executing a rapid charge upon the Dutchman, with loud shouts of defiance.

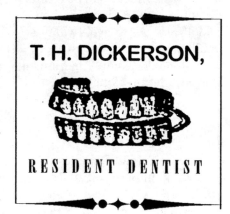

T. H. DICKERSON,

RESIDENT DENTIST

Hans seeing the enemy approaching, threw himself into an attitude of defense—drew his long pipe from his mouth, and poised it in the air to deal a deadly blow to the assailant. As Bill closed in, Hans brought down his pipe with a terrific force upon his pate—the fire flew in abundance—but as the negro's skull was the most invulnerable point of attack, the pipe was shattered into atoms, and the foe not disabled. The two came together, clasping each other firmly in their arms.

Now came the "tug of war." Both parties came to the earth—the darkey uppermost. Bill plunged his hands into Hans' long locks of hair, and

took a pull, a strong pull, and a pull altogether. Hans endeavored to obtain a grapple upon Bill's pate, but was defeated by the shortness of the wool. He then changed his system of war, and commenced belaboring him over the head with his fist, dealing a blow or two about the eyes, Bill all the time hanging on like Grim Death. But finding the darkey's head an impregnated citadel, and that it was impossible to make his eyes any blacker than they were before, Hans gave up in despair and cried most lustily for quarters.

The spectators at this point interfered and pulled Bill off by the legs, bringing with him in one hand a part of Hans' hair and in the other, a part of his shirt. The Dutchman arose from the earth with disheveled locks full of dirt, bloody nose and blackened eyes and went growling to his domicile, while the negro went off waving in triumph of his victory.

Thus ended an affair, which on ordinary occasions, would be forgotten in the tumultuous whirl of every day's excitement, but just at this crisis, its importance, viewed in a political light, is incalculable. This will add another, to the long catalog of Know Nothing outrages.

Here was a foreigner—an honest Dutchman—peaceable smoking his own tobacco in his own pipe upon his own door-step, basely assaulted by a native wooly head, and unmercifully licked. What glorious capital for Democratic stump speakers and editors! Won't the Grand Worm make himself busy? Wont the *Mirror* man rage? Wont he hold up the Dutchman's broken pipe in one hand and his torn short in the other, and call upon all his brother Sag Nichts to come and weep with him over so great a calamity?

It will be said that prominent Know Nothings stood by inciting the black imp to the attack, and encouraging him to pull the Dutchman's hair, and tear his shirt. Know Nothings, now look out for a terrible defeat;

John Smith, Reporter

P.S. I forgot to tell you, Mr. Editor, that Bill, is a boy about three feet and a quarter high, and weighs about 125 pounds being quite a "little nigger," while Hans is a full grown man, five and a half feet high and weighs from 200 to 250 lbs.

You can see from this, what foundation there is to the story which is being industriously circulated by the Grand Worm and his men, that the know Nothing employed Bill to attack the German because the latter was a foreigner and a Sag Nicht.

J.S.

Never judge one another, but attribute a good motive when you can.

Married.

On Thursday the 19th of August, Mr. George Postles to Miss Ann Waples, both of Montgomery Twp, Marion County, Ohio.

❖

On August 16th, Thomson W. Roberts of New Orleans, La to Miss Priscilla J. Mills of Marion Co., O.

Aug 31, 1855

☞ Edwin Wardin, son of John B. and Caroline E. Dumble, of this place died on the 26th inst, aged 2 years.

☞ We would say to our city fathers that an ordinance prohibiting hogs running at large in our streets would not come amiss. See to it.

Sep 7, 1855

Outrage upon an Old Citizen of Marion County.

We call the attention of the people of Marion county to the following facts, that they may see how one of their own number has been treated in one of the territories of the United States, for daring like a true man to express his honest opinions in favor of free speech, free soil, and free men.

The "one Pardee Butler" referred to is doubtless well known to many of our people, he having been formerly a resident of Marion county, where he has many friends who will heartily sympathize with him in his afflictions. Mr. B. is a preacher of the Discipline or Campbellite persuasion, and will be better known in the neighborhood of Letimberville where for a considerable time he faithfully followed his profession. He is an "actor" as well as a preacher of the great doctrine of Peace and nothing in his conduct in Kansas but accorded perfectly with that character.

"Great Excitement at Atchison— An Abolition Preacher Shipped on a Raft.

On Thursday evening last, one Pardee Butler arrived in town with a view of starting for the east, probably for the purpose of importing a fresh supply of Freesoilers from the penitentiary and pest holds of the Northern States. Finding it inconvenient to depart before morning,

he took lodging at the hotel and proceeded to visit numerous portions of our town, everywhere avowing himself a Freesoiler, and preaching the foulest of abolition heresies.

On the ensuing morning our townsmen assembled en masse and deeming the presence of such persons highly detrimental to the safety of our slave property, appointed a committee of two to wait on Mr. Butler and request his signature to the resolutions passed at the late proslavery meeting in Atchison. After perusing the said resolutions, Mr. Butler positively declined signing them and was instantly arrested by the committee.

After various plans for his disposal had been considered, it was finally decided to place him on a raft composed of two logs, firmly lashed together, that his baggage and a loaf of bread be given him and Mr. Butler was sent adrift on the great Missouri, with the letter R legibly printed on his forehead.

He was escorted some distance down the river by several of our citizens who seeing him pass several rock heaps in quite skillful manner, bade him adieu and returned to Atchison. Such treatment may be expected by all scoundrels visiting our town for the purpose of interfering with our time honored institutions."

Oct 19, 1855

Died—In Marion, October 4th, George Eldon, infant son of William and Lydia Clark of Van Wert, Ohio, aged three months and eighteen days.

Married.

On the 4th inst, at Pic Nic Vale, Mr. S.D. Welsh to Miss Mollie White.

❖

On the 5th Oct., at the house of David Mouser in Marion, Mr. Samuel Jones to Miss Louisa Mouser, all of Marion County, Ohio.

 During the past week three or four men have been killed on the B. & I. R. R. who were carelessly walking on the track.

Oct 26, 1855

 A train of nineteen passenger cars filled with soldiers and drawn by two locomotives, passed through this place lately, bound for the 'far west.'

Married

On the 11th Oct, Mr. Adam Bower to Miss Sarah Clark, all of Marion county, Ohio.

POETICAL

When lovely woman veils her bosom
With muslin fashionably thin,
What man with eyes could e'er refuse 'em
From casually peeping in?

And when his ardent gaze returning,
The dry goods heaves to deep drawn sighs,
Would not his fingers' ends be burning,
To press his hat down o'er his eyes!

Nov 9, 1855

EXHIBIT

Of the Receipts and Expenditures of Marion County, Ohio, from June 3, 1854 to june 3, 1855

Total Receipts 9,236.70

Total Expenditures 7,424.37

S.A. Griswold
Auditor, Marion, Co. O.

Nov 16, 1855

Caution.

I hereby warn all persons from trusting or harboring Martin Eager on my behalf as I will pay no debts of his contracting.
Hiram Eager

Nov 23, 1855

Married—On the 8th, Mr. Oscar Rawles to Miss Hellen Bowers, both of Marion co., Ohio.

❖

At the same time, Thomas Kerr to Caroline Clark, both of the same county and State.

Nov 30, 1855

Married,

On the 22d of Nov, Mr. Arnold Southwick of Marion Tp. to Miss Maria Harper of Montgomery Tp., Marion co., O.

❖

At the residence of Erastus Farnum, Nov. 6th, 1855, Mr. Thomas Patten to Mrs. Rosylla A. Gooding, all of Marion co., O.

Dec 21, 1855

Outrageous—During the past few days several persons, some of them ladies, have been frightened and in imminent danger from bullets discharged from the gun of some careless scapegrace. There is a law against the discharging of firearms within the cooperate limits of the village, therefore those guilty had better beware.

Jan 11, 1856

The Weather.

The cold period which commenced previous to the first day of January, 1856, and is not yet ended, has exceeded in intensity any winter which has ever been experienced in this region of the country, since thermometrical observations have been made.

Died.

At his residence in Marion, Ohio, on the 9th inst., Mr. A.P. Johnson of the firm of Davids and Johnson, aged 29 years, December 29, 1855. His illness, though of short duration, was severe, which he bore with christian fortitude and resignation until the last.

The deceased for the last eight years of his life was an exemplary member of the Baptist Church. In the death of Mr. J. the community have lost a good citizen and a useful man, a kind and beloved wife an affectionate husband.

Jan 18, 1856

Married—Mr. Cornelius Koons to Miss Susan L. Edmons, all of Big Island Tp. Marion county, O.

Jan 25, 1856

Married.

In Marion township on the 13th of January, 1856, Mr. Ammi Cluff and Miss Joanna Jump.

Feb 6, 1856

Fire in Caledonia!—The tavern owned by Mr. T.M. Anderson, of Caledonia, this county, was destroyed by fire on the night of the 31st ult. The building and nearly all the furniture was entirely consumed.

A tribute to the memory of Mrs. Emily K. wife of H.H. Harding, Esq. and daughter of Mrs. I. Kilbourn of Marion, Ohio who died at Nebraska city, Nebraska Territory, January 5th, 1856, aged 23 years.

Upon the dark records of Death we are called to write another name. "Emily"—quietly resigned to the stroke of the fell destroyer, another flower has been transplanted from earth to Heaven. A cherished and affectionate wife—a loved and loving daughter—a kind and gentle sister, and a pleasant associate has gone to that "bourne from whence no traveler returns."

No wasting of disease, no shadow from the silent hand fell round our sister to warn us of decay; suffering only a few short days the light of her young life went out, and calmly, quietly, without a murmur or a groan, she bid a long farewell to friends and earth with all its pleasant associations which once she loved so well. The unwearied attentions of a kind husband and friends, the devotion of love, and skill of Physicians availed not.

To her husband, who feels most keenly the bitter pangs of separation, we fain would whisper consolation. "Weep not for her," she's happy now. Be faithful, and when a few fleeting years have flown, your spirits shall again unite beyond "this vale of tears."

To our mother, who is again called to drink of sorrow's cup, we would say, serve thyself to walk unshrinkingly o'er life's thorny way, she was a Christian, and waits for thee in Heaven.

William Hare of Morrow co., was lately arrested and committed to jail, charged with having perpetuated a rape on the daughter of Mr. Conklin, 16 years old. The deed was committed last summer, whilst our blackberrying, he at the time threatening to shoot her if she told.

Feb 15, 1856

William Hare, confined in Morrow county jail on charge of rape, escaped on Saturday last, by picking the lock on the cell door. A reward of $25 is offered for his recapture.

Feb 22, 1856

Married.

In Findley, O., on the 19th inst., the Rev. J.A. Kellam of Marion, Ohio to Miss Martha J., daughter of Dr. J. Powell of Chesterville, Ohio.

On the 17th inst., Charles Augenstine to Miss Olive L. Pixley, both of Marion, Ohio.

Feb 29, 1856

A Man poisoned.

Our usually quiet town was thrown into a state of great excitement a few days ago by the rumor that a man had been poisoned in our midst.

The circumstances of the case are about as follows—about three weeks since a German named Brill was taken ill, and, notwithstanding the attending physician did not suppose from the symptoms, that he was in any danger, he died a few days after he had been attacked. About three days after his death, Mrs. Brill, his widow, married a man named John Reheis, who is said to have recently come from New York, and who professed to be buying butter and eggs for the eastern markets. This gave rise to the suspicion that Mr. Brill had come to his death by violence.

On Wednesday (20th inst.) the body was exhumed, the coroner sent for, a jury summoned, and an inquest held, when a *post mortem* examination took place under the supervision of Drs. Henderson, Irvine, and Watson, who decided that the man had died from the effects of arsenic.

On Friday, Rehies and his wife were arrested on suspicion and on Saturday they had a hearing before Esquire Ragan. When it was pretty satisfactory established that the man had been poisoned, that during his illness he had been nursed by no person but the prisoners, and also that a German woman had purchased arsenic at the Drug Store of Mr. Weisz in this place.

All these suspicious circumstances, and more were in evidence, and the general opinion seemed to be that they would be committed for trial, but the Attorney who conducted the prosecution was of the opinion that the evidence was not sufficient to justify the commitment of the prisoners, accordingly made a motion that they be discharged, in accordance with which they were released from custody.

Since writing the above, Dr. Irvine has returned from Cincinnat, where he had taken the stomach of the poisoned man for the purpose of having its contents analyzed by the most experienced and scientific chemists in the State. The investigation fully sustained our physicians in their suspicion that the man had been poisoned—a sufficient amount of Arsenic was found in the stomach to kill at least a dozen of men.

P. S.—Reheis and his wife have since been arrested and after another hearing before Mayor Mugg, the man was discharged and Mrs. R. was held in the sum of two thousand dollars to appear at the next term of the Court of Common Pleas for this county.

Mar 21, 1856

Married

On the evening of the 18th inst., at the residence of Bingham Allen Esq., Mr. William H. McWherter to Miss Fidelia A. Allen.

Married, in Sweed Point Boone Co., on the 7th inst, Mr. Erwin Wheeler to Miss Eliza J. Postle, of above place.

Notice.

With the present number our connection with the American ceases. Our patrons, no doubt, are to some extent prepared for the announcement. We at no time harbored a thought of our possessing the talent or ability required to conduct a public journal, but were necessarily through the mismanagement and desertion of our senior compelled to take upon ourself that responsibility. After twelve months trial we have found it to be impossible to meet the liabilities incurred in the purchase of the office.

Those of our subscribers who have made advance payments will be furnished the sheet of our successor until the expiration of the time paid for.

All to whom we are indebted will present their accounts. Those indebted to us, we hope will see the necessity of making immediate payment. We will be found at this office during the next two weeks, after which time the accounts will be placed in the proper hands for collection.

Jas. R. Appleton.

To the Public.

From Mr. Appleton's valedictory, in the present number the reader will learn that his connection with this paper as editor and proprietor has closed and hereafter it will be under the control of the undersigned.

As it is deemed desirable to make several material changes in the appearance, &c., of the paper to do which will occupy considerable time, no paper will be issued in the regular publication day of this week. The issue of the new series will commence on the 4th prox.,

from which time forward the patrons of the paper may confidently rely upon the regular weekly appearance of the paper.

J.W. Dumble.

Apr 11, 1856

Married.

On the 10th inst., John Long to Miss Hannah Snyder, all of Marion county.

In Marion on the 11th inst., Mr. Thomas A. Dempsey of Vesuvius Furnace, Lawrence county, Ohio to Miss Elizabeth Gruner of Marion, Ohio.

Died

In Pleasant Township, Marion county, O., April 3rd, 1856, Mrs. Hannah Fish, consort of Mr. Samuel Fish, aged 55 years and 4 months leaving a companion and 8 children to mourn their loss.

William her eldest son, was the first male child born in the town of Marion.

On the 30th ult., Margaret Epler, aged 19 years, 4 month and 7 days.

On the 1st inst., in the village of Marion, Mary Ann, wife of Mr. G. W. Lind, aged 22 years, 4 months and 22 days.

On the 1st inst., after a lingering illness, Jacob Young, aged about 36 years.

Apr 18, 1856

A Word in time.

It appears to us that the municipal authorities of our pleasant village have forgotten that cleanliness is essential to health.

It is a fact—to the shame of our citizens be it spoken—that with abundant facilities for drainage, the sewerage of Marion is so deficient that there are many places even in the business part of town, that are but receptacles for the accumulation of filth enough to poison the whole community during the entire warm season.

Gentlemen of the Town Council, you have the power to provide a remedy. If your power is exerted in season, you can, to a great degree, prevent a recurrence of the dreadful scenes witnessed in your midst in 1854. The people have placed their municipal interest in your hands, and will support you in all reasonable efforts to promote the general health, prosperity and happiness.

☞ George Patridge, convicted of theft during the present term of Court, has been sentenced to one year's imprisonment in the penitentiary.

Apr 25, 1856

☞ John R. Knapp, jr., has closed his connection with the *Mirror* as editor, which post he has filled for a number of years. P. Dombaugh assumes control as editor and S.C. Nichols as publisher. Both good boys, and we hope they may see the error of their ways before they become so hardened in (political) sin as the retiring editor.

May 2, 1856

Mayor's Address.

At our last meeting I called your attention to the following subjects: The first and most important, the propriety of employing a competent force under the direction of a trusty person to clean the streets and alleys before the settling in of warm weather.

Secondly, the establishing of grades on such streets as seemed to require it.

Thirdly, the propriety of securing suitable and making proper regulations for a market where everything should be weighed or measured before being sold, and thus all cause of complaint on the part of purchasers removed.

To these recommendations I am happy to say, the council promptly responded. By a resolution at our last meeting, the Mayor was authorized to employ a suitable force and proceed directly to clean the streets and allies; and accordingly he procured the services of Mr. John Quay, who took charge of several hands and is now actively employed in discharging that duty. But no money was placed in the hands of the mayor to pay those hands, many of whom are poor, and depend upon their daily labor for their support. I would suggest that a small sum of money—25 or 30 dollars— be appropriate for the purpose of paying such hands as cannot well wait the action of the council.

I would also call your attention to the subject of procuring grounds for a cemetery. There can not be any doubt but the wants of the community require a new and better place to inter the dead. The present burial place is already filled, and is too near the business portion of the town to afford that quiet believed to be essential to a resting place for the dead; and therefore can be but little doubt but the public expect and would heartily respond to a movement of that kind on the part of the town council.

Complaint is daily made from annoyance during the night, occasioned from noisy boys and men traversing our streets, singing, whooping, and swearing, evidently many times in a state of partial intoxication, rendering it unsafe for females to pass the streets, and preventing the sick and nervous from enjoying their necessary sleep. That species of nuisance should be abated, and I therefore recommend it to your serious consideration. How far that condition of things depends upon the ale and beer shops being kept open to a late hour, where persons can congregate to drink, I will not pretend to state; but that it exerts a great influence I can not doubt. Would it not be well to take measures under a heavy penalty to shut up such houses after the hour of ten o'clock at night; and also punish individuals keeping such houses by fine or imprisonment for selling any liquors to persons intoxicated or disorderly? The statute gives you full powers to regulate ale and beer shops; and I think the public peace requires prompt and stringent measures upon that subject.

Our town is at present infested with strange and suspicious persons without any visible means of livelihood, and we have reason to believe that are here for no good purpose. I have directed the Marshall and his assistants to keep vigilant watch upon their actions, and if detected in any unlawful business or occupation to arrest them at once.

T.B. Fisher, Mayor

Gambling and Vagrancy.

We have noticed for the last month or more, quite a number of strangers in our village, who appear to loaf about without any visible means of support, or usefulness to themselves or others. These individuals, it seems, are professional blacklegs, or in other words, gamblers—more properly called thieves, who steal their neighbors' money and reputation without any equivalent.

Our town, some years since, presented a spectacle which was humiliating; the remnants of the then blacklegs still exist in our midst. It would indeed seem that our place is a regular station upon the circuit of these wandering blacklegs. It is also a fact notorious that regular gambling houses are being fitted up in our midst, and others have existed for some time, where nightly meetings are held, and where the youth of the village learn to deal in cards and by degrees become infatuated with the same love of gambling as these older birds of prey.

It does seem to us that our corporate authorities should strive to interfere and scatter these vagrants from among us. The reputation of our village, its business, morals, and every thing that would induce enterprising and respectable strangers to locate with us, is in danger and every good citizen should see to it that this growing evil is removed.

May 9, 1856

The Dutch and Judge Metcalf

Week before last, a divorce case came off in Court, which created considerable interest. The parties were both German—a fact which gave rise to a rather singular and probably a rather new judicial ruling. The allegations which the husband, who made the application for the bill, had made against his *frow*, were adultery, and that she had proven herself guilty of gross neglect of duty as a wife, in keeping his house and household in bad order and being generally dirty. His proof seemed to be pretty strong—on the last point particularly so, but his Honor, Judge Metcalf, in deciding the case, held to the position that if the evidence was even sufficient for a divorce among the most of folks, it would not do in this case, as many of the Dutch were not expected to be as cleanly as other people and also that they, the Dutch, were not so virtuous as most people.

His honor illustrated his remarks by reference to the habits of many of the German population, describing them in numerous instances as living with a family of twelve in one small room, adjoining being the horse or cow stable and overhead the hay loft and chicken roost, such he said was a frequent occurrence in Northwestern Ohio.

However just the legal proposition may be, we hardly think Dutchmen will feel much flattered by the distinction which the Judge makes in their favor. In times of political turmoil, like these, when politicians live in eggshells, it would behoove his Honor to be somewhat cautious in the remarks he used towards a large and respectable portion of our people.

May 16, 1856

Married.

On the 8th inst., Reynolds Moses of Richwood, Ohio, to Miss Nancy E. Hill of Marion, Ohio.

GROCERY

I shall keep on hand at all times, sugars of all kinds, coffee, tea, tobacco, cigars, rope, bed cords, tubs, buckets, churns, nails, glass, fish, salt, nuts, raisins, sugar cured hams and beef. Best family flour from Marion Mills on hand at all times, Corn meal and candies &c., &c., and every thing nice for family use.

C.B. Smith

May 23, 1856

Died.

In this place on the 15th inst., Olive Catherine, infant daughter of E.P. and O.P.H. Copeland, aged 5 weeks and 2 days.

❖

In this place on the morning of the 24th inst., after a protracted illness, Mr. George R. Stanton, aged 36 years.

Jun 6, 1856

 This weather suggests ice cream, soda water, lemonade, linnen musent-mention 'ems, and such like. Wilson & Co. keep a good article of ice cream.

☞ The *Marion Eagle* is a continuation of the *Independent American* published in this place. We state this for the information of those who are sending us two of their papers in exchange. Advertisers east, who had dealings with the *Independent American* will please remember this change.

Jun 13, 1856

Independence Day.

The approach of the anniversary of our National Independence calls for the early adoption of measures to secure the celebration of the day in a becoming manner. The citizens of Marion county, favorable to the same, are requested to meet in the Court House, on Saturday the 14th inst., at early candle lighting, to make the necessary arrangements. Let there be a full attendance.

Died.

At Bloomfield, Marion county, Ohio, in the 38th year of her age, Martha, consort of Robert Patton and eldest daughter of N. & N. Hull of Waldo, Marion county, Ohio.

Mt. Gilead and Cardington papers please copy.

Jun 20, 1856

Crack! Bang! Ph-phiz-z-z-z!

The meeting called in our last, to make arrangements for celebrating the Fourth fizzled. Nobody was on hand and no candles were lit. No spark of enthusiasm was manifested by the crowd which failed to attend. Every body had something else to attend to that evening.

All in all, it was a glorious fizzle for the "glorious fourth."

Large Reward Offered.

Lost by a young lady of this place, a gold ear drop, an exact mate for which can be seen at this office. By leaving it at this office, the lucky finder, if a gentleman, will be rewarded by a kiss from the fair owner, and if a lady, will be rewarded by a kiss from our devil or ourself, at her own option.

Jul 11, 1856

Died,

In this village, on the 29th ult., Mrs. Elizabeth Bowen, wife of John Bowen, formerly of the city of Columbus, aged 23 years, The deceased was a consistent Christian, a member of the Methodist Episcopal Church and was highly esteemed by all who knew her.

Jul 18, 1856

Married.

On the 17th of July, 1856, Mr. Martin Berry to Miss Rebecca Arnold, all of Marion, Marion County, Ohio.

Thieves About!

A few evenings since the Post Office was broken into, and some fifty dollars worth of gold pens and holders, and other articles, with all the change in the drawer abstracted. The thieves forced an entrance through the window facing the alley.

Jul 25, 1856

Died.

Margaret, consort of Louis Gunn, died in Marion, Ohio, July 24th, 1856, seven o'clock A.M.

Aug 8, 1856

Married

In Middletown, Mr. Stephen Allen of Urbana to Mrs. Harriet Jones of Marion.

Aug 22, 1856

Died,

August 19th, 1856, Isaac W. Ulsh, son of Jacob Ulsh, aged 26 years, 4 months and 4 days.

Aug 29, 1856

Sad Deprivation.

We are sorry to state that our amiable friend Joe Sharitt has seen fit to deprive himself of a blessing which any a one would crave—that is, he stopped his paper at this office! To repair this loss to himself, we recommend Joe to water his whisky a little steeper than usual each morning! Between this and election, by using "whiskey and water" he may come out even, or at least drown the trouble he has occasioned himself by refusing to patronize us. Try it, Joe!

Sep 5, 1856

Obituary

Died of Cholera Morbus on the 4th of August, at the age of 37 years, Mrs. Julia Ann Lewis, wife of Porter Lewis, Esq. of Marion. Mrs. Lewis was a lady of intelligence, refinement and great excellence of character. She possessed a remarkably amiable and affectionate disposition which made her a favorite in the circle of her relations and the idol of a devoted husband and children.

Sep 19, 1856

Our Convention!
23,000 Live People in Marion!

Our village saw the greatest day of her life last Saturday.—The oldest inhabitant and the new comer, friend and foe, were alike taken by surprise, in the immense multitude which poured in upon us.—About half past nine, the delegations commenced gathering upon the hill to the South of town, and an hour later began their entrance into the place and until noon, one uninterrupted, closely packed stream of wagons, carriages, and horsemen, every means of conveyance being filled to its utmost capacity with men women and children, rolled in upon us, at which time the town was literally full.

It would take far more space than we can spare to describe the numerous novelties and attractions of the magnificent procession.—Foremost came a first rate representation of a woolly horse, with a flag on his head, bearing the motto, 'The woolly horse ahead.' Next rode thirty-two young ladies on horseback, all uniformed in appropriate garments of light complexion, except one representing unhappy Kansas, who was dressed in deep mourning. Then came troops of horsemen, young ladies representing the States in large wagons, of which we believe we counted seven, glee clubs, bands of music, an ox roasted whole, artillery representations of the mechanical branches on large platforms, the Pacific Rail Road in process of building, Border Ruffians giving vivid representations of Kansas doings, great teams of horses, one as a team of sixteen yoke, hauling a wagon containing over one hundred persons, and the whole interspersed with any quantity of common vehicles full of people, and bearing flags of every variety and device, there being over a thousand banners in the procession, the whole thing being closed up by a laughable burlesque on General Pierce's administration, performed by some boys with plenty of blacking on their faces, who drove an old team of horses to an old shackelly wagon, to which was attached an old sled behind, upon which a solitary melancholy looking individual was seated upon a whiskey barrel over which was the inscription, "The last of the Administration."

At twelve o'clock the mass moved down to the County Fair grounds, where after the thousands had partaken of an abundant free dinner, the speaking began. Five stands were prepared, and occupied with speaking throughout the afternoon.

One of the most interesting spectacles of the occasion to us, was to witness the large and very attentive audience which surrounded the German stand. We were not able to understand the language, but those who did told us the addresses were of the very highest order.

On the whole we are satisfied that ours has been the largest and best Convention of the kind held in Ohio this season. Marion has exhibited to the world that although small in body she has a great soul.

Sep 26, 1856

Married.

In Claridon Township on the 18th inst., Mr. William Underwood and Miss Caroline Shewey, all of Claridon Twp.

Married on the 23rd inst., Mr. J.D. Bricker to Miss J.G. Johns, both of this county.

Married—On the 16th inst., Wm. H. Moore to Miss Emily Farnham.

Married, on the evening of September 23d, 1856, Mr. Rolanda May to Mrs. Fanny Warner, all of Marion county, Ohio.

Died

Six miles North of Marion, Ohio, Sep 8, 1856, Lutitia, consort of Andrew Bending and daughter of Adam (deceased) and Sally Waits, aged 27 years and 7 months.

Also, in the same house, the next day, Sally, wife of Adam Waits (deceased) and Mother of Latitia Bending, aged 61 years.

The hand of affliction has truly fallen heavily upon this family. The former left a husband and two smiling children to mourn their loss— the latter a numerous family of sons and daughters, who are deprived of the counsels of a fond mother.

Oct 10, 1856

Married

On the 16th of September, A.B. Brice of Tarlton, Ohio to Miss E.V. Vose of Marion, Ohio.

On the same day, J.D. Peak to Miss Emma J. Vose, both of Marion.

On the 2nd of October, Rev. Isaac Newton of Delaware to Miss Susan B. Bell of Marion.

On the 2nd of October, at the house of Thomas Davids, Esq., Mr. J.B. Carpenter to Miss Christena Wolford, all of Marion county.

Oct 17, 1856

Married

In Scott Town, on the 7th inst., James Mahon of Marseilles, Wyandot Co, and Miss Phoeba Waples, of Scott Town, Marion County Ohio.

☞ The following Extra was issued from this office on Monday last, in reply to a batch of lies issued by the *Mirror*, secretly, under authority of Mr. Sharp.

To the Voters of Marion County

During the month of January, 1855 a "Law and order association" was formed in this place for the purpose of enforcing the Liquor law, of which association, the undersigned were members.

Mr. Alexander Sharp was approached by some of the members and solicited to become a member. Being informed as to its objects, he expressed a willingness to join; he signed and sent in the following application:

"I, A. Sharp, thus make application to become a member of the Law and Order association. And I hereby pledge my honor as a man that should I not become a member of said association, I will not divulge anything that may transpire during my presence at their Hall, the existence of such an association, nor the name of any person I may see present.

A. Sharp
January 1855."

The original, signed in Sharp's own hand writing, may be seen at the *Eagle* office by any person desirous of inspecting the same.

In pursuance of such application, Mr. Sharp was elected and admitted as a member, expressed his willingness to pay such assessments as might be levied upon him for the purpose of defraying expenses, paying costs &c., and was received in full membership in the order.

Prosecutions were commenced under the auspices of the association. Any individual who might be elected by the association, filed his affidavit, and the person making affidavit, was no more involved than any other member, for each and every one was as responsible as the person making affidavit. One was selected by the others, to begin proceedings, and was sustained by the others, including Mr. Sharp. If any prosecution failed, the costs were to be paid by assessment upon all the members, all including Mr. Sharp were bound to pay their proportionate share.

Mr. Sharp is now a member, in as full standing as any other, never having withdrawn, nor in any manner, to our knowledge, did he express himself as unfavorable to the association, or any of its objects, until in the last *Mirror* it was announced that he had reprimanded it.

But instead of repudiating them as the *Mirror* says, he shows his sympathy for the association and his willingness to engage in the prosecution of its objects, by entering himself as bail, on the 8th day of March, 1855, for the prosecution in the case of Joseph Anderson, of Larue.

In conclusion, we will state that the association was organized in good faith, for the purpose of stopping the illegal traffic of liquors and without any reference to the political organization of the country, and no distinctions being made as to the party connections of its members.

W.E. Kinnear
W.W. Bridge
J.E. Davis
B.H. Williams
John Gurley
Walter Willims.

I hereby certify that I was a member of the "Law and Order Association" of Marion Co. in the winter of 1854-5.

The object of the association was to bring to prosecution violators of the liquor law.

There were I think some seventy or seventy-five members of the association—one of whom was Mr. Sharp.

We regarded Mr. Sharp as a good active and judicious member. I do not know how many times I have seen Mr. Sharp present at the meetings of the association, but feel sure that I have seen him present at several different times.

R.C. Bowdish.

REMARKS

The course which has been pursued by A. Sharp and his organ, the *Democratic Mirror* in attacking the conduct of a number of our fellow citizens seems to require the publication of the foregoing articles from such citizens in their own defense, and the following statement of additional facts by us that justice may be done all parties concerned and the voters of the county be enabled to understand the truth of the case. It seems, about the beginning of the year 1855, a number of our citizens, believing the evils of intemperance

in our midst had become too great to be longer patiently borne, formed themselves into a society, called "The Law and Order Association," the sole object of which was to enforce the Liquor Law.

The existence of this society was preserved a secret, or at least was not generally known, until within a few days past, and then only did the fact become public, through Mr. Sharp and his friends. A suspicion having attacked to Mr. Sharp, that he was connected with this society, one or more gentlemen, against whom prosecutions had been commenced, applied to him for an explanation. Mr. Sharp equivocated, and denied all record evidence to prove any such charge. The gentlemen not being satisfied, and access being obtained to the records of the society, its constitution and by-laws were found to be signed by Mr. Sharp in his own hand-writing, together with his application for membership signed himself.

The next step in this matter consisted of publications in the papers—among them, an article appeared in the *Democratic Mirror* of the 19th inst., which the editor of that paper stated to be authored by Mr. Sharp, in which, while his membership is acknowledged, Mr. Sharp is sought to be extricated from responsibility growing out of his connection with the society, upon this apology that he was ignorant of its designs when he joined it; that he attended but one of its meetings, and then but a few minutes, and forthwith withdrew from it, as soon as he discovered its object, and never took an active part in its proceedings.

Now, as far as Mr. Sharp's course in the foregoing matter is concerned, we have nothing to say in consequence of his connection with the

"Law and Order Association." This is a free country, and Mr. Sharp has a perfect right to join in any movement his conscience approves. But some things in this connection we cannot approve, and for which we feel justified in arraigning him before the intelligent voters of Marion county, to whom he is now appealing for their support.

We must condemn the apology interposed by him in his own defence, of ignorance of the object of the society, when he joined it, and of immediate withdrawal therefrom since it is impossible to suppose such a thing of a man of Mr. Sharp's intelligence.

We must condemn Mr. Sharp for *double dealing* in attempting to obtain the favor and support of all parties upon this question and to deceive the voters as to his true position.

We would say, in conclusion, that neither Mr. Griswold, the candidate in opposition to Mr. Sharp, nor any other person on the Republican ticket, so far as we can learn, has had any connection with said "Law and Order Association," or with these publications.

Oct 24, 1856

Married

In Marion, Ohio, on the evening of the 12th inst., Mr. J.C. Johnson of Van Wert, Ohio and Miss Louisa J. Baker of Marion, Ohio.

At Delaware, O. on the 9th inst., Ethan A. Willey and Miss Rhoda J. Cunningham, all of Delaware.

Daring Robbery.

On Wednesday night last, some daring burglar entered the Daguerrean Room of William H. Moore on the third floor of the Bennett Block and carried off about $300 worth of stock, consisting of pictures, his Camera Obscura, &c. The rascal showed his good taste for the Fine Arts by taking some most exquisite female pictures.

Our County Fair

is progressing finely. The weather is rather gloomy, but this don't keep the people away. The entries are not large, but some of the stock is quite superior. Success to the cause.

Oct 31, 1856

Obituary.

We are called upon with sadness to record the sudden and unexpected death of our venerated fellow-citizen, William Bain. On last Thursday evening he was attacked with Apoplexy, while conversing with friends in J.E. Davids' Store. He was immediately carried to his residence and Drs. Bridge, Sweney and True called in, but all their efforts proved unavailing, and about 10 o'clock he expired.

Mr. Bain, we understand, had been a resident of Marion over thirty years and was the oldest Merchant in the place. He was one of the oldest, most active members and officers of the Presbyterian Church. He was one of our most enterprising, active and liberal citizens, and we have no doubt a good man in the best sense of this phrase. He was a man of very general reading and intelligence, and sterling good sense.

His funeral was attended by a vast concourse of people, near a thousand, we should judge, which showed the universal respect for his character, felt by the whole community. Thus one generation passes away and another comes, but we cannot always suppress the thought that as the venerated fathers pass off the stage, we, their sons, are scarcely worthy to meet the responsibilities and active lot of life in their place.

Married

Near Marseilles, at the house of Mr. Frost, on the 15th instant, Mr. J.B. Pool and Miss C.M. Woodard.

At the same time and place, H.B. Latham and Miss E.A. Woodard.

On the 20th inst., Mr. Benjamin Cornell and Miss Emma James, both of East Liberty, Logan county, Ohio.

Nov 7, 1856

Married

In Marion, Ohio, October 30th, Mr. John Morris to Miss Sarah Jane Ward, both of Delaware County, Ohio.

Nov 14, 1856

The Campaign Ended! Buchanan Elected!

The presidential contest is over.— The result is far different from that which we earnestly hoped and honestly believed it would be. Buchanan has carried all the Slave States, except Maryland, which has gone for

W. A. TURNEY

WATCHES, CLOCKS AND JEWELRY

Fillmore, and Pennsylvania, Indiana, New Jersey, and most probably Illinois have united their votes with the disunionists and slavery extentionists of the south.

This places the government for the next four years in the hands of the slavocracy. The bitter experiences of the last four years teach us too plainly what the future is to be unless the current of events shall be interrupted by the imposition of some unlooked for influences. We expect, as the result of this election, that the fair domain of Kansas, will be subdued to Slavery, before twelve months. We expect that the subjugation of and annexation of Nicaragua and Cuba will probably follow. We can see nothing in the world now to prevent these events, except the growing power, vigor and determination of the Republican party of the country. The great show of strength made by the party in the recent elections may cause the successful party to pause in their mad career of villainy and crime, but it is a bare possibility.

Sensible.

It is rumored that Mr. Buchanan does not intend to undertake the occupancy of the White House alone. He feels the necessity of a helpmate, and is said to have made arrangements for a joint tenancy with an accomplished southern widow who has already had the advantage of four years experience in that position. This is the most sensible thing we have heard of Buchanan's doing since the canvas opened.

Married

On the 18th inst., Mr. J.H. Foster to Miss Eliza Stephenson.

❖

On the 21st ult., Mr. George F. Franklin to Miss Harriet V. Beerbower, all of Marion, Ohio.

❖

On the 17th inst., Dr. McGuinnes of Wyandot county to Miss Susan Haldeman, of Marion County.

Nov 21, 1856

Married

On the 9th inst., Mr. Jacob Kise and Miss Elizabeth Byers, both of this county.

❖

On the 20th, William H. Mouser and Miss Hannah C. Owen, all of Marion Co., O.

❖

On the same day, Elijah Copeland of Lafayette Indiana (formerly of Marion Ohio) and Miss Lydia Amanda Baker of Marion Ohio.

Nov 28, 1856

 Queen Victoria is reported to be in an "interesting condition."

Married

November 20th, 1856, Mr. Elijah Copeland of Evansville, Indiana (formerly of Marion, Ohio) to Miss Lydia Amanda Baker of Marion Ohio.

❖

On the 23rd inst., Mr. John H. Johnston to Miss Melissa Walker, all of Marion county, Ohio.

Dec 5, 1856

Married.

On the 29th ult., N. Jerolaman of Des Moines Iowa and Miss Lizzie J. Williams of Marion.

❖

On the 17th ult., James H. Anderson, Esq. of Marion and Miss Princess A. Miller of Upper Sandusky.

Dec 17, 1856

December

Cold December is here, with her chilling blasts, embracing mother earth with icy hands and rendering blazing fires a necessary institution. Dreams are now flitting through the brains of our youngsters of well filled stockings, supplied by the generous hand of Santa Claus on Thursday next.

Jan 2, 1857

Married.

On the 24th of November, 1856, Mr. William Williams and Miss Angeline Essex, all of Marion county, Ohio.

Jan 9, 1857

Discontinued.

Wilson's Post Office in Bowling-green township, Marion county, has been discontinued by order of the Postmaster General. Our Bowling-green friends now get their mail matter partly at Larue in this county and partly in Essex in Union county. Slightly inconvenient we should think but we suppose the office would not pay.

More Victims.

A shipload of converts to Mormonism arrived at New York on the 1st. These people were primarily from Bristol. The Post says that the number of men and women is about equal, but there is a multitude of children. The men are not a strong, intelligent lot, but the women are *well made*, and many are handsome.

Parley P. Pratt and two other Mormon Elders, who are living in New York, visited this ship load and gave them their first lesson in Mormonism, which is to give an account of their means. The emigrants number 200, and will go to Utah in the spring.

 The first heavy snow of the season occurred on Friday night last. Bells and runners were in good demand on Saturday, notwithstanding the cold. Should the snow last, our livery stable men will reap a rich harvest, though horse-flesh does suffer some.

Jan 16, 1857

Died.

At the residence of her husband, Mr. Jacob Harshberger, on the morning of the 2d, inst., Mrs. Margaret Harshberger, aged 25 years, 4 months and 27 days.

Jan 23, 1857

Died.

On the 16th of January, 1857, Isabella M., consort of J.W. Boyd, aged 34 years and 3 months.

She leaves a kind husband and one little boy to mourn her untimely loss.

Jan 30, 1857

Died.

At his residence in Salt Rock township, Marion county, Ohio, on the morning of the 18th inst., Mr. George King, aged 64 years, 8 months and 3 days, leaving a wife and six children.

The deceased was a native of the county of Sussex, State of Delaware. Soon after the commencement of the war of 1812, he volunteered as one of the noble band of young men who agreed to hold themselves at all times in readiness to march to the defense of their country, in case of danger or invasion. Though not in frequent service, they were in frequent scenes of fatigue and peril. The deceased was present and assisted in repelling the attack upon Lewistown and with his companions done good service.

After the close of the war, he came to Pickaway county, Ohio, where he soon after married. He resided there until the spring of 1824, when he removed to this county and settled upon the farm where he died.

He was an affectionate husband, a kind father, an obliging neighbor, and good citizen.

He has been for several years a consistent member of the Presbyterian church and though quiet and retiring in his habits, his kindness of manner, benevolent disposition, and strict integrity was for him the confidence and esteem of a large circle of acquaintances.

Died at the residence of his mother of this place on the 27th inst, Benjamin F. Holmes, aged 20 years, 8 months and 8 days.

A Week About Town

Will satisfy any one that Marion though slow in improvement, is no less certainly on the advance in all that is calculated to make a county town comfortable or desirable. Our mercantile establishment, many of them, assume quite a city appearance. The windows of our broker establishments are well filled with the needful, which the men of credit, energy, and business capacity can get upon their own terms.

Our streets are in fine condition, yearly extending their accommodations to our citizens.

Our churches are fast assuming a comfortable exterior aspect while the evidence of genuine piety in the civil deportment of our citizens in the practical living exemplication of the walk and conversation of our people, manifest to the observer a sure index to the faithful administration of the word which adorns the interior. Though we are no priest worshippers, we feel disposed to say, that Marion may boast the possession of three or four of the clerical order who are, as all clergy men should be, living examples of the faith they preach.

Though much liquor is still dispensed by our grocery men, in violation of law—so long as drunkenness does no more offend the sight than at present, we believe in obeying the choice of public opinion, making that our law and the regulator of our conduct on that subject. We would that public opinion, with her iron heel, would grind the monster, Intemperance, to powder, yet, while it will not, we say preach and persuade. Let the force of your example, with your mild, yet firm precept, be against it, and against all avenues leading to it.

Our public houses are well filled and we but wish the buildings occupied as such were calculated to honor the keepers of them. Marion may boast of her landlords, though she be ashamed of her Hotels.

Of our physicians, we can say that they show wisdom by taking but little of their own physic, as that don't pay. The lawyers can most of them, speak for themselves.

Our county abounds with good livers; men who pay for and read the papers; making their homes the abode of intelligence, contentment and enterprise. Taking all in all, we look upon our town of Marion as one of the most comfortably situated places in the State, possessing the solid elements of true and lasting improvement, educational, religious, moral and social; the county at large as occupying a high eminence on the way of general prosperity; from our list of almost a thousand subscribers, we are induced to believe her political position is not in the back ground of her other important interests.

Feb 6, 1857

Deaths.

In this place on Saturday, January 24th 1857, Caroline, infant daughter of Henry and Bertha Harmon, aged two years and six months.

❖

Died—At the residence of his brother in this place, on the 1st day of February, 1857, Mr. Abram Young, aged 28 years and 3 months.

The subject of this sketch, for some years, has been a citizen of Marion, and his deportment was such that secured to him a large circle of warm friends. He was not only a good citizen, but an exemplary Christian.

False Census Returns from Utah.

Elder John Hyde, sent as a Mormon Missionary to the Sandwich Islands, has turned states evidence against the Saints and while denouncing their polygamy and villainy generally, charges them with falsifying the Census Returns of the Territory. He affirms that there are not half as many inhabitants in Utah as the census indicates. The names of deceased persons of immigrant disciples who never came to land

and of Mormons who long ago recanted their beastly creed and fled the country, were all retained and used to make the number of "10,000."

Feb 12, 1857

New Post Master.

Mr. J.B. Dumble has received the appointment of Post Master at this place; Mr. Dombaugh having resigned. John commenced his services in the Post Office by giving orders to the Clerk not to deliver the *Tribune*, unless subscribers names were written thereon. This will increase John's popularity among the Democracy, who are doing their utmost to curtail the circulation of Republican papers.

There is another class, however,— the business men of the place—who will not be so well pleased, and they will remember the man who refuses to deliver their papers.

The Post Master General, not wishing to shoulder the responsibility of detaining papers directed to the different Post Offices, left it to the option of the Post Master to deliver them or not. All Post Masters whose party spirit does not overtop their sense of right and Justice, will of course deliver them. Others who are prone to act narrow and contracted, can do as they choose. They should bear in mind, however, the fact that some people *do* cut off their noses to spite their faces.

Gone Up.

Sugar, potatoes, Butter, and in fact, everything in the eating line in Marion has gone up. It costs a cool sum to feed a small family now-a-days, and if the fuel and clothing

bills are counted up, a small fortune would be entirely inadequate for the support of even a small family. Let the necessaries of life keep on rising and see how long this place will prosper.

Things are so very high, a number of our young men who were about to commit matrimony, have declined doing so for the present, as they say it wont pay. Truly a very wise conclusion.

 The case of William G. Johnson vs. W. Smith in reference to the losing of a log chain, borrowed by the said Smith from the said Johnson, before Judge J. Moore, Justice of the Peace, on yesterday, was decided in favor of the plaintiff. The value of the chain was about $3.

Amusements.

Marion has long needed something in this line, to cheer the dull monotony of this dreary winter. Shows have been scarce; of concerts we have had none at all; and a dog fight will now bring out a crowd upon the pavement, and a fractious horse make a fortune for his owner at a dime a sight.

☞ The health of Marion is rapidly improving and we think a few days more will add the rose of health to a number of pale cheeks. This has been our greatest drawback to business, but it is being rapidly dispelled.

☞ A number of our citizens have laid up a good supply of ice, for the hot weather of '57, which will probably be along some time in the future.

W. A. TURNEY
Jeweler

Feb 19, 1857

 We notice large flocks of pidgeons flying over this place, going towards the South West in the morning, and the North East in the evening. The blue bird, that sure harbinger of Spring, has made his appearance, and crows and turkey-buzzard are seen sailing through the air. All these are sure indications of the near approach of Spring.

Show.

Well, we have been honored with a Show or Theater. Yankee Bierce was here with his troupe, and gave a performance every night for six nights, last week. Those who have a taste for such things, were no doubt on hand, and probably got their money back in witnessing the Tomfoolery of the performers.

The above show has started the fever among our boys and they have fitted up a room in the northern part of town and are daily practicing. Of course their delineations of different characters are truly tremendous! and when they start out to give public exhibitions of their awful feats, they will undoubtedly astonish the Natives.

Marriages.

Married —On the 12th instant, Mr. William H. James of Sergeant Bluffs, Iowa to Miss Louisa Epler of this place.

❖

Married—On the 12th instant, Mr. J.N. Pettit to Miss Ann E. Leatherberry, all of this place.

Deaths.

Died—In this village, on the morning of the 11th inst., Richard LeRoy Patten, son of Richard and Susan G. Patten, aged 19 years, 3 months and 14 days.

The subject of this sketch was a young man universally respected by all who knew him; and his sudden demise has not only spread a gloom over this community but produced the keenest pangs of sorrow in the hearts of his parents, to whom he was most dear. He is gone, he who, but a few days since was in the full enjoyment of health.

Died—Near this place, on the 7th inst., Mrs. Mahala Barnett, wife of Calvin Barnett, sen., aged 53 years, 5 months and 1 day.

Feb 26, 1857

A Change.

The *Mirror* last week made its appearance in a new head dress and under charge of a new firm. It is now edited by Thomas Jefferson Crawford and Andrew Jackson Crawford. If these two ancient locofoco names dont resuscitate the defunct party in Marion County, then there is no virtue in names and the posies to be found around country school houses would smell as sweet by any other name.

We welcome the brothers Crawford.

Mar 5, 1857

Deaths.

Died—At the residence of his parents, in this place, on the 21st ult., Clay W. Anderson, youngest son of Thomas J. and Nancy Anderson, aged 19 years, 4 months and 4 days.

The illness that resulted in the death of our friend Clay was a severe attack of the prevalent fever, of 17 days duration. The severity of the disease from the commencement of his sickness gave to his friends but small hope of his recovery, although at times the indications were favorable. Throughout the entire turn of his illness, not a murmur escaped his lips and when the lamps of death gathered upon his brow the most cheerful resignation pervaded his mind and he gave to his friends the strongest assurance that death had no terror for him.

Few young men possessed more amiable disposition or relied more upon their own powers for advancement than the deceased. On reaching his sixteenth year he commenced life for himself by teaching school in which occupation he gave a general satisfaction. In the fall of 1854 he accepted the place of teller in Durfee's Exchange Bank which position he occupied until his death. Those who came into business contact with him will not soon forget his amiable disposition and will long miss his familiar face from his accustomed place.

Mar 12, 1857

Dred Scott Case.

The reader will find the strange decision of this case, by the Supreme Court, in our columns today, reported by telegraph. The *Tribune*, in commenting on it, holds the following language:

The long trumpeted decision of the Supreme Court in the Dred Scott case was pronounced by Judge Taney on the 6th inst., having been held over from last year in order not too fragrantly to alarm and exasperate the Free States on the eve of an important Presidential election. Its cardinal points are reported as follows.

1. A negro because of his color, is denied the right of a citizen of the United States—even the right to sue in our Courts for the redress of the most flagrant wrongs.

2. A slave, being taken by his master into a Free State and thence returning under his master's sway, is not therefore entitled to his freedom.

3. Congress has no rightful power to prohibit Slavery in the Territories, hence the Missouri Compromise was unconstitutional.

This judgement annihilates all Compromises and brings us face to face with the great issue in the right shape.—Slavery implies slave laws—that is, laws sustaining and enforcing the claim of one man to own and sell another. In the absence of such laws, Slavery cannot exist.

This decision, we need hardly say, is entitled to just so much moral weight as would be the judgement of a majority of those congregated in any Washington bar-room.

NOTICE.

All subscribers to the Cincinnati *Gazette* will call at my store room for the papers—as the Post Master refuses to deliver them at the Post Office for the reason that the names are not written on each paper. I am willing to distribute this batch of papers as it takes but three minutes to write the names on each one. I don't think the Post Master's refusal to distribute these papers will have any tendency to suppress their circulation.

John E. Davids.

Deaths.

Died—On the 5th inst., in Bellefontaine, Logan County, after a painful and protracted illness, Mr. Orson N. Knapp, aged 42 years, 9 months and 5 days.

He has left a wife and a number of minor children together with a numerous circle of relatives and friends to mourn his departure.

Died—On the 8th inst., Annie Elizabeth, infant daughter of Rev. J.A. and Martha J. Kellam, aged 2 months and 12 days.

Marriages.

Married—In Greencamp township on the 6th inst., Mr. John Bratton to Miss Rosana McBride, all of Marion county, Ohio.

Married—In Claridon township on March 5th, 1857, Mr. Henry Dillon and Miss Elizabetha Munn, all of Marion county, Ohio.

Mar 19, 1857

Fire in Waldo township.

We learn from a gentleman who was present, that the residence of Samuel Wottring, in Waldo township was destroyed by fire, on the night of the 9th inst. A part of his household furniture was destroyed with the house. His loss was about five hundred dollars. No insurance.

Marriages.

Married—In Marion, in the 12th inst., Mr. Samuel Mahaffer to Miss Margaret Jane Campbell, all of Marion county.

In Greencamp township, on the 12th inst., Wilson Imbody to Miss Cynthia Berry, all of Marion co.

Married—In Waldo township, on the 16th inst., Jacob Strine to Miss Jane Waddle, all of Marion County.

Mar 26, 1857

End of the Volume!

This number of the *Eagle* closes the volume and the first year of its existence under our management. It is well known that when we took charge of the office, its patronage was at low ebb; its circulation small and daily becoming less and some weeks no papers at all appeared; and everything connected with the office gave evidence that its existence would soon he brought to a close.

Under all these unfavorable circumstances it was with no little fear and trembling that we engaged in the enterprise; but, relying on the assurance of the business men of the county that a Republican paper conducted with energy and issued properly would be sustained, we enlisted all our energies in the work.

Since we issued the first number of the *Eagle*, its circulation has been nearly doubled; its sphere of usefulness greatly extended and as a means of support it the publisher,

we think its business will compare favorable with any county paper in the State.

———————

☞ We are sorry to learn that the Postmaster at Marion, Ohio, who happens to be a brother of ours, has tried to but his brains out by refusing to deliver the *Tribune*, unless the names of the subscribers are written upon them. This is a direct attempt to curtail the liberty of the press, and shows plainly that if they had the power the locofocos would suppress the circulation of every paper that dares to question the supremacy and justness of Slavery.

The above is taken from the Mt. Gilead *Sentinel* edited by W.P. Dumble, a brother of ours. His remarks show plainly how he feels

on the Post Office question. But we are sorry to inform him that the little tyrant of a post master here has triumphed over the agents of the *Tribune* and Cincinnati *Gazette*; and now, very graciously condescends to deliver these papers, if the agents will call at the post office and write the names on them! The agents—Timothy Chase and John E. Davids—are thus made to 'knuckle down' to the post master, while he chuckles over the two slaves he has compelled to do his work.

———————

Marriages.

Married—In Greencamp township on the 19th inst., Mr. Theodore Bruce to Miss Charlotte Bell, all of Marion county.

Ketchams Improved IRON MOWER AND REAPER!

This celebrated combined machine is now on exhibition at the Hardware and Agricultural Depot of J.W. BAIN, Marion. Costing only $110 for Mower or $130 for Combined Machine.

Apr 2, 1857

Change of Name.

Our friends, we think, will agree with us, that the new title we have adopted for our paper is an improvement. Although the old name has long been honored by those who have successively published the paper, and although *"The Eagle"* has become a household word with the people of Marion county; yet the name signified nothing. Hence the change. And as we desire to keep the principles of Republicanism before the people, we think no better plan could have been adopted, than that of the word *"Republican"* at the head of our paper. The new paper we hope will be welcomed by every man in Marion county, who loves Republicanism—who hates slavery and tyranny—who detests patent locofocoism—and who is willing to give one dollar and fifty cents to the support of the faith that is in him.

Deaths.

Died—In Saltrock township, Marion county, Ohio, on the 14th of March, 1857, of dropsy, Mahlon Marsh, aged 63 years.

Apr 9, 1857

Deaths.

Died—In this place, on the 19th of March, 1857, Mr. John Venning, aged 24 years, 10 months.

Apr 16, 1857

Another Change.

The *Mirror* has experienced another change of proprietors. Andrew Jackson and Thomas Jefferson, late publishers have retired. But six short weeks have elapsed since we welcomed them as publishers of the *Mirror*: and now, alas! we are compelled to say, "Farewell, Brothers Campbell!"

The paper is now published by the 'Mirror Company'—consisting of the Post Master, the Cashier of Durfee's Exchange, and J.B. Dumble. These three, it is presumed, will make a strong team. We welcome the 'Mirror Company.'

Deaths.

Died—In Marion on the 31st day of March, Mary Elizabeth, infant daughter of Charles W. and Fanny Smith, aged 2 months and 28 days.

Died—In Marion, on the 1st of April, Mr. Samuel Hoxter, aged 22 years, 2 months, and 16 days.

Marriages.

Married—On the 30th of March, Mr. David McPherson, of Galion, Ohio to Miss Nancy McPherrin, of Marion county, Ohio.

Married—On the 2d of April, Mr. J.W. Engleman to Miss Catherine J. Smith, all of Marion county, O.

☞ Our city fathers have passed an Ordinance forbidding any one from using water out of the Public Cistern. Those who have duds that need washing, will feel the necessity of looking elsewhere for water. We opine, however, some water will ooze out of the Cistern aided by a bucket, one of these dark nights.

Apr 23, 1857

Fruit Prospects.

We are gratified to learn that the prospects for a good fruit crop are still quite favorable. About one half the peach buds are sound, and the trees will yield a fair crop provided disasters do not occur at a later period. Pears are also safe. Apples are uninjured. Early cherries are damaged, but others are not seriously affected. Grapes are in a good condition and promise a full average yield.

Spooks and Witches.

We hear of an interesting case occurring in Prospect township. A. rented a house from B. and refused to pay for it, whereupon B. sued for his money, and on the trial, testimony was given by A. going to show that the house was haunted. It was a jury trial and instead of B. getting the pay for his house, the jury rendered a verdict of fifteen dollars damage, in favor of A. So much for owning haunted houses for other people to live in! We thought the days of hobgoblins, spooks and ghosts were over with; but we were mistaken, as this verdict, rendered by four gentlemen of Prospect proves. We would like to publish full particulars of the case, from some one who will act as reporter.

☞ The Jury in the case of Michael Harrigan who was tried last week before Judge Whitely on a charge of murder in the second degree, rendered a verdict against the accused of assault and battery. His Honor fined him one hundred and seventy-five dollars and in addition, ordered him to be confined in the dungeon of the County Jail and fed on bread and water for ten days. This, we learn, is the full extent of the law.

Snow!

This town and vicinity was honored with a friendly visit from Col. Snow on the 19h inst. This is an unusual occurrence for this season of the year. The weather clerk, in making up his list of seasons for 1857, has omitted two of them at least, and is going to bless us with two, one of which is to be called Winter the 1st and the other Winter the 2nd. This omission will hardly suit every inhabitant of this mundane sphere, but as it is only about two months till the 12th of June next, when there will be a grand smash up of all things terrestrial, perhaps we can stand it until after that time. We enter our 'protest' however, against any more snow.

Another Fire!

The dwelling house of Mr. Joseph Nesbitt of Claridon township was destroyed by fire on Wednesday morning of last week. We learn that Mr. Nesbitt was in town at the time of the occurrence, and knew nothing of the affair until it was over. The house was new and large and Mr. Nesbitt's loss is therefore very heavy. There was a total loss both of the building and contents.

Died.

In Marion, Ohio, April 17th, James Wesley, infant son of Charles W. and Sarah J. Brown. Aged 2 years, 3 months and 24 days.

Apr 30, 1857

Marriages.

Married—On the 23rd inst., Mr. Joseph R. Oborn to Miss Catherine Barnhart—all of Richland Township, Marion county, Ohio.

Accident.

John Freeman, grocer of Mr. Victory fell from the gravel train on Saturday last and before he could recover himself, two cars passed over him, mashing one thigh and one ancle most horribly. Amputation was decided upon, but he was too much injured to withstand the painful operation and he died under it.

Mr. Freeman formerly resided near this place and we believe has relatives living here now. He was buried on Monday last by the Masonic fraternity of which he was a member.

The accident occurred at Mt. Victory.

Great Spook Trial.

Mr. Editor:—A trial took place in our township concerning the rent of a certain house in Middletown, which is said to be haunted with spooks, witches, spirits, demons or something unnatural, which renders it unfit for a family to live in—the rent of which is the cause of the present trial.

I will give you the testimony as it occurred in the trial as near as I can recollect.

The Defendant testified that he had heard sounds at different times like dogs fighting and running across the floor in the night. Also, that on the night of the 17th of December, 1856, clouds of fire and smoke appeared in the room with a flaming sword in the midst of it. The effect of the fire and smoke seemed almost to kill him—could scarcely breathe—could not move hand or foot, nor in any way help myself. A bad smell also pervaded the house, like some person dead and putrid. At different times noises were heard as if potatoes were thrown violently across the floor. Also said no consideration would force him to live in the house one day. A crock of new milk put in the buttery, would spoil in one hour, and would have that putrid smell.

First Witness for the defendant testified that the smell was very sickening one—that new milk would spoil. Also, that a young man stayed at the house when he lived in it—slept upstairs—heard something walking up and down the stairs like a man—which came to his bed and pulled the bed clothes from him. The young man halloed and witness got up and lit a candle—went upstairs, but nothing could be seen or heard—but found the young man pulling the clothes trying to keep on him, but they were already partly on the floor. He searched for the cause of the fright but could not find anything. The young man was so frightened that he left the house and went to the hotel. He believes there is something more than human about the house. Also states he is not afraid of spooks, witches, spirits, men, or the d---l.

Second Witness heard noises at different times—smelt the offensive smell—testified to the spoiling of new milk—searched the house at different times, but could find nothing; believed there was something troubling the house uncommon and unnatural.

Third Witness lives within about six rods of the house—was passing by one evening, with his son, when they heard a mournful groaning in the house, such as no human person could utter; and in about a month after, was passing by in the evening again—heard a noise similar to the first—saw large lights in and about the house, as large as a washing tub, at different times—was acquainted with the smell—satisfied that there was no real vermin about the house, for he had examined time and again—the cause of the trouble he did not know.

Fourth Witness heard unusual noises about the house—smelt bad smells, but knows no more about it.

Fifth Witness was only a witness of defendant tending plaintiff the money for the rent for the time he occupied the house. the plaintiff refusing to take it, and said he would have all or none—knows nothing about spooks.

Sixth Witness said he would not take a family of children in the house and live in it for any consideration. Never saw, heard or smelt anything—believes it all a humbug.

The Plaintiff testified that the defendant tendered him the rent money for the time he occupied the house, but refused to take it; and offered to take half of the money for the rent, being $25 for six months. The defendant refused to pay it, occupying the house only five weeks.

Thus ends the testimony in the trial. Now with regard to pleas in the case—Mr. John R. Knapp, of Marion, made the first in favor of the plaintiff. He did not say much; tried to say something, but of no use—all was "confusion and derangement." The second was made by the defendant himself. He made awful denunciations—so much so, that it would make the hair stand on end to hear him. Among other things he said he would go to jail and be carried out of the keyhole by worms before he would pay the rent, and so went on until he got perfectly enraged, when he took his seat, greatly excited.

The next plea was made by Esq. Dicks, of Prospect in favor of defendant—in which he tried hard to establish spooks and hob-goblins. The next plea was made by Mr. Osborn of Marion, in favor of plaintiff. His remarks were few but pointed. He appeared quite calm and composed.

Thus ends the great spook trial. Now for the decision. Well, the spooks got off victorious—the plaintiff had to pay the cost of suit; lose all the rent, and pay $15 damage! We cannot help saying hurrah for spooks forever! The reader will observe that we have something in our community uncommon! That we are a people to be looked up to as a very intelligent and progressive people! We are the first in the world to bring to light and establish the personality of spooks by judicial litigation!

We are ourself uncompromisingly skeptical:

Prospect.

May 7, 1857

Fortunate.

It has been demonstrated that the great comet will strike earth in the Border Ruffian region of Missouri. This is extremely fortunate and almost reconciles us to the general smash.

Deaths.

Died—In Caledonia on Sunday, April 26, Mr. Garry Clark in the 52d year of his age.

☞ May day visited us this year in rather an unruly manner. The rain fell while children settled around warm fires, wondering why they could not have a May party, as usual. But their ma's and pa's told them it was no use to grieve—they could have no May party until it cleared off.

This latter event has failed to come as yet; and when it does, we have no assurance that the children will have flowers, and green boughs, and nice fresh grass to play on; and it is feared that May parties this year will have to be postponed till June. However, when spring does come, the children will enjoy themselves. Confound that comet—when will it let us have some warm weather?

May 14, 1857

The New Game Law.

The new game law went into effect on Friday of last week. It is now unlawful for a man to kill in any manner, off his own premises, any deer or rabbit, or kill or destroy the eggs of any quail, partridge or pheasant, wild goose, duck, turkey, snipe, etc. The killing of robins, larks, thrush and cat-birds is prohibited at all times of the year. Birds of prey, crows, crow-blackbirds, red headed woodpeckers, etc., are not protected.

The intention of the law is to protect the various kinds of game during the season of their increase, and other birds at all times.

Acknowledgment.

The undersigned, in behalf of himself and family, hereby presents grateful acknowledgments to those gentlemen who, on the evening of the 1st inst., sent them a handsome donation of clothing, worth over one hundred dollars; and while they admire the taste and consideration manifested in the selection of the articles, and prize the goods for their intrinsic value, they do not fail to appreciate the kindly feeling, of which these gifts are the indices.

George B. Sturgis, Minister St. Paul's Church, Marion

May 21, 1857

Present Worth Having.

Lake Erie has been brought very near our town by means of railroad communication. Instead of receiving fish in wagons, slimy and half spoiled as formerly, we now get a supply fresh, packed in ice, the day after they are caught. We are reminded of this by recieving a large, nice, fresh muscalange, enough for several meals, from our friend Cy. Seibert—a present worth having when ham is fourteen cents a pound. Cy. receives fresh fish two or three times every week, and furnishes them at about half the price meat is selling for.

Jun 4, 1857

Obituary.

Died at the residence of his eldest daughter, Mrs. Jeffries in Spencer, Medina county, Ohio at 12 o'clock P.M. Friday, April 24, of disease of the lungs, Calvin Spencer, aged 78 years and 10 months.

The deceased was one of the early settlers in the Western Reserve. Born in Connecticut in 1778, he removed early in life to Greene county, N.Y., where he resided until past the meridian of life when he emigrated with his family in 1821 to Ohio, settling upon Black River thirty six miles south west of Cleveland where he resided up to the time of his death.

Married.

On the 21st ult., Col. J.B.W. Haynes of Richwood, Union county to Mary R. Convers of Pleasant Valley, Madison county, Ohio.

On the 28th ult., Dr. J.S. Cunningham of Urbana, Illinois to Miss Nancy A. Clark of Marion County, Ohio.

Gone

Brother Beckley, who was not elected county surveyor last fall, has pulled up stakes and gone to Kansas. We learn this interesting fact from some of his neighbors. The Democracy thus lose two standing candidates, merely because they would not elect them to office eternally. Take Warning!

Jun 11, 1857

The Fourth.

It seems the patriotism of the Marion folks all escaped at the celebration of the fourth of July, some two or three years since, and it has been impossible to collect enough together since that time, to make a respectable celebration. We hear of no effort being made here to secure a march in the hot sun, a sweltering oration and a free dinner of pickled beans and dried pumpkins; though we have heard of one fellow offering twenty-five dollars towards such a show, with the expectation of getting his money back by selling lager and poor lemonade!

That is a sort of patriotism that is commendable—it reaches way down through a fellow's heart, into his pocket!

Perhaps it is well enough that we have no such 'glorious time.' However, if we are to have a celebration, it is time we were making the arrangements. We merely alluded to the subject to draw attention to the fact that the fourth is near at hand. We are willing to engage in any laudable mode of celebrating the coming anniversary of our independence that our fellow citizens may see fit to make.

The Comet.

Next Saturday, the 13th, is the day set apart by astronomers for the collision between this mud-ball and the comet. The exhibition, however, will not come off. We learn by a dispatch from the man in the moon, that the fiery train struck one of the numerous worlds above, glanced off, and will pass this world at 17 minutes past 12 o'clock on Saturday next, leaving it about three-eights of a mile to the left.

The Chicken Trial.

This interesting case was, by some hocus-pocus of the lawyers, taken before his honor, Judge Snyder of the Probate Court on Wednesday afternoon last. We had intended to be on hand to give a report; but the sly, cunning lawyers stole a march on us, and when we went down street, on Thursday morning, to attend the trial, we heard that it was through with, and Ross discharged.

Of course no other result was anticipated; the idea that Hugh W. Ross, County Surveyor, could be guilty of stealing chickens probably never entering any man's head, only as a means of carrying out some petty spite or other ill feeling towards him. Mr. Ross stands acquitted of the charge, while his persecutor has been compelled to 'pay dear for the whistle.'

Daring Burglary!

On Friday night, the Banking office of J.S. Reed & Co. was broken open and an unsuccessful attempt made to force an entrance into their safe. Gun powder was freely used, as was quite a promiscuous kit of tools—among which were chisels, brace and bits, sledgehammer, &c.,

&c. The room when opened in the morning, was full of powder smoke, and in front and on the side of the safe, looked like a work shop.

The powder blew in the lining of the outside door, but did not affect the locks, otherwise than to render unlocking impossible by filling them with fire proof and fragments. Every bolt was firmly and honestly in its place; and all the sledging and wedging and prying and cutting and blowing did was to make a dirty looking room and to render it necessary to remove the door by main force.

This was done after an hour's hard work by four men, with the burglar's kit—to which it was found necessary to add an extra crowbar and a stick of timber. The inside doors of course were in good order. When it is remembered that the outside doors of a safe are relied on mainly for fire proof purposes, and that it is upon the carefully constructed inside doors that reliance is placed as protection from thieves, it will be seen that the burglars expended a hard night's work upon hopeless enterprise.

The noise of the explosion was heard by a number of our citizens, as was the sledging, but no one had an appreciation of what was going on. The safe, which so nobly resisted all efforts to blow it up and to sledge it to pieces, is one of Herring's Improved Fire and Burglar Proof make, whose three doors are secured by the most approved modern locks, among which is Hall's powder proof, and which was the one so severely tried.

It strikes us that a more reckless desperate, fool-hardy attempt at robbery never was made. Surrounded by dwelling houses, several persons

sleeping only a few feet from the safe, to use gun powder and sledges, regardless of noise or interruption, was simply folly. Burglarious visitors to the Marion County Bank hereafter will find company.

Married.

On Tuesday, June 2d, 1857, William Scofield of Marion County, Ohio to Miss Carrie E. Norris of Delaware County, Ohio.

Jun 18, 1857

1776! 1857!
July Fourth!

The citizens of Marion having resolved to celebrate in an appropriate manner the eighty-first anniversary of American Independence, the committee of arrangements submits the following:

A dinner will be prepared on the fair grounds, west of town, which it is proposed shall be furnished by the contributions of those participating in the festivities of the day. Our citizens are respectfully solicited to contribute from their abundance and all refreshments should be deposited in the court house by 8 o'clock on the morning of the 4th, where they will be taken charge of by the committee and placed upon the table.

The officers of the day will meet at the United States Hotel; the firemen at the engine house; the different schools at the stone school house; and citizens generally at the court house at 10 o'clock A.M. The procession will form at half past ten, under the direction of the Marshals in the following order:

Music.
Firemen—with Engine &c.
Officers of the day in Carriages.
Public Schools, Marshalled by the
Superintendent and Teachers.
Citizens.

The procession will move to the
Fair Grounds, when the following
exercises will take place:

1.—Music.
2.—Prayer.
3.—Music.
4.—Reading of Declaration.
5.—Music.
6.—Oration.
7.—Music.
8.—Benediction.

After which dinner will be served
up under direction of the committee.

It is proposed that the remainder of
the day be spent in such festivities
as the company may prefer, and the
whole to conclude, should the weather
permit, with a magnificent display
of fire works.

Jun 25, 1857

Married,

On the 24th ult., P.O. Sharpless and
Miss Mattie M.W. McIntyre, all of
Marion, Oh.

Jul 2, 1857

Married.

On the 30th ult., Mr. F.M. Anderson to Miss Sarah E. Geiger, all of
Marion County, Ohio.

❖

On the 30th ult., Mr. Isaac Wynn
to Miss Jane Thatcher, all of Marion county, Ohio.

 The planet Venus is now visible every clear day, about two
hours in advance of the sun. A
number of persons in town have
mistaken it for the comet, and
consequently 'nervous' people and
smoked glass are in greater demand
than they have been for some time.
A stranger coming into Marion,
would think it the fashion here to
carry the face up in the air, instead
of straight forward, as people usually do. Everybody is looking.

Jul 9, 1857

New Cemetery.

We notice that a cemetery association has at last been formed. Land
has been purchased by Mr. B.H.
Williams, being a portion of Mr.
James Bowen's farm, lying east of
the Delaware road, which is to be
offered to the association when
fully organized. We hope we have
seen nearly the last interment in the
old burying ground in the north east
corner of our village and that the
new association will go on with
energy to prepare and beautify a
spot for the final resting place of
our neighbors and friends.

There is no speculation about the
affair, as the law provides that all
moneys coming into the hands of
the association, after paying for the
land, shall be spent upon the premises. Those gentlemen, therefore,
who have associated for this purpose
are doing a work for our community, for which they should receive
our thanks and we wish the enterprise success.

We have nothing to say of the
proceedings of the Fourth—only
that they passed off to the satisfaction of all who took part in them.

Married.

On the 2d inst., Davis Taylor to
Miss Martha C. Smith, both of Salt
Rock township, Marion county,
Ohio.

Jul 16, 1857

Suicide.

Dr. J. Barnhart, of this place, committed suicide on Monday night
last, by cutting his throat with a
razor. His body was found in his
office, in the Bennett Block, on
Tuesday at noon.

He had been very much dissipated
for some time back, and while recovering from the effects of the liquor and opium, after his sprees,
would be partially delirious. It is
charitably supposed, that in one of
those temporary fits of insanity, he
committed the horrible deed. With
more truth, his murder might be
charged on the grog sellers who
thrive in Marion. And who tempted
him, for the base coin, to drink the
liquid fire, and ruin himself and
others—and this, too, against his
better judgement. And the liquor
sellers go on with their damaging
work, and are already selling liquor
to the next self-murderer. When
will it stop?

Dr. Barnhart—poor follow!—had
many warm friends, who have done
a great work to reform him, but all
to no purpose. His enemy was his
own weakness—and now that he is
gone, we feel constrained to drop
the sympathetic tear, and call down
the curses of all good men upon
those who worked his ruin. Peace
to his memory.

Accident.

Mr. Harvey Clingenpeel, clerk in Coffey's saloon was badly injured on Tuesday last, by being thrown from a colt. He was in the act of mounting, and by some means his clothes caught in a buckle on the saddle, and failing to get seated, the animal made a plunge and threw him. He struck on his head, injuring it severely, and also injuring his breast very badly. His wounds were dressed and in the evening he was removed to Mr. Coffey's residence.

☞ The weather is glorious. Nothing could be more auspicious for crops of all sorts. Grass redundant; corn is flourishing; and serials and vegetables of all descriptions promise an abundant harvest. We ought all of us to feel ashamed for having murmured at the last cold weather. Nature is wiser than man. Seed time and harvest never fail. Even the Comet demon is but a coward's bugbear.

Jul 23, 1857

A Mean Act.

Some wretch being possessed with a spirit meaner than the devil on Friday last shot and killed a fine young Durham heifer belonging to J.S. Copeland. This is too mean an act for the perpetrator to go unpunished, and we sincerely hope he may be discovered. Mr. Copeland offers a reward of twenty dollars for information that will lead to the conviction of the guilty.

☞ The young lady who burst into tears has been put together again.

Improvements in Marion.

Quite a number of improvements are going forward in Marion at the present time—a sure evidence of our growing prosperity. The Union School House is fast approaching completion and when done, will present a better appearance than any similar building we know of. Our market house has been commenced; and will be pushed forward as rapidly as possible; to be two stories high and finished off in the best style for marketing purposes, with a first class town hall above. A three story frame hotel will also soon be put under constructions.

A number of private dwellings are also in course of erection, giving employment to all our mechanics and bringing population, industry, and wealth to our town in abundance. Our boss workmen have their hands full, and are kept busy. Mr. E.D. Lindsey, boss plasterer, recently gave employment to six new hands, brought here from abroad. Mr. _____ informs us that he has more work than he can get hands for, and will give employment with good wages to half a dozen carpenters from abroad, if he can get them. No doubt others of our leading mechanics would give employment to workmen, if they were to be had. These are the kind of men to build up a community. Sober, hard-working, straightforward—when they commence an improvement, they soon finish it—and then there is an improvement worth speaking of. We wish there were more of them here.

Aug 6, 1857

Married.

On the 30th inst., Mr. Ezekiel Bacon to Miss Martha Folk, both of Marion county, Ohio.

On the 4th inst., Thomas McGuire of Bucyrus, Ohio to Mrs. Barbara B. Booth of Marion, Ohio.

Democratic Mirror Market

The above institution last week underwent another of those changes for which during the past year it has become so noted. The old (invisible) editor has withdrawn; and Mr. Addison Osborne, Esq., Attorney at law, &c., &c., assumed control of its columns, as Editor.

Mr. Osborne brings more character into the concern than any man who has had hold of it for years; but he won't last long—he is too 'meek and lamb-like'—to fill the measure of a locofoco editor, and the party will soon get tired of him. We desire him a full share of 'luck' pecuniarily; but politically, may he find editing the *Mirror* 'a hard road to travel.'

Another Robbery.

On Wednesday night of last week, the 29th of July, the store of T. Search, jr., of this place was broken into and about ten dollars—all there was in the drawer at the time—carried away. The scoundrels took no goods. An entrance was made through the front door, which is double, by placing a brace against the side containing the lock, with such force that the bolt of the lock was pushed out to the staple.

The rogues in this case go 'scot free' as it would be impossible to describe the money and they carried off nothing else whereby they could be detected. They are, however, suspicioned—and our citizens need only keep a closer watch to detect then in some other midnight excursion, and thus put an end to the system of robberies now occurring in Marion.

Still Another.

The money in the drawer of the clothing store of Messrs. Bartram & Grimm, merchant tailors of this place, was stolen out by a young man, who was kindly permitted to sleep there, on the night of Monday last, the 3d inst. He is a journeyman tailor, by the name of Brooks, and we believe hails from Bucyrus. He did not steal quite enough to send him to the penitentiary but enough to secure him a lodging in the 'Lewis House' of this place, if he is taken.

Crops in Marion County.

The crops of this county are doing finely. The weather could not be more auspicious. Corn is growing well—and most of it is far enough advanced to be out of the reach of frost, unless it comes very early.

Potatoes are coming in freely, nice large ones, at seventy-five cents per bushel. With half a chance they will be more abundant than ever before as there is no end to the breadth of land planted with them. They promise so well that farmers are already joking about them. Said one to an-

other the other day in our hearing, "This weather will destroy all the small potatoes." "Why how is that possible?" "By making them grow to be large ones!" said our friend; and the hearty laugh they both took over the joke showed that they relished the idea of having small potatos spoiled in this way.

MYSTERIOUS AFFAIR.
Death of a Strange Female by Poisoning.

Our usually quiet village was thrown into considerable excitement by the sudden and mysterious death of a strange female, on the evening of Wednesday, July 29th, at the house of our fellow townsman, F.C. Ruehrmund.

For the benefit of the public, and to correct a good many contradictory reports, which are afloat, we give below a condensed statement of the facts, as far as they are known, and which were obtained from a reliable source.

The woman was first seen in our village on Tuesday, July 28th, in the afternoon, apparently just coming from the cars, with a black satchel in her hand, and accompanied by a little girl about five years old. She was walking along the street, inquiring for a place to work; but did not succeed in obtaining one. Mr. Ruehrmund, indeed by pity and commiseration for her apparently helpless and distressed condition, finally took her home to his house where Mrs. Ruehrmund told her she could stay until she could look around and obtain a good home.

The deceased stated that her name was *Emerson*; that she was a widow; her husband had died five months

ago with the typhoid fever; her little girl was about five years old, and that they had lived at and come from Union; that she wanted to go to Cleveland, where an aunt of hers was living; but upon reaching Galion, she found that she had not money enough to reach Cleveland; she had therefore endeavored to get work in Galion, but on being unsuccessful, had returned to Marion.

Her deportment was modest and ladylike. She did not seem inclined to converse much; but would answer any question readily, and with a show of candor and truthfulness; and when questioned about her husband, &c., with so much sorrow, that it would excite the sympathies of the hearer very much.

She appeared to be in good health, and when asked whether she was able and willing to assist Mrs. Ruehrmund in her work about the house, replied in the affirmative.

On the evening of her death, she retired about 9 o'clock with her child to rest, and came down stairs again after a glass of water. Mrs. Ruehrmund also retired; but before getting into bed, heard a noise; thought it was the boys on the street; hoisted the window curtain to see whether there was fire anywhere, but could see nothing; and not hearing any more of the noise, fell asleep.

After while, while dosing or slumbering, she again heard the noise, and as she fancied, the voice of a child with it. The thought struck her then, whether it might not be the strange woman up stairs; she went to the foot of the stairs and inquired what was the matter; the woman answered: "O Lord!" Mrs. Ruehrmund then ran up stairs, and found the deceased in convulsions or spasms; threw some water in her face, took hold of her, and found her stiff.

Mrs. Ruehrmund then ran to Mr. Matthews' house, requesting Mr. Matthews to go for her husband; and from there to Mrs. Tharp's house, requesting her to come over. On her return, she found Mrs. A. H. Brown, who had heard the screams of the sufferer, and requested her to go up stairs with her.

When Mr. Ruehrmund reached his house, and found that the deceased was in extreme agony, he immediately started after a physician; but met Mr. Matthews a short distance from his house, who volunteered to call Dr. Christian, the family physician. Mr. Ruehrmund then returned to the bedside of the sufferer, who was lying in convulsions, or spasms, and uttering heart-rending screams. Mr. Ruehrmund requested her to be quiet; a doctor would soon be there and she would get better; whereupon she replied she could not help it. Mrs. Tharp and Mrs. Brown were present in the room, and remained there until the death of the sufferer.

The deceased asked the persons present to hold her, when Mr. Ruehrmund took hold of her wrists, and the ladies mentioned, of her feet; the spasms were so severe as to raise Mr. Ruehrmund completely off from the floor. She asked repeatedly for water, but on Mr. Ruehrmund attempting to raise her head to give her a drink, she screamed and said she could not be raised; he then tried to give her some water out of a spoon, but the deceased clenched her teeth and could not swallow.

Mrs. Ruehrmund had, previous to this last effort of her husband, succeeded in bringing a little water to the mouth of the sufferer, of which she swallowed a little, and which seemed to increase the spasms. On turning to the stand by the bedside, Mrs. Ruehrmund noticed a spoon lying there, when she remarked that she (the deceased) must have taken something, as there was a spoon.

Mrs. Ruehrmund asked her then if she had taken anything. She answered, "a quinine powder." On asking her who gave it to her—a doctor?—she replied "no—a man at Laramie Station." Mr. Ruehrmund then asked her what that man's name was—to which she made no reply, until the question was several times repeated, and until Mr. Ruehrmund had told her that he hoped she would not repay the kindness of giving a homeless, friendless woman a shelter, by bringing trouble over them; that there would likely be a judicial inquiry into this matter, and that it was very essential that the name of the person who gave her that powder should be known; when she, being again asked what his name was; said it was "Robbins." Being asked what his first name was, she replied "Edward," and on being questioned as to the desired purpose of the drug, stated it was for the purpose of destroying her child (she had a short time before stated that she was pregnant.)

She then said "send (or write) to Laramie Station, Shelby county, Ohio and the folks will come after my dear child." On being asked, what folks? She replied, "Holly's." It was evident from this that her real name had not been given at first—it was not *Emerson*, but *Nancy Holly*.

At this time no physician had come, and Mr. Ruehrmund, finding that she was sinking fast, started off after Dr. Sweney, but found two young men, who offered to go after the doctor.

When Mr. Ruehrmund returned to the sick room, he found her with the death rattle in her throat, just breathing her last.

Soon after Mr. Ruehrmund returned, and after her death, Dr. Sweney arrived, and with the assistance of Dr. Christian, preceded to make a *post mortem* examination, in the presence of the coroner and his jury.

After the body was examined, the stomach and its contents were carefully removed, and sealed up in a glass jar, in which condition it was carried by Dr. Sweney to the chemical laboratory in Cleveland Medical College, where it was analyzed by Prof. J. Lang Cassels, and found to contain a large quantity of strychnine—a medicine never used as an abortive, and only as a speedy, sure, and deadly poison.

A jury of inquest was called to examine into the cause of her death, when after a patient hearing of the facts above narrated, and after witnessing an examination of the body of the deceased, rendered the following verdict:

"We, the jury, after having heard the evidence and examined the body of the deceased, do find that the deceased came to her death by means of some deadly poison taken by her, at the residence of said Ruehrmund, on the evening of said 29th day of July.

We also find that said Nancy Holly, at the time of her death, was *enceinte*, and that said poison was probably taken by her with a view of producing an abortion, supposing it to be a medicine which would accomplish that result, and not understanding its deadly properties.

Also, that one Edward Robbins has been living upon terms of intimacy with said Nancy Holly, and has been immediately instrumental in producing the death of the said Nancy, having furnished her with the said poison, probably with an understanding of its properties, and contemplating the result produced."

On Thursday morning, deputy sheriff Lewis, with C. Martin started west with a warrant for the arrest of Robbins, whom they found, as stated by the deceased, near Laramie Station on the railroad. They also found a family by the name of Holly near the same place, who at once recognized the daguerreotype of the deceased. The body being yet unburied, was identified.

On Saturday, Robbins had his examination before Esq. Moore—the defence being conducted by P. Bunker, Esq. and the prosecution by prosecuting attorney James H. Anderson, and J.F. Hume, Esq. The defendant was bound over to the next term of the Court of Common Pleas, to answer the charge of murder.

On the examination he appeared much dejected, scarcely lifting his eyes from the floor, and frequently shedding tears.

This affair has caused deep feeling in our community, and more than one has been heard to talk of appealing to Judge Lynch; although no steps have been taken to interfere in the due course of the law.

Much credit is due to Sheriff Lewis and his assistant for the promptness displayed in securing the accused party and the evidence necessary to establish his guilt, which have proved the efficiency of Mr. Lewis as an officer.

A Card.

We received the following card from the brother of the unfortunate woman and he appeared as one whose mind has been trained aright, however deep the affliction he may be laboring under at present.

Mr. Editor:—It would be exceedingly ungrateful in us to leave Marion without expressing our warmest and most grateful thanks to the citizens for the sympathy and disinterested endeavors that have been so clearly manifested on this deeply melancholy occasion: This, we know, is a light compliment; but it is hoped may be acceptable. Such benevolence can only be rewarded, fully, by "Him who is the giver of every good and perfect gift." I speak in behalf of my mother and sister.

G.W. Holly

Aug 13, 1857

Threatening Letters.

The following letters were addressed to Mr. John Hughes, who, in partnership with Mr. Wallace Hoxter, has carried on the livery business in this place for some time. They were doubtless written with a view to frighten Mr. Hoxter out of business—which, in his unfortunate condition, it was very essential for him to continue.

They accomplished their object—not, however, until others were more frightened than he—and the firm have now dissolved. Mr. Hughes will continue at the old stand. Mr. Hoxter is thus thrown out of employment—but will soon open up again. As Mr. Hoxter has had two stables burned previous to this, we think it is time our citizens and officers should take the matter in hand, and, if possible, ferret our the scoundrels, and bring them to justice. But here are the letters—we give them *ver batem*.

No. 1.

MR. HUGHS you HAD BETTER look our FoR your DAMED thief PARDNER HAS PARTED MAN AND WIFE AND tHAy will HAVE REVNGE oR DyE.

No. 2.

Mr Hughes you had better get rid of that thief wal Hoxter as he has parted man and wife an had to Stables burned down now you had better get rid of him within two weeks or you will have another one burned down we dont want to destroy your property but we will have revenge in two weeks you had better take warning in time.

No. 3.

Mr. Hughs half of the time we give you is gone you have fair warning we will do what we say we will if we go to prison for life we will have revenge.

Aug 27, 1857

Improvements.

Messrs. J.S. Reed & Co. are making arrangements to tear away the old brick now known as the checkered store, and to replace it with a new and more modern building, better adapted to their business, which has outgrown it's accommodations. We hope Captain Hardy, who owns the remainder of the lot, will join, and that the result will be an ornament to our village and a pattern to those who improve hereafter.

"The old brick" whose approaching disappearance we announce above, is one of the "first settlers" and a history of its transformation from tavern to dwellings, from dwellings to stores, with a record of its merry frontier dances, its welcomes to new comers, its courtships and flirtations, its sorrows and crosses, its deaths, its cheap goods of the merchants, and its "most excellent-good-well-made-no-cotton-in-him clothes" dispensed by the descendants of Father Abraham, from under the old roof, would make quite a volume, and embrace much of the early history of our village.

Who will get up a history of Marion? Now is the time to gather up and preserve occurrences, while the original settlers are still living.

Sep 3, 1857

"Nothing to Wear"

The most scathing satire on fashionable dressing we have ever read, is now going the rounds of the press, under the above heading. The writer must certainly have paid a visit to Marion, or some town where the women dress the same as they do here—which consists of half dress and half undress. Here, at any time of day, on every street, may be seen women and girls with

"Nothing to wear!" Well, well we suppose,
Some ladies quite truly declare it,
For their habitual disuse of clothes
Above the waist sufficiently shows,
That there, at least as far as that goes,
They've "nothing to wear"—and they wear it.

Sep 17, 1857

Valedictory.

To the patrons of the *Republican*: having disposed of the Republican establishment, it is nothing more than right that I should say a few parting words to those who have supported me with their money and their influence, for the eighteen months last past. Nothing but an ardent desire for the welfare of the paper and the party in Marion county, could have induced me to sever the kind connections that have existed between myself and the Republicans of Marion county for the time I have been among you. It is unnecessary here to state the causes which have led me to take this step; suffice it now to say that they were of such a nature that had any of you placed in a similar position, I have not the least doubt you would have resolved on the same course.

In my intercourse with the citizens of Marion county, I have endeavored to deal justly and fairly with all. That I have erred at times, I have do doubt; and now that I am about to resign the post I have occupied at the head of the paper, I feel like saying to one and all, that I did so unintentionally; that if errors have been committed, they were errors of the head and not of the heart.

Regretting the necessity that has compelled me to abandon this post, in which you have so faithfully supported me, I return you my sincere thanks; and assure you that whatever my lot may be cast, whatever pursuits I may hereafter be engaged in, whatever associations surround me, I shall ever revert with pleasure to my brief connection with the gallant, true, and warm hearted Republicans of Marion county.

The paper will hereafter be edited by an older and more experienced brother, Mr. W. P. Dumble, a gentleman who is amply qualified to furnish you with a better paper than you had and whose long experience both as a printer and editor, is the best assurance that a paper inferior to none ever issued in Marion will be supplied at his hands. Give him your cordial; and united support.

J.W. Dumble

Married.—On the 14th inst., Mr. Lewis Trimble to Miss Georgiett Johnson, both of Marion, Ohio.

Sep 24, 1857

☞ Being but partially acquainted with the run of matters in this county as yet, of course we will leave undone many things that we should do, and do many things that we should leave undone. After we get the "hang" of the new schoolhouse, however, we flatter ourselves that we shall succeed in presenting our patrons with a paper that will meet their approval, and although it now has a circulation larger than any paper in Marion county ever attained since the dismemberment of the county, yet we know that a liberal patronage is the first requisite towards making a good paper.

Oct 1, 1857

The County Fair.
The Sixth Annual Fair of the Marion County Agricultural Society closed on Friday last, having occupied three days. The weather, throughout, was extremely favorable—being neither too warm nor too cold for comfort. Everything passed off smoothly, and upon the whole, the officers and managers of the Fair have just cause to be proud of the success which attended their efforts to make the exhibition interesting and instructive. The number in attendance each day was very large, showing conclusively that the people of our county are fully imbued with the progressive spirit of the age, and determined to keep up with the rest of the world in material progress.

☞ Mr. James Walker of Montgomery township, raised on his farm a water-melon weighing thirty-three pounds. He informs us he has larger ones yet growing on his patch.

Oct 15, 1857

Marriages.
Married—On the 7th inst., William K. Stockton and Miss Mary Jane Miller, all of this place.

Oct 22, 1857

Our paper.
The election being over, hereafter our readers may look for a more interesting paper, as we shall devote more of our space to miscellaneous reading. We shall endeavor to render our paper a vehicle for the dissemination of the latest news, useful information, and refined literature, and hope to render it a welcome visitor to the homes and firesides of Marion county.

Terrible Accident.
On Friday last, a son of Mr. Sampson Jones of this place, about 12 years of age, whilst engaged in driving the horses attached to the power of a threshing machine, got his leg entangled in the gearing, and before the horses could be stopped, it was literally ground to a pumice up to the knee. He was released as soon as possible, and the limb amputated by Dr. Bridge, assisted by Drs. Christian and others.

Bank Suspension.
The Bank of Marion suspended specie payment on Thursday last, Bill holders should not sacrifice anything on account of the suspension, as they are abundantly secured by public stock deposited in the State Treasury. The bills are as current here as the specie—being received by all our banking houses on deposit, or in payment of paper.

Oct 29, 1857

Horrible Affair.

We take the following item from a communication from Waldo, in this county:

A small boy, about twelve years of age, named John Smith, and living with Mr. John Wyatt, came to a horrible death on the evening of the 21st inst. He, in company with another boy, had been riding some horses to the creek, near by to water them, and was returning with them to the stable.

Coming to a gate, through which they had to pass, the little fellow, in getting off to open it, became entangled in the lines by one of his feet, and hung suspended with his head downward. The horse became frightened and started off, with the little fellow, at the top of its speed. He tried to regain his seat upon the horse's back, but failed. On went the affrighted animal, over and through fences.

The boy and horse were found in the woods, about two miles from the place where the horse started. He was considerably bruised and mangled, thou not so much so as would naturally be supposed in view of the circumstances.

Nov 5, 1857

Marriages.

On the 22d inst., In Richland township, Mr. George W. Rupp to Miss Elizabeth Barnhart, both of this county.

Nov 12, 1857

Marriages.

Married—On Thursday, the fifth inst., Mr. Justin H. Bunker to Miss Evaline Durfee, both of Marion, Ohio.

Nov 19, 1857

Marriages.

On Wednesday evening, Nov 4th, Mr. Jacob Daiky of Tipton, Iowa to Miss Jane Culbertson of Burlington at the residence of Dr. C.C. White.

From his old bachelor corner, the local sends greeting and good wishes to the fair bride, with many thanks for her kind remembrance—Hawkeye.

Nov 26, 1857

Case Continued.

Edward Robbins, charged with causing the death of Miss Nancy Holly by poison, in this place, a few months since, was arraigned at the late term of our Court of Common Pleas, when the case was continued on motion of prisoner's counsel, who claimed that several witnesses were absent, upon which testimony the prisoner relied for an acquittal.

Marriages.

On the 19th inst., R.R. Cameron to Miss M.E. Postle, all of Montgomery, Marion county, Ohio.

Dec 10, 1857

The Split in the Democratic Party.

The split in the ranks of the Democracy on the Kansas question seems now to be about complete. The northern press has come out almost unanimously in favor of rejecting the Calhoun Constitution. The President and his cabinet are well known to be in favor of its adoption by congress. The South, of course, will sustain the President, but without the aid of the northern wing nothing can be done. The war waxes hotter. It is refreshing to hear our northern Democrats shrieking for freedom. They go at it as earnestly as if they were used to it.

Marion County Agricultural Society.

The Agricultural Society of Marion County met in the Auditor's office, for the transaction of the annual business.

The following premiums were awarded, viz:—Best farm of 160 acres, D.S. Drake of Waldo Township; second best, Jacob Lee of Marion Tp.; best farm of 80 acres, M. Jacoby of Richland Tp.; second best, G. McWilliams of Marion Tp.

Dec 17, 1857

The Marion Cemetery Association.

This Association has purchased about forty-seven acres of ground for cemetery purposes. They have purchased more than they otherwise would have done, in order to acquire a desirable shape. And even making allowance for this, it is probable there will be a difference of opinion as to the necessity of purchasing so much. It must be borne in mind, however, that a considerable portion will be devoted to ornamental purposes, so as to make this final resting place of our friends and neighbors and *ourselves*, a place of agreeable resort for the cultivation of the memory of the departed, rather than a spot of gloom and sadness. It is possible that the Association have erred in this respect, but if so, it can hardly fail to be looked upon by them as an error of judgement, rather than a proceeding from any improper motive.

Owing to the precarious nature of the weather at this season of the year, the Trustees have not deemed it best to have a public sale this winter; yet as the present time is favorable to the removal of remains from other burial grounds, and as lots may be occasionally wanted for friends, previous to public dedication of the cemetery, they have resolved to allow any persons who choose, to purchase such lots as may please them, and a large number are therefore ready for disposal to those who may want them.

Married—In Marion, on the 13th inst., Henry Detwater of Clinton township and Mrs. Rachel Higgins of Marion.

Dec 24, 1857

Married—On the 17th inst., W. C. DeLong and Miss Sophia E. Banning, all of Larue, Marion co., Ohio.

In Marion, on the 21st inst., Mr. Henry W. Conrad of Pickaway county and Mrs. Catherine Corn, of Marion, O.

Our New School House.

The beautiful and liberal School Law has given an impetus to the cause of Education throughout our broad State, the effect of which will be felt for years to come, and the benefits of which generations of yet unborn will reap.

All over the State, spacious edifices are or have been erected in which the children of the rich and the poor alike, will obtain an education hitherto only within the reach of the favored children of affluence and wealth, without money and without price to them individually. The State has assumed the place of the parent, and extends to the forlorn children of adversity the same privileges that she does to those more favored ones within whose ranks we have hitherto been accustomed to look for our professional and scientific *savans*.

In every little village, the uncouth, primitive, log cabin school house have given way before the onward tread of the age, and in their place stately edifices are being reared that will long attest the liberality and the wisdom which inspired the friends of Free Education in the present age.

Under the supervision of our able and energetic Board of Education, we have rapidly approaching completion, a School House that will compare favorably with any in the State in regard to size, elegance, and convenience, and to give our readers at a distance some idea of it, we have collected a few facts which we deem worthy of record.

Its size, outside, is 93 feet in length by 66 feet 6 inches in breadth. The first floor is divided into four rooms 25 feet 3 inches in breadth by 36 feet 9 inches in length, designed for the Primary Departments. Two furnace rooms in which are placed the

furnaces for warming the different rooms, and a spacious hall 12 by 61 feet. The height of the story in the clear is 12 feet.

From the first to the second floor, access is to be had by means of two spacious flights of heavy stone steps with iron railing from the outside, in front and rear. At present two flights inside are used for that purpose. The second story is divided into four rooms 25 feet 3 inches by 36 feet 9 inches and two rooms 9 by 36 feet 9 inches. The four first mentioned are to be used as school rooms for different departments of the school. The two latter are recitation rooms. This story is also traversed by a hall 12 by 61 feet in size. This story is 14 feet in the clear.

Two flights of stairs inside lead to the third story, where we find four more school rooms of the same size of those already mentioned and two recitation rooms of a like size with those on the second floor. Here also, is another spacious hall, giving easy access to any of the rooms. This story is also 14 feet in the clear.

The fourth story is divided into a large hall of 61 feet 3 inches by 49 feet 6 inches, a room for the High School 36 feet 9 inches by 20 feet 9 inches, a Library Room, a dressing room for the large hall, and a hall leading to the dormitory 20 feet by 36 feet 9 inches. Height of this story is 18 feet 6 inches.

The height of the building to the deck roof is 75 feet. The deck roof is surmounted by an observatory, from which a beautiful view of the country for miles around can be obtained. The total height from the ground to the top of the dome of the observatory is 102 feet. From the fourth story access is had to the observatory by means of an easy flight of stairs and a hall, the dimensions of which has escaped our memory.

The different rooms are furnished off in a style strictly in keeping with the object for which the building was designed. The seating especially, we think admirably adapted to the purpose, combining durability with elegance, and affording much more comfort to the pupil than the old fashioned seats without backs.

Taking it as a whole, we think we have a School House that will compare favorably in every respect with any in the West. Attached to it are ample play grounds, which, in due season, will be properly laid off and embellished, rendering them attractive and agreeable. Our citizens should be proud of it, and each and every parent in the village should exercise great watchfulness that those committed to his care receive that benefit from it it was expected they would by those who have urged on the enterprise. Every parent should take a personal interest in it and aid in combatting every influence that would tend to destroy its usefulness, and ere long Marion will enjoy the proud reputation of having one of the best schools in the Union.

Dec 31, 1857

 Rev. G.B. Sturges, late Pastor of St. Paul's (Episcopal) Church, of this place, has removed to Gallipolis, O., having received a call from the Episcopal Church of that place. Mr. S., by his christian deportment and gentlemanly bearing during his residence here, has endeared himself to the entire community, and the best wishes of his acquaintances here attend him to his new home.

Marriages.

On the 28th inst., at the residence of the bride, Simon E. DeWolf and Miss Susan Busby, both of Marion.

❖

On the 17th inst., John Strawser to Miss Mary Ann Holverstott, all of Montgomery twp., Marion Co., O.

❖

In Marion, on the 24th inst., Mr. Moses Williams of Big Island to Miss Mary P. Johnson of Marion.

Jan 7, 1858

New Year.

New Year's day passed off very quietly here, although its advent was hailed with many noisy demonstrations—the night previous having been made hideous with the firing of guns, pistols, fire-crackers, &c., &c., and a stranger would have thought that the town had been taken by the Sepoys, who were engaged in an indiscriminate massacre of the inhabitants.

Jan 14, 1858

 On the 30th day of June last, there were only 346 names on the Revolutionary Pension Rolls at Washington. The number at the commencement was 55,000.

1857.

During the year that has just closed, there were 158 lives lost by fire in the United States; by steamboat accidents, 322; by Railroad accidents, 130; wounded by Railroad accidents, 530.

The Roads.

The public highways, in this part of the State, have been in such a woeful condition for a number of years. The bottom has fell clear out and they are almost impassible. Journeys, that usually consume two or three hours time, now convey a whole day. In fact traveling, save by rail, has almost entirely ceased. Everybody stays at home because they must, consequently, business has almost come to a stand still, and none of our farmers, even, venture to town, unless they are absolutely compelled to. A roaring blast from the north pole, accompanied by a liberal coat of snow, would receive a hearty welcome in "these parts" just now. Send it along.

Fire.

Yesterday, the 13 inst., a fire broke out in the north end of town, in a barn owned by John Hudson, and was burned to the ground. It was set on fire by some small boys who were in it lighting matches.

Jan 28, 1858

Marriages.

Married—On the 21st. inst., at the residence of the bride, in Marion, R.B. Holmes and Miss Maranda A. Tharp, both of this place.

On the 21st inst., at the Marion Hotel, Hugh B. Petty and Presilla E. Williams.

Feb 4, 1858

Revivals.

For some weeks past, an interesting revival of religion has been in progress at the M.E. Church, in this place. The altar is nightly crowded with penitents, and the meetings grow in interest as they progress.

A similar state of things exist at the United Brethren Church, and everything seems to indicate that the present winter will be a marked one in the history of Marion in consequence of the powerful revivals of religion with which her churches were favored.

Marriages.

Married—On the 28th inst., Mr. Allen Day to Miss Sarah J. Mears, both of Big Island Township, Marion county, O.

Died.

Died—At his residence in Pleasant township on the 25th inst., Rev. Jacob Klinfelter, aged 65 years.

Feb 11, 1858

Marriages.

In Marion, on the 9th inst., Mr. Israel Irey and Miss Margaret Bloxum.

Married—in Marion on the 2d inst., John Ehlers and Miss Eliza Russel.

Deaths.

Died—at his father's residence in Pleasant Tp., on the 2d inst., Mr. Benjamin Riley, aged 21y.

Died—at his residence in Waldo, Marion county, Ohio with Typhoid Pneumonia, Feb 1st, 1858, Andrew Stroub, at the advanced age of sixty years.

Feb 18, 1858

☞ Those who are in the habit of "tripping the light fantastic toe" will be pleased to learn that a public Ball comes off at the Davis House, in this place, on the evening of the 24 inst. The best of music has been secured, and those who attend will be sure to find everything just right.

Mar 4, 1858

Marriages.

On the 10th of February, Mr. John Sordon of Montgomery, to Miss Rachel E. Baker of Marion, all of Marion county, Ohio.

On the 14th of January, Mr. Jonas H. Mason to Miss Harriet C. Hatfield, both of Montgomery tp., Marion county, O.

Mar 11, 1858

Marriages,

On the 23rd ult., Wm. Potter of Bedford county, Pa., to Miss Sarah J. Luellen of Marion county, O.

On the 24th ult., Mr. L.P. Lewis to Mrs. Maria S. Bower, both of Marion, Marion county, O.

Mar 18, 1858

Married.

On the 3d day of March, Mr. Benjamin Vannatti of Wyandot county to Miss Patience Winslow of Grand township, Marion county, Ohio.

Died.

On the 13th inst., at her residence in Marion County, Mrs. Asenath Patten, wife of John Patten, aged 49 years, 4 months and 5 days.

Sister Patten was a member of the Methodist Episcopal Church for nearly thirty years, her piety never doubted. She was beloved by all who knew her. She was a good neighbor, kind companion, and an affectionate mother. After a long and protracted illness, she closed the labors and toils of this life and left a husband and three sons to mourn her loss.

Mar 25, 1858

Robbins Convicted.

As we are about going to press we learn that the trial of this man, which commenced on last Thursday morning in our Court of Common Pleas, and has taken up six full days, has terminated in a verdict of Guilty of Murder in the first degree. This case has created much interest and excitement in our community from the beginning, and consequently the trial has been largely attended by citizens of our own and other counties, and the result has been looked to with much anxiety. The case is undoubtedly one of the most curious in the annals of crime.

We shall, in our next issue, give a brief sketch of its most interesting features. The crime of which the accused, Edward Robbins, is found guilty, is, of killing Nancy Holly by poison.

Both parties lived in Shelby county, and the poison, strychnine, was furnished to the victim there, but taken in this county. Judge Lawrence has won increased reputation by the able and fair manner in which he has ruled throughout the trial. The accused has been both ably defended and prosecuted. The arguments, which commenced the first of this week, were made for the State by J.F. Hume, Esq., and Judge O. Bowen, and for the prisoner, by J.S. Conklin, of Sidney, P. Bunker and Jas.. H. Godman.

Married.

On the 14th inst., Eli Wapples to Miss Lovely Ellen Day of Big Island township, Marion county, Ohio.

On the 18th inst., Mr. Wm. M. Henderson to Miss Sarah E. Verden, all of Montgomery township, Marion county, O.

Apr 1, 1858

The State vs. Edward Robbins.

The Defendant was indicted for the murder of Nancy Holly by administering to her strychnine.

The death of Miss Holly took place in this town, on the 29th of July, 1857, at the house of Ferdinand C. Ruehrmund, a little before 11 o'clock in the evening. Her symptoms, while dying, and the subsequent examination of her stomach and its contents, established beyond doubt, that she was poisoned by strychnine.

The deceased was about 20 years of age, and in appearance quite healthy and beautiful. She was a resident of Shelby county, in this state, where her parents also resided. The defendant lived about ¼ of a mile from Miss Holly's residence, and had a wife and one child, and since his imprisonment his wife has borne him a second child.

The deceased had, for some three years been in the employment of the defendant as a servant girl in his house. The proof tended to show that great improprieties had been practiced by the defendant and Nancy, and she had been *enceinte* by him, and by his procurement was to leave home and go to Cleveland—that she left home on the 27th of July, 1857, and after going as far as Galion, her money become exhausted, and she returned to this place and endeavored to obtain employment, and was accepted into the family of Mr. Ruehrmund as a hired maid, on the 28th of July, where she remained until her death. On the afternoon of the 29th of July she disclosed to Mrs. R. that she expected to be confined in about three months.

She retired to bed that evening about 10 o'clock taking with her a tumbler of water and a spoon. Mrs. R., who had also retired, was soon awakened by her screams, and went into her chamber; found her in great agony, engaged in prayer, and saying that she must die. Efforts were made to get a physician to see her, but she expired before any could be obtained. She lived about 45 minutes after taking the poison, as near as could be ascertained. A *post mortem* examination, held by the coroner that night, confirmed what had been stated to Mrs. R. about her condition. A female child of full six months, it was certain, been like its mother, by human agency deprived of life!

Miss Holly, upon her death bed, made disclosures which led to the defendant's arrest. She and her family and the defendant were strangers in this place at the time she came here.

Robbins is a little over 30 years of age, as we infer from his appearance, and is rather short in stature, and of dark complexion. As to his place of nativity, family, or former pursuits, we have no positive information.

The evidence relied upon by the State consisting of the proof of various circumstances relating to the intercourse between the deceased and Robbins, and of statements made by her while dying as to the cause of her death, are at present withheld from publication by request of the court. When all of the questions involved in the issue are finally determined by the court, the whole evidence will be given to the public in pamphlet or newspaper form. Until then it seems proper, in justice to the prisoner, that the press remain silent as to the proof on what the verdict of guilty was found.

The case had gone to the Jury after a hearing occupying the time of the Court for seven days. The proceedings were protracted and thorough. The examination was minute and searching. On the part of the State we believe no effort was made to force a decision not warranted by the facts and attendant circumstances; and the defense was constructed with the greatest ability and zeal. Judge Lawrence's charge to the Jury was a model for clearness, precision, and impartiality.

The case was given to the Jury about 11 o'clock, on Wednesday, March 24th, and about 4 P.M. it was announced that a decision had been made. The Court House was soon filled to overflowing and conspicuous among the mass was the counsel in the case, and—"the observed of all observers"—the prisoner.

The latter to some extent, had, throughout the trial, appeared indifferent; yet a long continued anxiety had left traces upon his countenance that could not be mistaken, and the approach of the announcement of his fate seemed to quicken his feelings, and arouse them to a keener appreciation of his situation.

Upon the entrance of the Jury their decision was known without the utterance of a word. Individually their appearance indicated that they fully appreciated their position—that their lengthy deliberations had been candid—that their decision had been arrived at with a full knowledge of the responsibility that rested upon them, which was to set free, or else consign to an ignominious death a fellow citizen.

It is useless to disguise the fact that the public mind was prepared for the prompt rendition of the verdict given. The evidence in the case had left an impression of the defendant's guilt upon the minds of a large majority of those who heard it; indeed we may say the feeling was general.

The solemnity of the scene, during the polling of the Jury, we have never seen equaled. The breathless and decorous silence of the spectators, and the feeling manifested by the Court and Jury was commendable.

The thanks of the Court were publicly extended to the Jury who were immediately discharged, and the prisoner remanded to jail. We understand the counsel will move for a new trial today.

It having been announced by the Court that sentence would be pronounced at eleven o'clock on Saturday the 27th inst., when that hour arrived the Court House was densely crowded with people. Many ladies were present, and most if not all clergy men of the different religious denominations of our town were in attendance. Intense interest and anxiety seemed to pervade every mind.

Judge Lawrence then proceeded as follows: The defendant, Edward Robbins is now in Court. A motion has been filed by his counsel for a new trial and I understand counsel now submitts without argument.

Counsel—The motion is submitted.

By the Court—I have duly considered the motion for a new trial, and, after most mature consideration of the case in all its aspects, I am constrained to overrule it. The evidence in the case truly justifies the verdict in the jury. The defendant's guilt was proved beyond any reasonable doubt.

I have considered and reconsidered the charge given to the Jury upon the law of the case, and I feel that it was not only correct in every particular, but so written as to secure to the defendant every legal right to the fullest extent and at the same time direct the attention of the Jury to every consideration of both law and facts which could properly be suggested by the Court in his favor. Conscious of no error whatsoever, confident of the majesty of the law has been vindicated in a cause demanding it, the motion for a new trial is overruled.

SENTENCE BY THE COURT.

Edward Robbins, stand up. You have been indicted by the Grand Jury of Marion county for a high crime—the highest known to the laws of Ohio. The indictment charges you with murder in the first degree, by administering poison to Nancy Holly, of which she died on the 29th of July, 1857, in Marion county. Upon that indictment you have been tried by a Jury during the present term of this Court and the Jury have rendered a verdict against you; finding that you are guilty of murder in the first degree in the manner and form as you stand charged in all the counts of the indictment. Your counsel have filed a motion for a new trial, and after the most careful and mature consideration, that motion has been overruled buy the Court.

In the progress of your case which thus far has been fully and carefully considered, that point is now reached where it becomes the duty of the Court to pronounce the sentence of the law—the solemn and painful sentence of death. If you or your counsel now have anything to say why this last duty of the court shall not be performed—anything to say why the sentence should not be pronounced, you are now at liberty to say it. It is your right, and that of your counsel now to be heard. Have you anything to say why the sentence of the law should not be pronounced.

Here the prisoner remarked substantially as follows: All I have to say is that I do not know how the poor woman came by the medicine. The witnesses have not done me justice. There have been matters withheld and matters misrepresented, which would have thrown light on the subject. I admit that I have been faithfully tried and taking the evidence as you have it and as it was given to the jury, I have no reason to complain. If it would do any good I could and would make an explanation that would throw a different light upon it. I am not accustomed to speaking in public. This is the first time I ever spoke to so large an audience. I have nothing more to say.

The Court then proceeded:

The law has wisely provided many safeguards against improper convictions, and you have had the full benefit of them all.

A Grand Jury of 15 men upon their oaths, and upon full and satisfactory evidence presented their indictment against you, upon which you have been tried. Counsel of your choice has been assigned you, a Jury of candid, honest, intelligent, and impartial men, after hearing all the evidence, the arguments of counsel and the charge of court, attentively and patiently and after the most careful and mature consideration have found you guilty of murder in the first degree. With that verdict the court is satisfied. Upon the evidence it could not have been otherwise. You have had a full, fair and impartial trial. Your counsel

have conducted your defense with marked ability and fidelity. No consideration that could operate in your favor has been omitted.

In the performance of this unwelcome duty which I am now called upon to discharge, I have no disposition to add one pang to your already accumulated sorrows; but public justice demands on an occasion like this that I admonish you of the enormity of the points of which you have been found guilty.

You was a husband and a father of children, Nancy Holly was employed to aid in the labors of your household. Though she had been a frail and erring one, it was your duty to protect her and guard her purity. Save the error of her early womanhood, nothing is shown to mar her character, until you became the partner if not the instigator of still worse errors and even crimes, at the house which should have been sacred to your wife.

At last, to conceal the guilt of illicit intercourse you conceived the idea of sending Nancy Holly to Cleveland, deluding her with the belief that you had furnished her with a medicine to destroy an unoffending unborn innocent. With calculating depravity, you had prepared a fatal poison, and in the hope that would conceal your shame and Nancy Holly in one grave, you started her under an assumed name on an errand of crime. For want of money she stopped in Marion, and after a stay of one day, she took the fatal drug, not dreaming that in 45 minutes she would be numbered with the dead. The blood of a double murder cries to heaven for vengeance.

That murder was perpetrated upon a woman whose ruin you had completed, and upon the offspring of

your own illicit passion. It was perpetrated with poison—that most dreaded and horrid of all forms of taking human life. No warning prepared your victim in advance for the fate that awaited her. In fearful haste she was summoned to the bar of God.

But an all wise providence has so ordered it that enormous crimes can not be committed without leaving some evidence. I aver to these things now, not only in the hope that you may be induced to reflect on the errors of your past life, but still more to impress on the public mind the great truth that crime can not be concealed, for it is written that "the wages of sin is death." Let others, then, be warned by your example, and shun all evil for "the way of the transgressor is hard," and though guilt be concealed for a season, its ultimate detection is inevitable.

The object of punishment is not to avenge the crime committed, but to protect society from future crime, by depriving the offender of the means and power of doing wrong. The penalty of death, which you must soon suffer, is that provided by law to protect society from one whom, by crime, has forfeited his life.

While this is done in the forms prescribed by law it is proper that others should be warned by your example—should remember your fate, reflect on its consequences and shun the causes which have led to it. The evidence shows that your career of crime was not the result of the native prompting of a corrupt heart. Your evil passions were developed by intoxicating drinks, a course of intemperance had destroyed your better nature, and not until the image of God had thus been destroyed in your soul, did

But with all this there is yet hope. Death is but the separation of the mortal body from the immortal soul—it marks the era when "the dust shall return to dust, and the spirit to God who gave it." Your days on the earth are already numbered, and I entreat you to devote the remnant of your life to a preparation for the great future which you are soon to enter. Pray to our common Father in heaven, to watch over and protect your widowed wife. Implore that God who tempers the wind to the shorn lamb, to be a father to your fatherless children.

You will be allowed the visits of your friends, your counsel, and such of the clergy as you may desire, for your spiritual guidance and instruction.

It now only remains for me to pronounce the judgement for which the law has provided for your crime.

The sentence of the court is that you be removed hence to the jail of this county and there be safely kept until the 19th day of June A.D. 1858 and that on that day you be taken from said jail to the place of execution, where between the hours of 9 o'clock in the forenoon and 2 o'clock in the afternoon of that day, you be hanged by the neck until you are dead.

And may the Lord have mercy on your soul!

During the delivery of the sentence, there were many tearful eyes in the assemblage. The voice of the condemned when he spoke was tremulous, yet his utterance was distinct. He appeared to have nerved himself for the occasion—to have studied his part in the solemn role, and he enacted it with the utmost precision.

you reach the fatal point in human error where you conceived and executed the cruel act which makes you now the unhappy subject of these remarks.

In your wrongs you are not alone, for others have been contributed to the fruitful source of your guilt. But at last the day of retribution is at hand. An ignominious death on the scaffold awaits. That wife whose devotion was consecrated on the marriage altar, and who, in this trying hour, does not desert or forget you is to become an unprotected widow. Those children, who had a right to look to you for admonition, protection and support, are to become fatherless, but I hope not friendless.

The pangs of sorrow and shame will strike deep in the hearts of wife, children and friends. The contemplation of all this is painful, but it is true.

We watched his appearance closely during the recital of the wrongs he had committed, and the impressions made upon him, taking his countenance as an index, appeared to be but slight. At the close, the court, sheriff, many of the attorneys, and many of the spectators, were in tears. He seemed to have passed the agonizing point during the interval between the rendition of the verdict and his sentence, on which his thoughts have become familiarized. He left the court room with a firm step accompanied by the sheriff and his deputy only.

After the condemned had retired and the feeling had subsided, Judge remarked that he had been requested by the editors of Marion to permit the sentence to be published. This he said he should not do, if by any possibility it could prejudice a new trial in case the Supreme Court granted one.

Mr. Godman of prisoner's counsel, said that it would be better to publish it accurately than otherwise. The substance of it would be published by the editors, at all events. It did not state the evidence, and there can be no objection. All the counsel concurred.

The counsel for the prisoner presented a bill of exceptions, which was allowed by Judge Lawrence. An application will, we learn, be made to the Supreme Court, now in session, for a writ of error to reverse the sentence and judgement of the Common Pleas Court.

The grounds relied on, by the prisoner's counsel, in their motion for the writ of error, are, we understand, the following:

First—That the Court erred in admitting in evidence, to the Jury, the dying declarations of Nancy Holly.

Second—That the Court erroneously ruled that in an indictment for homicide, produced by poison, it is unnecessary to aver, or in the trial to prove, that the poison was given with the intent to kill, provided it be shown that the administration of it by the accused, was an intentional and premeditated act.

Third—Because the Court charged the Jury that if they found that the prisoner administered the poison, of which Nancy Holly died, that he so administered it unlawfully, purposely, and of deliberated and premeditated malice, knowing it to be a deadly poison, that he was guilty of murder in the first degree, and the jury could not find him guilty of any less crime.

Fourth—Because the Court instructed the Jury that it was the exclusive province of the Court to determine what the law is, and the Jury have no right to hold the law to be otherwise, in any particular, than as given to them by the court.

If in any of these particulars the Supreme Court shall be opinioned that manifest and substantial error was committed, the proceedings will be set aside, and a new trial granted. But, should that court approve and sustain the rulings of the Common Pleas Court, the prisoner will be executed to his sentence, on the 18th day of June next.

Married.

On the 25th inst., Mr. Elijah Rush of Claridon and Miss Sarah C. Arnold of Marion.

Court Doings.

The March term closed last Saturday; Judge Lawrence presiding. The term, owing to the Robbins murder case, mainly was taken up in criminal business. The following jury trials, we learned, have been had:

The State of Ohio *vs*. Martin Miller, Jr. Indictment for assault and battery on the person of James Linton, by testing the strength of his skull with a stone—verdict of guilty, and sentence of fine of $25.00 and costs.

State of Ohio *vs*. Edward Robbins, Indictment for murder in the first degree, by poisoning Nancy Holly—the particulars of this case are sufficiently given elsewhere—verdict of guilty, and sentence to be hung on 18th day of June next.

Thomas C. Dye *vs*. Joseph Linn and others. This was a civil action to recover damages for the breach of a contract, for the sale of 150 head of fat cattle, by the defendants refusing to take and pay for the cattle. The defense was that the cattle were not "fat." Much conflicting professional opinion of cattlemen was given, but the plaintiff seemed to have the weight of testimony in favor of the weight of his bullocks, as the Jury found that he was entitled to a verdict of $750.00 as damages; but as he already received $500.00 on his contract he got a judgement for $250.00.

Isaiah Lowe *vs*. William Delfart and Erie Wheeler. The plaintiff charged the defendants entering into a conspiracy to tramp up a charge against him, to induce him to leave the county, and to get his property into their possession under the form of a sale without consideration, in which he claimed they had, through certain not very proper contrivances, succeeded, and had proceeded to appropriate his property to their own use and concluded not to give it back; all of which rascally the defendants denied, but the Jury proved to be on the side of Lowe, as they gave him a verdict of $606.50.

Besides these, the ordinary number of divorce cases were disposed of, and other business by the court, including sundry actions to injoin the collection of School House taxes,.

Apr 15, 1858

Business Matters.

Last Saturday was a busy day with our mercantile friends. Our streets were crowded full of the teams and wagons of our agricultural friends, who, with their wives and daughters, had come to town to select from the well-filled shelves of our merchants, such goods as they were in want of. Proprietors and clerks were kept busy all day in supplying their various wants, and when night came there were about as tired a set of merchants and clerks in Marion as could be found in the State.

The fact is undeniable that there are more goods sold in Marion than in any of the surrounding county towns, and her trade is rapidly increasing as time rolls on. When our county becomes as thickly settles as most of those surrounding it, she will far outstrip all her rivals.

Married.

On the 11th inst., Perry Mouser to Miss Elizabeth J. Coonrad, both of Grand Prairie, Marion county, Ohio.

Heavy Rains.

This section of country has been favored with an overwhelming supply of rain since our last issue. It commenced raining on Saturday evening last, and up to the time of writing this, (Monday P.M.) there has been a constant succession of extremely heavy showers, deluging hill and plain. and swelling the streams into irresistible torrents. The effect will be to retard the spring work of the farmers and render the roads, which later were fast becoming settled, almost as bad as when winter broke up.

To Our Readers.

We feel that we owe an apology to the readers of the *Republican*, in consequence of the negligent manner in which the paper has been conducted during the past five or six weeks, having sold the paper with which we were formerly connected, and having had a business of seven or eight years to close up, we found it impossible to pay that attention to our duties here that we should have done. Having taken up our residence here, however, we shall in the future endeavor to make amends for the delinquencies of the past, by devoting our entire time and attention to the interests of the paper and its patrons. We shall, in particular, endeavor to render the *Republican* a faithful chronicler of the local news of the town and county, and to this end we would respectfully solicit the co-operation of our friends in all parts of the county.

Apr 22, 1858

Deaths.

On the 20th inst., in this place, Mrs. Jane Lindsay, aged 68 years.

Marriages.

On the 8th inst., at the residence of the bride, in Marion, Mr. John Bowen and Miss Priscilla A. Zuck.

On the 18th, Mr. C.A. Butler of St. Charles county, Wisconsin, to Mrs. Sarah E. Owen, of Claridon Tp., Marion county, O.

The Egg Trade in Marion

It is not many years since, that a merchant in Marion, almost hated the sight of a farmer wending his way to his store with a basket of eggs on his arm, because they were then a perfect drug here, and he knew that if he purchased them he was sure to loose on them no matter what the price, for the chances were as ten to one that he would have to throw away a portion of not all of them. But of late years, since the Railroads have made it profitable to ship them to the seaboard cities, the egg trade has loomed up in importance, until eggs have come to be regarded as the most marketable product of the country after butter and wheat.

Our thriving village annually sends to market an enormous quantity of these "vegetables," and yet but few of our citizens are aware of the magnitude of the trade. A single fact will enlighten them. In one month Messrs. Fight & Son shipped from this point, 560 barrels averaging eighty dozen per bbl! Cock-a-doodle-doo!

☞ And still it rains, rains, rains. There was a prospect that our agricultural friends would get their spring crops into the ground quite early, but owing to the immense quantity of rain that has fallen within the past fortnight, spring planting will be as late as usual. But there is no use of grumbling. It will all turn out for the best in the end.

Apr 29, 1858

To the *Republican.*

How much better it wold be if one denomination had charge of the Marion Union School. Then erroneous views of science, and morals, and politics, could, by comparison with discipline, be corrected and punished. Citizens of Marion, who are opposed to the old Board, which is badly mixed, and who would like to reform it by introducing uniformity, are requested to be at the Court House on Saturday evening.

Come out bigots and hot heads! Let us have a full meeting and run the old Board out.

Run Off! A Wheelbarrow, belonging to the United States House. The gentleman with whom it ran off will much oblige the landlord by letting it run back or he may "come to grief."

The Weather and Fruit.

Monday night was very cold, forming ice of a very considerable thickness and, we fear, destroying all prospect of a fruit crop this year. At least, it will not take many such to thoroughly cook our apples, pears, &c.

Honor the Dead.— Regard the Living!

We love to re-visit old haunts, to listen to old tales, to study the peculiarities of old times, and to shake again the warm hand of an old friend; and nothing more awakens in us emotions of subdued and melancholy pleasures than an hour of meditation in the "Old Grave Yard," where repose the ashes of the humble and the great, the timid and the brave, strangers and friends, beneath the bending willows, whose leaves drop tears over every grave alike, as the morning beam falls upon the "dew fresh earth."

In these days of improvements, the "Ornamental Cemetery" is taking the place of the too often neglected burying ground, and it is universally acknowledged that the home of the departed should be a cheerful and attractive spot.

But while we emulate the spirit that prompts to improvement in this regard we cannot look with any degree of allowance on the RUDE and CARELESS removal of bodies from their resting place in the old Grave Yard.

Only a day or two since, visitors to our village burying ground were shocked to see a grave from which a body had been removed, left unfilled and strewn around with fragments of the half-decayed box that contained the coffin. We think that removals at this season of the year, ought not to be allowed, but if they must be made, the greatest care should be taken to close the grave and to BURY EVERY THING that was in contact with the coffin or box. Those who reside in the immediate vicinity of the old burying ground are particularly anxious that proper care should be used to preserve the health of themselves and families.

Marion County 33 Years Ago.

We have before us a copy of the Duplicate of Marion county for the year 1824, being over a third of a century ago. It covers nine whole pages and three fractions of pages, of a book about the size of a small day-book. The land in the county was not duplicated in townships, but was all put together, the only distinction being "Virginia Military" and "Congress Lands." The Auditor at that time was our esteemed citizen Col. H. Gorton, who still lives in our midst a witness of the vast change that has been wrought in our county since he made up the first Duplicate. The whole number of acres returned for taxation that year was 24,000. The number of tax payers was 172. There appears to have been no personal property returned for taxation that year. Among the names of the tax payers, we recognize one who figured conspicuously in the early history of the State, and who filled many important stations under her community, and finally becoming her Governor. We mean Governor Duncan M. Arthur, formerly of Chilocothe. In looking over the list we do not find the name of any person who is now a resident of our town. There are doubtless the names of persons in it who then resided here, but have either died or removed to other parts of the Union.

The Duplicate of 1825 covers eight whole pages and four fractions. The whole number of tax payers this year was 155. Isaac DeWitt is put down as owning 161 acres which lies adjoining the present town of Melthina in Morrow county. He was killed several years ago by lightning. James Taylor of Newport, Ky. is put down for over four thousand acre at about one dollar per acre.

Costs and Expenses Connected with Case of the State vs. Robbins, (Charge of Murder) to-wit:

For Inquest and funeral expenses of Nancy Holly,	54.37
For Postmortum examination in Marion,	30.00
For Expenses of physician to Cleveland and analysation of stomach of deceased,	51.00
For Expenses of Prosecuting Attorney in search of testimony for State,	22.40
For fees and allowance of officers and witnesses,	295.65
For fees of Jurors challenged and excused,	75.35
For fees and board of Jurors on trial,	207.35
For Clothing and Bible for prisioner,	8.85
For Allowance to J.F. Hume assisting Prosecuting Attorney,	125.00
For Allowance to P. Bunker for defending prisioner,	125.00
Fow Allowance to J. S. Conklin for defending prisioner,	125.00
	1119.97

In 1826 the Duplicate for the first time was made up by townships. Township No. 1 was called Washington, since cut off and formed a township in Morrow county. Among the tax payers in the township of that time were Benjamin Sharrock and Nehemiah Story, both of whom are still living there. For the first time, also, personal property appeared in the Duplicate this year, but the term as then used, only applied to horses and cattle.

No. 2 was called Scott township, and remains that name yet, although it does not now embrace the same boundaries as it did then. From the remarks of the Auditor, we learn that in 1826 there were no taxable lands in Scott. Nineteen persons paid tax on personal property, among them were John Beckley, Adam Hipsher, James H. Larabee and Henry Parcel, some of whose descendants still reside there.

No. 3 was Grand Prairie in which there were 22 land holders and 24 who owned taxable personal property. Among the land holders we notice the name of Geo. H. Bussy,

of this place, who was taxed on 154 acres of land valued at $132 on which there was levied $2.44. The said land is now probably worth $5000. We also noticed the name of Moses Kirby, John Kirby and Wm. B. Swinerton.

No. 4 was called Salt Rock and still bears that name, although the boundaries have been changed. In 1826 there were only 8 persons in the township who paid taxes on land, and 43 who paid taxes on personal property. Amongst those paying taxes on personal property was W.W. Concklin of this place who was taxed on 2 horses and 18 head of cattle. The largest landholder in the township then, was George Kimmell, who owned 1930 acres valued at $1294. The same land is now worth probably $30,000.

No. 5 was Grand township, the borders of which have been changed since its formation. In 1826 it embraced original townships 4 and 5, and the Virginia Military Land lying due south of it in Marion county as we learn from the Auditor's heading of the Duplicate. There

were forty-three land holders in the township who owned 21,261 acres valued $2508, 5 among whom were William Brownlee, Walter Dan, Charles Lewis, Thomas Miller, and James Taylor.

No. 6 was Big Island township, being original township 5 in range 4. In this township in 1826 there were 15 land owners holding 2449 acres valued at 2644 dollars on which there was levied $38.95. Among the names owning land there were C. Brady, at present a resident of this place, David Brady, William Brady, Riverius Messenger and Alson Norton.

No 7 was Centre township being original township 5 in range 15. Since then its name has been changed to Marion. In 1826 there were 25 persons owning land outside the town, in the township amounting to 2657 ¼ acres valued at $3459. In the original town of Marion as laid out by Eber Baker, Esq. there were 38 persons holding lots, the balance being by the proprietor. Among those holding lots who are still living here we notice the names of T.J. Anderson, G.H. Busby, H. Gorton, Dr. G. Holloway and N. Peters.

No. 8 was Claridon. In it there were then 23 land holders holding 1314 acres. Col. Kilbourne appears to be the largest lot owner in the town.

No. 9 was Canaan township, since set off to Morrow county.

No. 10 was Morwin township since included in Morrow county and called Cardington.

No. 11 was Richland township. In 1826 there was 23 persons in the township who were owners of real estate.

No. 12 was Pleasant township. We notice F. Biggerstaff, F. Farnam, E. Farnus, S. Gooding, J. Gooding, C. Gooding and J. Ideman.

No. 13 was called Grand Camp. There were 26 land holders, including James Taylor, with 1860 acres.

These facts are interesting as showing the progress that has been made in the last third of a century.

May 6, 1858

The New Cemetery.

Quite a large number of lots have been taken in the new Cemetery, and the Association are energetically, at work laying out walks and carriage roads, and planting trees and shrubbery, and the lot holders are sparing neither pains or expense in beautifying their lots, and ere long we will have a cemetery that will compare favorably in point of beauty and adornment with that of any town or village in Ohio.

School Election.

The election for Directors of our Union School, which came off on Tuesday last resulted in the choice of the following gentlemen, viz: For three years; B.H. Williams and E. Peters, Esqs. For one year; O. Patten and T.B. Fisher, Esqs. The opposition vote was very slight, and the result shows that our citizens generally are well satisfied with the School as at present constituted, and are determined not to make any change, in which, we think they are wise.

Desperate Rencontre.

We learn that on Saturday evening last a difficulty between two Irishmen in this place, which ended in a fight, during which one of the combatants named Dewey, had his leg broken and his ancle dislocated. From the information we have received, Dewey was entirely blameless, having only interfered to prevent one Irishman from striking another when the fellow turned upon him, knocked him down and inflicted upon him the injuries detailed above. The sufferer was carried home, and is now as comfortable as the painful nature of his wounds will admit.

It is time that these disgraceful and murderous Irish rows were put down by the strong arm of the law. They are a disgrace to the town, and every good citizen should render his assistance in doing away with the evil. If they can not be put down in one way, try another. If peaceable measures will not accomplish the object, USE MEASURES THAT WILL do it. Better, far better, that a few of these ruffians should be stretched out than the good name of our town should be sacrificed and peaceable, unoffending citizens murdered whilst striving to vindicate the majesty of the law.

Fatal Accident.

We learn from the *Marshall county* (Iowa) *Express* that Mr. Hiram C. Kennedy, who, it states formerly resided in Caledonia, in this county, was killed by the accidental discharge of his rifle, within six miles of Marietta, Iowa, on the 16th ult. The circumstances attending his death, as detailed by the *Express* were as follows:

On the afternoon of the 16th, seventeen young men, from Waterloo, Iowa, passed through this place, on their way to Kansas. When they arrived on the banks of the Minerva they halted to camp for the night, when one of the party Hiram C. Kennedy, seeing a flock of ducks in the creek, went to a wagon to get his gun. The gun was partly covered up with goods, and while Mr. K. was in the act of pulling it out, muzzle foremost, the piece was accidentally discharged and he received the contents in his breast, the ball passing through the lower portion of the left lobe of the lungs, near the heart. He lived about six hours after the accident, and was rational and able to talk up to the last moment of life.

Explanatory

As there has been some feeling created in certain quarters by the publication of a communication in our last issue relative to the Election for Directors that has just passed, we wish to state that in giving publicity to that article, we pursued the course that we have always observed since our connection with the press, that is, to permit the free discussion through our columns of all public questions, without reference to our own opinion in regard to those questions. This course, we conceive the only proper one, and we shall adhere to it in all cases. The gentlemen who feel aggrieved by the publication of the article referred to, would have been very indignant had we refused to publish an article advocating THEIR side of the question at issue, and yet we had just as much right to reject one as the other.

Free discussion never hurt a good cause yet, and we think when the gentlemen referred to, come to reflect, they will see that we have pursued the only proper course, and exonerate us from all blame in the matter.

Wrong.

Since the process of vacating the old grave yard commenced, many horrible stories have been set afloat in community in regard to persons being buried alive, as indicated by the positions in which corpses have been found. Every one of those stories, so far as we could ascertain, were without foundation, and whether they were set afloat from malicious motives, or for the purpose of hoaxing others, they have no doubt shocked the feelings of those having friends buried there.

Let the motives be what it may, it is wrong to put such stories in circulation, unless they are absolutely true, for even to raise a SUSPICION in a sensitive mind that a friend had been buried alive, is to drive it to distraction. Let us have no more of them.

Marriages.

Married on the 21 inst., Mr. Amaziah Wortman to Miss Mary A. Zeller, all of Claridon Tp., Marion county, O.

May 20, 1858

A Hurricane.

On Monday last a terrific hurricane swept over the southern portion of Crawford and northern portion of Marion counties, sweeping away fences and buildings in its destructive course. At Galion it is reported a church and tower were blown down, and several other buildings injured, and a train of cars standing on the side-track, set in motion which ran over a german; crushing his arm. A portion of the storm swept over our town, doing no damage so far as we can learn, save blowing some boards off the spire of the Episcopal Church, one of which penetrated the house of Mr. S.A. Griswold, but done no further damage.

☞ The Mayor held a public levee in Tuesday evening, and was visited by a couple of gentlemen, father and son, who were arrested, the first for being intoxicated and the latter for resisting the officers when taking his sire. The old man was lodged in the calaboase until the "sober second thought" had assumed full sway, when he was brought out and fined $5 and costs. The young man was fined $10 and costs.

After the young man was arrested some person struck him a severe blow on the head with a club, causing it to bleed profusely. This was entirely wrong, for officers have no right to use any more force than is necessary to a faithful discharge of their duty. Any thing beyond this is needless cruelty, and should be severely reprehended by every lover of justice.

To Be Repaired.

Our Town Council have contracted with two gentlemen of Galion, practical and experienced machinists, to repair our Fire Engine, the air chest of which bursted at a trial of the "machine" a few months ago. In this they are right, for, as at present situated, we are without any means whatever, wherewith to stay the ravages of a fire, should one break out.

The Robbins Case.

This (Thursday,) is the day set for hearing the Robbins case in the Supreme Court, on error. Mr. Bunker, one of his counsel, left for Columbus on yesterday morning to attend to the case upon the part of the prisoner. We have not heard what points the prisoner's counsel intend to rely upon in the effort to reverse the proceedings in the Court of Common Pleas. We shall, probably, hear in a few days what the result is.

May 27, 1858

Rain, Rain, Rain!

We do not recollect a spring for years, during which so much rain fell, as there has during the present one up to this time. For the past forty days, shower has succeeded shower, until the earth, has become thoroughly saturated, and the husbandman begins to despair of the promised seed-time. The first of June is almost here, and as yet scarcely any corn at all has been planted. Indeed, a great many farmers have all their plowing to do, and spring work will have to be done up in a bunch. We hope a change for the better will take place soon.

Police Court.

The Mayor had two cases before him on Thursday last, both being on the charge of "Drunk." They were sent to the calaboose to cool off awhile, when they were brought out and fined $5 and cost each.

The Circus.

Last Thursday was a terribly stormy day, and the roads being almost impassable, Dan Rice's Circus failed to reach here in time to fulfill their afternoon's engagement. Several of his wagons were badly "used up" in the contest with the mud and water, and he was compelled to ask aid of the people in the line of his route. In the evening however, he was greeted with a full house, and everything passed off pleasantly. Dan's institution is a great one, and should be patronized by all lovers of the "ring."

Jun 3, 1858

Marion Atheneum,

Is the name of an association formed in our town during the past winter. Judging from the manner and spirit in which their exercises, debating especially, were conducted at their last meeting, we have no hesitancy in saying it is worthy of commendation, and is calculated to do much good. It is just the thing our young men have needed for some time past. The Society have expended considerable money in fitting their room in Bennett's Block, and yet they lack a book case and other conveniences. They are collecting a good library, and if any one of our citizens have any books which they may choose to give or lend them, they will be well cared for, and returned when called for.

Sudden Death.

Yesterday morning Mrs. Butler, relict of the late Joel D. Butler, who has been slightly ill for the past two weeks, was found dead in her bed. When first discovered, the body was still warm, but all efforts to resuscitate her proved unavailing. Mrs. B. was one of our oldest citizens, and was much respected in the circle of her acquaintance. She leaves several children, to battle alone with the sorrows and trials of their life, unaided by the counsels and encouragement of a mother.

Died.

In this place, at the Freese House, on 1st inst., of Congestion of the Brain, B.V. Meeks aged 28 years, 9 months and 1 day.

Mr. M. was a resident of Miami county, Ohio, where his parents reside. Business having called him hither, he made his home with friend Freese, and by his urbanity and social qualities won many friends, who join with his relatives in mingling their tears over his untimely death. His remains were taken to Miami county for burial.

Storm.

Quite a heavy wind-storm passed over the northern portion of this township on Monday last, leveling fences, orchards, and forests in its track. The storm was about half a mile in width, and ran from south west to north-east. We heard of no buildings being damaged, save the cider-press of Mr. E. Bowdish, the roof of which was torn off and carried some fifteen or twenty rods. This is certainly one of the most remarkable years for hurricanes we have had recently.

The Robbins Case- New Trial

We learn from a gentleman of our town, who returned from Columbus on Friday last, that the Supreme Court have, after two weeks deliberation, set aside the verdict rendered in the Robbins case in the Court of Common Pleas. It will be recollected that Robbins was convicted at the March term of murder in the first degree, by administering strychnine to one Nancy Holly, in July last. The poison, the deceased stated in her death-bed, was given to her by Robbins, (with whom she had previously had sexual intercourse) for the purpose of procuring an abortion.

On the trial, Judge Lawrence charged the Jury that if they found that the prisoner gave the deceased the poison for the purpose of producing an abortion, and death resulted therefrom, they should find him guilty of murder in the first degree. This the Supreme Court decided to be erroneous—that the Jury should have had the power to return a verdict, upon such a showing, of murder in the first or second degree, or of manslaughter, just as they saw proper. They, therefore, set aside the verdict rendered in the Court below, and remanded the case for another trial. This will come off, it is supposed, at the next term of the Court of Common Pleas.

New Bakery.

Our friend, Wilson, who as Marshal of our town, has proven himself a terror to evil doers, has just opened a new bakery on the east side of Main street.

Supreme Court of Ohio.

Decision in the Robbins Case.

L.J. Critchfield, Reporter.

Edward Robbins vs. The State of Ohio.

Writ of error to reverse the judgement of the Court of Common Pleas of Marion county.

Thomas W. Bartley, Chief Justice, held:

1. That a party indicted for murder in the first degree, had no right, under the present state of the law, to elect to be tried in the district court, as he had, under the former constitution of the State.

2. The rule, that a judgement on a general verdict of guilty on an indictment containing several counts, some of which are good and some bad, will be sustained, it not appearing from the record, that the defendant was prejudiced by the introduction of evidence under the bad counts.

3. Evidence of dying declarations are not excluded by the constitutional provision, that the accused shall be allowed to meet the witnesses face to face—the objection to such evidence going to the competency of the evidence, and not to the competency of the witness.

4. It is essential to the admissibility of dying declarations as evidence, that it should be made to appear to the court by preliminary evidence, not only that they were made in *articula morta*, but also made under a sense of impending death, which excludes from the mind of the dying person all hope or expectation of recovery.

5. In all jury trials, it is the peculiar providence of the jury to determine the questions of fact and that of the court to determine the questions of law presented, and in the trial of a criminal cause, it is the duty of the jury to receive the law as determined by the court, and no juror can rightfully disregard the law as declared in the instructions of the court to the jury.

6. The overt act of homicide by administering poison, within the meaning of the law, consists not simply in prescribing or furnishing the poison, but also in directing and

causing it to be taken, so that, if the poison be prescribed and furnished in one county to a person, who carried it into another county, and there, under the directions given, takes it and becomes poisoned and dies of the poison, the administering is consummated, and the crime committed, if committed at all, in the county where the person is poisoned.

7. Where a drug is administered to a woman pregnant with a quick child, with intent, not to kill the woman, but to produce abortion, and the woman dies from the effects of the drug, the offense cannot constitute murder in the first degree under the criminal statute of this State.

8. In case of homicide by administering poison, or causing the same to be done, the accused cannot be convicted of murder in the first degree, where there was no purpose or intent to kill the person poisoned, inasmuch as the statute of this State has had purpose of intent to kill an essential element of that degree of homicide for which the punishment of death is inflicted.

9. Murder at common law has been superseded by our statutory provisions in relation to homicide. Inasmuch as the language of the law has undeniably made malicious purpose to kill essential in all murder in the second degree, it could not have been the reasonable intent of the law to punish any kind of unintentional killing, or killing by misadventure, with death.

Judgement of the common pleas of Marion county reversed, and case remanded.

Justices Joseph R. Swan and Jacob Brinkerhoff dissented from the eighth and ninth propositions, holding that killing another in the perpetration of rape, arson, robbery, or burglary, is murder in the first degree; and every evil intent necessary to constitute murder in the first degree in such cases is, in law, incontrovertibly implied.

Court of Common Pleas- State Cases Disposed of

The State cases on the Docket of the late term of the Court of Common Pleas of this county were disposed of as follows:

The State of Ohio vs. Jno. A. Gustin alias Jno. Chew. Assault and Battery with intent to kill. Continued.

The State of Ohio vs. The same Defendant. Indictment for Bigamy—Same disposition.

The State of Ohio vs. John Cardiff. Indictment for Grand Larceny. Same disposition.

The State of Ohio vs. Thomas Horrgan. Indictment for Murder in the Second Degree. Same disposition.

The State of Ohio vs. M. Miller, Jr., Edward Barr and Jacob Coffee. For playing the game of Poker, with cards, for money. Defendants recognized in $100 each and case continued.

The State of Ohio vs. Fred Freese. For keeping a room in which Intoxicating Liquors were sold. Defendant recognized in $200 and case continued.

The State of Ohio vs. Joseph Anderson. For keeping a room in which Intoxicating Liquors were sold. Settled by Prosecuting Attorney; defendant paying $20 into county treasury and costs of prosecution.

The State of Ohio vs. B. Hussey and J. Martin. For selling intoxicating Liquors. Settled; defendant to pay $20 and costs of prosecution.

The State of Ohio vs. Jno. Gantzhom and Samuel Wickizer. For keeping Grocery where Intoxicating Liquors were sold. Settled; defendants paying $75 and costs of suit.

The State of Ohio vs. Timothy Fahey. Same offense. Defendant recognized in $200 and case continued.

The State of Ohio vs. Fred Freese. For permitting rooms to be used for Gambling. Continued.

The State of Ohio vs. the same. For permitting games other than athletic to be played in his tavern. Continued.

The State of Ohio vs. Patrick Kelly. For keeping Grocery for the sale of Intoxicating Liquors. Defendant recognized in $200 and case continued.

The State of Ohio vs. Andrew Friesinger. For keeping Grocery to sell Intoxicating Liquors. Settled; defendant paying costs.

Jun 10, 1858

Special Term of the Court.

A special term of the Court of Common Pleas of this county will commence on the 25th inst. This Special Term is to be held, chiefly, for the purpose of arranging some preliminaries in regard to the Robbins case, so that he can be tried at the next regular term thereafter.

Marriages.

On the 27th ult., Mr. Oliver R. Austin to Miss Amillia Reeding, both of Big Island Tp., Marion county, Ohio.

In Marion, on the 1st inst., Mr. J. W. Gorton and Miss Annette C. McWherter, both of Marion, Ohio.

Jun 17, 1858

Poor Tray.

On Sunday night last, some fiend in human shape, instigated by the Father of all Evil, doubtless, prepared a quantity of strychnined meat, and scattered it all over town.

The consequence was, that before the sun had gone down on that eventful (dog) day, some score or more of the canine inhabitants of our beautiful town had fallen "wictims" to the fiendish malice of the midnight assassin. The wail of sorrow "was heard in the land," and the younger portions of the masculine and feminine persuasions mourned heavily and "would not be comforted," for Towser and Tray and Carlo, and numerous other household deities "were not," for they had gone "where the good dogs go." Many were the conjectures as to who were the authors of this dark tragedy, but, we fear, the mystery which now envelopes it will not be cleared up until the dark secrets for the Town Council chamber are dragged to the light!

P.S.—Skeezicks predicts that dog chains will immediately advance in price, whilst bologna and other sausages will become dog cheap.

Narrow Escape.

On Monday morning last, as a little child of Dr. Fischer's, in company with his grandmother, was passing along the sidewalk near the Dr.'s residence, it picked up a piece of half-dried meat and was just in the act of putting it in its mouth, when it was taken from it, and, upon examination, was found to be entirely covered with strychnine.

One moment more, and its doom would have been sealed irrevocably. The fiend or fiends who throw such things in the way of children, if discovered, should be severely punished.

Wild Pidgeons.

Just at this time, the "Pidgeon Fever" is raging severely in this section, and every man who can furnish himself with anything in the "shooting" line, is taking a "shoot" for the woods for the purpose of shooting pidgeons if he don't shoot himself in the neck. The birds are said to be in first-rate order, being fat, young and tender. They most generally resort to places where stock has been fed, and are very easily approached. Those who are fond of them, should pitch in at once.

Died.

Entered into rest, on Friday, the 20th inst., after a long and painful illness, George F. Cooper, in the 20th year of his age.

Death from Sun Stroke

We learn that an Irish laborer on the B. & I. R. R. was killed by sun stroke at Larue on Saturday last. Persons laboring in the sun during this extreme hot weather, should be careful not to overheat themselves, as a fatal result is almost sure to follow.

 On Monday night last, just as we were "passing away" into the "land of dreams," we were brought back to this "mundane sphere" by the sweet strains of the "Marion Orchestra." To the gentlemen who thus favored us we return our sincere thanks, and hope that "oft in the stilly night" their Æolian strains may wake us from our slumbers.

The Baptist Church.

On Monday last we visited the Baptist Church, and were surprised to find it completely transformed into one of the handsomest churches in the place. The building has been raised eighteen inches—a new foundation put under it—a platform built in front, two new doors made, and newly seated. A very handsome pulpit has been erected and an orchestra for the choir. The walls have been papered, carpets laid on the floor, and, in short, every effort has been made to render the church pleasant, and inviting. In this the congregation, seconded by the zealous efforts of their Pastor, Rev. S.D. Bates, have been entirely successful. The amount expended in making these improvements was about $500, contributed by our citizens generally.

Marriages.

On the 26th inst., Mr. Henry L. Rudolph Hulster and Miss Caroline Emmons, both of Big Island Township, Marion county, O.

❖

On the 24th ult., Mr. Gebhard Brorkin to Miss Sophia Gracely, all of Richland Township.

Be Careful of your Horses.

Persons engaged in working horses cannot be too careful of them during this extreme hot weather. Within the past week, we have heard of four or five that dropped dead in the harness. The difficulty is, that their danger is not apt to be seen until they drop dead with scarcely a struggle. Drive moderately, water often, and "blow" them every fifteen or twenty minutes.

Crops.

There is no longer any doubt but that the wheat crop in this county will be a heavy one. It stands thick on the ground, the heads well filled and the berry plump. Oats also look first-rate, and the yield will be up to, if not ahead, of that of other years. Corn is just making its appearance above ground, but if we have a late fall the yield, per acre, will be a good one. The next two months will tell the story. Potatoes look about as well as usual, thank St. Patrick.

Sad Accident.

On Friday afternoon last, David Harriman, aged about 18, son of Charles Harriman, of Green Camp township, in this county, was drowned whilst bathing in the Scioto. It appears that the deceased, in company with some younger boys, went into the river, and being unable to swim, was floating about on a rail, when it either slipped from under him or was pulled away by some one of his comrades in sport, and the water being deep, he instantly sank to rise no more.

Pidgeons and the Corn.

We learn that the pidgeons in many localities in this county are literally sweeping the late planted corn fields clean, pulling up the stalks and devouring every grain. One man lost sixteen acres, another eighteen, another ten, and so on. They cannot be driven away, for when fired at, they only rise to light again within a few rods. Hundreds and thousands of them have been slaughtered within a few days, by our citizens, but the numbers do not seem to diminish in the least.

Marriages in Marion County.

Since the 1st day of July, A.D. 1857, the probate Judge of this county has issued 177 marriage licenses. Consequently, since that time 354 people have passed form "single misery" to that of "double-blessedness" within our borders. This, considering our population, is doing right well and indicates a heavy increase in the way of population in old Marion.

Jul 8, 1858

High School Exhibition.

The pupils of the High School Department of our Union School acquitted themselves handsomely at their exhibition on Friday last. The audience was large and attentive and the receipts must have been considerable. Some of the pupils display a very considerable share of talent as stage performers, and show that they have been thoroughly drilled by their tutors.

Another Death from Coup de Soliel.

We learn that a German resident of Pleasant township was killed by Coup de Soliel or sun stroke, one day last week. Persons laboring in this hot sun should be very careful not to overdo or overheat themselves.

The weather and Crops.

Since our last issue we have had several glorious showers of rain, and they have put an entire new face upon vegetation. Oats are filling finely, and stand thick on the ground. Wheat is made, and the crop will be a very heavy one—the heaviest one that has been cut in this county for many years. Grass is heavy, and the supply will be abundant. Corn that is up at all, looks first-rate—is growing finely, and we venture the prediction that there will be more good sound Corn raised in this county this year than there was last.

The farmers are now busily engaged in cutting their wheat, and, as we stated before, the crop is a glorious one. Taking every thing together, the prospect for the farmer is good—first-rate, and any one who grumbles at it, don't deserve to have any crops at all.

Destructive Fire.

On Friday morning last, about 7 o'clock the Prospect Steam Grist Mill located in Middletown, in this county, took fire in the boiler-room, and before the flames could be got under, the mills were totally consumed, together with two adjoining dwelling houses and a doctor's shop. One of the dwelling houses was occupied by Mr. R. Patten, late of this place, who succeeded in saving his household goods in a damaged condition. To prevent the further spread of the flames, the Lutheran church was partially destroyed.

The mill was one of the finest in the county, and was owned by a joint-stock company, and was valued at $10,000. There was no insurance upon them, and their destruction will be severely felt by the citizens of that neighborhood, who will now have to go miles to get their grinding done.

The entire loss was about $12,000, and there was no insurance as far as we can learn. This will be a severe blow to Middletown, which had lately become quite a business point, and the sufferers are entitled to the sympathy of the public generally. We hope the owners of the mill will conclude to rebuild it without delay, as it is a great convenience to that part of the county.

Exhibitions, Plays &c.

We give place to the following communication, not because we approve of its sentiments entirely, but because it relates to a matter in which the public are deeply interested. So far as we are personally concerned, we should feel inclined to take the opposite side of the question but, on that account we do not feel at liberty to choke down discussion on the subject. If the speaking of Dialogues, or even of Plays, by the pupils of our schools, is wrong, it is time that fact should be established, and if not, then let an effort be made to counteract the erroneous opinion entertained, honestly by many on the subject. These results can only be reached through ample, honest and free discussion, and to facilitate their realization we lay before our readers the following, from the pen of one of our leading citizens. We hope some one will take up the appropriate side of the question.

Our Union School.

A Tax-payer and parent would like to say he is ready to cry "enough," and beg the teachers of our schools to cease their efforts to "get off" theatrical plays and spending their time, for which we are paying enormous prices, in some better way than daubing scenes for these performances.

I do not want and will not permit my daughter to take a part with these young fellows in being educated and trained to act on the public stage, these silly love stories.

And to such of our citizens as desire to witness them, I, for one, would rather contribute something to retain the act of vagabonds who are now exhibiting such plays, near the Depot, to remain a few weeks in Marion. Then the minds of our children would not be turned inside out some weeks before each farce which comes off at the close of our terms.

Parents, what do you say to this new mode of educating the heels instead of the heads.

Teachers and Board, give our children sound principles, and a moral bias against "the appearance of evil," and a good elementary discipline—but from every consideration, don't contaminate the soul with that which can only lead to the third tier.

Parent.

Jul 15, 1858

Accident.

On Monday morning last, whilst Mr. Eber Baker, an old and much respected citizen of this place, was endeavoring to drive a bull belonging to him away from a water-trough, the animal suddenly made a lunge at him, knocking him down and breaking some of his ribs. At last account, he was as comfortable as could be expected, considering the nature of his hurts.

Jul 22, 1858

Northern Lunatic Asylum.

Owing to the neglect of the late Locofoco Legislature to appropriate a sufficient amount of money to defray the current expenses of the Northern Lunatic Asylum, the Board of Directors have determined to close it during the months of September and October, and send the patients home.

☞We often hear of a widow mending her condition by repairing.

Broke Jail
$50.00 Reward.

On Wednesday night last, or, rather Thursday morning, John Sparks, confined in jail on a charge of Grand Larceny, broke out, by picking a hole through the wall of the upper story of the jail, and letting himself down to the ground with a bed-cord. He is about 5 feet 10 inches high, 22 years old, hair light and somewhat curly, complexion light, countenance bad, round-faced, had on a black oil-cloth cap and hairy coat. The Sheriff has been diligent in his efforts to re-arrest him, and has once or twice succeeded in getting on his track, but he is still at large, and the Sheriff offers a reward of $50.00 for his arrest and confinement until our authorities can get him again.

Jul 29, 1858

☞ We learn that one Nicholas Onselman was bound over by Esq. Christ, of Richland Township a few days since, for committing an assault with intent to kill, by shooting in that township.

Obituary.

Died—In this place, on the 26th inst., after a lingering illness, which she bore with great fortitude, Mrs. Julia, consort of John W. Bain, aged 34 years, 1 month and 14 days.

Husband, son and daughter she sweetly resigned to the care of him "who doeth all things well."

Mrs. Bain was born in Galia Co., Ohio, June 12th, 1824. On the 29th of July, 1851, she was united in marriage with him who has recently followed her to her last resting place and mourns a loss which earth cannot repair. May Heaven's blessing rest on him and the little ones.

Irish Row.—On Saturday evening last three or four Irishmen, some of them under the influence of rotgut corn juce, got into a row in or near a liquor shanty in the alley north of the Freese House and brickbats, lime-stones and Irish claret were distributed around promiscuously until Marshal Wilson appeared on the scene of action, when all of them cut dust but one, who was arrested and fined by the Mayor $5 and costs. Subsequently another one was taken and put through the same course. Both paid their fines, and promised to keep clear of whisky and Irish WEDDINGS in the future.

Elopement—It is stated that on Monday evening last a THING in the shape of a man who has been living in this place for some months past, deserted his wife, and eloped with a "grass widow." What aggravates his villainy is, the fact that his wife is a comparative stranger here, and, in feeble health. We hope the scoundrel who could thus desert her whom he had sworn to cherish and protect, and leave her to the cold charity of strangers, away from friends and home, may meet with speedy and condign punishment. He must be a villain of the deepest dye.

And to make her situation entirely unendurable, we are informed that his brother has, since he left, taken most of the furniture from his sister-in-law, and evicted her from the premises, although he had no right whatever to interfere with her. Tar and feathers ought to be in active demand in this neighborhood.

Aug 12, 1858

Married.

At Little Sandusky, on the 8th inst., Mr. Sanford Wilson, of Marion, and Miss Isabella Wilmoth of the former place.

Aug 19, 1858

The Court House Fence.

After making a survey of the thing by courtesy called a fence which surrounds the Court House lot, our neighbor says that "a single day's work by a practical mechanic will preserve the court yard from depredation for a year or two longer." We have no doubt this is so. By nailing props to each panel and letting them extend out over the pavement they will probably stand for "a year or two," but how would it look?

It is true our taxes are high, but will they not be just as heavy next year, and the next? If so, then when will we be able to build it? Why, a tax of a half a dollar on each tax-payer would more than be sufficient, and who so small as to grumble at it? The Court House and yard belong to the people of the county and they have pride enough to be willing to pay for beautifying and preserving it.

Aug 26, 1858

Deaths.

Died—On the 28th inst., at the residence of O.J. Johnson in this place, Mrs. Julia Mills, in the 69th year of her age.

Mother Mills was born in the State of Pennsylvania in the year 1789, and was brought up in the State of New York. Her maiden name was Julia Wells, and she was married to Richard Mills in 1809. In August, 1815, she emigrated with her husband to Chilicothe, Ohio, where they lived until the next Spring. They then removed to McArthurstown, then Athens but now Vinton county. In 1818 they removed to Franklin county, Ohio, and in February, 1822, they came to this county. This county was then very wild and new, being but the second year of its settlement. The two succeeding years brought with them many hardships and privations, which Mother Mills, in common with the frontier settlers, had to endure. The Fall of 1823, called the sickly season, was especially trying to the new settler. Some of her friends, and many of her acquaintances, at that time fell in death, while others fled from the country in terror and returned no more. In the Fall of 1828, they moved on to a small farm ¼ of a mile north of town. In July, 1834, mother Mills was left a widow. Her husband, Dr. R. Mills, fell in death away from home and among strangers, by that dreadful scourge of mankind, Asiatic Cholera. She lived in a state of widdowhood one month over twenty-four years. She was the mother of 7 children, 5 boys and 2 girls.

For forty years she has been a faithful and devoted member of the M.E. Church. Her last sickness was Lung Fever, and lasted but six days.

Marriages.

Married—On the 12th inst., Mr. Francis M. Sargent to Miss Pernina J. Southwick.

Destructive Fire.

We regret to learn that the Store of Messrs. Search & Dumble, in Caledonia, in this county was destroyed by fire on Wednesday morning last about 1 o'clock A.M. The loss is supposed to be about $6,000, no insurance.

Sep 2, 1858

Court House Fence.

As the building of the Court House fence might cause a severe pressure in money market, we have concluded not to have it built just yet. Those, therefore, who have been hovering for fear their pockets might be affected, can, dismiss their fears.

Tax-payers will return thanks for our lenity!

County Fair.

Let everybody and his wife remember that our County Fair commences on the 23d inst, and continues three days. The Fair promises to be the best one ever held in the county.

 The largest Pole knocks the persimmons, they say, and we suppose the same is true of the largest corn-stalk. Mr. A.D. Bretz, of Grand Prairie township informs us that he found a stalk of corn in his field which measured 16 feet 9 inches in height. it had three well-filled ears on it, besides, two half-filled ones. The top ear was 10 feet from the ground.

Sep 9, 1858

Marriages.

On the 6th inst., in Marion, Ohio, the Rev. Henry H. Messenger and Miss Gertrude Jane Turney.

Mr. Messenger is a late Graduate of Kenyon College and of the Theological Seminary of the Prot. Episcopal Church at Gambier. He was ordained Deacon a few months since, and in company with his amiable partner intends to set sail in a short time for Cape Palmas on the western coast of Africa, to labor as missionaries in connection with the flourishing Mission of the Prot. Episcopal Church.

❖

On Thursday, August 26, 1858, Rev. R. Lawrence, of the Delaware Conference, to Miss R.J. Hiett, of Fremont, O.

Repairing Sidewalks.

We are glad to see that our citizens in different parts of the town are repairing their plank walks and putting them in order. A plank walk, the end of every other plank in which is loose and sticking above the general surface is worse than no walk at all, and is absolutely dangerous. Therefore, we hope the repairing will go on until every plank walk in town is put in complete order.

Our Town—Its Business, its Necessities, &c.

In making the remarks which follow, we wish it distinctly understood that we refer to no particular person or institution, but speak generally, and if any misstatements are made, we shall be happy to correct them. Our aim is to benefit our beautiful town and fertile county, by pointing out what we conceive to be errors in business matters and suggesting their remedy.

There is, probably, not a county in the State where a Bank would pay as well as in ours. Large amounts of money are used by our business men, and it is a well established fact that no bank has ever lost a dollar by a Marion county man. Over $300,000 are now in use here, borrowed from banks and money-lenders. The average cost to the borrower is 16 to 18 per cent.! The only bank in the county is unable to supply but a small portion of the demand. By paying large interest on deposits, these modern institutions gather up all the loose money in the county, and Shylock himself might take a new degree if he could know the terms upon which they "discount" to their devoted customers. Twenty and thirty day New York Bills are the rule, and cost the borrower 25 to 33 per cent.

That any county can prosper where business men are drained by usurers, as ours are, no one believes. That the present condition of our "money facilities" is not all wrong, no sane person can doubt. Compare Delaware, with her two heavy banks, ready to accommodate her business men upon fair terms, her busy shops, factories and mills, her handsome buildings, her neat streets, her thriving schools, her beautiful Cemetery, so admiringly looked after—compare all this to Marion! Our only foundry closed, not so much as a hoe-handle made in the county. Tributary to neighboring county towns—to this one for stoves, to that one for thrashing machines, brooms, rakes, and cradles. Even water melons were selling on our streets a few days since brought from Delaware county!

If a drover wants to use a thousand dollars, and is unwilling to pay 18 per cent for it, he, too must go to the next county town.

Our old Grave yard, surrounded by dwellings, and the entrance to which is through a well-ornamented barn-yard, and which is full already to repletion, is considered good enough, and is still used, although a new Cemetery is open to the public. Rumholes and gambling houses are plenty, and well known, and yet the law passes by on the other side, and these pest houses are quietly going on, demoralizing the young and confirming the old in idleness.

Some parts of our town are given up to the stock hog business. A pen is built on a street or alley, a six-foot nosed breeding sow placed therein. Directly the sow is turned out with a dozen pigs, squealing after her to steal their living, polluting side-walks, daubing up fences, distributing fleas and filth in every direction, destroying gardens, aggravating christians, and raising ned generally. The sale of the pigs, and the chawing of the carcass of the old sow which is filled with shot, pitch-fork stabs and dog-bites, induces the breeders to continue the trade.

With money at 20 to 25 per cent all enterprise is smothered, borrowers and lenders "dry up," buildings are neglected, work-shops are closed, religion dies out, hearts harden and close to all kindly feelings or desire of progress or improvement. Every other building may be a hog-pen, a rum-hole or a saloon. "Twenty per cent pays," and who cares for aught else?

Let the money of the county be concentrated into a bank of $200,000 capital, established to lend money to our business men upon fair terms, and not to borrow at extreme and dangerous rates, for the purpose of lending again at usurous rates, and speculation in western lands and lots. Let every lot owner plant out shade trees. Let the moral part of the community (and they are vastly in the majority) unite to suppress the haunts of vagabonds. Pass corporation laws which shall extinguish the hog trade, and enforce cleanliness. When these things are done, you will see manufactures springing up in our midst, and noisy shops, handsome buildings, busy streets, and general thrift and improvement will be seen in Marion. Without a change, dog fennel, nettles, hog pens, shavers, rum-holes and misers will take the town.

Sep 16, 1858

Improper Conduct.

On Saturday evening last a couple of *women* who are presumed to have arrived at the age of discre-

tion—for one of them has been married for several years—were engaged in the *lady-like(?)* occupation of stretching a rope across one of our most frequented pavements, and watching its effects in tripping up unsuspecting pedestrians. They must have anticipated a large amount of fun, for, notwithstanding the coldness and darkness of the night, they continued at their posts until 10 o'clock. A repetition of the offence will be followed by a full exposure, for, to say the least of it, it is not only a very undignified, but also a very dangerous experiment.

Marriages.

On the 9th inst., Mr. Ebenezer Cory and Miss Mary B. Pangburn, all of this county.

On the same day, Mr. Harrison Word and Miss Margaret Seater, all this co.

On the 19th inst, Mr. Victor J. Taylor and Miss Emeline Payne, all of this Co.

Died.

Died at the residence of her father in Delaware, Ohio on Thursday the 9th inst., of Eryhipcles, Miss Elizabeth Wildbahn, in the 29th year of her age.

The deceased was well known in Marion where she spent the happy hours of her childhood and youth. Miss W. gave early indication of a taste for learning and she graduated in 1857 at the Washington Female College with distinguished honor. She was for some time a teacher in the mathematics department in the Delaware Female College.

Sep 30, 1858

Marriages.

On the 25th inst., at Indianapolis, Mr. S. Peckenpaugh, of Marion, O., and Miss Mary E. Grafton, of the former place.

On the 22d inst., Mr. Simeon Ward and Miss Nancy J. Brady, all of Big Island tp., Marion county.

Marion County Fair.

The Ninth Annual Fair of our county has just closed, and we are pleased to hear on all sides that it was decidedly the best Fair ever held in this county; not only in regard to numbers that attended, estimated at from 4,000 to 5,000 persons, but for the number and superior quality of the stock exhibited; every pen was well filled, and a dozen or more wanted.

There were several persons scaled the high fence, but in almost every instance they were taken by the constables in waiting; they were fined from 40¢ (being double the price of a ticket) to $1.00, and, without exception, the fines were paid.

There were hundreds of small farmers, mechanics and laborers, that daily purchased their tickets and come in like honorable men, as they were, the contrast between these, and a few farmers worth thousands, to tens of thousands of dollars, who set on their horses, or stood up in their wagons, outside, and anxiously strained their necks and eyes in looking over the high fence, rather than contribute a mite to the expenses of the Society, looked ridiculously small and as unhappy as "fish out of water."

MCLEAN'S
Strengthing
CORDIAL

Before taking,

The County Convention.

The Republican County Convention, which met at the court house on last Monday was one of the fullest we have had for years. Everything passed off harmoniously and the nominations were effected without strife or contention.

The ticket put in nomination is one of the best that has been offered to the people of Marion county for years, and we have no doubt but that it will be triumphantly elected.

Our candidate for Auditor,

Louis F. Raichley,

Is a citizen of this place, having spent his whole life here. His qualifications for the office for which he has been nominated, are of a very superior character, and it is conceded by all that he will make one of the best County Auditors Marion or any other county ever had.

Nelson C. Mitchell,

Our candidate for Recorder, is a citizen of Claridon township, where he was born, and where he has spent the largest portion of his life. He is a true blue Republican—is well qualified for the office, will be triumphantly elected, if we all do our duty.

Noah Gillespie,

Is an old resident of Grand Township, where he is universally esteemed for his sterling good sense, his unflinching integrity, and his superior business qualifications. If elected, and we have no doubt of it, he will carefully guard the interests of the people, and make one of the best Commissioners we have had for many years.

Jacob R. Neff,

Our nominee for Infirmary Director, is a prominent citizen of Salt Rock Township, among whose citizens he ranks among the best. His qualifications for the office for which he is a candidate are of a superior character, and his careful attention to his own business shows that he will be ever watchful of the interests of the people of the county as connected with the County Infirmary.

— and —
Blood Purifying
REMEDY

After taking.

William B. Davis,

The nominee for Coroner, is a citizen of Prospect township. The office of Coroner is not of very great importance in itself but it may be of importance in case of the death of the Sheriff before the expiration of his term, when the incumbent of the former office would succeed to the latter. Hence it is important that the office should be filed by a man of the right political proclivities, and we hope every Republican in the county will be as careful to vote for Coroner as for any other office.

Oct 14, 1858

Death's Doings— Original Statistics

In our travels we collect facts in the grave-yards, copying the ages from the memorials, distinguishing between males and females and thus getting the average age of each sex and the extent of mortality among the children. We give a few examples this month for Marion, Ohio:

Males	192
Females	204
Total	396

Average Age Males	18½
Average Age Females	17½
both	18

Infants	36
Under 5 years	181

The number of males and females between the ages of 16 and 40, is as follows:

Males	44	Females	54

Oct 21, 1858

Accident at Wyandott Co. Fair.

We regret to learn that a horse belonging to Sheriff Lewis, of this place, whilst being driven around the ring at the Wyandott county Fair, by Mr. B. Kent, of this place, became suddenly frightened from some unexplained cause, tore the sulky to pieces and making a dash into the crowd, severely injured a lady and gentleman who were setting in their buggy looking at the trotting. The lady had her arm broke and was somewhat bruised otherwise. The gentleman was severely wounded in the head, and the doctors, we learn, despair of his recovery. No blame, we learn, can be attached to either Mr. Kent or Sheriff Lewis, as the horse was going along very quietly when he took fright and was never know to be vicious before.

The Robbins Case

Just as we go to press we learn that the Jury in the case of the State of Ohio vs. Edward Robbins, (charged with murdering Nancy Holly by Poisoning in July 1857,) by consent of counsel, have returned a verdict of "Guilty of murder in the Second Degree," the penalty of which is imprisonment in the Penitentiary for life.

Marriages.

On the 13th inst., Mr. J.J. Boyd and Miss Eva G. Gorton, both of Marion.

On the 19th inst., in this place, Mr. Gilbert Counterman and Miss Mary S. Luke, all of this county.

Oct 28, 1858

Balloon Passing Over Town.

Some boys, who were out east of town on Friday last, gathering hickory nuts, report that they saw a large balloon sailing towards the North. Whence the ærial traveller came from and whither it went, we are not at present advised.

Nov 4, 1858

Sentence of Robbins.

On Saturday P.M. last, after disposing of some other business, Judge Lawrence ordered Robbins, who had been convicted of Murder in the Second Degree, by poisoning Nancy Holly, to be brought into Court for sentence. In reply to the usual question, whether he had anything to say why sentence should not be passed upon him, he said, in effect:

"I am innocent of intending to bring about the result that has been. I have nothing more to say."

Judge Lawrence then said:

Edward Robbins, stand up:

The verdict of the Jury is, that you are guilty of Murder in the Second Degree. With that verdict you have every reason to be satisfied. You have had every guaranty, and every aid which the law could furnish in your behalf. You have been defended by counsel of rare ability and with unsurpassed fidelity. The prosecution has been conducted with equal fidelity, but with a commendable disposition to seek no advantage except that justified by the law and the evidence. That you are guilty of a high crime against the laws of God and man, I entertain no doubt.

No palliating circumstances relieve your crime of its unwonted enormity. You was a husband and the father of children. In your own household Nancy Holly became your servant, and claimed your protection. In that sacred circle. she became the erring victim of your lust. When her shame and yours must soon become manifest, if not already so, her parents were induced to indulge the mistaken belief that she was seeking the hospital shelter of a relative, while you persuaded her to go among strangers, deluded with the idea that you had furnished a medicine that would destroy the unborn fruits of your illicit passion. She did so:—took the fatal drug, and, with no warning preparation, was hastened into eternity. The guilt of a double murder rests upon you.

At last you are here, a spared monument of your wrongs, about to enter a prison for life, under circumstances which forbid all hope of Executive pardon. Another is added to the daily accumulating evidences that crime can rarely ever escape detection and punishment. Let others, then, warned by your example, shun the vices and temptations that lead to ruin. By the sentence of the law, you are now forever shut out from the world around you. You are lost to that wife who has never forsaken you. You are lost to those children who had a right to the kindly protection, care, and future of a father. But, with all this, there is yet hope, mercy is the darling attitude of God.

I earnestly entreat you to profit, even now, by the misfortunes that have befallen you. Implore the Father of all mercies, to change your heart. Have faith in the merits of the Redeemer. Devote the residue of your life to the practice of every christian virtue. With a christian's hope, the captive of a gloomy prison is more free, more useful, more happy, than one who enjoys freedom only to pollute the world and condemn the ordinance of God and man.

The sentence of the court is, that you be imprisoned in the penitentiary of this state, and kept at hard labor during life, no part of the time to be in solitary confinement, and that you pay the costs of prosecution.

During the reading of the sentence, the prisoner seemed entirely unmoved, and was apparently unconcerned as any one of the vast multitude which surrounded him. After sentence had been passed, he conversed for a few moments with Mr. Conklin, of Sidney, Ohio, one of his counsel, and was then removed by the Sheriff to jail, which place he left on Monday morning last, in charge of the Sheriff and his deputy, to enter upon his life long sentence in the penitentiary.

The Trial of Robbins,

Cost the people of Marion county over $2,000, of which they will probably receive back from the State about one fourth. A losing operation, that.

Nov 11, 1858

Dedication of Marion Cemetery

The Cemetery Association deem it proper, on this occasion, to make a brief statement of their organization and of their subsequent proceedings, in order that a distinct understanding of the whole matter may be had, and that unfounded impressions, if entertained, may be corrected.

It is hardly necessary to remark that previously to the commencement of this enterprise, the want of a new, more commodious, and more tasteful place of burial for the dead, further removed from the immediate vicinity of the village was greatly felt. The old burying ground had served its day and generation, and fulfilled its mission. It is true that many lingering memories cluster around its enclosure. There, many of "the rude fathers of the hamlet sleep." But these interesting and we may say even sacred reminiscences could not serve to shut out entirely the fact, that in the growth of our town it had become too near the houses of any of our citizen, to near for the purity of the atmosphere, and too near for the purity of our veins of water which feed the neighboring wells, running as they do, over a superficial bed of limestone.

Not only was it too near the village, but its dimensions were too contracted to admit of its being used, for any length of time for the purpose which it was originally intended.

The lots themselves, too, although suitable to the circumstances and the time in which they were laid out, were too small and many of them too inaccessible to admit of that growing taste for embellishment with trees, shrubs and flowers, which marks the spirit of our time, and which is so evident a token of refinement in feeling; seeking, as it does, to transform the cold, angular, barren and gloomy spot of earth, into a graceful lawn which shall be a place of cheerful, pleasant and even attractive resort.

The depth of the soil, moreover, in the old burying ground is such that many of the graves cannot be sunk over 2 feet and a half without blasting the rock, and many are the bodies in that graveyard now, which are not covered with earth over twenty inches, and this within the corporate limits of the village of Marion. These reasons, more or less known by our citizens, gave rise to the call on all sides for efficient steps to be taken for the purchase of ground for a new cemetery. Our public papers urged, too, the fact that great attention was paid to new and spacious cemeteries in other villages not larger than our own. And that a decent pride or respect for our own village should lead us not to be behind our neighbors, or behind the age in which we live.

The consequence of all this was that repeated attempts were made within the last few years to procure grounds at a convenient distance, for a new city of the dead. Nothing practical was done however until last year.

On the 3d day of July, 1857, a preliminary meeting was held by the citizens of Marion who were desirous that an effort should be made for the immediate purchase of lands. Fourteen gentlemen entered into articles of association, held their meeting for the election of officers on the 26th of that month, and when their proceedings were recorded in the recorders office of the county, on the 12th day of August following, they became a body corporate under the general cemetery law of the state.

To the original number of members were shortly afterwards added five more, so that the present number is nineteen.

This comprehended all of the enterprising citizens of our village, that could be found to willing to undertake, practically, and with something more than idle declamation, the self denying, and in many quarters the thankless task of preparing a cemetery. The association, thus incorporated, were desirous of purchasing land immediately for this purpose. As a corporation, they had no means, no resources. The law contemplates both donations and loans, the latter not to exceed ten thousand dollars.

Of donations, the corporation has received none. For the purchase of land, therefore, it was necessary to borrow money to meet the fist payments, and to give obligations for the deferred payments. It was also necessary to borrow money for the payment of labor required to be performed in order to clear up the land and put it in condition to sell the lots. For these purposes, some two thousand dollars have been borrowed, on the notes of the association, and the deferred payments on the land amount to some $2,500 more. Not far from $700 have been expended for labor alone, and $200 for surveying.

The whole amount of land within the Cemetery enclosure is about 17½ acres. About 2¾ acres of this were sold to the Catholic congregation, for their exclusive use as a cemetery. Also, an arrangement was made with the township of Marion, of the following nature: In as much as the whole people of the township were, in a measure, as much interested as the associated corporation, as it was a public enterprise and of no more benefit to the members than to every other citizen, and as the law allowed the purchase of five acres by the Trustees of the township, it was considered right that the public should bear a portion of the preliminary burden, and should become interested to the amount of $500. This would enable the Trustees of the township to set apart such a portion as they might see proper for the use of the poor, as required by law, and retain the remainder for sale. As the portion selected by them occupied a central position in the cemetery, it was acknowledged by them to be proper that the whole grounds should be subject to those reasonable regulations and laws which are common to all cemeteries and which would produce unity in its supervision. The township, in this manner, assists in the enterprise, furnishes a portion of ground for the use for the poor, and retains another portion for future sale.

It may be the impression, and doubtless it has been the thought of some, that too much land has been purchased. In reference to this it may be remarked, that it is impossible to select a suitable piece of ground, within a convenient distance of the town, which shall contain enough land in one contiguous body. Any selection of a proper site must necessarily comprehend much waste land, if any regard whatever be paid to the symmetry of its form. It must be remembered that we are purchasing land, not alone for the use of the present generation, but in part at least for posterity. They at least will thank us, if there should be found some now who think that our ideas are too extensive and magnificent. Fifty years hence these grounds will be considered limited. It has been the common fault, the result we may add of a common delusion, incident to the frailty of human feeling, to anticipate that the advancing army, pressing on to the grave, will, it may be, march forward henceforth, with unbroken ranks and straggling columns, rather than with the accelerated and augmented tide that derives impetus from increased population. Deceive not yourselves with the thought that the dead will not multiply. The common experience respecting all graveyards, even of the one in our own village, and of all cemeteries, is, that in a few short years more land is wanted for the accumulating nation of the dead.

More land, where the mute remains shall be safe from the vandalism of so called public improvements, which not infrequently lay their iron track directly through our most venerable graveyards, and carelessly throw aside the dust of those whose memory has passed away. The belief and the judgement of our association is, that we have not too much land, especially when we consider that our cemetery is designed to accommodate a larger scope of country, and a wider circle of those who shall need a final resting place from the toils of life.

Nor are those portions properly regarded as waste which are unfit for burial. The groves that will spring up, the flowers and shrubs that will be cultivated in these parts of the grounds will but minister to a rational regard and respect for the memory of those who are gone. They will contribute to give variety, interest, even though a mournful interest, to the passing loiterer, whose feelings may be softened and subdued by the rustle of the trees or the delicacy of the flowers, while he muses upon the mutations and uncertainties of life, the past, the present and the future, secure from the intrusions of a busy, a heedless, a selfish world.

As to the amount of progress that has been made in advancing this enterprise, we may properly refer to the grounds that are before you. The whole is in its incipient stage, and yet already the winding avenues, streets, and walks may almost lead you "in wandering mazes lost." Already the hillocks, scattered here and there denote that some that were but recently in our midst and warm with life, have been laid here in their narrow house. But a short distance from us lies one, who, as an old citizen, was active

and energetic in whatever would contribute to the improvement of our village. He is gone from the active scenes of life, and all that remains of Thomas Henderson lies upon the brow of Prospect Hill. Yonder, upon the Mound, reposes what was earthly of other fathers of the village. Benjamin Williams, William Bain, James Williams, Curtis Allen, were names are familiar in the village annals. And the marble already marks, or shortly will, the name of Walters, of Reed, of Stokes, of Lindsey, of Davis, of Jameson, of Minerva Williams, of Laura Patten, of Julia Bain, of Harshberger, of Cooper, and of many who had not reached mature age. Nor will it detract from the pleasures of imagination, to suppose that their forms rest more serenely beneath those neatly shorn lawns, and springing evergreens of Sunny Side and Terrace Bank. Your walk among them will show what has already been done, in the very infancy of our enterprise.

To return a moment to the nature of our organization. We have no stock, requiring dividends; we disdain the idea of speculating in matters of so sacred a nature as those pertaining to the mansions of the dead. The receipts are applied to the payment of loans of money for the first advances, as before stated, and to the debts incurred for necessary labor, to fit the grounds for sale. We have already devoted, and we anticipate in the future to devote much time, thought, care, to an enterprise in which every citizen is really as much interested as we are. We have so far been careful to avoid the occasion of a charge of unworthy motives, and private ends. In privileges we have placed ourselves on a level with every other citizen. We have bought our lots, (so far as any have bought them,) at the same

prices and in the same manner as others have and the privilege of purchasing. And when we make them on the faith of men not unknown in the community, and of whose responsibility and honor all are capable of judging.

Of that class of chronic grumblers and fault finders, whose natural proclivity is to complain of every new idea and every new enterprise, and who are therefore incurable, we have nothing to say but to express the hope that when they reach their final home on earth, they may rest in peace.

To any responsible class of men who think they can carry on an enterprise of this kind with more wisdom and energy, we will gladly assign all our title and interest. In the meantime we ask the cooperation of those who desire to advance the interests of our town, village and community.

Married,

In Marion, on the 31, inst., Mr. James M. Howard and Miss Anna J. Carson, both of Rusheylvania, Logan County, Ohio.

A Singing Mouse.

Mr. Bruck, of the firm of Bruck & Leonard, Druggists, of this place, caught in a wire trap on Tuesday evening last, a musical mouse. The little fellow will troll of a tune equal to the best Canary. It has been heard singing about the store ever since last winter, but all previous attempts to capture it failed. It is truly a great curiosity.

Burglary.

We learn that the store of Mr. W. Cummings, in Berwick, in this county, was broken open on the evening of the 21st ult., and robbed of between $50 and $75 in specie. The thief or thieves first tried to get in by cutting a hole in the door and removing the bolt, but failing in this, they effected an entrance by prying open a window. Let our citizens be on their guard, for there is, no doubt, scores of thieves prowling through the country.

Nov 18, 1858

Turkey and Babies.

A modest young gentleman at a dinner party, put the following conundrum: "Why are most people who eat turkey like babies?" No reply. The modest man blushed, and would have backed out, but finally gave this reason: "Because they are fond of the breast." Two middle aged ladies fainted, and the remains of the young man were carried out by the coroner.

Mammoth Turnips.

Mr. J. Walker, of Green Camp township, brought into our office, on Saturday last, two Turnips, which were natural curiosities. One of them measured 28½ inches in circumference, and weighed full nine pounds. The other 1½ inches less in circumference and weighed ½ pound less. They were solid and juicy and sweet throughout, and were not pithy and dry, as overgrown vegetables usually are. They were truly monsters, and, we think, cannot be beat easily.

Married.

In Prospect township, on the 11th inst., Mr. Humphrey M. Moore and Miss Elizabeth A. Greek, both of this county.

On the 14th inst., Mr. Wm. H. Scribner to Miss L.M. Owen, both of Claridon township, Marion county, Ohio.

Nov 25, 1858

Marion Cemetery.

The Odd Fellows have purchased a fine lot in the new burying ground, and intend improving and ornamenting it at once. We understand that quite a number of lots have been sold since the dedication, and that removals from the old burying ground have again commenced.

Those engaged in removing should carefully re-fill the old graces, and leave the ground as smooth and orderly as possible. It strikes us that the corporation should appoint a medical committee to examine the old grave yard and report as to the effect of further internments almost in the midst of town, upon the health of the place. The only difficulty will be to get a committee of doctors to visit their former patients, knowing as they do that their pills and drugs have been largely instrumental in filling the grounds up.

Snow Sleighing.

Within the past forty-eight hours (being from Sunday morning) the clerk of the weather has enrobed the form of mother earth in a mantle of snow four inches in depth, and the merry jingle of sleigh bells in our streets shows that a portion, at least, of our people possessing time and facilities for indulging in the exhilarating amusement of sleighing. At the hour we write it is still snowing, and old winter seems to be fully installed on his icy throne.

Married,

On the 28th day of Oct., 1858, Mr. Abraham Stagg of Hope, Ohio, to Miss Maggie Harrison, formerly of this place.

On the 18th inst., John A. Hawk and Miss Elizabeth Ann Marsh, both of Salt Rock Township, Marion Co., O.

Dec 2, 1858

Public Lectures.

We notice that a great many of our sister county towns have prepared, or are preparing to have a course of public Lectures delivered during the winter, and we think the citizens of Marion ought to take some steps toward effecting the same object. If means enough cannot be raised to procure the services of foreign Lecturers, let the service of home talent be substituted. We have gentlemen in our midst who are amply qualified to entertain an audience, and whose Lectures would be interesting and instructive. Who will move in this matter first.

☞ Woman has found her true 'sphere,' at last—it is about twenty-seven feet around and is made of hoop and crinoline.

Improvements.

Brother Thompson, of the *Delaware Gazette*, thus sums up the improvements that have recently been made in the capital city of his bailiwick:

"Mr. Shoub has built a new board fence extending from his house to his barn—that Mr. Martin has just put up a sign at his tailor shop—that Mr. Evans has erected a new stable—and that a pavement has been laid before Mr. Seibold's Grocery...."

The improvements in this place are fully up to those in our sister town. Jerry O'Donohue has added two boards—taken after night from a pile his neighbor "lost" in his backyard—to his pig-pen to prevent the "baste" from getting out. Patrick O'Shane has cut two saw logs for lumber to cover his hen roost. Cathleen O'Shaughnessy has weatherboarded the hole in Micky's blue coat with a nice piece of red flannel, a portion of a petti-skirt-coat that mysteriously disappeared from a clothes-line between two days and dos't hang out as much in the morning as it did at night.

A native citizen, born in this country, said he would build a stable as soon as B. & I. R.R. Stock rose to par, and another one (a Rhinelander) is determined to put another hoop to his Krout barrel as soon as he can get the hoop pole from Hardin county by the A. & G.W. Railroad. These we believe, are all the improvements that have been made here the past season, and they show that ere long all the available building space adjoining town will be taken up.

Clean the Side-Walks.

The city Fathers should see that the side walks are cleared after a fall of snow, in a reasonable time; and to secure this greatly to be desired reform, I suggest an ordinance, requiring each occupant of premises to clean his side walk, and a proper share of any street crossing. To be enforced by proper inducements. There is great comfort in a clean side walk, while one six inches deep with slush, is a great nuisance. Pedestrian.

A Fire—Almost.

On Tuesday evening last, about 9 o'clock P.M., the barn of the Freese House was discovered to be on fire. By prompt exertions, it was extinguished before any serious damage was done.

Destruction of Hogs.

We are sorry to hear that about fifty hogs belonging to Mr. W. Biggerstaff were smothered to death in the B. & I. R.R. cattle yard on Monday night last by laying on each other. Damage estimated at about $150.

Nice Cattle.

On Wednesday last Col. E. Messenger, shipped from this point 44 head of as nice cattle as it has been our fortune to see for some time. They were three-year old grades, and were in superb condition, and if the New Yorkers grumble at such beef, they ought to be fed on scalawag beef for a year and a day. They were fed by Mr. Thomas Dye, whose farm lays in Marion and Wyandot counties, and do great credit to him as a feeder.

Marion County Agricultural Society.

We lay before our readers in today's paper an exhibit of the financial transactions of the Marion County Agricultural Society during the past year. On Saturday last a large number of the members of the Society met in the County Treasurer's office, and elected the following officers to serve during the ensuing year:

President.—Everett Messenger;
Vice President.—Paten Hord;
Secretary.—A.D. Matthews;
Treasurer.—Ebenezer Peters;
Directors: William Thew, David Pettit, A. Travenner, C. Smith, J. Lee.

Marriages.

On Thursday, the 25th ult., 1858, Mr. David T. Bruck to Miss Mary H. Baker, both of Marion, O.

On the 22 ult., at the residence of Mr. S.L. Johnson, Mr. Martin V.B. Barnhart to Miss Emma V. Johnson, all of Prospect tp, Marion co., O.

Dec 9, 1858

Terrible Occurrence— Two Children Burned to Death.

It becomes our painful duty to record the death, by burning, of two children named Heald, one a boy and one a girl, whose parents reside in Richland Township, in this county. The particulars of this sad affair, as near as we can learn them, are as follows: On Friday afternoon last the mother of the children, visited a relative, taking two children with her and leaving two at home. In the evening the father left home for the purpose of filling an appointment to preach in the neighborhood, leaving the children alone. About 7½ o'clock the neighbors discovered the house to be on fire, and when they arrived, the children were seen laying on the floor, they and the room being all in a blaze. How the house caught on fire, and why the children were prevented from leaving the house are questions that cannot now be answered. The ages of the children were, one 4 and the other 7.

Marriages.

In Marion, on the 1st inst., Mr. Jonathan Smith and Mrs. Sarah D. Britton, both of Hardin Co., O.

Dec 16, 1858

Dobbs

Says that if the people of our town go to the trouble of scrapping up the mud on our streets into piles, it is but mere justice that the corporation authorities should haul it off. Dobbs is right in that, certain.

Desperate Affray.

A desperate affray came off in this place on last Thursday evening, between an ex penitentiary convict named Partridge and a tanner named McPherson. The latter attacked the former with a "dummy" and inflicted several wounds upon his head, cutting it to the bone. Partridge retaliated with a knife cutting McPherson severely in the hands and face.

McPherson was arrested and taken before the Mayor, who bound him over in the sum of $200 to appear at the next term of the Court of

Common Pleas of this county. Things are coming to a pretty pass when deadly weapons are used in our most public streets, and we hope all who resort to them may be punished to the extent of the law.

Fire.

We are sorry to learn that the steam saw mill of J.C. Emery five miles west of Marion on the B. & I. R.R. was destroyed by fire on last Thursday evening. Loss about $1500. The origin of the fire is not known.

Nice.

How nice it is to keep three or four needle nosed hogs to run around town breaking into peoples' gardens and rooting up their pavements. For a specimen of their "paving" operations see West Street.

Dec 23, 1858

Ancient Relic

On our table before us lays a relic of "ye olden time" in the history of our beautiful village, in the shape of a newspaper, *The Saturday Visitor and Marion Intelligencer*, dated Saturday morning Feb 1, 1840, G. & A. Shrung Editors and Proprietors. The *Visitor* was about the size of the *Republican*, the advertisements and reading matter being both set in the same size type. Among the businessmen here who advertised in it, and who are in this vicinity at present are R. Patten, J.S. Reed, J.H. Godman, E. Peters, G.H. Busby, John Bartrum.

Among the advertisements we notice which were the offspring of the very angry feelings which animated the two parties into which the

citizens of the town were at the time divided. One is headed "Anti-Abolition Meeting," and the other "Freedom of Speech." They were caused by a debate which took place up the "Marion Lyceum," then in full blast. The everlasting slavery question was brought up by some means and the sentiments expressed by those who took ground against slavery were so offensive to a portion of the citizens that the town was divided into two angry and warring factions. We well remember that at one meeting of the Lyseum, while some person was speaking on the slavery question and against slavery, that those were opposed to the arguments being uttered broke out into hisses, yells, boots stamping until the court house trembled to its foundation and the riot was only quelled by the appearance the venerable Curtis Allen, at the time Mayor of the village, who had been sent for to restore order. The Call headed "Anti-Abolition," was signed by nineteen then prominent citizens, but as the feelings then aroused, have long since passed away, together with many of those in whose bosom they then throbbed, we forebear inserting them here. The other call was signed by only "Many" but who they were we have no way of knowing.

Altogether, the *Visitor* has a very familiar look that carries us back to the days of "auld lang syne." Many who read it as it made its weekly appearance have passed away together with one of the proprietors, but its memory cherished by numbers of our older citizens, whose heads have been frosted by the hands of time since it made its appearance. An humble, unpretending sheet issued before steam and lightening had revolutionized the world, it had served its day and generation, but there are still many among us who would glance with pleasure over its dingy columns whilst longing memories would carry them swiftly back "o the days and scenes of other years."

Marriages.

On the 14th instant, Mr. David Gray and Miss Lucinda Vanhauter, both of Scott Town, Marion co., O.

On the 29th ult., Thomas Thompkins and Mrs. Losina Cullison, all of this county.

On the 11th ult., at the residence of her mother, Mr. Abraham H. Kepler and Miss Emeline Garrison.

On the 2d inst., Mr. John E. Lefevre and Miss Mary J. Tunis, all of this county.

On the 16th inst., Mr. Jacob Harshberger and Miss Jane Tharp, all of this place.

Deaths.

In this place on the 17th inst., Henry Joseph, son of Michael and Mary Muntsinger, aged 3 years, 4 months and 5 days.

Dec 30, 1858

Marriages.

On the 22d inst., M.M. Wheeler to Miss Olive P.O. Mason, all of Montgomery tp., Marion co., O.

Christmas

Passed off in this place "about as usual." Young America being engaged in reporting to each other the visits of Santa Claus to their stockings the previous evening, and in dilating upon the various nice things he deposited there, and in fireing *feu de joies* of fire-crackers, pistols, &c, whilst the "children of a larger growth" contented themselves with firing volleys of roast Turkey, chickens, "4th proof," "old rye" &c, and so on down their throats, though we saw but one drunken man during the day. And thus passed the Christmas in Marion, in 1858. May we all witness many happy returns of the day.

☞ 'Tis an old saying that "a bare Christmas makes a fat grave-yard." If this be true, this year will be a very unhealthy one, for the ground in this section is as bare as the bottom of a darkies foot.

Sales of Real Estate.

We learn from Mr. John W. Bain, that he has, within the past three or four weeks, sold to different persons nearly $1500 worth of lots in his Addition to the town, on the hill. As these lots were all sold to persons who intend building on them, it speaks well for the prosperity of our town, and shows that, with a return of good times, we may expect to see its borders rapidly extended.

Jan 6, 1859

Marriages.

On the 20th ult., Mr. David J. Bowers and Miss Julia E. Vanarsdall, the former of Wyandot and the latter of Marion county, Ohio.

Deaths.

Died, at Lyons, N.Y., on Sunday morning, Nov. 29th of dysentery, Miss Mary Jameson, aged 31 years. Miss Jameson was the sister of our esteemed fellow citizen David Jameson and was a young lady who by a very rare combination of talent, modesty, dignity and unaffected piety, had endeared herself in a wide circle of friends.

She had just graduated at the Musical Academy of Lyon, having attained to the highest standard of success in her profession, and was preparing to take charge of the Musical Department of an Academy in Pennsylvania, when she was cut down by death, disappointing the fond expectations of her friends. She died a most triumphant christian death. She has left behind some musical compositions which attest her rare abilities in her profession.

Jan 13, 1859

Marriages.

On the 9th inst., in Green Camp, Mr. James H. Johnston of Green Camp, and Miss Martha J. Hutchason, of Marion.

On the 7th inst., Mr. George Ballantine and Miss Sarah Jane Wynn, all of this place.

The Coldest Morning of the Season.

Last Saturday morning was the coldest morning of the season, the thermometer standing at 8° below zero at sunrise. The contrast between the extreme rigor of such weather and the spring-like mildness which had previously pre-vailed, was great, and caused "ye people" to stick as close to the fire as possible.

Heavy Tax Payers.

We give below a list of the heaviest tax payers in Marion county, together with the amounts paid by each, for the year 1858:—

C. Brady	$428.45
S.S. Bennett	351.31
O. Bowen	540.37
J.S. Copeland	300.97
W.W. Conklin	379.36
E. Messenger	151.80
A. Monnet	513.79
E. Peters	158.18
N. Peters	265.86
D. Pettit	349.70
Landy Shoots	346.28
E. Sharpless	91.26
Patten & Wallace	551.42
J.S. Reed & Co.	924.20
E. Hardy & Co.	946.96
Bank of Marion	746.13

Crime &c., in Marion County.

From the report of the Prosecuting Attorney of this county to the Attorney General of the State, we gather the following fact:

Indictments pending	15
Found during the year	27
Convictions	14
Acquittals	4
Nolle Prosequis	1
Total Costs	427.35
Costs collected	169.37
Costs collectable	150.33
Costs not collectable	47.65
Costs paid by county	45.02
Fines Assessed	272.50
Fines collected	142.50
Fines collectable	110.00
Penitentiary for life	1
Fines and imprisonment	8
Fines	4

The convictions were for the following crimes: Murder in 2d degree, 1; sale of intoxicating liquors, 8; assault and battery, 1; keeping tavern without license, 3.

Jan 20, 1859

Bound Over.

On Friday last, Mr. J. Honecker, of Bowlinggreen township, was examined before Esq. Moore, of this place, and bound over to take his trial on the Court of Common Pleas on the charge of selling intoxicating liquors to be drank on the premises.

J.E. Fouke, of Green Camp, who was examined on a similar charge before the same magistrate, was discharged.

Removing Cancers.

We saw last week, a Cancer which had been removed from the face of a Mr. Drown, who resides in Montgomery township, by Dr. Sweeney, of this place. The Cancer was situated on the right side of the nose, just below the eye, and affected a portion of the face about one inch in circumference. Mr. Drown stated to us that it had been about five years since it first made its appearance in the form of a small sore which gradually increased in size up to this time, attended by sharp prickling or piercing pain. The Cancer was removed with a plaster or preparation that caused but little pain. In the case spoken of the cure seems to be almost perfect.

Marriages.

On the 13th inst., Abraham Smith to Miss Rachel C. Crabb, both of Salt Rock township, Marion Co., O.

Deaths.

W.D. Bridge, son of Dr. W.W. and P.M. Bridge, died January 12th, 1859, aged 4 years, 7 months and 19 days. Disease, croup.

Jan 27, 1859

Marriages.

On the 20th inst., Ezra G.G. Bartram to Miss Magdalena Smith, all of Montgomery, Marion county, O.

On the 22d inst., Mr. Joseph W. Cone, Jr., and Miss Priscilla Redman, all of Marion, O.

On the 17th inst., Mr. Clegget C. Ridgway of Hardin co., to Mrs. Caroline Davids of Marion co.

On the 20th inst., by Newton Messenger, J.P., Samuel C. Smith and Miss Lucy A. Messenger, of Big Island township, Marion Co., O.

On the 24th inst., Martin V. Brady and Miss Betsy Brady, of Big Island Township, Marion co., Ohio.

Deaths.

On the 23d inst., William Harper, youngest son of W.M. and Kate Hardy, aged 3 years and 9 months.

Estates Administered.

During the year ending December 1, 1858, there were thirty wills admitted to Probate in this county.

Marriages in Marion County.

During the year ending December 31, 1858, there were issued from the Probate Court of Marion county 174 Marriage Licenses, being a larger number than was ever issued before, in the same period of time since the organization of the court.

Preparing to Leave.

We understand that our fellow townsman, and late editor of the Mirror, John R. Knapp. has purchased the *Hillsborough Gazette*, and will take charge of that paper on the 1st day of April next. John wields a racy pen, and will undoubtedly make a first-rate paper, bating its red-mouthed Locofocism, which, with him, is a matter of course. We wish him all kinds of success, political excepted.

Feb 3, 1859

Agricultural Premiums.

At a meeting of the Board of managers of the Marion county agricultural Society, the Board awarded to Mr. Jacoby, of Richland township, $3 for having produced the best field of Corn during the year 1858. The measurement of the ground, and grain were both certified to by Mr. Jacoby and two other persons. the yield on the acre was 97½ bushels of shelled corn.

Mr. William Oborn, also of Richland township was awarded $2 for having raised the second best acre of Corn. The yield was 88½ bushels of shelled Corn.

These were large yields, but we learn that Mr. Henry Wolf, of Salt Rock township, raised 120 bushels on one acre of ground, but not hav-

ing complied with the conditions affixed by the Board, they could take no notice of it.

Accident.

Our old friend, Jacob Baker, of Pleasant township, was thrown from his horse last week, and severely but not dangerously cut on the head.

Aliens Naturalized.

During the year 1858, there were twenty-eight aliens naturalized by the Court of Common Pleas of this county.

Feb 10, 1859

Miscellaneous.

Butternut Pie—One quart of milk, two eggs, a coffee cupful of pulverized butternut meats, and a little sugar and nutmeg.

Wigs—Half a pint of warm milk, three quarters of a pound of flour, three spoonful of yeast. Let it rise, and work into it four ounces each of sugar and butter, and a few caraway seeds. Bake quick.

An Excellent Common Fried Cake—One cupful of sugar, one cupful of cream, three eggs, some cinnamon or nutmeg, and a tea-spoonful of saleratus. Cut in jumbles or in strips, and twist and fry in lard.

Milk Toast—Boil a pint of rich milk with a tablespoon of butter, and one of flour. Have ready, in a dish, eight or ten slices of bread, toasted., Pour the milk over them hot, and cover it until it goes to the table.

Great Robbery and Failure.

On Thursday last Mr. Gordon McWilliams, who resides near this place, and who has for some years past, been engaged in buying and shipping stock to New York, Philadelphia, &c., returned from the latter place and reported that he had been robbed of $3,000 somewhere between that city and this place.

This announcement caused great excitement in the community and as he was largely involved, his sureties and other creditors demanded that he should secure them so far as his property would reach, which he done.

There are all sorts of stories afloat in regard to the matter, and days must elapse ere the truth will be made public. Many of our farmers hold his paper, from whom he had bought stock on time, and it is thus almost impossible to ascertain, with any certainty, the amount of his indebtedness; some put it at $15,000; others at $20,000.

Some few believe that he has been really robbed, whilst the great majority have no faith whatever in his story. Where the truth is between these two extremes, we cannot pretend to say.

Revivals.

We learn that a powerful revival of religion has been in progress for some time past in the Methodist Episcopal Church in Middletown, in this county, and that between twenty and thirty have united with the church.

We also learn that a religious awakening has taken place in Larue, in this county, and that quite a number have united with the Baptist Church of that place.

The protracted meeting which commenced in the Methodist Episcopal Church in this place some three weeks since, is still in progress, and quite a number have been converted.

Feb 17, 1859

Married.

On the 15th inst., at the residence of William J. Woods, Mr. William Simpson to Miss Lucetta Seiples, all of Marion co.

Mr. G. Williams.

This gentleman, by some strange perverseness of perception, conceives that in the paragraph in our last we intended to charge him with the commission of some heinous crime, though by what process of ratiocination he arrives at such a conclusion, we cannot imagine. We had no intention of doing him any injury, and we have yet to learn that our statement was false in any particular.

This being the case, we think him and his friends should stop and consider before they make themselves entirely ridiculous in the eyes of all sensible men. We have already stated to Mr. McW. that we had no intention of injuring him, and if after this, himself and his friends chose to consider us as their personal enemy, they can do so, but they will find that we are not to be deterred from stating the truth by threats of personal violence, loss of patronage, &c.

Died.

In this place on Saturday the 12th inst., of Putrid Sore Throat, Harvey, son of W.M. and Kate Hardy, aged 6 years and 9 months.

Thus, within the space of three short weeks, these parents have been bereaved of two beautiful and interesting children, and their fireside and hearts make desolate by the dispensation of Providence.

Feb 24, 1859

Died.

On the 8th inst., of chronic affection of the heart and lungs, Mrs. Sarah Bowdish, consort of Mr. Elijah Bowdish, aged about 66 years.

Mrs. Bowdish was among the early settlers of the county and leaves a large circle of friends and an affectionate family to mourn her loss. She, for many years, had been a member of the Free Will Baptist Church.

At his residence in Montgomery township, Marion county, Ohio, on the 14th inst., Mr. McMurray Johnson in the 76th year of his age.

Ground Hog Day.

Some of our cotemporaries have a good deal to say about "Ground Hog Day," lately, keeping up a senseless gabble about it, the weather, &c., &c. It appears to be of as much interest to them, almost, as that other great day—"All fool's Day!"

Married.

On the 17th inst., at the residence of the bride, Mr. William M. Thompson of Findlay, Ohio and Miss Eliza J. Livenspire of this place.

Mar 3, 1859

Retired.

Mr. S.A. Griswold, who has served as County Auditor for four years last past, retired on Tuesday last. We venture to say that no gentleman ever filled that office in this county who gave better satisfaction than Mr. G. Attentive, accommodating, careful of the public interest, correct in the discharge of his perplexing duties, we feel assured that the citizens of our county, without distinction of party, will regret his absence from the court house.

Married.

On the 24th ult., Mr. William Davis, formerly of Virginia, and Miss Margaret Metz, of this county.

Convicted.

Patrick Kelly, of this place, was convicted on Monday last, of keeping a place of public resort where liquors were sold to be drank on the premises. He has not been sentenced yet.

Marion Bakery.

Messrs. Wilson have added new facilities to their establishment and are prepared to supply Families with superb Bread, Cakes, Crackers, &c., on very reasonable terms. They have pitched that Billiard Table overboard, and the establishment is now conducted in a manner none can take offense at.

Street Crossings.

We hope our City Fathers, at their meeting this evening will devote some attention to the subject of Street Crossings. Some of them are in a wretched condition. For instance, those on the public square should be all taken up and laid down anew. In their present condition they are a nuisance and an annoyance to all who use them. Another fault is, that most of them are on a level with, or below the surface of the street, and the consequence is, that they are generally about as muddy as the street itself. Let them be put in good order for the use of the public.

A Bride and a Corpse.

On the 10th ult., Mr. John Bivens, of Middletown, in this Co., was married to Miss A.M. Tuck of Prattsville, Greene county, Ohio and in one hour and a half thereafter she was a corpse. Married to the husband of her choice, in so short a space, death claimed her as his bride, and bore her away from the husband of an hour.

Revival.

We learn from one of the members, that a revival has been in progress for some weeks past in the Allright Church, in Richland Tp., in this county, and some twelve or fourteen have been converted.

Mar 10, 1859

Married.

On the 1st inst., John W. Stayner and Miss Ellen Williams, all of Salt Rock, this county.

On the 2d inst., Samuel Shrigley and Miss Sarah J. Andrews, all of this county.

Accident.

Barney Hoes, formerly connected with C. Howard's Mill, in this place, but lately an employee of the Olentangy Iron Works, Delaware, Ohio, was severely, if not fatally injured, yesterday week, by the breaking of an engine whilst in motion.

Profitable Trip.

Mr. P. Lee and wife, of Salt Rock arrived in this place one day last week with a load of marketing which put into his purse over $100, of which they had prepared with their own hands, although the old gentleman has passed the three-score-and-ten post. This fact allows that our farmers can at least make good wages by raising family marketing, and we hope to see more of them engage in a business which cannot fail, at any time, to be highly remunerative.

The Grand Jury

Were in session all last week, and, we understand, disposed of an immense amount of business. Some thirty indictments of various crimes were found—a number unprecedented in the annals of the court. We were not aware that crime was on the increase in our midst, as this result would seem to indicate.

Imprisoned.

On Thursday last the Court of Common Pleas took up the case of Frederick S. Freese, convicted at the October term, 1858, of said Court, of keeping a place of public resort, where liquors were sold to be drank on the premises. Judge Lawrence ordered the sentence passed on defendant at said October term to be carried out, viz: Defendant to pay a fine of $50 and be imprisoned in the county jail twenty days. This created an intense excitement in the community, which was heightened by the announcement that defendant had escaped from the hands of the Sheriff. He was subsequently found by the Sheriff and taken to jail.

Threats were freely made that he should never go to jail—that the jail would be town down, &c, but, to the credit of our citizens, as a law abiding people, the officers were not interfered with nor was the jail molested. This was indicative of sound judgement, for, whatever we may, individually, think of the Liquor Law or any other law, it is our duty as good citizens, to obey its commands. And however hard we may think Mr. Freese's case, we should recollect that he has had a fair and impartial trial, and has been pronounced by a jury of his fellow citizens, guilty of violating the laws of his country.

Mar 17, 1859

Married.

On the 13th inst., Mr. John R. Garberson, Esq., Clerk of the Courts of Marion county and Miss Sarah Curtis.

Heavy Robbery.

We are sorry to learn that Mr. N.C. Mitchell treasurer of Claridon township in this county, was robbed of $500 belonging to the township, on last saturday night. The circumstances appending the robbery, as near as we can learn them, are as follows: Mr. M. had been absent from home quite late that evening drawing some deeds for some persons in the neighborhood. On returning home, he immediately went to bed, hanging his coat, in a side pocket of which was a memorandum book containing $600 of his own private funds, on a peg and laid his pants on or near the bed, they containing the $500 taken.

Some time during the night the mortar was picked out between the logs near the door, so as to admit of reaching in and shoving back the bolt. The thief or thieves then entered, and carried away the coat and pants. In taking down the coat, luckily the memorandum book and contents fell out on to the bed, and were overlooked. The coat was dropped outside the house near the gate, where it was found next morning. The pants were carried some distance farther, rifled of their contents, and left on the ground.

This was certainly a bold operation. So far as we can learn at present, no clue has yet been found which seems likely to lead to the detection of the person or persons engaged in this daring robbery.

Died.

In this township, on the 11th inst., Mary E., daughter of Abram and Ann Mouser, aged 17 years, 11 months and 14 days.

The Liquor Cases.

Patrick Kelly, convicted of a violation of the Liquor Law at the late term of Court, was sentenced to pay a fine of $50 and be imprisoned ten days. He is now serving out the sentence.

Martin Miller, Sr., convicted at the October Term, 1858, was also committed in pursuance of a sentence of ten days imprisonment and a fine of $50.

— Diebold, also convicted at the October Term, had the same sentence passed upon him. He has not yet been committed.

Wm. Carey's case was disposed of in like manner, with the exception that the forfeiture of his appearance bond was respited until the May Term.

Several cases were compromised by the defendants paying a fine of $50 and costs, and agreeing not to sell any more in violation of law.

Mar 24, 1859

Died.

In Marion, on the 15th inst., of congestion of the stomach and bowels, Mrs. Ann M., consort of Mr. James Davidson.

Mrs. Davidson has been a resident of Marion co., for nearly 30 years, and been a consistent member of the F. W. Baptist church a large portion of the time.

Thieves About.

We learn from our friend, C.B. Smith, on the corner of Main and North Streets that his smoke house was broken into on Saturday night last, and twelve pieces of meat—in all about 200 lbs—taken therefrom. He has no clue to the thieves, as yet, but we hope that they may be caught and brought to justice, as this sort of thing is becoming altogether too common in our town for comfort. Keep a sharp look out for your smoke house.

Apr 14, 1859

☞ The waters in this section of the State have been higher within a few days than they have been for some years previous.

Fire—Stable Burned—Diabolical Attempt at Incendiarism—Intense Excitement—Threats of Lynch Law!

On Thursday morning, about 4 o'clock A.M., our citizens were roused from their slumbers by the dead alarm of "Fire!" and on rushing out, the stable of Mr. John Siebert, on West street, was discovered to be on fire. The flames spread rapidly, and soon enveloped the whole building, rendering furtile all attempts to save it. When the fire first broke out, the wind was from the west, and it seemed almost certain that the flames would sweep through Capt. Hardy's premises, immediately adjoining on the east, and thus, reach the stores and warehouses on Main Street, when beyond all question, the destruction of property would have been immense. Fortunately, at this critical juncture, the wind veered round to the south-west, and thus the impending catastrophe was averted.

Soon after the fire commenced, three kegs of powder exploded, which had been stored for safe keeping in the stable, throwing firebrands, coals and sparks on to the Presbyterian Church, immediately north of the stable. In a moment the roof and steeple were blazing in several places, but by the superhuman exertions and daring of some of our citizens, the flames were extinguished and the church saved. Judge Bartram's residence, north of the church, also took fire but was saved. Thus, fortunately, the conflagration was confined to the building in which it commenced, though if the wind had not so providentially changed, the better portion of the business part of town would now be shouldering ruins. As it is, the loss does not exceed $500, on which there was no insurance.

The circumstances attending this fire were such as to leave no doubt in the minds of our citizens but that it had been kindled by the torch of the incendiary, and immediately upon their becoming known, the most intense excitement pervaded all classes, and threats were made by many if the fiend or fiends could be discovered Judge Lynch should pass upon their cases. These threats were not confined to any particular class, but were made by some of our most substantial citizens.

The excitement that created, was greatly intensified by the announcement about 9 o'clock A.M., that an attempt had also been made to burn the residence of T. Fahey on Main street. An "infernal machine," composed of powder, shavings, punk, or something like it, and paper, tied up with white wrapping cord, was found shoved in between the weather-boarding and plastering. It had been lighted, but, fortunately, had gone out without firing the building—Had it ignited the building, the loss of property would have been immense, and, in all probability, life, too, would have been lost. Within seven feet of where this torch was placed, five small children were sleeping, and if the fiends who placed it there had been successful in their hellish designs, a portion, if not all of them, would inevitably have been burned.

By this time the suspicions of our citizens had settled on two persons as the incendiaries, and, upon searching their usual haunt, a torch, *exactly* a fac similie in every respect of the one found under Fahey's house, was found in a back room. In addition, it was known to a portion of our citizens that these two persons, with some others, had been engaged in a drunken orgie the previous night, and had been undoubtedly in a situation to commit almost any crime which might cross their phrensied minds.

A warrant was consequently sworn out by John Siebert, before mayor Davids, and the officers arrested George Patridge, white,—an old penitentiary convict—and—Andrew Pierce, colored, his crony. While proceeding to the village prison with them, the officers were followed by a large crowd of our citizens, many of whom cried out, Lynch them. Lynch them! No attempt, however, was made to take them out of the hands of the officers.

About 10 A.M., they were taken in the court house for an examination before the Mayor. A large and excited crowd immediately filled the court room, and listened with breathless attention to the examination. J.H. Anderson, Esq., conducted the prosecution in an able manner, the prisoners had no counsel. A large number of witnesses were examined, but no evidence was elicited *directly* connecting the prisoners with the incendiarism, but circumstances were brought to light which leave but little doubt as to the guilt of the prisoners, and they were bound over for their appearance at the next term of the Court of Common Pleas in the sum of $1000 each; failing to give which, they were committed to the county jail.

Our town has long been infested with a class of men who bode no good to any community in which they settle. To clear these out should first be attended to. Steps should then be taken to effectually protect the town from the torch of the midnight incendiary and murderer. Efforts should then be made to elicit testimony in regard to this fire, and if the guilty ones have been arrested, to insure their conviction. This must be done, or it will not be long ere our beautiful village will fall a prey to a conflagration kindled by fiends in human form. Forewarned, forearmed! Let *honest* men combine and rid the town of penitentiary birds, and thus save it from destruction.

Marriages.

In Berwick on the 7th inst., Mr. Henry Bowdish and Miss Sarah Moore, both of Marion.

On the 7th inst., Mr. Paul G. Harvey to Miss Sarah E. Campbell, all of this township.

Death on the Cars.

On Saturday afternoon last a German whose name was afterwards ascertained to be Frederick Ackerman, took passage at Crestline on the B. & I. Railroad train for Indianapolis. Whilst in Galion, he was attacked with hemorhage of the Lungs. Soon after leaving there he was removed to the emigrant car, and the Conductor and a portion of the passengers paid him all the attention that the circumstances would admit of, but death ensued before the train reached this place, and those in charge of it left the body at the depot.

Upon learning of this fact, John Moore, Justice of the Peace for this township, acting as Coroner for the time being, immediately summoned a jury, and proceeded to hold an inquest on the body.

After examining one or two witnesses, Dr. Sweeney, who made a post mortem examination of the body, gave it as his opinion that death was caused by hemorhage of the lungs. The jury returned a verdict in accordance with these facts.

There was found upon the deceased something over $20 in money, three letters directed to Emil Harmon Meisser, Belleville, St. Claire Co, Ill., John Harmon, Ockoo P.O. Washington county, Ill., and Augustus Pentash, Nashville, Ockoo P.O. Ill. There was also a passport issued by one of the German Governments and a number of other articles. These were handed over to the Probate Judge to be disposed of as he sees proper.

The remains were buried in the new Cemetery on Sunday last.

The Fire.

Every good citizen should consider himself a special Vigilance Committee of one to ferret out and bring to justice the persons or persons who have recently attempted to burn the town. There should also be a reward of some magnitude offered for testimony that will point out and insure the conviction of the guilty ones. A few dollars had better be expended in this way, rather than suffer further and greater losses. Who will lead off in this manner.

Main Street.

We are glad to see that our business men on Main street are cleaning up the mud in front of their premises and having it hauled away. The spring trade will soon open, and our friends from the country will be glad to be able to do up their business in town without floundering through seas of filth.

Another thing: hot weather is approaching, and, for the health of the town, the mass of filth that now cumbers its streets and alleys should be cleaned up.

Apr 21, 1859

Our County Infirmary.

Upon inquiry, we learn from Superintendent Jones, that the number of paupers now supported at public charge in the County Infirmary is twenty-five. This is a large number, when the sparseness of the population of the county is considered, and their support is a burden upon our tax payers not easy to be borne.

Marriages.

On the 31st, Isaiah C. Jones to Miss J. Hinaman, both of this county.

On the same day, Mr. John W. Malone to Miss Catherine Burtsfield, all of this county.

On the same day, at the residence of John Cunningham, Esq., Joseph Uncapher to Miss Kesiah Cunningham, all of this county.

On the 17th inst., Samuel Snyder Jr., to Miss Adaline Haine, both of Marion Co., O.

News.

Items of interest are as scarce this week as white black birds. If someone would only hang themselves, shoot some body else, or run away with some other body's wife, or set a house on fire, or steal a horse, it would greatly relieve us, and place us under a thousand obligations.

☞ Two or three persons have lately left this place for Pike's Peak. They are the only ones that we know of, who have left this county for that region, as the fever does not rage very extensively here.

Barn Burned.

The large barn on the farm of widow McClain, near Bowsherville, was struck by lightning on the evening of the 16th inst., and entirely consumed. There were two horses in the barn at the time, one of which was burned to death and the other severely injured.

Curious.

A piece of brown paper, folded and placed between the upper lip and gum, will stop bleeding at the nose almost instantaneously.

Accidents.

Major W.E. Hardy, of this place, was thrown from his horse, on Monday last, and severely though not dangerously injured.

And a man named Gracely was also thrown from his horse on Friday last, and his head badly cut.

A woman from the region of Berwick, attempted to steal a lot of goods from Lucas & Sefner's store on Saturday last, but was caught in the act, and, after being admonished, was allowed to leave. She had far better pay two prices for her finery, than procure it in that way.

May 5, 1859

The New market Ordinance,

Went into effective operation on Monday last, and the butchers, we understand, have all taken stalls in the new Market House. All fresh meat, poultry, eggs, butter, fruit, and vegetables sold within the corporate limits on Market days—Tuesdays, Thursdays and Saturdays of each week—must be sold at the market house, within the regular market hours, which are established as follows: From 5 to 9 o'clock A.M. from the 1st of April to the 1st of October, and from 6 to 10 o'clock, A.M. from the 1st of October to the 1st day of April.

Persons who have attended market during market hours, and who have produce undisposed of, have the privilege of selling it after market hours. The sale of fresh meat by the quarter, and potatoes and apples in quantities of five bushels and upwards is not prohibited however. Persons violating the Market Ordinance are subject to a fine of not less than one nor more than ten dollars.

We hope our farmers and others, who have produce to sell, will make it a point to attend the market regularly, as we are satisfied the interest of both classes will be largely enhanced by thus bringing the producer and consumer together, as the per centage of all go betweens is thus saved.

May 12, 1859

Obituary.

Died on the 26th inst., of Typhoid fever at the residence of his brother-in-law, Dr. J.H. Carpenter, John M. Anderson, son of John Anderson, Esq., of this place in the 20th year of his age.

May 19, 1859

☞ Can any of our readers give us any information in regard to the far-famed Hungarian Grass? When, and how should it be planted? how much will it yield per acre, and where can the pure seed be obtained? Who can give us any information upon these points? Answer soon or it will be too late to do any good this season.

Died.

In Waldo Township, on the 8th inst., of erysipelas, John Moses, in the 90th year of his age.

Matrimonial.

By an examination of the record, we learn that the Probate Judge of this county, has issued 40 marriage licenses since the 1st day of January last. So we suppose that during that time eighty persons have left the State of Ohio and gone to the State of matrimony. Joy go with them.

☞ Those of our farmers who have vegetables, poultry, butter, eggs, &c., to sell, should make it a point to attend the village market, where they can dispose of their stuff readily, without the trouble of peddling it around, and at highly remunerative prices.

May 26, 1859

Desperate Assault.

On Sunday evening last, about half past nine o'clock, Filander Pierce assaulted his wife on the streets near the public square with a slung shot, or some other murderous weapon. The woman was beat and bruised in a most shocking manner, and there is little doubt but that he would have killed her if others had not come to her rescue. One of these, a young man, was compelled to flee for his life, as the drunken fiend turned all his rage upon him for interfering to prevent him killing his wife. After some trouble, Pierce was arrested by the village Marshal, and committed to the village prison.

Married.

On the 22 inst., in Green Camp Township, Mr. John J. Cade and Miss Christena Hawkins, all of this county.

Jun 2, 1859

Attempt to Break Jail.

Patridge and Strode, who are confined in the same cell in our county jail, made an attempt to regain their freedom on Thursday evening last, between 11 and 12 o'clock. Fortunately, Sheriff Lewis heard them at the work, and calling assistance, he soon had them secured again. An hour longer would probably have let them out.

Married.

On the 13th, at Wis., Mr. Osten March to Miss Harriet G. Lane of Marion co., O.

Jun 9, 1859

Home Again.

C.W. Brown, of this place, who started for Pike's Peak some weeks since, after traveling some hundreds of miles across the Plains, and meeting with hundreds of half-starved wretches on their way back from the mines, returned to the States again, and arrived here a few days ago, fully satisfied with his gold hunting experience.

Heavy Frost.

On Sunday night last, a heavy frost fell in this region, destroying gardens in a terrible manner. Beans, tomatos, corn, potatos, &c., were thoroughly cooked and looked as if they had been scorched by fire.

We fear, indeed we know, that an immense amount of damage has been done in the corn fields in which the corn was up. Thousands and tens of thousands of acres will have to be re-planted. Fortunately, there is time to do this, and by Saturday evening next, the ground will be nearly re-planted. A great many fields in which the corn was not yet up, have, of course, escaped. That which has been killed can be re-planted, and then it will be from fifteen to twenty days ahead of the crop of last year.

We fear that a great deal of the wheat has been killed, as much of it was just in blossom, and therefore, easily killed. In many fields the heads are pretty well filled, and where this is the case, we do not think much damage has been done.

Another Change.

Another change has been made in the *Mirror* establishment, Mr. Osborne having sold his interest to a Mr. Hodder, who assumes control of the editorial department. We wish both the outgoing and incoming editors all kinds of success but political.

Jun 16, 1859

☞ On yesterday morning the boarders at the Marion Hotel, were surprised to find that their landlord, one Smith, was missing, together with his clerk, who was his father-in-law. It was soon ascertained that Smith had taken the 5 A.M. train for the east, and has probably gone to parts unknown.

We understand that he has left many of our citizens in the lurch for small amounts. We do not know what arrangements have been made in regard to the matter, but we notice that the house is open, and business going on as usual. Marion is a fast town, decidedly.

General Jail Delivery— Escape of Strode and Partridge—$100.

On Wednesday night last, George Strode, confined in our county jail on a charge of burglary and George Patridge, confined on two charges of arson and attempted arson effected their escape, and have gone to parts unknown. The manner in which they made their escape shows the most determined perseverance, indomitable courage and superior mechanical skill. They were confined together in the western cell on the first floor. They first bored off a portion of the two inch plank with which the cells are sheeted all over. They had next to cut off two pieces of timber 9 inches square, which was done in the most efficient manner, the auger cutting as true as a die. Between this timber and the ground on which the jail stands, there is a space of some eighteen inches or two foot. This was filled with small stones and cemented together with water lime. This they dug through till they reached the foundation wall nearly in the center of the building and running east and west. Burrowing through with herculean labor, they worked on till they reached the western wall of the building which they did under the door of the hall entering the Sheriff's department from the cells. Piercing through this wall, they shoved the steps aside and were free.

The first intimation the sheriff had of the escape was the next morning when the attendant of the cells informed him that these two prisoners refused to receive the water for their morning ablation. He immediately passed around the building to see if they had broke out. He passed around it twice before he discovered their place of exit, when noticing that the steps did not occupy their usual position, and there discovered what he was in search of, and upon examining the cell it presented the appearance of a stone quarry, there being at least a wagon load of stone if not more piled within it. The bed tick upon which they slept was full of the chips made by boring through the timber. Around the cell the following documents were found which evidence great deliberation on the part of the fugitives if nothing else;

Take Notice,

Do not think hard of us because we take the leave of you Sheriff you have treated us well but do not think hard of us for doing what we have God knows we worked hard for our liberty and should not like to do the same over we have been five days accomplishing our design being as the wheat crops have failed we thought it was enough for the county to do to board our friends upstairs for my part i am not guilty of that mean act of burning and i hope when I am guilty of that trick I will be lynched.

Good day or night

George Partridge

I am not going away because I am afraid to stand my trial it is because I do not want to lay in this limestone cell I want to be out to breathe the sweet fresh air and to carry the comforts of this yielding summer o sweet liberty there is nothing to equal it god knows i am not guilty of that cursed mean trick of burning property i hope the man or men or persons that did burn this barn that I am blamed for will be found out and have to suffer the worst penalty of the law I do not blame anyone for taking me up but blame the prosecuting attorney for putting our trial off.

George Partridge

We went out at about 9 o'clock on the 8th of june I leaver my respects to John and Mary for their kindness They gave us all we wanted to eat and drink.

George Partridge

I have studied the matter over and I have come to the conclusion leg bail is the bail i can give so farewell.

George Partridge

It will be noticed that in the first epistle Partridge says that they were five days in breaking out. We can hardly think this is true, for on the day previous to their escape the

Sheriff directed his assistant to swept their cell clean in every part, which the latter declares he faithfully done and he failed to notice anything unusual about the floor or elsewhere. If they were five days in effecting their design the floor must have been cut and many of the cemented stones loosened on the day the Sheriff's assistant swept the cell. How was this concealed from him. There is nothing in the appearance of the timbers and planking which solves this problem.

The only tool the prisoners had to work—or the only one they left behind was an auger two inches in diameter, which was so fixed that it would answer for boring or picking. This was probably furnished by some friends outside, as the windows of the jail outside and in the cells are so arranged that tools, &c. could be easily passed in. If they had other tools they carried them away with them, as no others can be found on the premises.

The county commissioners being in session, they immediately informed the Sheriff to offer a reward of $100 for the arrest of the two and their return to the county jail. It is to be hoped that they will both be returned to their old quarters soon, as they are both dangerous and vicious men.

Jun 23, 1859

Died.

on the 14th inst., Mary Frances, daughter of William F. and Mary Harvey, in the 12th year of her age.

Recapture of Partridge.

On Friday evening last, George Partridge, who, in company with Strode, escaped from our county Jail on the night of the 8th inst., was returned to his old quarters, having been recaptured at Delphos, in Van Wert county. At our request, he wrote out the following account of his escape and recapture, which we judge to be not far from the truth:

As there are so many different stories told about the length of time Strode and myself were at the work of boring and digging out of the Marion Jail, I will now make a true statement of the whole affair. On the third of June we first spoke of getting out under the floor. Strode said he was a carpenter, and he knowed it was not going to be much of a job to bore through the floor, for, said he, the joist that the floors system are one foot and a half apart and two inches thick. So I concluded that if such was the case, we were just as good as out. So we kept on talking and planning until the next Tuesday, the 7th of June, when we commenced work. I went to tuning the old fiddle and Strode went to whetting his auger. He spat on his hands and I rosited my bow, and I played while Strode bored in order to drown the sound of the auger. No person could have heard the auger at work, nor even have mistrusted that such work was going on, Strode bored a few holes, and to our great astonishment, we found the job more difficult than Strode, the carpenter, apprehended.

We found the joist that he spoke of as being a foot and a half apart and two inches thick, a foot square and close together. We went on with our work a while on this day, the 7th, and then we gathered up every shaving that was to be seen, and put them in our straw bed, and then we put some old clothes we had over the place that we were boring through, so that no man could have proved any thing of the kind. There is no person that would of mistrusted any such thing as boring through the floor the way we had it fixed. We also had our boots throwed under the bed carelessly. We then put our works off until Wednesday, the 8th that sheriff and his hired hand came in our cell and swept out under the bed but that did not disturb the old clothes and boots which he nor no other man would think it any use to move because there is the place where dirty clothes is most always kept. The hole that we put through the floor is under the head of the bed and in the back corner. We did not lift the logs out until after the Sheriff and his man had been in and done what they do every morning or every other morning, that is, sweep out and attend to the buckets. We then on the afternoon of the 8th, lifted the logs out and commenced working at the stone. We found the stone loose, so that we made great headway through the wall. We made no noise that could be heard, for the stone were easily moved. While Strode was at work, I could listen to see if I could hear him at work, but I could not; nor could he hear me when I was at work.

We made our escape the same evening about 10 o'clock. Put all our work together, and we were but very little over a day breaking out. The note I left stated that were "five days in accomplishing our design," by which I did not mean that we were at work for 5 days but that we were that length of time doing the wind work. The Sheriff was very watchful; indeed, more so than any sheriff I have ever been under, and you all know that I have had the good luck to be elected a number of times and he gives the men under his control plenty to eat and drink just such as his own table affords. For my part, I have boarded with Sheriff Lewis a great deal, and I always found him very strict about the jail and he was always through the jail every day to see if things were all right. There is no sheriff that is going to pull the bed out every day and move the old shirts, and scratch all over the floor to see if he can find a place where there is a hole bored through. It is the last thing any man would think of doing, and no one could blame Sheriff Lewis for our escape. Because there was no noise made, and most of the work was done after he had made his daily visit. This is all true, and you can judge for your selves whether any one should be blamed. It is true that Strode and myself dug out, and it is just as true that I got in again, easier than I got out. I seen hard times when I was out wandering around in the night and lying in the woods, with no company but the mosquitos, which are always ready to take the last drop of blood a poor devil has.

Geo. Partridge.

Jul 7, 1859

Frost-Something Unparalleled.

Sunday night last was a cold one—cold enough, at least, to make fires necessary to comfort. The wind blew from the north and seemed laden with the frosts of winter rather than the balmy zephyrs of mid summer. And the early riser on Monday morning found the fences, &c, covered with a heavy white frost. Fortunately the earth retained sufficient warmth to enable it to throw off the frost and convert it into dew, or we might again be mourning over the destruction of the corn crop and garden vegetables. This is certainly a remarkable season so far. It excels any that we remember for years for its coldness.

The Fourth

Passed off very quietly, so far as this place was concerned. The Firemen turned out, and had a short parade. A large number of persons visited Boyce's Garden, and passed the time very pleasantly admiring its beauties. Business was generally suspended during most of the day, most of our establishments being closed.

The most attractive feature of the day, was the School Exhibition and Pic Nic, on the farm of Mr. M. Page, in the north western portion of this township. The schools which took part, were taught by Misses Warner, Gorton and Connoyer, and we are assured by gentlemen who were present, that the pupils evinced the most thorough training, and reflected the greatest credit upon their teachers by the correctness with which they discharged their tasks.

Prof. Olmsted, of our Union school, delivered an eloquent address, to which the immense crowd numbering 1,500 to 2,000 listened with the most rapt attention. Everything passed off with the utmost decorum, and all who were present were highly satisfied with the manner in which they had been entertained.

Jul 14, 1859

Sunday School Pic Nic.

On Wednesday of last week, the M.E. Sunday School. of this place, went on a Pic Nic Excursion to a beautiful grove some two miles this side of Galion.

The officers of the B. & I. Railroad furnished a special train for the occasion upon such treasonable terms as to put it within the power of every member of the School to par-

ticipate in the festivities of the occasion, and some 100 Teachers, Scholars and visitors took part in the same. The day was very pleasant, and the little folks returned home highly delighted with the pleasant re-union.

Not the least accident occurred, and by 5 o'clock P.M. all the scholars reached their homes safe and sound.

Those who planned and conducted the excursion, are entitled to great credit for the manner in which it passed off, and we hope such excursions may be made as often as once a year at least.

Married.

On the 6th inst., Mr. John S. Dudley of Marion township and Miss Sarah A. Randall of Marion.

Deaths.

Died—At his residence in Richland township, in this county on the 26th ult., Wm. Fisher, aged 52 years.

The disease which caused his death was that known as Milk Sickness. His brother is Dr. Fisher.

On the 30th ult., Silas Bennett, adopted child of William and Ann Eliza Fisher in the 11th year of his age.

On the 8th inst., Ann Eliza, relict of William Fisher, aged 35 years.

Extraordinary Fatality.

The circumstances attending the death of Mr. Wm. Fisher, which event is recorded in another column of to day's paper, were such as to demonstrate in the most forcible manner the malignancy of that mysterious disease popularly known as "Milk Sickness" or the "Trembles." His tenant named Gilson, was first attacked, and died. Mr. F. himself was the next victim, and then his wife and two adopted children were taken ill. Of these three cases two terminated fatally, and the last advices we had from there stated that Mrs. Gilson, wife of the first victim, was just breathing her last,—five cases out of six having a fatal termination. The best medical skill our country affords was exerted in behalf of the unfortunate family, but their systems had become so thoroughly saturated with the deadly poison that the remedies employed seemed to have no effect whatever.

These unexpected deaths have spread a deep gloom over the neighborhood in which they occurred, as Mr. Fisher and his family were very highly respected by all who had the pleasure of their acquaintance.

Jul 21, 1859

☞ Last Monday was a scorcher. The sun seemed to fairly blaze, whilst the *pave* felt as though heated by internal fires. Oh, for a dashing, revivifying shower.

An Old Settler Gone.

Mr. David Bush, one of the oldest settlers of this part of the State, died in this place on Sunday night last.

Drowned.

A young man named Ponser was drowned in Rush Creek, Bowling-green Tp., this county, on last Sunday week, whilst bathing.

Jul 28, 1859

Large Timothy.

Mr. B.F. Shoots, of Grand Prairie Tp., brought into our office last week a head of timothy which measured 12½ inches in length. Considering the extreme drouth which has so long parched our pastures and meadows, this is an extraordinary growth, and we doubt whether it can be beat in the county.

Married.

On the 23th inst., at the residence of Mr. Plummer, Mr. Jacob Boyer and Miss Elizabeth Snyder, both of Pleasant township, this county.

Aug 4, 1859

Sheep Killed—Heavy Tax.

By the Assessor's returns to the county Auditor, we learn that during the year previous to the last assessment of personal property, there were killed and wounded in this county, by dogs, the following number of sheep:

Killed,	999
Wounded,	791
Total,	1790

These sheep were valued at $2,248, and that amount may be set down as the Dog Tax paid yearly by the farmers of Marion county. And still the Legislature will not levy a tax on the worthless curs that cause this immense loss.

☞ No recent occurrence has caused as much regret in this community as the death, on Saturday last, of Mr. Jacob Mouser, lately connected with the Stock Bank of this place. He was a young man who possessed the faculty of endearing himself to those with whom he associated, in a more than ordinary degree. His death is universally regretted. Peace be to his ashes.

Aug 11, 1859

Accident.

Mr. William Baker, formerly a resident of this township, but now of Big Island, and his daughter, were both severely injured by being kicked by a horse a few days since. They are both recovering.

☞ A Hurricane passed over a portion of Big Island township a few days since, destroying fences, hay stacks, fruit and forest trees in its track. The house of Mr. Metts was partially unroofed by it.

Aug 18, 1859

Probably Fatal Affray.

A desperate fight came off on the Railroad track near Caledonia last week, between two men named respectively Ozenbaugh and Young. The cause of the quarrel was a pint flask, and both were said to have been drunk at the time. They quarreled as to which should get the flask filled. They were seen to fight two or three different times, and soon after Young was found with his skull badly shattered, his nose broken, several of his teeth knocked out, and bleeding profusely. He was removed to Caledonia and his wounds dressed.

Subsequently a warrant was issued by Esq. Underwood of Claridon Tp., for his arrest upon a charge of assault and battery. Upon his examination, it was proved that Young assaulted Ozenbaugh first, and, therefore the latter was discharged.

At the time of our last advice from him, Young was pretty low, and his recovery is very doubtful. Should he die, Ozenbaugh will probably have to attend his trial upon a more serious charge than that upon which he has already been examined.

Aug 25, 1859

Sudden Death.

On Tuesday morning last, Mr. Simon Huggins, an old and esteemed citizen of this county, residing a short distance east of this place was found lying in his doorway, apparently in a fit, and in a short time thereafter he died. He leaves a large circle of friends and relatives to mourn his loss.

Married.

On the 4th inst., Mr. John T. Little of Springfield, O., and Miss Harriet Morgan, of Montgomery Tp., this county.

On the 20th inst., at the United States Hotel in Marion, Mr. Charles P. Meinger and Miss Eliza Ann Hart, both of Caledonia, Marion county.

Sep 1, 1859

Died.

In Marion on the 27th ult., of a disease of the throat, Emma Louise, oldest daughter of Daniel E. and Sarah Krause, aged 11 years, 5 months and 17 days.

Brilliant Display.

A brilliant display of the auroro borealis, or northern lights, took place on Sunday night last. The bright flashes shot up from the northwest and northeast until they met in the zenith, rendering the evening as luminous as if the queen of night was shining in her glory. The display attracted universal attention, and was beautiful beyond expression.

Serious Accident.

On Thursday last whilst they were engaged in repairing Mr. Jameson's Cabinet Shop the scaffold gave way under them, and precipitated to the ground Mr. Burt Cooper, and Mr. J. Sosey, the distance being some fifteen to twenty feet. Fortunately Mr. S. caught his arm upon a cross-piece, which broke his fall somewhat, or he might have been seriously injured, as he struck the ground with such force as to burst his boots.

Mr. Cooper struck the ground with such force as to severely injure his spine. He was taken up insensible and carried to his mother's residence, and medical aid procured. He soon revived, and is now doing as well as could be expected.

An Artesian Well.

Mr. Geo. Rhoades, of Big Island Tp., informs us that in digging a well on his farm in Salt Rock Township, he was fortunate enough to secure a perfect Artesian Well with but very little expense. He dug down sixteen feet, and then bored twenty feet more when suddenly the auger dropped down about six inches, and upon taking it out, the water followed so rapidly as to fill the well. He has since inserted a wooden pipe in the bore, and the stream is so strong as to throw the water three feet above the surface of the ground. It certainly is a valuable acquisition to friend R's farm.

Mayors Court.

On Wednesday last week a man named Gillett was arrested for violating the Market Ordinance. The Recorder, in the absence of the Mayor, fined him one dollar and costs.

☞ The brilliant phenomena of Sunday night seems to have been caused by electricity, as the telegraphic wires over a large area of country became so charged with it, as to prevent the transmission of dispatches.

Sep 8, 1859

New Mayor.

Dr. Fisher, having resigned his post as Mayor, the Council appointed J.E. Davids in his stead. Mr. D. has accepted the appointment and entered upon the duties of his office.

Married.

At her father's residence near Little Sandusky, on Thursday the 1st inst., Mr. David S. Bretz of Marion Co., to Miss Jane Ann Coon of Wyandot Co.

Sep 22, 1859

Died.

In this place, on the 10th inst., of Consumption, Elizabeth, consort of John Hughes, aged 52 years.

She was a woman of strong mind—pleasant in her intercourse with others, and was greatly beloved by a wide circle of friends who feel that in her death they have sustained an irreparable loss.

On the 10th inst., of Dyspepsia, at the residence of Mr. Walter Williams, in Allenton, Mo., Mrs. T.D. Clark, aged 39 years, 11 months and 10 days.

Mrs. Clark had been a citizen of this place thirty-four years.

An Irish Row

Occurred on Monday last at the Grocery of Father Kelly, on the corner of East and North streets, near the Depot, in which several awful black eyes were given through the medium of steel knuckles, &c. The authorities should see that the parcipitators in these disgraceful exhibitions are severely punished.

Pickpockets About.

During the fair, the swell mob gentry were quite active in carrying on their nefarious business. On the second day, a Mrs. Hornby was robbed of $45 in money and notes to the amount of $700; Mrs. Uncapher of $6, and Mrs. Coonrod of $8, besides some others whose names we did not learn. No arrests were made as there was no clue to guide the officers in their effort to fetter out the light-fingered gentry.

P.S.—On the last day, we are informed, some four or five others paid tribute to the skill of those thievish gentry, among whom were our friends D.H. Harvey and T. Harvey, the former in the amount of $19, and the latter about $5.

Serious Accident.

On Friday last a child of Mr. J.L. Smith, who resides about one and a half miles east of this place, about two years old, was attacked by a sow, and so severely bitten that its life is despaired of. He would, undoubtedly, have been killed had not his little brother came to his rescue, who succeeded in driving off the furious beast.

Married.

On the 20th inst., in this place, Mr. Oscar D. German, of Mt. Gilead, and Miss Ann Randall of this place.

Our county Fair.

This annual Jubilee of our Agriculturalists and Merchants commenced on Wednesday of last week. The weather was propitious throughout, indeed, too much so for a moderate shower would have added to the general comfort of the crowd present by laying the clouds of dust which filled the air.

The show of stock, mechanical and agricultural products was very good, though probably not much in advance of other years. The frosts and drouth of the past summer, if they had no other effect, discouraged our farmers, so that competition in several classes was not so keen as it would have been. But still, after making a proper allowance for these, the show of vegetables, fruits and cereals was excellent. Nicer potatoes never tickled the palate of the epicure with their mealy treasures, whilst pumpkins, squashes, beets, melons, onions, &c., DEMANDED euconiums from the passer-by upon their mammoth proportions. Huge ears of corn gave abundant promise of the plentiful crop which is just now ripening on our luxuriant plains, and plump grained Mediterranean and white wheat hinted at the snow white loaves which will crown our boards dung the coming year, notwithstanding the disastrous visitation of the Fourth of June last.

The exhibition of horses was peculiarly excellent, and visitors from other counties were forced to acknowledge that in that department we were equal, if not superior to any county in this section of our State.

In cattle, sheep, &c., of course the show was good, though not better than at some previous Fairs nor do we think as many animals were exhibited as last year, owing to certain causes of which many are cognizant. Our county is peculiarly a stock county and self interest will compel our farmers to make use of every means in their power to increase the value of their stock.

But one competitor appearing to contend for the premiums offered, the exhibition of Lady's equestrianism was uninteresting and excited no interest whatever.

The exercises closed with a foot race for a purse of $6, which was contended for by five or six young men, who, at the end of the round, looked as if they had been rolled in corn meal and powdered with buck wheat flour.

The receipts, we learn, were about $560, being the largest amount ever received at any one Fair since the organization of the Society.

Sep 29, 1859

Accident.

A little boy of Mr. Britton's fell down W.H. More's steps on Monday last and severely gashed his forehead.

Married.

On the 27th inst., at New Caanan, Conn., Mr. A.H. Kline of this place and Miss Louisa M. Hutton of the former state.

Oct 6, 1859

Our County Jail!

As some of the voters of the county are inclined to blame Sheriff Lewis for the escaping of prisoners from our Jail, we have been to the trouble of hunting up the evidence that those escapes arose more from the defective construction of the building than from the Sheriff's carelessness or neglect of duty. This statement is borne out by the fact that prisoners have escaped under every Sheriff, nearly, that has charge of the Jail since its construction. Nor do prisoners only escape only from the Marion county jail. The Jail of Morrow county is constructed upon the same plan exactly that ours is here, and prisoners are constantly escaping from it.

Epler vs. Lewis.

The last *Mirror* makes a desperate onslaught upon Sheriff Lewis, because of the escape of Sparks, Strode and Partridge. He had better let that matter alone, because Epler has a record of escapes that has not quite passed out of memory. During his service two prisoners, one named Weirick, and another whose name is not recollected, made their escape together by making a wooden key and unlocking the door with it. Weirick was subsequently re-arrested by C. Martin, of this place, E. Barton, now Sheriff of Morrow county, and another person. The other one, we believe, was never recaptured.

But, during Epler's service there was another escape took place which, up to this day, has never been explained. A black-leg named Wilson, was arrested for passing counterfeit money at the card-table, He made his escape from the jail, and did not leave a single mark to indicate how he got out. The floor was not bored through; he did not dig through the walls; the bars were not cut off; no false key was made, nor was the lock picked, nor any of the usual modes of jail-breaking resorted to, and yet he got out, and the question is, how did he get out! Every prisoner who has got out under Sheriff Lewis, has left some mark to show how he got out, but, this man Wilson did not, and, to this day, the mystery remains as impenetrable as ever.

Married.

At the United States House on the 2d inst., R.S. Rice to Miss Cordelia Fickel, all of Marion township.

Carriages for the Sick and Infirm.

The Republicans of every township have carriages provided to bring out the sick and infirm who may not otherwise be able to come.

Mammoth Sweet Potatos.

For twenty years past, our old friend Jesse Walker, has been famous in these parts for his superior Sweet Potatoes and mammoth melons. A few days ago he presented himself at our office door, with two monstrous Sweet Potatoes, which he presented to the printer, well knowing that he had no money to buy such luxuries. Having the curiosity to ascertain how much they weighed, we tried them, one weighing two pounds and one ounce and the other two ounces heavier.

The Fogies in Office!
From Everlasting to Everlasting!
WILSON, EPLER, HAIN!

Since the adjournment of the Democratic County Convention, we have been searching among the musty records in the court house to prepare a history of the official sops what have been gulped down in this county by the three inveterate office-holders named above, but, in truth, we had to go so far back in the history of the county that we almost got beyond the purview of the records. We found that these three men, during a generation past, have almost constantly either been in office or seeking office. The first named above, Richard Wilson, has been a pensioner upon the people's treasury so long that "the memory of man runneth not to the contrary!" He first makes his appearance upon the county records as an office-seeker in 1833, more than a quarter of a century ago, when he was elected County Treasurer. From that day up till TO DAY, he has almost annually, presented himself for some portion of official droppings.If he is re-elected Representative (of which, however, there is not much probability) and serves his term out, he will have held office altogether

TWENTY-SIX YEARS!

Or during the life-time, almost, of a generation of men. One would think that being in office for a generation, would satisfy any reasonable man, but after serving that long, this man presents himself before the people this Fall for another two-years lease of Office. Voters of Marion County, have you not done enough for him?

DAVID EPLER.

This man's official history extends back even further than does that of Wilson, and commences in 1830.

For TWENTY-NINE YEARS past, with the exception of short intervals, he has been fattening upon official spoils, until he seems to think that he ought to have a perpetual suck at the public teat!

Every young Democrat in the county should ponder well these figures. Epler, Wilson and Hain can hold office year after year and year after year for the life-time of a generation, they seeming to think it a matter of course, but if such men as Cricket, Woolly, Biggerstaff or Guthrey present themselves for a small share of the support of the party, these inveterate office-holders and their friends, shove them aside saying, "you can't run;" you must stand back till we and our administrators and their administrators are dead, and then, if our ghosts don't return, you may have a chance to get a nomination. It makes no difference how well qualified you are, we old Hunkers here in town won't support you, and you must stand back, But to go on with our record of these old suckers:

HENRY HAIN

Although a younger man in politics than the other two, yet Henry, if he lives, bids fair to hang on to the public teat about as long as any of 'em. He held office and has been a candidate since 1843.

Thus we see that these three men have actually held office in this county

FORTY-FIVE YEARS!

Or nearly half a century, and if they had been elected every time they were candidates and had served their times out they would have been in office

SEVENTY-TWO YEARS!

Their day, however, is now past, and this Fall they will be laid on the shelf for good. Mark that!

Oct 13, 1859

Marion County Election.
Entire Republican Ticket Defeated, save Representative and Coroner!

This morning we have the disagreeable duty of announcing the defeat of our entire county ticket on Tuesday last, with the exception of Representative and Coroner.

Mr. J.A. Carter, for Representative, has a majority of 20, and Mr. B. Little, for Coroner, a majority of 40. Dr. T. B. Fisher, for Senator, has a majority of 3 in the county, also. Sheriff W.B. Lewis is defeated by 5 votes. The rest of the County Ticket is defeated by majorities ranging from 50 to 165.

For this untoward result, the Republicans alone are to blame. If they had all voted the straight Ticket, and had all came out to vote, our Ticket would have been elected by the usual majority. Another great cause of our defeat was the importance of Irish votes. In this township alone, some forty or fifty Irishmen voted who were utter strangers to our oldest citizens. Whisky was as free as water for them all day long, and, brutally drunk, they were led up to the polls like so many cattle, a Locofoco ticket put into their hands, and they compelled to vote it.

Married.

On the 9th inst., James Davidson and Mrs. Sarah J. Miller, all of this place.

Oct 20, 1859

Sunday School in Marion Co.

By an article from the pen of W.H. Dyer, Agent of the American Sunday School Union, left in our office some time since, which was unfortunately mislaid, we gather the following facts in regard to the Sunday Schools of this county, the denominations to which they belong; their number and the number of scholars enrolled in each one:

No.	Denominations	Teachrs	Scholars
1	Christian	3	42
1	Disciple	6	40
1	Episcopal	6	40
2	Free Will Baptist	11	75
7	German schools of different denominations	39	264
11	Meth. Episcopal	95	700
1	Prot. Methodist	5	40
1	Presbyterian	14	70
6	United Brethren	49	246
11	Union Sun. Schls	83	495
43		307	2010

A Natural Curiosity.

Mr. Nelson Walker of Pleasant Township, brought us a roll of butter weighing 1¼ th lbs., made from the milk of a heifer 2½ years old, that has never had a calf! Of this latter fact he can speak with entire certainty, as he has had possession of the heifer from the time it was calved. The butter was yellow and rich, and tasted as natural as any other butter we ever tasted.

Oct 27, 1859

Married.

In Marion, on the 25th inst., Edward L. Palmer of Baltimore, Md., and Miss Susan C. Boyd of Marion.

Died.

At Marion, on the 20th inst., of Consumption, Miss Anna Elizabeth Holmes, at the early age of 21 years.

The memory of so gentle and lovely one who has so lately fallen in our midst, should not be allowed to fade from memory without some tribute to her unobtrusive virtues. She possessed great natural reserve of character. It was natural for her to draw a thin veil between herself and the world.

Fond and affectionate mother, who so long and uneaasily ministered to your affected one, rejoice that she is gathered as a lamb to the bosom of her Saviour.

In this township, on the 15th inst., of putrid sore throat, David, son of Benjamin D. and Patsy Pettit, aged seven years, two months and two days.

David was a sprightly, amiable child who had endeared himself to a large circle of friends by his generous and affectionate disposition.

The Harper's Ferry Affair.

This is one of the most astounding affairs on record! That a mere handful of mad fanatics should attempt to revolutionize two large and powerful States, is sufficient evidence of their insanity to place the affair in its proper light.

The attempt of a few dishonest Locofoco papers to stigmatize the Republican party on account of this outbreak, will only be laughed to scorn by honest men of all parties. Not one of the insurgents nor their abettors, so far as their names have been made public, have ever belonged to the Republican party, but, on the contrary, some of them have been its most bitter opponents. As for the leader of the expedition, Capt. John Brown, he has long been regarded by those most intimate with him as a monomaniac in the full sense of the term, made such by the Border Ruffians of Missouri. One of his boys was put to death by these hell-hounds after being tortured in every conceivable manner, and from that time his father has sworn vengeance upon slaveholders everywhere.

Therefore, the Border Ruffians of Missouri, headed by "drunken Davy Atchison," and backed by Presidents Pierce and Buchanan, are responsible for this outbreak of fanaticism, and for it they should be held to a strict account.

Nov 3, 1859

Married.

In Green camp Township, on the 30th ult., Mr. Trenton C. Grigsby of Prospect Township, and Miss Elizabeth Humphries of the former place.

Nov 10, 1859

Crowded.

Our streets were JAMMED on last Saturday with vehicles and horses, and it was a general remark that there had not been as many people in town on an ordinary day for a year as there was on last Saturday. Our business places were all crowded, and a large amount of money changed hands. The indications are that the season of stagnation is over, and that we will have better times hereafter. Do make it be.

Pot Shooters—
Game Butchers—
The Tresspass Law—
The Course Farmers
Should Pursue.

We understand that the county is full of hunters from Cincinnati, Cleveland, and other cities, sent out by the restaurant and eating-house keepers of those places to slaughter the game of the country, for the purpose of providing delicate tit bits for the customers of the aforesaid restaurants &c. These fellows pay no attention to the rules of hunting, their only object to kill as much game as possible. Hence they slaughter the game by wholesale, and will certainly exterminate certain species of it if a stop is not put to their wholesale slaughter. Several farmers, we understand, have attempted to drive these interlopers off of their premises, but were insolently called upon to show their deeds, &c., before they would leave. Our advice to every land owner in the county, who is troubled by them, is, to give them fair warning to leave, and if they do not do so, then to proceed to the nearest Justice of the Peace, and have them arrested for tresspass. If a few of them are put through in this way, the balance will be a little more careful how they impose upon decent people.

Mammoth Apple.

Mr. N. Christman, of Big Island township sent us last week, two Newton Pippins which were perfect mammoths, each weighing twenty ounces, and measuring—we don't know how much. They were good to look at, and the boys, who devoured one of them, after prodigious efforts, pronounced them first-rate to "take."

Deaths.

In Marion, on the 8th inst., of lung fever, Mrs. Betsy A. Abbott, aged 45 years.

Mrs. Abbott was born in Montgomery county, N.Y., and has resided most of her life in Oneida county of the same state. Owing to an affliction of the lungs, she came to Marion two years since, hoping, by a change of climate, to enjoy improved health. During her brief residence here she has, by her industry, uniform kindness and piety, secured the respect and high esteem of all who became acquainted with her. The community deeply mourn her loss, both as an active citizen, doing a successful Millinery business, and also as an ernest friend and Christian. She has been a member, for many years, of the Baptist church.

In this place, on the 4th inst., of Putrid sore throat, Lewy Adolphus, son of David and Mary W. Jamison, aged 3 years, 7 months and 4 days.

Hoaxed—Who Done It?

A few evenings since, a large number of men residing hereabouts, together with something less than four hundred boys in various stages of development, assembled at the depot for the purpose of seeing a certain portion of the U.S. Regular army, said to number 600 rank and file, which, rumor said, was on its way to Harper's Ferry, to put down old John Brown, who had taken that town, and shook the ground, till the people all around 'thar' thought the end of time had come.

As it happened, the train was behind time that evening, but the children all, "those of a larger growth"

as well as those of a smaller, waited patiently, and at last the train dashed up snorting fire and leaving flame. An examination was instantly commenced for "those troops," but by the time they had searched all through the train "and each and every car thereof," save and except the can or engine, it began to get through "the wool" of the crowd, that there was a hoax out somewhere in that vicinity, which caused the old 'uns to slip away for their homes without saying a word, while the young 'uns shouted "a bore!" "a bore!" with such hearty good will that it added considerably to the chagrin of their elders, and gave the news of the hoax a general circulation.

Some few of the more obtuse still think "the soldiers will come," and watch each train as closely as the terrible old "Honnas" kept his prisoners in the arsenal.

Nov 17, 1859

Houses of Ill-Fame, &c.

One of our subscribers inquires of us if there are any LEGAL means by which the houses of ill-fame in our midst can be abolished. He says they they are ruining numbers of our most promising young men and breaking up the peace of numerous families in our midst and spreading moral disease and death all around. Although we make no pretensions to being posted on the subject, we must say that we know of no LEGAL means to accomplish the object he aims at. There may be, however, some nevertheless, and "A Subscriber" had better consult some legal gentleman on the subject.

Married.

In Pleasant township on the 14th inst., at the residence of Mr. Samuel Fish, Esq., Mr. Hiram W. Riley, of Marion and Miss Hannah C. Fish, of the former place.

Nov 24, 1859

Houses of Ill-Fame, &c.

Mr. Editor:—We noticed in your paper of last week that one of your subscribers was making inquires of you "if there are any LEGAL means by which the Houses of ill fame in our midst can be abolished." Not knowing there are any such houses in our midst, we nevertheless can inform your inquiring friend, that there are LEGAL means not only for abolishing houses of ill-fame but for punishing vagrants, common prostitutes, and persons disturbing the peace of our village. There are two LEGAL means, one by indictment before the Grand Jury, and the other by an ordinance passed by the town council. Incorporated villages have power to provide that all vagrants, common prostitutes, and persons disturbing the peace of such village, shall, on conviction thereof, be punished by imprisonment for such period as may be provided by ordinance not exceeding sixty days. Our citizens know their rights, let them demand them.

Petty Thieving.—Seems to be on the increase as winter approaches. The kitchen of E.D. Lindsey was entered one night last week and between three and four dollars worth of provisions stolen. Our citizens generally should keep a strict watch and if they find any of these thieving gentry prowling among their premises give them a load of fine shot about the legs.

Died.—Mr. George Rupp, an old esteemed citizen of Pleasant township in this county, died on Tuesday last, after an illness of several weeks duration.

Mail Agent Elopement.—Erkeman, formerly a resident of this place, and who has lately been acting as a U.S. Mail Agent on the Mad River Railroad, has eloped, taken with him the wife of a citizen of Sandusky City, and leaving his own with eight children to take care of. It is also strongly suspected that he had made very free with the mails as several valuable letters have been lost on that route during the past year. It is supposed that he has left the country for the purpose of more securely enjoying his illegal gains and illicit love.

Married.

On the 18th inst., at the residence of Charles High, Esq., of this place, John Klee, of Delaware county, to Miss Caroline Coleman of Marion Co.

On the 3d inst., at the residence of the brides father, Mr. G. B. Smith, of Bellefontaine, and Miss Celeslia E. Gray, of Middlefield, Ohio.

Dec 1, 1859

Burglary.

We understand that the store of Mr. Lewis Trimble, at Scottown, in this county, was broken open a few nights since, and robbed of $200 worth of Goods. No clue to the perpetrators has as yet been obtained, although suspicions points to certain ones as the guilty parties.

Sent Up.

A colored gentleman was arrested one evening last week for 'hooking' a couple of pounds of cheese from Muntsinger. He was taken before Esquire Anderson, who ordered him to pay a fine of $5 and costs, failing; to do which, he was lodged in the county jail.

Serious Accident.

We regret to learn that a Son of Mr. Ault, Cashier of the Marion Bank seriously wounded himself whilst out gaming on the 24th ult. In loading his gun, the charge became fast when part way down the barrel of his gun, and, in endeavoring to get it out, by working with the ram-rod, the gun went off, forcing the ram rod through his hand. The wound, though a serious one, will not seriously maim him.

Married.

On Tuesday evening, Nov. 28th, Mr. Wm. B. Merriman of Findley, O., to Miss Mary A. Lindsey, of Marion, O.

Dec 8, 1859

Sudden Destruction.

On Monday morning last, while the court house bell was ringing, the huge Centre Piece in the Court Room suddenly fell, bringing the huge chandelier down with, breaking up the chairs and desks considerably. The entire damage done will not fall short of $100, which our tax payers will have to foot.

Died Like a Man.

Capt. Brown died like a brave man. On the way to the scaffold, and whilst on the scaffold not a muscle moved, not a nerve trembled, but, calm and serene as a summer's morning, the brave old man met his fate.

On the way to the scaffold, he wrote on a slip of paper, and gave it to one of the gentlemen accompanying him, a sentence to the effect that he once believed that Slavery could be put down by moral suasion, but that his views had changed, and he now thought that a great deal of blood would be shed ere that end was accomplished. Who dare say that his words will not prove prophetic.

Married.

On the 1st inst., Mr. Amos Taylor and Sarah N. Martin, both of Marion county, Ohio.

Dec 15, 1859

Died.

On the 5th inst., in Grand Prairie township, of Putrid Sore Throat, James, son of John A. and Mary Carter, aged 3 years and 3 months.

In Allegan, Mich., Nov 21st., at the residence of his son, Carlos Baker, of abscess of the lungs, Mr. Ebenezer Baker, aged 74 years.

The deceased was one of the first settlers of Delaware, Ohio. He subsequently removed to Marion, Ohio, thence to this place.— *Allegan Register*

Dec 22, 1859

Splendid Sleighing.

On Saturday last the snow fell nearly all day long, and on Sunday it done the same most of the time, and the consequence is, that we now have the very best of sleighing in this region. And, judging from the continuous tintinnabulation of the bells, our people are disposed to make the most of it. We hope that while it continues those of our subscribers who have promised to bring us wood, will make use of the occasion and bring it right along, and thus ensure the best wishes of the printer for their happiness and prosperity.

Married.

In Marion, on the 19th inst., Mr, Frederick Hall of DeKalb county, O. and Miss Margaret McNeil of Marion.

Died.

On the 7th inst, at the residence of his father in Salt Rock township, in this county, Henry C. Lee, in the 20th year of his age.

He leaves many friends to mourn his departure.

Dec 29, 1859

Our Jail.

Is about full again of worthless vagabonds, who are thus made a burden to our tax payers.

Desperate Affray.

On Sunday last the peace and quiet of our village was disturbed by an affray which commenced at Simon Pierce's Barber Shop. The parties engaged were Philander Pierce and James Gunn, mulattos, employed in the shop, and a shoemaker named Cameron, alias Old Virginia." During the fray young Pierce was knocked down on his knees by Cameron, who, in his turn, was badly cut on the head by a razor or some other sharp instrument, and with a heavy hickory cane. The two mulattos were at once arrested by officer Bishop, who conveyed them before the Mayor, who committed them until Monday morning when they were taken before him, and, after an examination, they were held for their appearance at the next Court in the sum of $50 cash, failing to give which they were committed.

Cameron was fined $5 and costs for being drunk and to stand committed until he paid or secured the payment of said fine and costs.

Jan 5, 1860

The Sheriffality.

On Tuesday last, the Commissioners of the County met at the Court house for the purpose of accepting the official bond of David Epler, Sheriff elect of this County. Upon an inspection of the bond presented, it was found imperfect in this, that the bondsman would pay *fifteen hundred* and there stopped, not stating whether it would be dollars, sawlogs, rails or what not.

Another difficulty arose. A law passed in 1854 declares that Sheriffs must give bond and qualify themselves within ten days after receiving their commission. This Mr. Epler failed to do. He received his Commission on the 10th day of December and did not offer to qualify until the 3d day of January.

The Commissioners advised with the best counsel they could get, and it is understood that they have determined to pursue this course, to wit: They are to have a special meeting next Saturday when Mr. Epler will present another bond which they will refuse to receive and then he is to carry the case to the Supreme Court, and have the matter authoritatively settled. Till a decision is thus had, the old Sheriff, Lewis, will hold over.

Serious Accident.

We regret to learn that Mr. S. Peckenpaugh, the B.& I. R.R. Agent at this station, had his arm broken on yesterday whilst engaged in shipping some stock at the cattle yards. The injury was promptly attended to, and he is now as comfortable as could be expected. We hope he may soon be able to resume his duties.

The Weather.

The people of this part of the universe are favored with weather of nearly Arctic severity. The thermometer ranges, during the nights, at from 8 to 17 degrees below zero. The sleighing is superb, and is well improved, notwithstanding the severity of the weather.

Accident.

We regret to learn that Mr. W.H. Thomas, Publisher of the *Mirror*, fell from his Press on Saturday last, and severely wounded himself on the face on a pair of scissors. Dr. Sweeney was called, who dressed the wound, and Mr. T. is at present tolerably comfortable.

Married.

At the residence of Alexander Shorn, on 29th ult., W.R. Gooding to Miss Ann E. Moon, all of Marion Tp.

At the Marion House in Marion, on the 31st ult., Mr. Horatio Clingerman of Essex, Union Co., O. and Miss Lucy E. Bauckins of Middletown.

On the 2d inst., Mr. Joseph Curtis of Richland County, Ohio and Mrs. Mary Hornby of this county.

Jan 12, 1860

Locked Up.

A Mr. Julius Baker was given lodgings in the county boarding house last week, having been bound over to take his trial in the Court of Common Pleas on a charge of having stolen 44 head of Sheep from Col. Conklin's farm in Salt Rock twp.

Mr. Epler's Case.

The Commissioners met at the Auditor's office on Saturday last, when Mr. Epler presented another bond, which two of the Commissioners, Messrs. Gillespie and Idleman, after conferring with the best legal counsel at hand, decided was not presented within the time prescribed by the statute, and therefore refused to receive it. Mr. Harvey, the other member of the Board, held that the bond was presented in time, and entered his protest against the action of the other two Commissioners in rejecting it.

The course pursued by the majority is the only safe one, as, if Mr. Epler is legally entitled to the office, he will only be kept out of it a short time, whilst if he is not, it would be foolish and criminal to give it to him.

Jan 19, 1860

Married.

In Marion, at the Marion House on the 2d inst., Mr. James F. Quay of this place to Miss Mary J. Walton, of Scott Twp., this county.

On the 13th inst., at the residence of Mr. Jacob J. Idleman, of Waldo, Elija W. Thompson and Miss Samantha Idleman.

Look Out for Thieves.

Within a short time past, quite a number of clothes lines in different parts of town have been robbed of their contents by nocturnal prowlers. We trust that those who are addicted to this petty and annoying thieving will be caught and severely punished.

Another Head Off.

We understand that the Postmaster at Mt. Gilead, Mr. High, has been removed, and Mr. J.B. Dumble, late of this place, has been appointed in his stead. This is doing pretty well for a yearling.

Mr. Epler's Case.

Mr. Epler having retained Judge Bowen to prosecute his case in the Supreme Court, that gentleman has commenced proceedings against Sheriff Lewis to make him show by what authority he now holds the office of Sheriff of Marion county. J.H. Godman, Esq., has been retained on the other side, and, by agreement of counsel, we learn, the case is set for hearing on Saturday next, the 21st.

Jan 26, 1860

Mr. Epler's Card.

The last *Mirror* contains a Card from the Sheriff elect, which indicates that when he penned it he was in a bad humor with himself and everybody else.

Our brief notice of his case week before last, seems to have aroused his ire, tho there was nothing in it that any reasonable man could object to. The word "criminal" which he seems to object to the strongest has no application to him whatever. We merely intended to say that if the Commissioners really doubted his legal right to hold the office, they would be criminally neglectful of the interests of community if they permitted him to take the office, and thus opened the door to endless litigation in the future. In this, we think, every right minded man will agree with us. And further, we are free to say that if the Commissioners could give him the office without violating the law and their oaths of office, they should do so. But the mere fact that he was elected, is no reason why they should give him the office in violation of law. There are certain other things requisite beside the mere election. Certain laws must be complied with and conformed to, and unless they are, the Commissioners might as well permit a person who had not been elected to take the office as one who had been.

So far as Mr. Slick is concerned we have to say: We never said one word to him in regard to his signing Epler's bond, nor any others of his sureties. We suppose Mr. Slick withdrew from the bond because he feared he might be injured pecuniarily, and wished to retreat in time. The talk about his turning pale, &c, is balderdash and beneath the dignity of a man.

Married.

On the 24th inst., Mr. John M. Camp of Bement, Illinois and Miss Sarah M. Holm of this place.

On the 24th inst., at Westfield, Morrow county, Ohio, J.B. Trimble to Miss H.P. Goodhue, both of Westfield.

On the 18th inst., Mr. William Fauroat and Miss Aceniah Fowler, all of Salt Rock township.

Feb 2, 1860

Mr. Epler's Case.

On Tuesday last the Supreme Court announced its decision in this case. They decided in favor of Epler, and the Commissioners will meet to day for the purpose of accepting his bond.

Larue and Thereabouts.

We made a flying trip to Larue on Monday last, and found the citizens of that village, as usual, intent on making their "pile," and taking things just as easy as they know how. We found Green's Store chock full of goods, which his accommodating clerks were selling to his numberous customers about as fast as they could tie them up. Seth himself was *non est*, and it was reported, *sub rosa*, that he had gone east to lay in a stock of calico!

Dr. Copeland is practicing medicine on the "independent" system, is full of the spirit of General Jackson, and chock full of Republicanism.

Mr. Franklin, late of Pickaway county, is making havoc among the timber on the site of the celebrated town of Winnemac, and will soon have a fine farm opened there. Like a sensible man, as he is, he subscribed for the *Republican*, and paid in advance. Mr. F. is a valuable acquisition to Montgomery township, and will make his mark there if he lives. West of the warehouse we found a man piling up "Oregon currency," i.e. hoop poles—the trade in which article amounts to no inconsiderable sum in the course of a year.

Friend Rainey is keeping the Union House, sets a good table, and is doing a good business. Upon the whole, Larue is a thriving little place, and if she don't get a back set, will cut no inconsiderable figure hereafter.

Asking to be Incorporated.

A large number of the residents of Larue have petitioned the Legislature to incorporate their town. This is done to restrain the rampageous "Oregonians."

Married

On the 29 ult., Mr. Oliver Mitchell of Logan County to Miss Eliza Jane Burt of Marion County.

On the 1st inst., at Middletown, Mr. George Gast to Miss Margaret Idleman, both of this county.

On the 27th inst., at the brides residence, Mr. Frederick Otho to Miss Mary Wieder, both of Middletown, this county.

Feb 9, 1860

Married

On the 5th inst., at the American House, Mr. Elza Pool to Miss Mary Jane Davis, both of this county.

Feb 16, 1860

 Mrs. H.E. Pilcher, formerly a resident of this place, died in Delaware on the 3d inst.

Accident.

We regret to learn that a daughter of Mr. Holm, of this place, had her collar-bone broken on Monday last, whilst engaged with others in a play on the grounds of the Union School.

Died.

On Friday morning, Feb'y. 10th, of Consumption, Mrs. Mary Brown, aged 68 years and 12 days.

Mrs. Brown was born in Broomfield, Mass. and moved to Ohio in 1840. She was much respected by those who knew her and her death is regretted by a large circle of friends.

"Thoap."

The "Quaker City Soap Man," was in town on Tuesday last, mounted a buggy in front of the American House, told a few yarns, gathered a crowd, raised a laugh, opened his stock and sold a large quantity of his soap at only a dime a cake. So eager were the crowd to get the "thoap" that he could hardly take their dimes fast enough, whilst in the stores around them a better article of soap could be purchased for just one-half the price. But people are bound to be humbugged, and we suppose the "thoap" man might just as well do it as anybody else.

Married

On the 31st ult., Mr. James Culbertson and Miss Narcissus Halderman, all of this place.

Feb 23, 1860

Business Activity.

On Saturday last our streets were crowded and jammed with sleighs and wagons from the country. About 1 P.M. we counted ninety-eight sleighs and wagons on Main and Centre streets. Our merchants were busy all day, and a large amount of goods must have been sold. Matters are undoubtedly changing for the better in Marion.

Big Island.

Considerable excitement has been created in this township by an alleged case of abduction. As the matter is to undergo a judicial investigation, we forbear making any comments upon it.

Mar 1, 1860

Marriages.

In Crestline, Ohio, on Wednesday, Feb'y. 22d, Mr. S.R. Green of Larue, to Miss Fannie J., only daughter of Samuel C. Freeman, of Fort Wayne, Ind.

On the 2d of February, Mr. Frederick W. Bleil to Miss Charity A. Drake, both of Grand Prairie township, Marion county.

On the 23d day of February, Mr. Thomas S. Henderson to Miss Sarah R. Lindsey, all of Montgomery township, Marion county, Ohio.

Deaths.

On Thursday, February 23d, 1860 at 4 o'clock P.M. of Scarlet Fever, Emerson, son of Rev. J.M. and Hannah Heller, aged 16 months and 21 days.

Emerson was a little twin brother; he has left his sister Mary to join the angels.

Marriages in 1859.

By an examination of the official record, we learn that the Probate Court of this county issued, during the year ending December 31, 1859, 122 marriage licenses.

Fire.

On Wednesday evening last, about 7½ o'clock, the residence of B.H. Williams, on the hill south of town, was discovered to be on fire. The fire was first discovered in the garret, and in a place where it was hard to get at, but, by the untiring exertions of many of our citizens the flames were finally arrested, though not until a portion of the roof was burned to a cinder. The damage we have heard estimated at from $150 to $200, which is more than covered by a policy in the Hartford Insurance Company.

Terrible Hurricane.

On Wednesday afternoon last this section of country was visited by a hurricane which did a vast amount of damage in its passage. It had been blowing a strong gale most of the afternoon, but about 4½ o'clock it greatly increased in violence. The air was filled with flying fragments of fences, boards, roofs, trees, &c., and, at one time, it seemed as if unlimited destruction would ensue.

South of this place, we hear of fences being prostrated by the hundred rod—on some farms scarcely a panel is left standing, whilst on others the damage is not so extensive. In town it partially destroyed a frame building belonging to Mr. Gurley, on the corner of Main and South streets. From a number of chimneys, loose bricks were blown down on the pavement below, greatly endangering the passersby. Fortunately no one was hurt by them.

Continuing its course northwest-wardly, it unroofed the southern portion of the County Infirmary crushing in the south gable-end in its furious career. The gable end, being composed of brick, crushed through the ceiling of the upper story of the portion of the Infirmary occupied by Superintendent Jones and his family, but fortunately no person was injured, though some of the furniture was badly injured. The main portion of the building occupied by the paupers, is said to be considerably shattered, though not so much so as to render it unsafe to the occupants.

An Eccentric Fe-Male Woman

Made her appearance in our town last week in the character of a Lecturer on ----- well we don't know exactly what, but it was not on Woman's Rights or Free Love, as her printed bills abundantly showed. She was about six feet high, more or less; had a complexion like a brass kettle, a nose like a razor, a stride like a giraffe and a dog like "Snarleyow."

She felt some heads, expended some Phrenology, diddled the green 'uns, purchased some cod fish, lammed her dog for a juvenile indiscretion, and took the midnight train on Saturday evening for Bellefontaine, after delivering a Lecture unparalleled in the history of the world.

Mar 8, 1860

Marriages.

In Claridon Tp., on the 28th of February, Mr. John Brockelsby and Miss Mariah Squibb.

Deaths.

In Green camp Township, on the 1st inst., of Typhoid Fever, John C. Berry, aged 36 years and four days.

Mar 15, 1860

Marriages.

At Caledonia, on Sunday, the 4th inst., Mr. Abner Nickols of Cardington to Miss Margaret Jane Zuck of Marion, Ohio.

Deaths.

In Berwick, in this county, on the 14th inst., of Winter Fever, after a short illness, William Cummings, aged 40 years, 2 months, and 13 days. Esquire Cummings was one of the most respected citizens of the southern portion of the county and his death will be deeply deplored by his friends and neighbors.

Mar 22, 1860

Our Town—It's Prospects.

The business prospects of our town are better this spring than they have been for several years past. Every business room has been taken up and will be occupied during the coming year, and there are not near so many empty tenant houses as there have been heretofore. Several new business establishments will open on the first of April, and matters seem to have changed for the better within the last few months.

Marriages.

On the 15th inst, Mr. George W. Riley and Miss Phama Sullivan, all of Marion County.

On the 15th inst., Mr. John D. Davidson and Miss Hannah Fauroat, all of Salt Rock Tp., Marion Co.

A Large Funeral—Deep Sorrow,

The death of Mr. W. Cummins, a citizen of Berwick, in this county, which we briefly announced in our last, seemed to cast a general gloom over the whole community wherever he was known. His remains were followed to the grave by one of the largest processions ever seen in our county. Elder Bates, Pastor of the Baptist Church in this place, preached an eloquent and impressive funeral discourse.

Nor is it any wonder that the death of Mr. Cummins is deeply regretted by the community in which he lived. As a citizen, a neighbor, a friend, a husband and a father, he discharged all his duties in such a manner as to win the praise of all whose good opinion is worth anything. It is not known that he had an enemy in the world, and surely he was the enemy of none. The vacancy caused by his sudden death will be hard to fill, while to the widow and her fatherless children no one can fill his place as he filled it.

Fire.

On Saturday evening last at about 10½ o'clock P.M. an alarm of fire was caused by the burning of an old cabin a short distance west of town near where the A. & G.W. Road crosses the Kenton Road. It was unoccupied and has been for some time, and it was undoubtedly set on fire, tho' for what purpose can not be divined. The object might have been plunder, and as we have numerous hard cases about town, it may be as well to keep an eye on the numerous "gentlemen of leisure" who are "lying around loose" about here.

Our Fair Grounds.

Happening out west of town the other day, we noticed that our county Fair Grounds were in a deplorable condition. A large portion of the fence has been blown down and the hogs, having free access to the grounds, have rooted them completely over, and a large amount of labor will be required to put them in proper order. The officers of the Society should at once have the fence rebuilt, and all other necessary repairing done, or before Fall the whole thing will become a complete ruin.

Mar 29, 1860

Closing Exercises.

Of the Marion High School, for the Winter Term of 1860, on Friday, March 30th at 1½ o'clock, P.M.

Orations
Latin Salutatory .... John Dunlap
Who are the Honored .... John Gauser
Honor .... E. Baker
Thoughts of the Future ...... Geo. Christian

Compositions
1859 .... Jay Williams
Hope .... L.D. Bowen
Prejudice .... J.S. Reed
Our Lives are
What we Make Them ....James Clark

Rehearsals
Misses Williams, Hoxter, Shields, Brockelsby, and Anderson

Orations
Agriculture .... H. Jump
Disunion .... C.E. Baker

Compositions
Commerce.......................... L. Anderson

Young Ladies' Paper

Orations
Progress .... M. Bowen
America and Americans .... J. Stokes
The Impending Crisis ...... W.B. Raymond
Valedictory .... C. Conklin

Marriages,

On the 15th last, at the residence of the brides father, near Middletown, Mr. William F. Bevis to Miss Sarah Jane Worline.

On the 25th inst., Mr. Wm. N. Hain of Middletown and Miss Anna Winterhalter, of Marion.

Deaths.

In Richland Tp. in this county, on the 30th inst., of consumption, Mariah, consort of Henry Klinefelter, in the 30th year of her age.

The deceased was an affectionate wife, a kind mother and a consistent christian.

Superior Job Work,

We invite the attention of our business men to the superior posters we have printed in the *Republican* Job Office within the last ten days, for the business houses of Underwood & Hunter, Caledonia: J. Fribley, J.B. Williams, Phelps & Hale, Marion; bills for Mr. McKinstry, of Claridon, Mr. Gast, of Middletown, and circulars for Phillips & Davis, of this place, all of which, we think, will compare favorable with Job Work of the same kind turned out at any country office in Ohio.

Church Festival,

The members of the Catholic Church in this place, will have a Festival at the City Hall, on the evening of Easter Monday, being the 9th proximo, the proceeds of which are to be appropriated to fencing the Catholic burying grounds in the new Cemetery.

What Others Say of Us.

Brother Millikin, of the *Washington Herald*, appears to have had his eyes open, whilst visiting our town a short time since, and in his paper of the 29th ult., speaks as follows in regard to it:

"We also visited the pleasant village of Marion, county seat of Marion county. In our more youthful days, we published and edited a Whig paper in this village, for the space of four years, and used to be acquainted with everybody in the entire county, but, on our return there a few days since, we found things materially changed. The place had grown vastly, and the faces were all strange; even those with whom we had been familiar had changed. Some had grown old; some fat; some lean; some with hair bleached white; some pious and some wicked. The change to as one who had not seen many of these old friends for a term of years, was great indeed."

Fire—United states House Burned.

On Yesterday morning, the United States Hotel in this place, owned by P. Loebrich, and occupied by Mr. R. Gray, late of the Cardington Exchange, was discovered to be on fire in the upper story. The alarm was given, and our citizens rushed to the rescue. Situated as the Hotel was and surrounded, almost, by frame buildings, save on the South side, it was feared that an immense amount of damage would be done before the flames could be arrested. Fortunately a short time after the fire broke out a heavy shower of rain commenced, which not only dampened the surrounding buildings, but allayed the wind, and in a great measure prevented the spread of the flames.

On the south side of the hotel, and in immediate contact with it, was a brick house owned and occupied by Mr. Loebrich as a grocery and bakery. This building was cleared of its contents in a few minutes and by the untiring exertions of our citizens it was saved, though somewhat damaged by the water and by tearing out the counters, shelving, &c.

Immediately north of the hotel and one rod from it, was a one story frame occupied by the grocery stores of J. French & T. Fahey. Still south of these and connected with them was a two story frame building occupied as a residence by T. Fahey. All these buildings were cleared of their contents under the apprehension that they would be destroyed. They were saved, however, after several hours of severe exertion upon the part of our citizens. Their contents were somewhat damaged by their hasty removal though not more so than would reasonably be expected under the circumstances.

Thus the entire loss by the conflagration was confined to the hotel and the damage done to goods by their removal. This result is surprising when we consider the means on hand for checking and combatting a fire, the situation of the surrounding buildings, &c., and shows that our citizens worked like heroes. Even the ladies lent a hand and done efficient service in passing water, saving goods, &c.

During the progress of the fire a number of persons met with accidents by which they were more or less injured though not seriously. Mr. W. Garrett was knocked off of one of the buildings at the rear of the hotel and had his upper lip cut through besides being badly jarred. Several were injured by the throwing of empty buckets, and we hope that at future fires more care will be exercised in this respect than there was on this occasion.

Mr. Gray's case is a particularly hard one. He had just taken possession of the United States House and is now thrown out of business. By his manly bearing and strict attention to business he had made an excellent impression on our citizens, and no doubt would have been very popular as a landlord. We understood that efforts are making to fit up the old Depot House so that he may commence business again. We hope this may be done, and that Mr. G. may be induced to remain amongst us.

Married.

April 4th, at the residence of the brides mother, Mr. David S. Jones and Miss Leonora M. Adams, both of Marion, O.

In Marion, on the 1st inst., Mr. James A. Watson and Miss Catherine Hook, both of Marion county, O.

At the Marion House on the 31st ult., Mr. Samuel Leeper of Kenton, Harlin county and Mrs. Elizabeth Lanier of this county.

On the 3d inst., Nathaniel Redd and Susan Sult, all of Marion county, O.

The Catholic Festival.

The Catholic Festival at the City Hall on Monday evening last was an occasion of great hilarity and sociability, whilst, at the same time, everything was conducted with the strictest propriety and good order. The Supper prepared by the ladies of the Catholic Church was a superb one, and elicited unbounded commendations from all who partook of it.

The attendance was very large, considering the inclemency of the weather and embraced members of nearly all denominations and many non-professors. Eloquent Speeches were made by Dr. Fisher, Prof. Olmsted and others. In short, the whole affair was conducted in such a manner that the most fastidious could not take exceptions to it and the company broke up about twelve o'clock, highly pleased with each other and with the festival which had called them together. The nett proceeds, we are happy to learn, will amount to over $150, which will enable the congregation not only to fence their burying ground but also to ornament the grounds as they should be.

The Fire—Stealing.

We are somewhat surprised to learn, as we do from Messrs. French, Gray and Fahey, that they each had a large amount of goods stolen during the progress of the late fire. The wretch who would steal a man's property under the pretence of helping to save it from the flames, would commit any other crime if opportunity offered. We did not suppose we had such persons in our midst. The town authorities should detail a number of persons to guard any property that may be carted into the street to save it from fire.

A Visit to the Marion School.

From the *Morrow Sentinel*.

Mr. Editor:—I was highly pleased with a visit to the Marion Schools during the fore part of last week. The building occupied by the schools is a large four story brick; of no great pretensions to architectural beauty, but well and strongly constructed. This I consider an important item in a School House—that it be firmly, plainly and substantially built. Our Marion friends have built their house large enough to meet the wants of the school for many years, and have taken care that everything should be solid and firm.

The basement contains two large rooms used as reception rooms where hats, bonnets and the like are left—a room where small children and those residing at a distance can stay and eat their dinners—a room for fuel and two furnaces. We then ascended the broad and solid oaken stairs to the second story where we find the Primary and Secondary Schools, the Superintendent's Office, and a room used as a music.

Upon the third floor we find the Intermediate, Grammar and High School and several recitation rooms. The fourth is devoted to a hall large enough to seat fifteen hundred persons. In this the exhibitions, lectures and the like are held. This seems a feature worthy of all commendation and one whose merits will be seen by all who have experience in holding exhibitions in Churches, Court Houses and other places, intended for widely different purposes.

All the rooms are furnished with chairs supported by iron pedestals, and where desks are needed they are single, made of cherry, and supported in the same manner.

The school is under the care of that accomplished educator, Mr. E.B. Olmsted, assisted by an able corps of teachers. The discipline though mild, is thorough and most excellent order is secured, not only in the rooms but upon the grounds.

So full control have the teachers that none of the out-buildings are at all defaced, nor are any of the shrubs or trees upon the grounds injured.

The walk to the front door is bordered upon both sides with rose bushes and other flowering shrubs, and I was told that a rose was scarcely ever plucked although five hundred children pass within a reach of them every day of the flower season.

The attainments of the various classes and the success of the teachers in imparting knowledge, though not so remarkable as the order, were still excellent.

I met the results which are to be expected where school rooms are kept scrupulously clean and neat, and where trained teachers govern and instruct, guided by an experienced Superintendent and blessed with the confidence of intelligent patrons.

I was much pleased with the examination of one of the Primary Schools. The well trained teacher, the well dressed and intelligent children, the order and quiet of the room, as well as its neat and house-like aspect, made a scene to which I was not surprised to see that the parents reported.

I was also much impressed with the excellence of the Intermediate School which is under the care of Mrs. Hume. The reading in this in very good, and great care is taken to prevent hesitation, miscalling and the "singing tone."

The High School, under the care of Mrs. Olmsted is a remarkably quiet and orderly school, and will compare favorable with any in the country.

The attendance is an uncommonly high per cent of the whole number of scholars within the district.

I look upon the school as very successful and as signal instance of what can be effected by the combined influence of the Teachers, the Board and the Patrons,

Yours, &c.,

W. Watkins.

Sup't. Mt. Gilead School.

Marriages.

On the 27th ult., in Tully township, Mr. John A. Duncan to Miss Elizabeth Welbourn.

On the 5th inst., Mr. Henry Powell to Miss Cyntha Ann Thatcher, both of Green Camp township.

On the 3d inst., Mr. Robert Straw to Miss Sarah Jane Garrison, both of Green camp township.

Apr 19, 1860

Deaths.

At his residence in Montgomery township, Marion County, on the 15th of March, Mr. Joseph Anderson in the 55th year of his age.

Mr. Anderson was among the first settlers of this township. As a husband he was kind and affectionate, as a father, he was tender and very indulgent, as a neighbor he was generous, obliging and kind-hearted.

Marriages.

On the 15th inst., at the residence of Mr. Robert Hopkins in Pleasant township, Mr. James C. Clay to Miss Nancy J. Hopkins.

Burglaries,

On Friday night last a number of burglaries were committed in this place, though in not one instance was there any very great amount of property stolen.

Mr. J. Strelitz's Clothing Store was entered by prying open a shutter and raising the lower sash. Three or four coats worth from $20 to $30 were taken. The gun smith shop of Mr. J. Hefner, was entered in a similar manner, and a revolver worth $15 stolen. The barn of Mr. S. Frame was entered by breaking the lock and a lot of corn taken. Our citizens should be on the lookout for these midnight depradators and should try to bring them to justice if possible.

Apr 26, 1860

Prisoner Escaped—Gross Carelessness.

On Friday night last, Julius C. Baker, confined in our county jail on a charge of sheep stealing, made his escape by sawing off some of the bars of the eastern window in the south end of the jail. It appears that he had not been confined in the cell that night, and was thus enabled to carry out a long cherished scheme for escaping. In the day time, since his confinement, he has been permitted access to the hall running around the cells, and it was probably during this time that he cut off the bars, and when the proper time come, had everything ready for his departure.

The democracy last fall, tried to make a great deal of capital against Sheriff Lewis out of the escape of Partridge and Strode. Now look at the difference between their escape and Baker's. They broke out of the cell, where prisoners confined on penitentiary charges should be kept. Baker is allowed to be out of the cell after night, Lewis never had an imitation that his prisoners were trying to escape, and hence was not put on his guard. Epler, on the other hand, we learn, found a short time before Baker escaped, a lot of provisions which he had secreted for the purpose of sustaining him when he should make his escape. This should have put him on his guard, and a strict scrutiny of the jail should have followed. None was made, however, and the prisoner escaped. Lewis's prisoners escaped by means the least likely in the world to be thought of or detected, whilst Baker took the most obvious means possible.

The people can now see how much they gained by making the change. We told them that Epler had permitted prisoners to escape when Sheriff before, and in one instance at least not a single mark was left to show how the prisoner did escape, and, so we prophesied, it would be again, and scarcely three months have elapsed after Epler took the office before our words were made good. Nor will this be the last case of the kind. Inefficiency has marked every step of the new administration thus far, and it will continue to be so until the end. Mark that.

Lecture.

Mr. C.M. Sherman will deliver a public lecture this evening at the court house. Subject: Life. Admittance free. Boys excluded.

The Marion Cemetery—Great Improvements—Dastardly Outrages.

We learn that the cemetery association have been making considerable improvements on their grounds this spring. They have set out between one and two hundred beautiful trees, and a large number of shrubs, and otherwise beautified and adorned their grounds. Their Sexton is constantly at work making improvements and no expenses will be spared in making this last resting place of the dead pleasant and inviting, and in their efforts in this behalf, our citizens who are not connected with the association should countenance and support them as far as they consistently can. Should the board be enabled to carry out their designs in full, the cemetery will be a credit to our town and an honor to those who projected and perfected it.

We are pained to learn either some thoughtless boys or some rascally boys have defaced several tombstones in the cemetery, broken the miniatures affixed to others, and destroyed many of the growing shrubs. Whoever it may be who ruthlessly invades the sanctity of the tomb, and defaces or destroys the tokens of affection and love placed on the last resting place of the dead by the living, we trust they may be detected and severely punished for their sacrilegious crimes.

A Fire Almost—Narrow Escape.

On Monday last the dwelling of Mr. T.J. Magruder, on West street, narrowly escaped destruction by fire. Whilst the family were engaged in the upper portion of the house, a spark from a stove ignited a basket of clothing in the kitchen, and before the fact was discovered, the flames had destroyed a dining table, and badly charred the casing around a window. The flames were finally subdued by the neighbors and the building rescued from imminent destruction.

Marriages.

On the 21st of April, Mr. Cyril G. Miles to Miss Anna Douce.

May 3, 1860

Died,

In Marion, on the 27th ult., Mrs. Eliza M. Johnson, aged 70 years.

May 10, 1860

Married,

On the 3d inst., at the residence of the bride, 2¼ miles south east of Marion, Rev. W.W. Winter of the Delaware Conference, and Miss Laura E. Clark.

Died.

At the residence of his father in Marseilles, Levi J. Lavennfire, aged 21 years.

May 17, 1860

Off for Chicago

Quite a number of our live Republicans have availed themselves of the low fare offered by the B.& I. Railroad, and have gone to Chicago to attend the great National Republican Convention. From the indications before us we are inclined to think that this will be one of the largest political gatherings the country has ever seen.

The Grey House

Our friend Grey, having fitted up the Depot House and renovated it from top to bottom, will be ready to receive guests by next week, when, we hope, he will receive a liberal share of patronage.

Married.

In Caledonia, on the 13th inst., Hiram A. Koons to Miss Sarah L. Bell.

May 24, 1860

Married.

Cyrus M. Finney and Miss Christina Yarr, all of this place.

May 31, 1860

Baker Re-Captured

Officer Lutz arrived on the 25th inst. from the West having in charge Julius Baker, charged with Sheep stealing, who made his escape from the county Jail a few weeks since. He captured him in Whitley county, Indiana, having got track of him by a letter Baker wrote to his wife and which laid in the Marion Post Office for several days. Mr. Lutz is entitled to great credit for recapturing this fugitive from justice.

Died.

In Marion, on the 13th inst., Mrs. Margaret Raichley, nearly 75 years of age. She was a native of Shenandoah Co., Virginia but came to Ohio in the earliest settlement. She has been a resident of Marion nearly 24 years.

Jun 7, 1860

Married.

At the residence of the bride's parents, in Marion, on the 5th inst., Mr. E. G. Allen and Miss Mary Anna Baker.

In Findley, Ohio, on the 29th of May, Mr. John W. Bain of Marion, O. to Miss Mary Monnett.

On the 31st ult, at the brides residence, Haywood Howison to Mary Kenechel.

On the 30th ult., at the residence of the brides father, three miles west of Caledonia, Mr. Alfred F. Dawes to Maria Reed.

Jun 14, 1860

Extensive Sheep Stealing!—A Daring Villain!

Our county has lately been the scene of some extensive sheep-stealing, the facts connected with which are unparalleled in the history of rascality. Some two or three weeks since Messrs. Robert Carr and ___ Caldwell, who reside in the northeast part of the county, and who are extensive sheep growers and wool raisers, missed about 150 head of fine sheep from their flocks. As they could not find that they had strayed away or died from disease they naturally concluded that they had been stolen and immediately took measures to recover them. They got on track of a drove answering the description of theirs and following it found they had been shipped at Caledonia on the B & I R.R. for Cleveland. Following on they overwhelmed them at Galion and here they might have caught the thief with the stray sheep in his possession if they had exercised no caution. The sheep were on the cars and the train was about ready to start and Mr. Carr, making his presence known in such a way that all around knew what his business was and it being dark, the thief took the alarm and escaped. Messrs. Carr and Caldwell identified the sheep and took them home.

This is the boldest effort at rascality we have heard of lately. That a man should go to the fields of two farmers, take out between one and two hundred head of the sheep with the owners brand on each one of them, drive them 7 or 8 miles through a thickly settled county, many of the people being acquainted with their owner's marks, take them to a town of twenty three hundred inhabitants and here publicly ship them, shows a hardihood unparalleled almost exceeds belief. We trust the daring scoundrel may yet be overtaken and brought to justice. Every farmer is interested in ferreting out the rascals and securing their proper punishment.

P.S.—Since writing the above, we learned that Mr. F. Campbell who resided some 2 miles west of this place, had some about 70 head of sheep stolen, retraced them into the hands of a Mr. Rouse, of Bucryus who had got them off the cars at Gallion, claiming them as his own he having had some stolen also. When he found them they had been sheared, thus rendering it more difficult to identify them. Nevertheless, himself and one or two others who had seen them on Mr. C's place made it so apparent that the sheep were Mr. C's that they were surrendered to him, he permitting Rouse to retain the wool rather than be compelled to test ownership of the sheep in the Courts.

This thing of sheep stealing has been reduced to a system hereabouts, and we might mention numerous other instances. Our farmers should be uniting in their efforts to put a stop to it, for if it is allowed to go on, the business of wool raising will have to be abandoned in great measure. Every drove of sheep that passes along the road should be closely scrutinized so that pursuit may be rendered more easy and recapture more certain. A description of those who have charge of each drove should also be secured if possible and by those means sheep stealing will be made a rather difficult business.

Serious Accident.

A serious accident occurred in this place on Monday last, about 11 A.M., by which several persons were injured. The persons injured were T.J. Anderson, M.O. Pixley, M. Pixley, F. Saiter, and a German who was working for M.O. Pixley. The four latter were engaged in putting on a new roof and eave trough on the residence of Mr. Anderson, who was superintending them, when the scaffold on which they were all standing suddenly gave away, precipitating four of them to the ground, a distance of eighteen or twenty feet.

Mr. Anderson was severely if not fatally injured, having a leg, and arm, and one rib broken, and, it is feared that he has sustained internal injury sufficient of endangering his life. Mr. Saiter had his arm badly bruised, and was considerably jarred by the fall. Young Mr. Pixley was badly jarred, and it is feared that he has been severely injured internally. The German was cut on the forehead but escaped with less injury than any of the others. Mr. M.O. Pixley made a very narrow escape. Feeling the scaffold give way beneath him, he instinctively grasped a ladder, which in falling, threw him through a window into the house, by which he escaped with but very little hurt.

The physicians report Mr. Anderson's condition to be very critical, and it is very probable that he is fatally injured. How any of them escaped without broken limbs, or fatal hurts seems almost miraculous. We trust this serious accident will induce our mechanics generally who have to work up off the ground, to take more care in building their scaffolds and see that they are properly braced and made secure beyond the possibility of a doubt. An other course will lead to a repetition of accidents like that detailed above.

At Home

Mr. T.C. Bowen, son of Hon. O. Bowen, of this place, who has been a member of the National Naval Academy in Annapolis, Md., during the past three years, arrived at home on Monday last.

Jun 21, 1860

Married.

Mr. John Schneider to Louisa Moyer, both of Marion, Ohio.

❖

On the 11th inst., Mr. Solomon Kemmerel and Miss Susan Fluelling both of Big Island Township, Marion Co., Ohio.

 All of those who were injured by the falling of the scaffold at Judge Anderson house last week are about, attending to their ordinary business save the Judge himself who however is getting along as comfortably as could be expected.

Retired.

Mr. Thomas, late Publisher of the *Democratic Mirror*, in this place, has sold out his interest of that paper to Mr. _____ Spooner, of Cleveland. We trust the retiring and incoming Publishers both may meet with all sorts of good luck, save political.

Jun 28, 1860

Our County Infirmary.

During the last ten days, the Directors of our County infrimary have been visiting the infirmiries of the neighboring counties for the purpose of seeing if they can discern some regulation that could help in the management of ours. There is a general feeling among the citizens of the county that the cost of maintaining our paupers is too great and they would be glad to see a strict system of economy introduced into its management.

The First Lincoln Pole in Marion County.

The first Lincoln pole raised in Marion county, was set up in the North part of town on last Thursday evening by Mr. M.O. Pixley and his neighbors. The pole is a beautiful one, being forty-eight feet high and straight as an arrow. From it flows a beautiful flag bearing the names of Lincoln and Hamlin for the live Republicans of the North end.

Caution.

Whereas my wife, Sarah Marenda Payne has left by bed and board without just cause or provocation, this is to notify all persons not to trust or harbor her on my account as I will pay no debts of her contracting after this date.

David J. Payne

Jul 12, 1860

Marriages.

In Claridon on the 1st., Columbus Sickle and Miss Mary A. Hipsher.

Jul 19, 1860

Severely Wounded.

On Saturday evening last, whilst the Misses Halden and Patten of this place were riding in the south part of town, the steed of the latter became frightened and ran away with her and finally threw her with such force as to inflict a severe wound upon the head that, although the wound was a severe one, the skull was not fractured. The patient is now doing well and will soon be round again. Whilst the horse was running, Miss P. had presence of mind enough to disengage her feet from the stirrups and this probably saved herself from a fatal injury.

Lucky.

Mr. "Phil" Pierce having imbibed about thirteen inches of "never fail" whilst at the Lake during the excursion yesterday, undertook, on the return trip to but the bridge across Scioto river at Larue off the track. The result was Philander would have been instantly killed if the breakmen hadn't noticed him as he rolled off the end of the car. He was "booted" into a "box-car" until the train arrived at Marion.

Jul 26, 1860

Splendid Meteor.

A large and beautiful meteor was seem here on Friday evening last. The head of it seemed to be about the size of a water bucket, and the tail about ten feet in length, apparently. Some ten to fifteen seconds relapsed from the time it was first seen until it passed out of sight.

The same meteor was also seen at Cleveland, Buffalo and New York. It was seen here about 9¼ o'clock.

Killed by Lightning

Mr. E. Peters of this place had a fine yearling mule colt killed by lightning, on Saturday morning. It and three or four other were standing under a tree in the pasture, and the lightning passed down the tree, knocking several of them on to their knees, but all recovered save one.

☞It is said that Brigham Young, for the Mormons, proposes to sell out Salt Lake City, and emigrate to British or Russian America.

The Fourth at Boyce's.

Boyce will be prepared to entertain company at his beautiful garden on the 4th in superb style. Refreshments of various kinds will be served up to those who wish them and a Balloon ascension will take place in the evening.

In short the Fourth will be celebrated in good, old fashioned style at Boyce's and all who wish to can participate.

Aug 2, 1860

Desperate Affray—Man Stabbed!

We learn from Dr. Tyler that a desperate affray occurred in Middletown in this county on Saturday last, during which a young man named Carr was so severely stabbed that his recovery is extremely doubtful. The circumstances attending the affray, as we learn them, were as follows:

Young Carr was engaged in taking care of B. Lauer, son of a hotel keeper in Middletown, who was sick. Some two or three persons (among whom was one who goes by the name of Dutch Jake) were engaged in drinking and quarreling in the bar room of the hotel, when young Carr stepped to the door, and requested them not make so much noise, as it disturbed Lauer. Thereupon they all pitched onto him, when he knocked all three down. He then returned to the sick man's room, where he remained a few moments, when he stepped out on to the porch, where they had gone to.

As soon as they perceived him, one of the party remarked "there's the d——d s–n of a b——h." and all again him. He resisted as well as he was able, but finally retreated into the setting room, where they renewed the attack upon him, and finally got him down, and during the melee he was stabbed twice, once in the right side of the breast, between the fifth and sixth ribs, the knife running in the direction of the heart, and once on the arm. Dr. Powers, who is attending the wounded man, gives it as his opinion that the chances are very much against his recovery.

The assailants of young Carr were subsequently arrested and taken before Esq. Dix, when it appearing that the stabbing was in all probability done by "Dutch Jake," he, together with another man, were bound over to the Court of Common Pleas, the former in the sum of $500, the latter in $300.

Killed.

Mr. G. Foster had a valuable cow killed by lightning on Sunday morning last, whilst standing under a tree the northeast part of town.

Bucyrus.

The census taker returns the population of Bucyrus at 3,542 souls. Our citizenship can judge from this the benefit of encouraging people to locate in a town and especially can they see by it the benefit of aiding in building up manufacturing institutions. Marion to day might just as well as not have occupied the position that Bucyrus does, if her capitalists had made the right use of their means.

Hodder Thrashed.

On Saturday evening last, Mr. T. H. Hodder editor of the *Marion Mirror* was whopped by J. Johnson Esq. of this place. The difficulty as we learn had no connection whatever with politics, but was caused by an insult offered by Hodder to a lady relative of Mr. Johnson's and if the facts are as stated to us, the only wonder is that the thrashee got off as easily as he did. The affray caused some excitement, and immediately afterwards Mr. Johnson was arrested and taken before Mayor Davids who after an examination, bound him over to appear at the next term of the Court of Common Please when he at once gave bail for his appearance thereat.

The Erie Sewing Machine!

Mr. J.R. Knapp, Jr., is Agent for this Machine, for this county, and has it on exhibition at his residence on East Street three doors South of the M.E. Church. It makes two stitches at each revolution, or 2000 stitches per minute! Price—$20 with foot power and a walnut or Iron Stand, or $15 with hand power. Call and see it.

Aug 9, 1860

Serious Accident.

We regret to learn that one day last week, Mr. Henry Smith of Big Island township, whilst engaged in running his threshing machine had his right arm so severely injured that amputation probably will have to be performed. The particulars attending this unfortunate occurrence as we learn them are that the horse power attached to the machine had been stopped, but that the cylinder was still revolving rapidly, and in attempting to oil some parts of the machinery, Mr. S's arm was drawn between two cog wheels connected with the tumbling shaft by which nearly all the flesh on his arm between the wrist and the elbow was crushed off. Fortunately no bones were broken and there is a probability that the arm may be saved.

Dr. Davis is attending the patient, and has some hopes that amputation may be avoided. Mr. S. is in moderate circumstances and this accident will fall with crushing force upon himself and his family. We trust he will speedily recover from his injury.

Marriages.

On the 31st ult., in Kenton, Mr. Jos. F. Fouke, Esq. of Marion and Miss Jane Cope of Hardin county.

Deaths.

On the 15th day of July at his residence near Marion, Mr. James Cunningham, aged 57 years, 9 months and 20 days.

He leaves an affectionate companion and eight children to mourn the loss of so kind a father, yet some of them rejoice in this that their loss is his eternal gain.

Some of his children are yet unreligious, but I cannot think that their father and mothers prayers will be lost. I hope that God's blessing will continue with this family, that they all may meet as an undivided family around our Father's throne in Heaven.

Rev. W. Martin

❖

In this place, on Friday evening, the 5th inst., of Putrid Sore Throat, Willie G., son of H.C. and Kate Godman, aged five years, six months and fourteen days.

Willie was a sweet child, soft and tender in his disposition as an infant. He was loved by all his little playmates and many were the tearful eyes and the little sobs in the infant class Sabbath morning when the teacher said "Willie is dead!" Willie loved his class and teacher, and long will she remember how earnestly he listened while she talked of Jesus and Heaven.

Sudden Death.

Mr. Snider, son of the undertaker of this county who resided with his parents on their farm, south of town who was about 33 years old died very suddenly on Sunday evening last. We have not learned of a certainty what was the occasion of his sudden demise.

Poisoning Dogs.

Some person or persons have taken upon himself or themselves the duty of Dog Killer, and are engaged in killing off the canine race by poison. Who they are we know not, but suppose they must either desire to destroy the dogs with an eye to petty thieving or else are animated by a spirit of pure cussiness which should entitle them to a whipping at the catt's tail or a coat of tar and feathers.

 We regret to learn that a young man maned Coran whose parents reside on Sheriff Epler's farm in Big Island Tp., was severly injured on Monday last by his slipping and falling off a load of hay on to a pitch fork which caused a slight wound on his hip and a severe one on the breast which, it is feared, may cost him his life.

Killed by Lightning.

We regret to learn that Mr. Elias Washburn, a respected citizen of Salt Rock township, was instantly killed by lightning whilst at work on his farm on Tuesday last. We have not learned any particulars in regard to that unfortunate event.

Aug 16, 1860

A Queer Accident.

On Sunday night last, a man who was sleeping in an upper room of a house in the north part of town, got up whilst in a "discumfuscated" state, busted a window and got out on to a shed from which he fell to the ground, breaking his hip. Dr. Bridge reduced the dislocation and the patient is now doing as well as could be expected.

☞ We regret to learn that Mr. H. Knable, one of the proprietors of the Planing Mill in this place, had three of his fingers cut off whilst attending the machinery Monday last.

Deplorable Accident.

On Saturday last, whilst the Douglas Democracy were engaged in raising the last splice of their pole, the rope to which it was suspended suddenly broke and the pole fell to the ground, striking down in its fall four persons, viz: Mr. Hezekiah Millizer, whose scalp was badly cut and his skull fractured. Very strong hopes are felt that he will fully recover from his injuries.

A lad named Seymour, aged eleven years had his skull fractured so terribly that he died at seven o'clock next morning and was buried on Monday morning at 10 o'clock. Mr. Heiner received a cut on the eye brow, but not severe enough to hurt him badly. One or two others received small hurts, but were not materially hurt.

Marriages.

On the 15th, Mr. A.R. Swisher of Bellefontaine and Miss Mattie T. Randall of this place.

Deaths

On July 20th, at Claridon, Bettie Thew Brocklesby, aged 20 years.

Aug 23, 1860

Deaths.

Died on Aug. 11 at the residence of her mother, Mrs. A.M. Patton near Elizaville, Kentucky, Lucinda Jane, wife of C. Bryant of Indianapolis, aged 27 years and 4 days.

Marriages

At the residence of Mrs. Helen Showers on the 21st, Mr. W.A. Walker and Miss Susan Showers, all of this county.

In Marion, on the 11th, Mr. William Reese and Miss Mary Jane Winemiller, all of this county.

Aug 30, 1860

Accident in Marion.—We regret to learn that in consequence of a rope breaking while the Democracy of Marion were raising a pole on Saturday last, a lad named Hanford Seymour was fatally and a Mr. Millizer seriously injured. The former died on Sunday morning. No blame was attached to any one.—*Mt. Gilead Messenger.*

But blame should attach to some one, neighbour, for the rope which broke and let the pole fall, by which, young Seymour was killed, was known to be perfectly rotten, (having been tried at the raising of the Republican pole a week or two pervious and found wanting), and the gentleman who owned it warned the person who borrowed it of him that it was rotten, and made him promise that it should not be used where any strain of weight would come upon it, and not satisfied with that, he went to the person who was bossing the job, and repeated the warning. The warning was disregarded, the rope broke, and the result is known. Who is responsible?

Deaths.

Died.—On the 13th inst., in Shakelee Minnesota, Mrs. Eliza Darlington, wife of Cary A. Darlington, formerly of this place, aged 56 years.

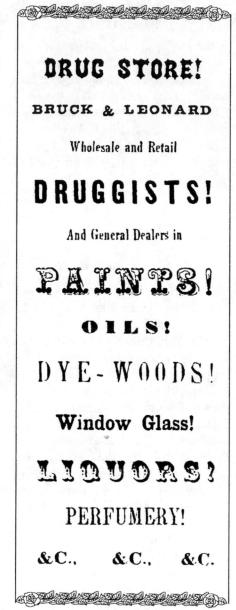
A Narrow Escape.

On Monday morning last, a very wild three year old colt, belonging to Mr. A. Sims, who resides north east of this place four or five miles, and which was in charge of a professional trainer here, broke away from him and ran furiously up Main St. just as the morning freight train from the east was crossing said street. It never paused in its mad career for a moment, and jumped on to a platform car when in motion. The consequence was that it took his feet from under him, and he fell onto his side on the car, and from thence fell to the ground. It then regained its feet and ran up the Railroad to West street and down West street to South street, where it was recaptured. Every one expected to see it either killed or so badly injured as to render it worthless, but it escaped without a scratch almost.

Sep 6, 1860

Deaths.

In Grand Prairie Township, on the 2d inst., of sore throat, Mary Ann Davidson, aged nearly 10 years.

Oct 4, 1860

Married.

On September 27th, P. Phillips and Miss Ollie Clark, all of Marion.

Deaths.

On the 4th at his residence in Claridon township, Jacob T. Holverstott.

Oct 11, 1860

Marion County.

The result of the election in this county is a complete Locofoco triumph—they having elected every one of the county officers. The Republicans struggled nobly, and brought out the largest vote they ever had in the county, but the Locofocos largely increased their unprecedentedly large vote of 1859 and awed the platter. All sorts of means were used to compel voters to support their ticket; direct and downright coercion among the rest. We shall have something more to say upon this subject hereafter.

The Fraud Palpable.

That the citizens of Marion county— those who love in it and pay its taxes—may see and know that the late election here was an outrageous fraud upon the sanctity of the ballot box, we give the following figures, from the record:

The last enumeration of white male inhabitants over twenty-one years old, shows that there were but 3016. Which includes all that are unnaturalized, who must number nearly or quite 100.

At the late election there were 3114 VOTES POLLED, showing that were NINETY EIGHT more votes polled than there are white males over 21 in the county, and we must remember that there must have been from 50 to 100 who did not vote. In the face of such figures, who can believe that Cricket, Gray, Dombaugh, Rosencrance, and Courts have a just right to hold the offices to which they claim they are elected? Let honest voters answer.

Oct 18, 1860

Mr. Editor:—I would call the attention of the Democracy of Marion county to the matter of damages sustained by me whilst assisting to raise the Hickory Pole in August last. I was promised pay for all my lost time and enough to pay my Doctor's bills. As yet I have not received one cent. I am a poor man and support myself and family by my labor. Such promises, I find, are more readily made than redeemed. If I am not paid the full amount of my damages soon, you will hear from me again.

Hez. Millizer.

Mr. Millizer is a poor hard working man and should be paid his damages. Toe the mark, gentlemen.

Gas Works in Marion.

Under the auspices of Mr. Harvey who, we believe, erected the Gas Works in Bucyrus, an effort is now being made to organize a Gas Company in this place. The amount of the capital stock is fixed at $12,000, of which amount Mr. H. has subscribed $4,000. At present about two thirds of the stock is taken and if the remainder is subscribed soon, the necessary works will be erected this Fall yet. As the Works would undoubtedly prove a great benefit to our town, and the returns for the investment reasonably remunerative, we trust the remainder of the stock will be speedily taken and the works put in train for completion.

Oct 25, 1860

An Old Republican

At the late election in this Tp., Mr. Abram Zuck, who is nearly 90 years old was present and voted the straight Republican ticket. The young men vote the Republican ticket because it is the party of the future—a young, growing and liberal party. The old men vote the same ticket because its principles are the same as those sustained by Jefferson, Madison and Jackson when they first begun to vote.

Convicted.

Julius Baker was tried for stealing 44 head of sheep from Col. W.W. Conklin of this place, in January last, by the Court of Common Pleas now in session here, on Monday last, and on Tuesday morning the Jury returned a verdict of guilty of Grand Larceny. He will be sent to the Penitentiary.

Married.

On Saturday, Oct. 21, in Marion, Mr. Hezekiah McRill and Miss Maria Sweitzer, both of this county.

Nov 1, 1860

Married.

In Pleasant township, Oct. 22th, Mr. E. Howard to Miss M. Hiles of Marion county.

October 22d, in Green Camp, J.E. Longacre and Miss S.J. Northland, all of Marion County.

October 13th, Daniel Kirts and Miss Maria Canouse.

October 28th, Harvey Canouse and Miss Lovey Jane Riley, all of Marion county.

Deaths.

Died—October 27th, Mary, only daughter of J.W. and Mary Bain, aged 6 years.

Nov 8, 1860

Married.

On the 1st inst., at the residence of Wm. Clark, Mr. Sylvester R. Gooding to Miss Martha M. Clark, both of this county.

On the 1st inst., at the Methodist Parsonage in Marion, Mr. A. C. Fletcher and Miss R.E. Owen, both of this county.

Obituary.

Mrs. Margaret Turney was born in Hempfield township, Westmoreland county, Pa. on the 20th of June, 1793. She was the daughter of Rev. John William Weber, being blest with the training and example of pious parents, she remembers her creator in the days of her youth. At the age of fifteen, she made a public profession of her faith in Christ, and joined the German Reformed Church.

She was married to Joseph Turney December 7th, 1811, with whom she lived in the bands of christian love until the close of her life. She was the mother of eleven children, all living. She came with her husband to the state of Ohio in 1819, where she remained till her death, which occurred on Saturday evening, October 27th, 1860. Her health was somewhat feeble through the winter season, but she was not severely ill until the first week in April, since which she was confined (most of the time) to her room and bed.

Nov 15, 1860

Married.

In Marion on the 13th inst., Mr. L.F. Raichley and Miss Elizabetha Kelly, both of Marion.

In Tully township, on the 4th inst., at the residence of the bride, James McCafforey to Miss Eveline Bell.

Nov 22, 1860

Married.

In Claridon Tp., on the 15th inst., James E. Roach of Morrow County and Miss Mary M. Underwood of Claridon Tp., Marion County, O.

Local Affairs.

Improvement is now the order of the day in Marion. A larger number of buildings have been erected within the past eight months than there were during the pervious two years. All departments of business are more lively and give strong evidence that we have in a great measure, at least, recovered from the disastrous effects of the crash of 1857. Business men are more hopeful and cheerful and anticipate better times than they have been struggling through. Real estate is more lively than it has been, and if it does not command better prices, it is, at least more salable. We have heard of more transfers within the last three months than in the previous twelve.

All our business rooms are fully occupied, and we almost weekly hear of new branches of trade and manufacture about to be started. The great crop of the present year has placed our business men in easier circumstances, and has done much to resuscitate that confidence between man and man which is the soul of trade and speculation.

Everything indicates that Marion is about to enter upon a new era of prosperity, and if her people will make a good use of the advantages they possess, she will more than recover the ground she has lost in the race with her sister towns.

Nov 29, 1860

The Bank Panic

Still grows in intensity, and threatens to become as overwhelming as that of 1857. And it has all arisen from the fact that a few traitors will not acquiesce in the constitutional election of a President.

Married.

November 22, Mr. Solomon Dunklebarger and Miss Lydia Daniels, all of Richland township.

Look Out.

Somebody with very long fingers has been playing "foul" with the fowls of the people in the north end of town. Better look out, or the shoulder grabber will be after you.

Dec 6, 1860

Deaths.

In this place on the 29th ult., of Putrid sore throat, Jessie F., daughter of Wm. B. and Ann Lewis, aged 2 years, 11 months and 28 days.

Married.

On Thanksgiving Day, near Middletown, Mr. I.N. Riley and Miss D.H. Greek, both of Marion County.

On the 2d inst., Mr. A.F. Davis and Miss Hannah P. Eaton, all of this county.

On Thanksgiving day, at the residence of the brides brother, Mr. Samuel L. Rayle to Miss Priscilla Uncapher.

On the 29th of November, Mr. Lafayette Fletcher and Miss Ann Brockelsby, all of Claridon township.

On the 29th of November, Mr. James Vestal to Miss Emily Davis, all of Marion County.

YE GREAT ELECTION!

Ye mauls which knocked ye Persimmons on ye day of ye election.

Ye man with ye rail, yclept Honest Old Abe.

"My Gur-reat Principle."

Dec 13, 1860

Married.

On the 4th inst., Mr. Hugh V. Davidson to Miss Cyntha Farout, all of Salt Rock Township.

Burglary.

On Tuesday night last the residence of B.H. Williams of this place was burglariously entered and some $50 or $60 worth of Jewelry stolen from the inmates. Our citizens will do well to keep a sharp look out for the light-fingered gentry just now.

☞ By the terms of the contract, the iron fence around the court house square is to be completed by the first of next month. When finished, it will add much to the appearance of the square.

Dec 20, 1860

The County Infirmary.

We understand that the Directors of the County Infirmary have appointed Mr. Benjamin Baker of Prospect Tp. Superintendent of the County Infirmary, *vice* Mr. Jones, whose term will expire on the 31st inst. Mr. J. has been a faithful and capable office, always carefully guarding the Interests of the county, and, at the same time, doing full justice to the Inmates.

Died.

Of diphtheria at Piqua, Ohio, on Monday, December 9th, 1860, Grafton M. only child of S. and M.E.G. Peckenpaugh, of this place, aged 14 months and 4 days. (*Lebanon Star* please copy.)

Married.

On the 18th inst., Mr. James Fletcher to Miss Jane Porter.

Dec 27, 1860

More Outrages.

Messrs. Solomon and Samuel Epley, formerly citizens of this place, but who have lately been working at their trade—carpenters—in Tennessee and Mississippi, arrived at home on Tuesday evening last, having been expelled from Panola county, in the last named State, for no other crime than that of being Northern men.

"Mr. S.H. Epley, Sir, after some mature reflection upon the political sentiments you uttered in our midst favoring Black Republicanism, we, as Vigilance Committee of Batesville, deem it our duty to notify you that we wish you to leave here on tomorrow morning's train for Memphis.

Respectfully,

J.M. Sherford,

Sam. Daegfus,

W.B. Carouthers,

Vigilance Committee of Batesville."

Married.

On the 20th inst., Mr. Daniel Baker to Miss Sarah J. Luke, both of this county.

In Pleasant township, on the 19th inst., Mr. N.A. Shawn and Miss E. Newton, both of Marion Co.

Jan 3, 1861

Married.

On the 1st, inst., Thomas W. Thompson of Muskegon co., O. and Miss Emily A. Cricket of this place.

On December 25th, John Brocklesby to Miss Alice Welborn, both of Marion co.

Golden Wedding.

On Tuesday last, Samuel and Elmira Scribner, of this place, and old residents of this county, celebrated the 51st anniversary of their marriage. They were joined in marriage, Jan. 1st, 1810, by John Carpenter, Esq., of Liberty Township., Delaware county, Ohio.

At the late anniversary, they had the pleasure of sitting at the table with eight of their nine children (who were also accompanied by a limited number of their forty-four Grandchildren.) The occasion was very agreeable to all present. Long may they and the other pioneers of our State, who have "made the wilderness to blossom as a rose," live to enjoy the blessings they done so much to secure.

Fearful Riot and Bloodshed.

On Tuesday last our town was the scene of a fearful riot, which resulted in bloodshed, though, we believe, no person was fatally injured. The particulars as near as we can give them are about as follows:

On Monday evening Mr. Charles Partridge had some difficulty with an Irishman named John O'Reagan.

They finally come to blows, and two or three other Irishmen interfering, Partridge got the worst of it. The next day the latter's brother, Henry Partridge, in company with two young men named Wilkins and Herriman, came to town to spend New Year's. About 3½ P.M. of that day, the two Partridges, Wilkins, and Herriman were at the grocery of Mr. T. Fahey, and were about starting home, when Herriman was assaulted by someone of the Irishmen, and a general assault was made upon the party. The two Partridges finally retreated into Pierce's barber shop, followed by some half dozen or more Irishmen. Charles Partridge managed to escape out of the front door as the Irishmen rushed in. Henry Partridge, however, run back around the barber shop and into a small room in the building occupied by George Birk as a grocery. He had previously been badly beaten, and here four or five Irishmen found him and beat him till he was a perfect gore of blood.

During the progress of the fray, Herriman was knocked down four or five times with stones and brickbats and young Wilkins was also badly beaten, and brickbats, stones, clubs, &c. flew around thick as hail for a few moments, endangering the lives of disinterested spectators, and the wonder is that we have not the painful duty of recording the violent death of one or more persons. Several of the Irishmen were also wounded, but none of them dangerously.

After the fray was over, Officer Johnson collected a posse and proceeded to arrest the principle offenders against the peace and quietude of our town. Two brothers, Irishmen, named O'Donnell, undertook to resist after they were taken to the village prison, and were somewhat roughly handled by the posse before they were rendered tractable. Another one named Michael Ryan, drew a knife and tried to stab Officer Johnson, but a rap over the head with a "billy" in the hands of one of the Marshall's assistants, soon rendered him tractable, and while the knife was taken from him, in doing which, a man had his finger badly cut with it.

The prisoners are to have an examination today (Wednesday) at 10 A.M. when we will probably gather further particulars.

P.S. Since writing the above, John O'Reagan and two persons named O'Donnell, brothers, were tried before Mayor Davids on a charge of riot, and then plead guilty and each were fined $10 and costs. Subsequently, three other persons, Anthony Flaherty, Michael Ryan and Patrick Ryan plead guilty to the same charge and were fined a like amount as the three first named. We also understand that warrants are out for the arrest of the Partridges, Herriman and Wilkins, and they will probably be taken to-day or to-morrow.

Jan 10, 1861

The Hour and the Peril.

We do not wish to be considered alarmists, but we feel that the country is in deadly peril, and that we stand on the outermost verge of civil war. For years past, the storm has been gathering, and the election of Lincoln has been seized upon as a pretext for carrying out a purpose matured and cherished for long years. Since that event, traitors have been busy, and treason has stalked abroad unrebuked. Already has one State, so far as she can, rent the bonds which bound her to her sister States, and declared herself independent of the Government she herself helped to form. We repeat, the hour is full of deadly peril, and it is time the sovereign people should take cognizance of our situation. Whilst we write, a contest may have been begun at Charleston that will entail more of woe upon the world than any other event in its history. It is time that people arouse from their false security and examine carefully all the difficulties which surround us at the present time. They should act calmly, coolly and promptly. They should meet in their sovereign capacity and instruct their servants as to their wishes in these trying times. They should speak in terms that cannot be misunderstood. It is no time to choose phrases. Whatever is done must be down now. The people of every county in the North should rally at once, and proclaim to the world the position they will occupy in the coming contest. The friends of the Union should make themselves known. They should act in concert and act effectually. If the North will only speak out harmoniously and decidedly, they can do much to save the Union. Their rulers will hear and obey them, and traitors will know what they have to expect.

We hope the people of our county will move in this matter at once. Let a meeting be called, and let us know who are for and who are against the Union. Let us have a Union Mass Meeting without respect to party.

Old Abe in Marion.

It is just possible that his numerous admirers here will have the pleasure of seeing the President elect in Marion. From Springfield, his most direct route to the capital is via Terre Haute, Indianapolis, Marion, Pittsburgh, &c. *Springfield Journal* says he has not determined which route he will take, and he is as likely to take the most direct one as not.

A Noble Horse.

We are pleased to learn that Messrs. E. Messenger, D. Pettit and V.D. Pettit of this county and T.C. Dye of Wyandot county, have purchased the celebrated Rogish draft horse, "Bold Lancastershire," who was imported from England by Washington Beals & Co., of Pennsylvania, in August last. This celebrated horse is one of the largest, if not the largest, horse in the world. He is full 17 hands high and will be seven years old next spring. He is what would be called a black roan, and when in good condition weighs 1800 lbs.

The new proprietors have re-christened him John C. Heenan, and stock raisers in this section of Ohio, by their enterprise and liberality, will have an opportunity of introducing some of the best blood in the world. John C. Heenan is a thorough draft horse and whilst possessing tremendous muscular power, he has, at the same time, great activity, and more than average speed and good temper. It is a well known fact that the horses of this section are entirely too small for the labor they have to perform and any enterprise which lead to the introduction of a larger breed is one that should be commended and seconded by every true lover of the horse and we trust that the gentlemen who have thus stepped forward and secured to our horse raisers the services of such a horse as John C. Heenan may reap a rich reward.

Died.

Near this place, on the 8th inst., Calista, wife of D.H. Harvey, in the 33d year of her age.

She was much respected by all her acquaintances and her death is deplored by a large circle of relatives.

"EASY WASHER."

The undersigned takes this method of informing the people of this county that he has made arrangements for the manufacture of the celebrated "Easy Washer." Determining it altogether unnecessary to give a detailed account of the merits of this machine, will briefly state that it is a complete machine in itself, doing away with the necessity of using an ordinary washboard to complete the work.

R.L. Linn, Proprietor.

TESTIMONIALS,

I have tried the Easy Washer and find it an excellent Machine in every respect and believe its merits can scarcely be overstated. It washes fast and clean and works very easy. It does not spoil or damage the clothes, either by staining, rust, or hard scrubbing. It seems all that any person could wish for in a washing Machine.

Mrs. Chas. Mincinberg, Marion

This is to certify that I am using the Easy Washer and can conscientiously recommend it as a complete washing Machine. The dirtiest garment needs scarcely any extra rubbing and there is little or no wear on the clothes. I find it especially what any Lady wants—a very easy washer and will add that I have bought one, and do not want a better Machine.

Mrs. C.B. Mann, Marion

Married.

On the 1st inst., Chas. D. Moore and Miss Joanna Fouke, all of this county.

On the 10th inst., Martin Kistler and Miss Christina Briggle, all of this co.

On December 29th, John Roakley and Miss Frederika Kirch, all of this county.

At the residence of her mother in this place on the 30th ult., George H. Riggle to Miss Lizzie Randall.

Sudden Death.

Mrs. Thompson, wife of J.M.C. Thompson, of Salt Rock Tp., in this county, died very suddenly last week of heart disease. She rose about 3 o'clock on the morning of her death and sat by the fire for some moments, and then returned to bed where her husband was lying awake. After her return to bed, he fell asleep and slept some time, and upon waking up, he found her dead by his side. She was much respected among her acquaintances, and leaves a large circle of relatives to mourn her sudden departure.

Infirmary Directors Vs. Dr. Bridge.

We have received from Dr. Bridge in regard to the allowance of his bill for attending on David Loyd, who fell from the second story of a house in the North part of town in July last and dislocated his hip. It appears that there are some persons who deem the Dr.'s bill for the services rendered in the case as too high, and censure the Infirmary Directors for allowing it. Hear both sides, and then judge.

The New Year's Row.

This morning, (Monday) Charles and Henry Partridge and Lafayette Harriman, who were engaged in the affray in this place on New Year's Day, came into town and surrendered themselves into the custody of the Mayor. Subsequently, a charge of assault and battery was preferred against them by Mr. A. Flaherty, and, as the defense wished to call the Mayor as a witness, the case was transferred to Esq. Anderson's docket, and the examination fixed for tomorrow.

Tuesday—the plaintiffs appeared before Esq. Anderson this morning at 10 o'clock, with counsel, and no one appearing against them, they were discharged.

Important Arrests.

Two men, named, respectively, Church and Sherwood, pinchbeck jewelry peddlers, were arrested in this place on Thursday evening last, by the Sheriff of Crawford county, on a charge of forgery. It seems that they forged a check on one of the banks in Bucyrus, and presented it for payment, but having a suspicious appearance, it was not paid, and they then sold it to an outsider. The arrest broke up a nice little arrangement which one of then had effected for a travelling tour in company with a female institution of our town.

Jan 17, 1861

The *Mirror* and the New Year's Row

In the last issue of the *Mirror*, a dastardly appeal is made to the prejudices of our Irish citizens and an attempt made to create the impression that we had purposely misrepresented their conduct during the melee mentioned for the purpose of prejudicing them in the eyes of the community generally. In reply to this it is sufficient to say that every statement made in our article of January 3d was amply sustained by the testimony of nearly every witness before Mayor Davids. Our object was to tell the truth, let it hit where it might. And we defy the *Mirror* to produce a single witness who followed that row all through, as we did, who will tell the truth and contradict one of our statements.

Married.

On the 10th inst., at the residence of Dr. Harrington, Newark O., J.W. Boyd of Marion Co. to Miss Mary E. Rhodes of Licking Co., Ohio.

On the 15th inst., Mr. John B. Culk and Miss Catharine Strine.

Ed. *Republican.*—Whilst at home during holidays, I was informed that some of the non tax payers of Marion county—those that pay nothing make the most noise—had been abusing the Infirmary Directors for allowing me $75 ($5 out of that amount to be paid to Dr. Johnson, and $3 to Dr. Davis.) After deducting said amount, it leaves $67.00 for my surgical and medical attendance on one David Lloyd, who, on the night of July 3, 1860, fell from the second story window of a house occupied by Mr. Fahey. Distance of fall, about 14 feet, lighting on the trochanter major and pelvis of the left side, producing a dislocation of the femur and fracture of the acetabulum. Twelve hours after the accident I saw the patient and, without saying anything about the symptoms, &c, became satisfied that the case was a critical one, and the patient ex-

tremely liable to be a cripple for life. I procured the assistance of Drs. Johnson and Davis, and, with their capable assistance, I was enabled to reduce the dislocation and bring the legs to an equal length.

There was much difficulty in keeping the head of the femur in place. Perseverance for over forty days crowned my efforts with success. Between forty-five and fifty days after the accident the patient was removed to the County Infirmary. On the 25th day of December last the patient was able to walk without the assistance of crutches. Taking the case in all its meaning, the recovery with scarcely any lameness is more than could be expected by the surgeon. As to the bill, Mr. Grumbler, if you should meet with a like misfortune, call on Dr. Bridge, and he will charge you according to your ability to pay.

David Lloyd was a non-resident of Marion county—had met with a very grave misfortune. What was to be done? Let him die or be a cripple during life—to be supported by the county, or render him relief? Mr. Grumbler says that it was right to give him aid, but you charged too much. When you apply to the legal profession, you expect them to charge in accordance with the importance of the case and the ability to pay. For a grave offense, such as would imprison a criminal during life, $75.00 would be a mere nothing. $500 would be a small fee to be cleared, provided the client was as able to pay as Marion county. David Lloyd was not saved from prison, but he was saved from being helpless during life.

Mr. Grumbler says that Drs. ought to doctor for nothing and not charge it to the county to increase our taxes. As long as it is expected for a Doc-

tor to pay for what he buys, you must expect them to be paid for their professional services.

W.W. Bridge, M.D.

Jan 24, 1861

War Movements

A letter received by one of our most respected citizens from a man who is now residing—at Annapolis, Md., says that strange things are going in in that quarter—that all the guns at the Naval Academy have been removed and placed on board the Constitution—that steamers are heard in the bay every night, though nothing extraordinary takes place in the day time—and that great preparations of a warlike character are evidently making for some purpose.

Jan 31, 1861

Stabbing at Middletown.

We learn that an affray occurred at Middletown in this county at a religious meeting on Monday evening last, during which Mr. Samuel Mounts was stabbed in the breast by a young man named Griffith. Griffith, it seems, was making some disturbance, when Mr. Mounts remonstrated with him upon the impropriety of his conduct. A scuffle ensued and Mounts ejected Griffith from the house, when Griffith struck at him twice with a knife a painful but not serious wound.

☞ The trial of John J. Cade and Newton Blynn, on the charge of Grand Larceny, by stealing a lot of jewelry in Larue in September last, in our Court of Common Pleas terminated last evening in the acquittal of the latter and the finding of the former guilty of Petty Larceny.

Died.

On the 25th inst., at the residence of her daughter in Berwick, Mrs. Mary Patten, aged 78 years, 10 months and several days.

Married.

On the 14th, Mr. James C. Rhoads and Miss Anna Wilson, both of Scottown, Marion County.

January 24th, Thomas H. Carter and Emma F. Winslow, both of this county.

Feb 7, 1861

Burglars About.

On Sunday night last the dwellings of several of our citizens were entered by a burglar or burglars. Mr. J. Ullman was robbed of $180 in money and a gold watch. Mr. J.E. Leonard, a boarder at the Marion Hotel was robbed of $10 in money and a gold watch. Mr. Wm. Medey, who occupied a room in his mother's boarding house, also lost a small sum of money. The residence of Mr. John Ault was also entered but nothing was taken therefrom. An attempt was made to enter the residence of E. Peters, but the burglar, becoming alarmed, fled.

The operator was certainly a bold one, as Mr. Ullman's watch and money were taken from within reach of the bed where himself and wife were sleeping. Most of the rooms of the Marion Hotel were entered, but none of the boarders lost anything, save Mr. Leonard. We trust the thief or thieves may be discovered and brought to justice.

Serious Accident.

We regret to learn that Mr. C. Weishman, an employee on the farm of Mr. J.C. Lee, adjoining town on the West, was severely injured one day last week by the bursting of a shot gun he discharged. One of his thumbs was blown entirely off and he was severely wounded on the side of his face and head. A portion of his jaw bone being carried away. Although suffering severely we are pleased to learn that there is no danger of the injury proving fatal.

Trial for Passing Counterfeit Money.

Mr. _____ Monroe, who has been confined in our county jail on a charge of passing counterfeit money in Larue, in August 1860, was tried in the Court of Common Pleas last week and the Jury after being out a short time, failed to agree, and were discharged. The accused proved a most excellent character from boyhood up to the present time. He was ably defended by Messrs J.H. & H.C. Godman.

The New Fence,

Around the court-house square is completed so far as contemplated by the original design, save putting in some stone under the fence. The Commissioners now have it in consideration whether it would be best to extend along the eastern line of the square in place of the board fence which they first designed placing there. As it now stands, it cost from $1,200 to $1,500.

Died.

Of Diptheria, January 24th after a severe illness of two weeks, Mary Alice, only daughter of P.K. and C. Francis, aged 9 years, 2 months and 17 days.

Feb 14, 1861

Improvements in Marion.

During the coming summer several valuable improvements will be made in our village. Messrs. Fite intend putting up a large building on the northeast corner of East and Centre Streets, which they will use for their business as Egg and Butter packers. Messrs. Lucas & Sefner will erect a large and well appointed Warehouse on the corner of Main street and the B & I Railroad. They intend, as heretofore, to do a large produce and Forwarding business.

Mr. D. Scott is, we understand, taking measures for the erection of a building for the manufacture of buttons. As this is a new branch of business in this part of Ohio, Mr. S, deserves great credit for his enterprising and liberal spirit.

A number of good sized dwelling houses will also be erected during the coming summer, and, on the whole, the coming season promises to be one of at least average prosperity to our village.

Married.

On the 14th inst., at the residence of the bride's father, in Marion, Ohio, Mr. T.H. Hodder, Editor of the *Marion County Mirror* to Miss Mattie Lee Saiter.

Died.

In Eldorado, Fayette Co., Iowa, May 31, 1860, Mary E. Baker, daughter of Artemas N. and Matilda Baker, formerly of Marion, Ohio.

Feb 21, 1861

For Washington.

Several of our citizens have determined to visit Washington to witness the Inauguration of Mr. Lincoln. There will be tens of thousands of people present at that interesting ceremony.

The Festival,

Our Firemen had a most inclement evening for their Festival and hence the turn-out was rather slim. They had a beautiful table prepared for their friends, loaded with the choicest delicacies and had everything ready on their part for a tip top affair, and we were truly sorry that so few were present, not only on account of the useless preparation but because this backwardness has a tendency to discourage the Firemen from taking an interest in having the town thoroughly prepared against attacks of the devouring element. If property owners wish to have it protected from fire, they must do their part and not rely altogether upon its being taken care of by those who have no interest in it whatever.

Military Meeting.

We are requested to announce that a meeting will be held at Scottown on Saturday, the 23d inst., for the purpose of forming a military Company. All favorable to the foundation of such a Company are invited to be present.

Married.

On the 14th inst. in Scott township at the residence of Wm. Hill, Mr. Horace P. Johnes of Bucyrus, Crawford County and Miss Ellen Rosencrancon of this county.

On the 16th at the residence of M.A. Lincoln, Christopher Wilkins to Miss Mary C. Smith, both of this place.

On the 17th, Russell Southwick and Miss Rosanna White.

Died.

At the residence of her son-in-law, in this place on the 18th inst., Catharine Lucas, aged 73 years, 1 month and 18 days.

On the 10th in Pleasant township of Diptheria, Samuel, son of John R. and Mary M. Yerr, aged 5 years, 7 months and 5 days.

Mar 7, 1861

The New Administration.

Before this paper goes to press, the new Administration chosen by the people in November last, will have been inaugurated and entered upon the discharge of its duties. At no time since the adoption of the constitution has there been so critical a period as the present one, and to surmount the difficulties which lie in the way of the new administration, will require the vary highest order of statesmanship and tact, and if Mr. Lincoln and his constitutional advisors succeeded in doing it, they will be entitled to the thanks of patriots in all sections and of all parties.

A portion of the States of the Confederacy have assumed a hostile attitude toward the General Government, and, on paper, have thrown off their allegiance to it. They have seized the property of that government; its forts and arsenals; its dockyards and branch mints, and in various other ways have set its authority at defiance.

The country expects the new administration to meet this treason with a firm front; to reduce the rebels to subjection, and to enforce the laws throughout the whole union. It is not expected that the country is to be rushed into a civil war without reflection, but it is expected that traitors will be punished and the laws enforced in all quarters. The people are tired of temporizing cowardly policy, and they want to see the question whether we have a Government or not definitively settled.

Married.

On the 31st inst., Mr. Thomas Lushbaugh and Miss Julia McDanels, both of this County.

Mar 14, 1861

Licked Again–That So Well Earned!

On Tuesday evening last, the editor of the *Democratic Mirror*, of this place, T.H. Hodder, was soundly flogged by Hon. O. Bowen, in consequence of a scurrilous attack made on the latter in the *Mirror* of Feb 28. Ever since his advent here, this man Hodder has made it his business to assail the character of such private citizens as happened to incur his ire, and has not scrupled to make the private affairs of citizens of our town matter for comment and animadversion in the columns of the paper which he happens to control. And especially has he singled out Judge Bowen as an object for his evil vituperation and slander. Time and again has he charged the latter with high crimes and misdemeanors, until forbearance ceased to be a virtue, and the result is, the castigation mentioned above. And the verdict of all fair-minded men, of all parties, is, "served him right."

A Word of Public Explanation.

For the *Marion County Republican*.

An occurrence which took place in one of the streets of this town on Tuesday afternoon, the 12th instant, may justify, from me, some explanation which led to it.

On the 19th of April, 1860, Thomas Hodder, the editor of the *Democratic Mirror*, without a shadow of provocation, published a malicious libel against me, in reference to the late State Treasury defalcation of Breslin and Gibson, and in the 26th of the same month he reiterated the charges in the same paper. I took no notice of these abusive and unprovoked attacks, but allowed them to pass, by simply expressing an intimation that another publication of similar charges in his paper would be answered by a personal chastisement of the author. This determination of mine was communicated to Hodder, and the libel was not, for a time, repeated. I hoped that his recklessness, and disregard of common propriety and decency might be improved by study and reflection, and that his malicious desire to malign private character might be modified and perhaps subdued by the counsel of his friends, and his paper cease to be, what it had notoriously become, the vehicle of the coarsest and most unscrupulous personal slander.

Neither the public, nor myself, have realized the fulfillment of these hopes. The lapse of time has not seemed to change the depraved nature of Hodder. He seems unwilling to acknowledge any law but that of the professional and degraded vilifier of private citizens. It is impossible for him to reach the standard of a semi-respectable publisher of a country newspaper.

On the 25th of February last, I left home, in company with one of my sons, to witness the Inauguration of President Lincoln at Washington, and to visit another son, who is at school in Annapolis. On the 28th of the same month, Hodder published in the *Democratic Mirror* an editorial article, which I copy in full. It is as follows:

"Office Seekers.

On last Tuesday the following gentlemen from the county and village started for Washington to see "Old Abe." Dr. Copeland, Harvey Peters, John J. Williams, Judge Anderson and Judge Bowen. Messrs. Hood, Johnson, and Davids started in the same crowd, but go to New York for goods; although we shouldn't be surprised if the latter gentleman found himself in Abraham's bosom before his return to the bosom of his family.

The following is said to be the programme lain out for Old Abe for the above gentlemen, which if not strictly lived up to, it is supposed, will create a muss in the camp. For minister to the Guano Islands, Dr. Copeland; for Minister to Utah, Harvey Peters; for Minister to the Cannibal Islands, John J. Williams; for Indian Agency to the Kickapoo, Poera, Flat Head, Long Heel, Knock Knee, Lantern Jawed, Long Legged, Slab Sided, Piankeshaw, Kaskaski, Wea, Obejibews, and Ossawattomie tribes of Indians, Judge Anderson; for Grand Handler and *Keeper* of the

Public Moneys, Judge Bowen, late of the firm of Bowen, Gibson, and Breslin. We learn that Jim Anderson, who started for Washington a week in advance of the others, has secured an appointment as Special bearer of Dispatches to his Sable Majesty the Emperor of Hayti."

I returned home late on the evening of the 7th of March. I do not take the *Mirror*, nor do I read anything it contains, unless it be some paragraph to which my attention is directed by others, or some legal notice which has an exclusive place in its columns. About three o'clock on Tuesday afternoon, the 12th inst., a friend handed to me a copy of the *Mirror*, and pointed me to the article which I have quoted above. It was a republication of the old slander in more direct terms. This was the first time I had seen it. Acting from first impulse, upon the resolution which I had previously adopted and believing that I had at command no other remedy—that I could not, by any of the usual legal proceedings, obtain adequate redress for the injury I had received from the hand of an irresponsible and infamous libeler, I went immediately in pursuit of Hodder, but did not find him for some half or three quarters of an hour. I finally met him on the south west corner of Main and Centre streets, and in the presence of a goodly number of spectators, I chastised him with a *cane*, and endeavored to, and trust I did, *beat* into him some respect for truth and decency, which all other experiments had failed to reach him.

I am not an advocate of street brawls, or, as a general rule, of the higher law made of redress. But an evil may become so great: a nuisance may become so intolerable—its putridity so destructive to the health, public welfare and morals of the community, that abatement by physical force becomes and is the only appropriate remedy. This remedy is given to me by the Common Law. In all proper cases we may avail ourselves of it. Hodder's unfounded and criminal accusations against me, presented such proper case. I have publicly chastised a confirmed and untiring defamer of private character and thereby performed a duty to myself and to the community, through which his slanders are circulated, and for doing that I ask the approval of all good citizens.

O. Bowen.

Married.

On the 16th ult., Mr. Christopher Wilkins to Miss Mary C. Smith, all of this county.

Died.

Of Pulmonary Consumption in her eighteenth year at the residence of her father in Marion county Ohio, Harriet O. McLellen.

At the residence of her son-in-law, Col. E. Messenger in Big Island Twp. on the 20th ult., Mrs. Jane Johnson in the 72nd year of her age.

Mar 21, 1861

Died.

At the residence of her father in Marion, on the 10th inst., of Typhoid Fever, Mary Sharp, aged 18 years and 4 months.

Married.

On the 3d inst., Mr. George Learn-hard and Miss Christina Augustine.

On the 21st, Henry L. Lacy and Miss Sarah E. Landon.

Serious Accident.

We regret to learn that Mr. William Barker, son of Mr. J.H. Barker of this place, who has been acting as a brakesman on a freight train on the B & I Railroad, for some time past, met with a serious accident early on Tuesday morning last, near Union. Whilst looking out at one side of the train, his head came in contact with the target of a switch, while the train was running at nearly full speed, and he was knocked off on to the ground, breaking one of his legs and crushing one of his hips.

Dr. Bridge of this place, and some of his relatives immediately started to his relief, and he was brought home yesterday.

Fort Sumter.

No order has been given yet for the evacuation of this fortress, but it will undoubtedly be done in the course of a few days.

INDEX

A

Abbott Betsy A. 172
Ackerman Frederick 160; Sanford J. 34
Adams Leonora M. 180; Margaret 33; Rebecca Ann 80
Adinman T.W. 91
Albrecht 49
Alexander J.S. 49
Allen Bingham 96; Corydon 43; Curtis 149, 152; E.G. 184; Fidelia A. 96; Samuel 20; Stephen 99; Stephen B. 40
Amburg A. 71; Lizzie 71
Ames 86; O. 49
Anderson 8, 179, 194; Clay W. 107; F.M. 115; J.H. 160; James H. 104, 119; Jim 198; John 26, 36, 38, 161; John M. 161; Joseph 101, 138, 182; L. 179; Martha 26, 70; Minerva J. 36; Nancy 107; Orrel E.I. 67; T.J. 7, 76, 134, 184; T.M. 95; Thomas J. 107
Andrew Tamsey 50
Andrews John B. 67; Sarah J. 157
Angel H.N. 167
Applebaugh 19; Wm. R. 25, 88
Appleton James R. iv; Jas. R. 96
Armstrong James D. 88; Matthew 90
Arnold Rebecca 99; Sarah C. 130
Artherton Allen 41
Arthur Duncan M. 132; Harriet 49; Harriet F. 67
Asbury Elsa B. 80; Francis S. 80; Hugh I. 80
Ashbaugh Frederick 4; Matilda 4; Oliver Marion 4; Orrilla Mirium 4
Atchison Davy 171
Augenstein Ernestine 80
Augenstine Charles 95
Auginbaugh John 9
Augustine Christina 199
Ault 49, 173; H.M. 51; J. 68; John 196
Austin Oliver R. 138; Sylvester 48

B

Bacon Ezekiel 116; Perry C. 49
Bain 10, 19, 80; Charlotte 4; J.W. 71, 78, 109, 190; John, Jr. 71; John W. 57, 141, 153, 184; Julia 141, 149; Mary 190; William 58, 103, 149; Wm. 7
Baines R. 49
Baker 82; A.N. 2; Allen D. 37; Artemas N. 197; Benjamin 37, 44, 47, 191; C.E. 179; Carlos 174; Daniel 192; E. 179; Ebenezer 174; Eber 7, 25, 133, 141; Eliza 35; Elizabeth 22, 37; Ellmore C. 22; H.W. 2, 22; Henry Ellis 22; Horace W. 22, 50; Isabella 62; Jacob 62, 155; Julius 175, 183, 189; Julius C. 182; Louisa J. 102; Lydia 25; Lydia Amanda 104; Mary Anna 184; Mary E. 197; Mary H. 151; Matilda 197; Mindwell 5; Nancy Jane 48; Oscar 45; Rachel E. 125; William 166; William M. 38
Baldwin T. 49
Ball Allen 16
Ballantine George 154
Ballentine John 38; Saml. R. 82
Balloon 63, 146, 186
Banning Sophia E. 123
Bardott B. 79
Bare Adam 70
Barker 50, 87; J.H. 88, 199; James 85; James H. 87; William 199
Barnet George 25
Barnett Calvin 107; Louisa 61; Mahala 107; Mariah 55; William O. 29
Barnhart 87; Catherine 111; Elizabeth 122; J. 35, 115; Martin V.B. 151; Susan E. 87
Barnum P.T. 65
Barr Edward 138
Bartley Thomas W. 137
Barton E. 169
Bartram 117, 159; Ezra G.G. 155; J. 86; J.W. 76; John 7; John W. 52; Mary Jane 34; Sarah 49
Bartrum John 152

Batch J.S. 47; Joshua S. 38
Bates 179; Dexter S. 58; Lydia 62; S.D. 139
Bauckins Lucy E. 175
Bay Ruth 18; Thomas 2
Bean D.J. iv, 37; Dabney Jackson 72; James M. 40; M.P. 19, 35; Ursula L. 35
Beaver Abraham 43
Bechtel Mary 70
Beckley 113; John 133
Beckman Joseph 38
Beebe James R. 34
Beede Phebe Jane 67
Beerbower Harriet V. 104; Samuel 76
Beesley J. 49
Bell Charlotte 109; Eveline 190; Hiram 49; Sarah L. 183; Susan B. 101
Bender T. 49
Bending Andrew 101; Lutitia 101
Bennet 74
Bennett Harriet A. 18; Julius 60; S.S. 7, 154
Berger Catharine 48; Samantha 62
Bering Jacob 80
Berry Calvin 70; Charles 74; Cynthia 108; Harman 55; John 39; John C. 178; Martin 99; Samuel 39
Bevis William F. 179
Bible Society 28
Bierce Yankee 107
Biggerstaff 170; F. 134; Nancy 32; Samuel 3; W. 151; Wm. 62
Biggs Helen Adeline 60; James M. 60; Sarah J. 60
Birk George 192
Bishop 174
Bivens John 157
Blackford John R. 49
Bleil Frederick W. 177
Blocksom Martha 25; Samuel 49
Bloxum Margaret 125
Blynn Newton 195
Bodeman C.A. 62
Bolander John 62; Samuel 66
Bolton Elizabeth A. 43; James 28
Bonaparte Napoleon 82

Booth 79; Barbara B. 116; D.J. 80; Jacob 30

Bossler Marcus 49

Bounds Julian 39

Bowden Hannah 79

Bowdish E. 136; Elijah 68, 156; Henry 160; R.C. 68, 102; Samuel 48; Sarah 156; Sarah E. 43

Bowe Edwin R. 55

Bowen 176, 198; Elizabeth 99; James 115; John 99, 131; L.D. 179; Lydia 8, 25; M. 179; O. 126, 154, 185, 197, 199; Olias 31; Ozias 8, 25; Platt Ralston Spencer 8; T.C. 185

Bower Adam 94; Maria S. 125

Bowers David J. 153; G.W. 39; Hellen 94

Bowes Maria J. 21

Boyce 186

Boyd Isabella M. 105; J.J. 146; J.W. 7, 105, 195; Joseph, Sen. 2, 21; M.E. 92; Susan C. 171

Boyer Jacob 166

Brady A.D. 80; Betsy 155; C. 133, 154; David 49, 133; J. 39; Lavina 50; Martin V. 155; Nancy J. 144; Willaim W. 49; William 133

Bratton John 108; Rachel 49

Breman W. 49

Breslin 198

Bretz A.D. 143; David S. 168

Brewer Emery 38

Brice A.B. 101; Wm. K. 28

Bricker J.D. 100

Bridge 36, 68, 121, 187, 194, 199; P.M. 155; Rachel 36; W.D. 155; W.W. 102, 155, 195

Briggle Christina 194

Brill 95

Brinkerhoff Jacob 137

Britton 169; Dewit C. 47; Sarah D. 152

Brockelsby 179; Ann 191; John 178

Brocklesby Bettie Thew 188; John 192

Brooks 117

Brorkin Gebhard 139

Brown A.H. 34, 118; Abigail M. 21; Albert 19; Bellona 34; C.W. 60, 162; Charles W. 111; James Wesley 111; John 171, 172, 174; Mary 177; Minerva 14; Sarah J. 111; Wm. 3, 7

Brownlee Archibald 10; James 5; Jane L. 10; Ruth 5; William 133

Bruce Theodore 109

Bruck 149, 188; David T. 151

Bryant C. 188; Lucinda Jane 188

Buchanan 103, 104

Buck J. 49

Buckingham Elizabeth 23

Buffington O. 22

Bunker 43, 88, 123, 135; Ella Imogene 21; Hannah 71; Justin H. 122; P. 7, 21, 119, 126, 133; Peleg 59, 61, 71, 86; R.H. 21

Bunn 39

Bunnel Christene 34

Burgess John 24

Burgis A.M. 24

Burnham James F. 87

Burnison James 29; Samuel 49

Burns Nathan 53

Burr E. 32; George Griswold 32; H.G. 32

Burt Eliza Jane 177

Burtsfield Catherine 161; John 23

Busby Eliza 10; Eveline 10; G.H. 7, 14, 63, 134, 152; George H. 10; H. 16; Jane E. 16; Lucretia 81; Paulina E. 14; Susan 124

Bush David 166

Bushey Mary Ann 44

Bussy Geo. H. 133

Butler 136; C.A. 131; J.D. 7; Joel D. 136; Mary M. 26; Pardee 93; Thomas 26; Wm. A. 62

Byers Elizabeth 104

C

Cade John J. 162, 195

Cadwalader Edward J. 48

Caig Joseph 64

Caldwell 184

Calhoun 122

California 35, 36, 39, 42, 44, 45, 47, 50, 52, 53, 55, 65

Calvert James 49

Cameron 174; R.R. 122

Camp Benjamin S. 63; John M. 176; M.M. 44

Campbell Andrew Jackson 110; F. 184; George W. 18; Margaret Jane 108; Sarah E. 160; Thomas Jefferson 110

Canderbeck 11

Canouse Harvey 190; Maria 190

Cardiff John 138

Carey 3; J.W. 49; Wm. 158

Carney C. 49

Carouthers W.B. 192

Carpenter Alonzo 35; J.B. 101; J.H. 161; James H. 36; John 192

Carr 186; Elizabeth 53; Margaret 14; Robert 53, 184

Carson Anna J. 149

Carter J.A. 170; James 174; John A. 174; Mary 174; Thomas H. 196

Case Eliza Ann 60

Cassels J. Lang 118

Catholics 79

Cemetery 5, 55, 68, 97, 115, 122, 132, 134, 135, 143, 146, 147, 150, 183

Census 42, 52, 59, 71, 106

Chambers John 39; Violet 45

Chard Jas. 49

Chase Timothy 109

Cherry C.W. 49, 67; Theresa 67

Chesney William M. 43

Chew Jno. 137, 138

Cholera. *See* Disease

Christ 141

Christian 118, 121; Geo. 179; Johannes 50; John M. 14

Christman N. 172

Christmas 153

Christy A. 49

Church 194

Circus 65, 136

Civil War 195, 199

Clark 41, 79; B.F. 27, 64; Caroline 94; E.H. 46; Ellen 36; Enoch 48; Garry 112; George Eldon 93; Isaac B. 45; James 119, 179; John F. 2; John G. 20; Juliet C. 49; Laura E. 183; Lydia 93; Martha M. 190; Milton 80; Nancy A. 113; Ollie 189; R.O. 62; Rebecca Ann 62; Riley 62; Rufus 73; Sarah 94; T.D. 168; William 93; Wm. 190

Clay 2; Ann 29; James C. 182

Cleveland Kingsley 49

Clingenpeel Harvey 116

Clingerman Horatio 175

Cluff Ammi 95

Cochran M.B. 70; R.H. 45

Coffee Jacob 138

Coffey 116

Coffier Christina 73

Eavley Frederick 66
Edmons Susan L. 94
Ehlers John 125
Elder Ann 34
Eleatt Susan C. 88
Elling George 80
Elliott Alexander 20; Autumn iii; Caroline E. 20; D.W. 59, 62; David iii; Roger iii; Vera iii
Ellis L.F. 62
Elwell Thomas 5
Emerson 117
Emery J.C. 152
Emmons Caroline 139
Engleman J.W. 110
Ensminger D. 60; Sarah E. 60
Epler 33, 169, 175, 176; David 7, 19, 35, 170, 175; Louisa 107; Margaret 96; Ursula L. 19, 35
Epley Adam 44; S.H. 192; Samuel 192; Solomon 192; Solomon D. 90
Erkeman 173
Essex Angeline 104; Elizabeth Ann 67; Martha 51
Eustice Daniel 31
Evans 151; Joel M. 29
Everett William 2, 5
Ewings Robt. 80

F

Fahey 181, 195; T. 159, 180, 192; Timothy 138
Fair 74, 103, 121, 143, 144, 168, 179
Farnam F. 134
Farnham Emily 100
Farnum Erastus 94
Farnus E. 134
Farout Cyntha 191
Fashion 54, 55, 56, 89, 120, 150
Fauke Jane Amanda 67
Fauroat Hannah 178; William 176
Fellows J. 49
Fenzell Louisa 9
Ferris Elijah L. 23
Fickel Cordelia 169
Fickle Louisa 14; Sarah 46
Fillmore Millard 32
Finney Cyrus M. 183
Fire 13, 32, 41, 66, 67, 88, 89, 95, 108, 111, 124, 140, 151, 152, 159, 160, 161, 178, 179, 180, 181, 183
Fischer 138
Fish 96; Hannah 69, 96; Hannah C. 173; Ruby S. 86; Samuel 69,

96, 173; Samuel F. 69; Susan Emily 39; William N. 29
Fisher 63, 66, 74, 165, 168, 181; Ann Eliza 165; Silas Bennett 165; T.B. 29, 32, 61, 97, 134, 167, 170; T.R. 7; William 165; Wm. 39, 165, 166
Fisk A.D. 84
Fite 196
Flaherty A. 194; Anthony 193
Fletcher A.C. 190; J. 49; James 192; John 49; Lafayette 191
Flood 20, 21
Fluelling Susan 185
Folk Martha 116
Ford James M. 34; Seabury 32
Foreman George 66; Malinda 16
Forrest Edwin 58
Fosher Ann 63
Foster G. 186; J.H. 104
Fouke J.E. 154; Joanna 194; Jos. F. 187
Fowler Aceniah 176
Frame S. 182
Francis C. 196; Mary Alice 196; P.K. 196
Franklin 176; George F. 104
Frederick John, Jr. 10; Mary 10
Free Eva Elizabeth 62
Freeman Daniel F. 32; Fannie J. 177; John 111; Samuel C. 177
Freese Fred 138; Frederick S. 158
Frelinghuysen 2
French 181; J. 180
Fribley Elizabeth 87; J. 179
Fries John 20
Friesinger Andrew 138
Frost 103
Fulkerson E. Janny 67
Fuller D.T. 2; William 88

G

Gaberson John 64; Rosanna 64
Gaffield Anna 8
Galley 64
Galphinism 66
Gantzhom Jno. 138
Garberson John R. 158
Garrett W. 180
Garrison Emeline 153; Sarah Jane 182
Gast 179; George 177
Gauser John 179
Geiger Ann 167; Sarah E. 115

German Oscar D. 168
Germans 50, 92, 98
Ghosts 110, 111
Gibson 198
Gillespie 175; Ellenor 12; Evan 9; Noah 25, 145
Gillett 167
Gillis Samuel 49
Gillit John M. 49
Gilmer Emily 40
Gilson 166
Godman 88, 130; Ann Eliza 12; Ann S. 9, 12; H.C. 187, 196; Hannah 45; Henry C. 66; J.H. 152, 176, 196; James H. 9, 12; James Mortimer 9; Jas. H. 7, 45, 126; John C. 7; Joseph 49; Kate 187; William 49; Willie G. 187
Gold 35, 36, 39, 42, 44, 45, 47, 52
Goodell A.L. 71
Goodhue H.P. 176
Gooding C. 134; Christopher C. 22; J. 134; Mary E. 70; Rosylla A. 94; S. 134; Sylvester 2; Sylvester R. 190; W.R. 175
Gorton 49, 165; Alfe 57; Eva G. 146; H. 2, 132, 134; Hezekiah 57; J.W. 138; Mary C. 51; Olive 57; Philander 53
Gottshal Maria 66
Gracely 161; Sophia 139
Grafton Mary E. 144; Samuel 57, 63
Graham 70; Mariah W. 30; Martha 87
Granger Henry 45
Grapes Catherine 73; Lucinda 43
Grassley Caroline 27
Graves Mary 50; Mary Jane 58
Graveyard. See Cemetery
Gray 181, 189; Celeslia E. 173; David 153; James P. 19; R. 180; Sarah E. 24
Greek D.H. 191; Elizabeth A. 150
Green S.R. 177; Seth 176
Gregory 65; J. 49
Grey 183; James P. 43
Griffith 76, 195
Grigsby Trenton C. 171
Grimm 117
Griswold 16, 23, 102; Caroline M. 11; Ezra 25; Martin 49; Matilda O.M. 11; Ruth 25; S.A. iv, 2, 24, 38, 41, 50, 67, 94, 135, 157; V.M. 31; Victor M. 11
Gruber Elizabeth 20

Gruner Elizabeth 96
Gumpf George 49
Gunn James 174; Lewis 69; Louis 99; Mahala 12
Gurley 178; John 19, 102; Kate 79; L.B. 53
Gustin Jno. A. 137, 138
Guthrey 170

H

Hadsly Jacob 73
Hahn Charles 22
Hain Adam 63; Henry 7, 170; Mary M. 3; Samuel 50; Susan 29; Wm. N. 179
Haine Adaline 161
Haines Leah 50
Haldeman 45, 51; C. 2; Harriet 84; Henry iv, 45, 63, 67, 84; I. 82; Isaac 45, 69, 84; J. 49; John 54; L. 76; Levi Olmsted 76; Loretta M. 41; M.A. 76; Mariah 45; Rachel 54; Susan 104
Halden 185
Halderman Narcissus 177
Hale 179
Hall Frederick 174; Julia 57
Haltbill A.B. 77
Hamler Samuel 49
Hamlin 185; John 28
Hanby E. 50
Hanse Maria W. 25; Samuel 25
Harding Emily K. 95; H.H. 90, 95
Hardy 120, 159; E. 154; E.F. 7; Harvey 156; John 71; Joseph T. 31; Kate 56, 155, 156; Laura Elizabeth 56; Phebe 76; Phebe D. 71; Sarah G. 71; W.E. 161; W.H. 31; W.M. 56, 155, 156; William Harper 155
Hare William 95
Harmon Bertha 106; Caroline 106; Henry 106; John 160
Harper Maria 94
Harrigan Michael 110
Harriman Charles 139; David 139; Lafayette 194
Harrington 195
Harrison Maggie 150
Harsh Adam 24
Harshberger 149; Jacob 77, 105, 153; Margaret 105
Hart Eliza Ann 167
Hartzell Jonas 38

Harvey 175, 189; D.H. 168, 193; James M. 86; Mary 164; Mary Frances 164; Paul G. 160; T. 168; William F. 164
Hatch Edward D. 71
Hatfield Ann 53; Harriet C. 125
Hattan James 15
Havens James 34
Hawk John A. 150
Hawkins Christena 162
Haxter Wallace 38
Haynes J.B.W. 113
Heald 151
Heartman Samuel 50
Heenan John C. 193
Heese William 27
Hefner J. 182
Heiner 188
Heisler Letitia M. 82
Heller Emerson 177; Hannah 177; J.M. 177; Mary 177
Helwick Jane 34
Henderson 95; Margaret 26; Thomas 26, 149; Thomas S. 177; Wm. M. 126
Henkle Philip 41
Henry Peter J. 50
Herbert Benjamin 27; Margaret 27; Sarah Ann 27
Herrick Elijah 69; Sarah 69
Herriman 192
Hess John 14
Hiett R.J. 143
Higgins Cordelia 70; Joseph 5; Mary 90; Rachel 123; Waterman 91; Watrman H. 49
High 176; Charles 173
Hiles M. 190
Hill Nancy E. 98; Wm. 197
Hilliard 36
Hills Chauncey 27
Himmelreich Frederica 66
Hinaman Frederick 45; J. 161
Hind 54
Hipsher Adam 133; Mary A. 185
Hitchcock 65
Hite Elizabeth 39
Hodder 163; T.H. 186, 196, 197; Thomas 198
Hoddy Ethelinda 45; Monroe 91
Hodeman 84
Hoes Barney 157
Hoffman Jacob F. 10; John 10
Holderman John 10
Holler Kate 84

Holloway 58; G. 134; Geo. 74; James 74
Holly G.W. 119; Nancy 118, 122, 126, 130, 133, 136, 146
Holm 177; Sarah M. 176
Holmes 82; Anna Elizabeth 171; Benjamin F. 105; Charles 82; R.B. 125; S.W. 60; Susan E. 35; William, Jr. 2
Holverstot 66; Jacob 80
Holverstott Jacob T. 189; Mary Ann 124
Homes Eliza W. 87; Samuel 87; Susan E. 87
Honecker J. 154
Hook Catherine 180
Hooker Charles 57
Hoover Mary 62
Hopkins Archibald 70; John F. 62; Nancy J. 182; Robert 182; Robert, Jr. 84
Hord N.G. 79; Paten 151
Hornby 168; Mary 175
Horrgan Thomas 138
House Mary Jane 11
Houseworth Rachael 27
Howard C. 157; E. 190; H. 24; James M. 149
Howison Haywood 184
Hoxter 179; Frederick 60; M.P. 167; Samuel 110; Wallace 120; Wallser 66
Hoxtor Sarah Jane 58
Hudson John 124
Huffman Prudence 74
Huggins John 32; Laura 59; Nancy J. 76; Simon 59, 167; Susan 59
Hughes Elizabeth 168; Jane T. 44; John 120, 168; Wm. R. 77
Hughey Alexander 29
Hull E.T. 57; George W. 5; Martha 99; N. 99; William 43
Hulster Henry L. Rudolph 139
Hume 86, 181; J.F. 119, 126, 133
Humphrey Jane 29
Humphries Elizabeth 171
Hunter 179
Hurd 69
Hussey B. 138
Hutchason Martha J. 154
Huttler Jacob 66
Hutton Louisa M. 169

I

Ideman J. 134
Idle Fredrie 50
Idleman 20, 21, 175; C. 2; Jacob 20; Jacob J. 175; Margaret 177; Samantha 175; Silas 81
Imbody Wilson 108
Indians 47
Infirmary 160, 162, 185, 191
Ireland 21, 22, 31
Irey Charles Hamilton 30; Enos 7; Israel 125; Samuel 30
Irvine 95, 96

J

Jackson 176
Jacobee 73
Jacoby 155; M. 122
Jail 33, 56, 182
James Aviah 25; Betsy 66; Emma 103; Isaac E. 66; Martin V.H. 66; Susannah 25; William H. 107
Jameson 149, 167; David 34, 84, 154; Elizabeth 34; Mary 34, 154
Jamison David 172; Lewy Adolphus 172; Mary W. 172
Jeffery 60
Jeffries 113
Jerolaman N. 104
Johnes Horace P. 197
Johns J.G. 100
Johnson 35, 86, 87, 192, 195; A.P. 92, 94; Dorcas 35; Eliza M. 183; Emma V. 151; Georgiett 121; Hezakiah 14; J. 186; J.C. 102; Jane 199; Margaret L. 66; Maria 44; Mary P. 124; McMurray 156; O.J. 85, 142; R. 167; Richard H. 16; S.L. 151; Sarah Jane 36; Thomas 76; William G. 106; Wm. C. 85
Johnston James H. 154; John H. 104
Jolley E. 4, 5
Jones 41, 69, 121, 160, 178, 191; A.M. 50; Becca M. 91; David S. 180; Elizabeth 31; Harriet 91, 99; Isaiah C. 161; Jacob 29; Lydia C. 14; Sampson 121; Samuel 94; Sarah Jane 66
Jump Elizabeth 74; H. 179; Joanna 95; Shelby 74
Jurey Abner 50; John 50
Justice Martha 19

K

Kagg Jos. 12
Kastner Christiana 41
Keese Samuel 39
Kellam Annie Elizabeth 108; J.A. 95, 108; Martha J. 108
Keller John 80
Kelley Alfred 3; Frances Sina 14
Kelly 168; Adaline 52; Elizabeth 190; Henry 70; Patrick 138, 157, 158
Kemmerel Solomon 185
Kendrick William L. 77; Wm. L. 7
Kenechel Mary 184
Kennedy Agnes J. 83; Christena 23; Hiram C. 134
Kent B. 146
Kepler Abraham H. 153
Kepner Nicholas 44
Kerner Andrew 26
Kerns Benjamin 31; Sarah 31
Kerr Elizabeth 2; Thomas 94
Ketcham 109
Kibben 18
Kilbourn Emily 90, 95; I. 95
Kilbourne 134
Kimmell George 133
King George 19, 70, 105; Harriet C. 80; Nancy F. 19; Samuel H. 47
Kingman Matilda 53
Kinnear 74, 76; W.E. 102
Kirby John 133; Moses 133
Kirch Frederika 194
Kirts Daniel 190
Kise Jacob 104
Kistler Martin 194
Kleinguenther 82
Kline A.H. 169
Klinefelter Henry 179; Mariah 179
Klineknicht Catherine 80
Klinfelter Jacob 125
Knable H. 188
Knapp 65, 68; Calvin W. 40; J.R. 7, 72; J.R., Jr. 187; John 78; John R. 87, 112, 155; John R., Jr. 87, 97; John R., Sen. 38; Orson N. 108; R.A. 12, 14
Konkle Frances V. 40
Koons Cornelius 94; Hiram A. 183
Kopler Edward 37
Kraner Anches 33; John 25, 80; John, Jr. 85; William 33
Krause Daniel E. 167; Emma Louise 167; Sarah 167

L

Lacy Henry L. 199
Lake Anna H. 5
Lakin John Q. 2
Lambett Robert 2
Landon Sarah E. 199
Lane Harriet G. 162
Lanier Elizabeth 180
Lapham Arthur 39; Cynthia 38
Larabee James H. 133
Larcomb Moses 20
Larue Wm. 50
Lasar 63
Lassar 62; Henry S. 61
Latham H.B. 103
Lauer B. 186
Laughry John 50
Lavennfire Levi J. 183
Law Mary 88; Samuel 60, 88
Lawrence 126, 127, 130, 136, 146, 158; George 70; R. 143; Richard 36
Layton Richard C. 46
Leach Alva 32
Learnhard George 199
Leatherberry 59; Ann E. 107; N.M. 20
Lee Benjamin F. 76; J. 151; J.C. 196; Jacob 28, 122; Martin 80; P. 157; Sarah Ann 80
Leeper Samuel 180
Lefevre John E. 153
Leffingwell Hannah 24
Lehner Christian 80
Leonard 149, 177, 188; J.E. 196; John F. 153
Lerch Morvin 23
Lesnet Lafayette 45
Lewis 117, 119, 146, 162, 169, 175, 176, 182; Ann 191; Charles 133; Electe L. 5; Jessie F. 191; John 163; Julia Ann 100; L.P. 125; Mary 163; Porter 100; W.B. 170; Wm. B. 191
Lichtenberger Hannah 73
Lidgard Johnson 53
Likens California 33; James 33, 50
Lincoln 185, 191, 197; Abe 193; M.A. 197
Lind G.W. 96; George W. 65; Mary Ann 96
Lindsay Jane 131

Lindsey 149; E.D. 116, 173; Elder 72; Elder D. 34; Mary A. 173; Sarah R. 177
Lingral Mathew 51
Linn Joseph 130; R.L. 194
Linton James 130
Little 73; B. 170; Eliza W. 18; Elizabeth W. 18; John T. 167; Leonard 50; Lyman 85; Rodolphus 85; William 18
Littleton Almira 50
Livenspire Eliza J. 157
Lloyd David 195
Lobrich Philip 11
Lockwood 70; A.P. 28, 34
Loebrich P. 180
Long John 96
Longacre J.E. 190
Loren William 26
Lowe Daniel 91; Isaiah 91, 130
Loyd David 194
Lucas 161, 196; Catharine 11; Catherine 197
Luellen Sarah J. 125
Lugenbeel 13; William 13
Luke Mary S. 146; Sarah J. 192
Lumbert Robert F. 27, 33; Sarah Ann 27
Lushbaugh Thomas 197
Lutz 183
Lynn Daniel 4; George 85
Lyone Marcy 62

M

Madison A.W. 39; Augustus 73
Magruder T.I. 87; T.J. 183
Mahaffer Samuel 108
Mahon James 101
Maiz Mariah 32
Malone Elizabeth 14; John W. 161
Manahan Aron 44
Manby Thomas 37
Mann 58; C.B. 37, 51, 194
Mansur Samuel 28
March Osten 162
Marion Joshua 4
Marlow Levi 73
Marsh Elizabeth Ann 150; Mahlon 110; Susannah 18
Martin 151; Abel 162; C. 169; Chris. 85; Christopher 73; Elizabeth 39; J. 138; Mary Jane 57; Sarah N. 174; W. 187

Mason Beulah C. 16; J. 66; Jonas H. 125; Joseph 2; Lucinda A. 91; Mary P. 66; Olive P.O. 153
Matthews 118; A.D. 24, 151
May Charlotte 43; John 84; Rolanda 100
Maynard Chas. 39
McAtee Emily O. 18
McBee Sophronia S. 22
McBride Rosana 108
McCafforey James 190
McCan John 50
McClain 161
McClasky Philip 43
McClosky Julia Ann 50
McCoy William 43
McCully James 16
McDanels Julia 197
McFarland Archibald 14
McGaven Hugh C. 25
McGuinnes 104
McGuire Thomas 116
McIntire Eliza M. 31
McIntyre Mattie M.W. 115
McKelvy Martha 62; Nancy 34
McKibbin James 26, 30; Mary M. 26
McKinstry 179
McLean 145
McLellen Harriet O. 199
McMann Anna 82
McNab Peter 79
McNeal Allen 4; Ann 62; Belinda 66; Roxy 77; Samuel A. 70
McNeil Margaret 174
McNulty C.J. 16
McPherrin Nancy 110; Samuel 26
McPherson 63, 152; David 110
McRill Hezekiah 190
McWherter 32; Almira 55; Annette C. 138; Elizabeth 40; Julia Ann 43; William H. 96
McWilliams Elizabeth 57; F.G. 57; G. 122; Gordon 156; James 44, 82, 87; Maryann 82; Pauline 57
McWright A. 18; Petnanda E. 18
Mears George N. 36; Sarah J. 125
Medey Wm. 196
Meeks B.V. 136
Mehhefey Robert 85
Meinger Charles P. 167
Meisser Emil Harmon 160
Meliger Isaac 50
Mergenhaler John 80
Merriman Charles 43; George 21; Rachel 43; Wm. B. 173

Merritt Sarah J. 16
Mesick Maria C. 63
Messenger Antha 20; E. 151, 154, 193, 199; Everett 151; Henry H. 143; Lucy A. 155; Newton 155; Riverius 133
Metcalf 98
Metts 166
Metz Margaret 157
Metzger Philip 80; Philipine 80
Mexican War 15, 16, 19, 22, 30, 31
Miles Cyril G. 183
Miley Mary Ann 65; William, Sr. 60
Milker John W. 48
Miller 45; Charles F. 71; Emeline 19; John 50; John W. 44, 48, 53, 77; M., Jr. 138; Martin 130; Martin Jr. 12; Martin, Sr. 158; Mary Jane 121; Merica 43; Princess A. 104; Sarah 69; Sarah J. 170; Sarah M. 44; Thomas 133; William Albert 44; William F. 80; William H. 44
Millikin 180
Milliser Jacob 50
Millizer 188; Hez. 189; Hezekiah 188
Mills Ellie 90; Hiram 5; J.H. 63; Julia 142; Mary Ann 60; Priscilla J. 93; R. 142
Mincinberg Chas. 194
Miner Wm. 50
Mitchel Nelson C. 57
Mitchell N.C. 158; Nelson C. 145; Oliver 177; Wm. 84
Monday Hannah M. 80; Julia A. 66; Thomas 67
Monnet A. 154
Monnett Mary 184
Monroe 196
Moon Ann E. 175
Moore 61, 86, 119, 154; Benjamin 2; Chas. D. 194; David C. 80; Elsa B. 80; Francis S. Asbury 80; Fred iii; Hugh I. 80; Humphrey M. 150; John 38, 85, 160; John Jr. 2; Margaret R. 80; Marguerite iii; Phebe Lucretia 80; Sarah 160; William 74; William H. 103; Wm. H. 100
More W.H. 169
Morgan Harriet 167
Morison Elizabeth 70
Mormons 4, 11, 12, 14, 104, 106
Morral John 50
Morrall Milton 23

Morris Eley 74; John 103; Joseph 75; Stephen 35
Morrow County 30
Morton 21
Moses Job 119; John 162; Marshall W. 88; Reynolds 98
Moulon Emilie 153
Mount Sarah 62
Mounts Mary Ann 7; Rachael 31; Samuel 195
Mouser Abagail 45; Abram 158; Ann 158; David 94; Jacob 166; Louisa 94; Mary E. 158; Perry 131; Silas M. 11; William H. 104; Wm. J. 26
Moyer Louisa 185; Margaret 60
Mugg 96
Munn Elizabetha 108
Muntsinger 173; Henry Joseph 153; Mary 153; Michael 153
Murder 32, 35, 55, 95, 117
Myers 58; Catherine 74; Sarah 62

N

Neel Joseph 12
Neff Abraham 14; Geo. F. 50; Jacob R. 145
Negros 55, 56, 59, 92
Nellans Sarah Ann 84
Newson Sarah 22
Newton E. 192; Isaac 101
Nichols Benjamin 24; Jacob 39; Nathan 22; S.C. 97
Nicholson John 37
Nickols Abner 178
Nimiller Henry 50
Noble 74; Barbary 50; William 13
Norris Carrie E. 114
Northland S.J. 190
Norton Alson 2, 30, 37, 57, 133; J.C. 55; John C. 57; O.P.H. 30; Stephen 57

O

Oborn Joseph R. 111; William 155
O'Donnell 192
Olds Isaac C. 4
Olmsted 165, 181; A.J. 167; E.B. 167, 181
Onselman Nicholas 141
O'Reagan John 192
Orr Sarah 65

Osborn 112
Osborne 163; Addison 116
Otho Frederick 177
Overdier Caroline 12
Owen Catherine 86; Hannah C. 104; L.M. 150; R.E. 190; Sarah E. 131
Owens Emeline C. 25; Hiram 18
Ozenbaugh 166

P

Page M. 165
Palmer Edward L. 171
Palmerton Chancy D. 58
Pangburn Mary B. 144
Parcel Henry 133; Jane M. 42
Parcell John 5
Parnhart Margaret 70
Partridge 152, 169, 182; Charles 192, 194; George 164; Henry 192, 194
Patridge 162; George 159, 163
Patten 154, 174, 185; Asenath 125; Assenath 38; Emery 78; Hosea 85; John 38, 125; Laura 27, 149; Mary 196; Mary Ann 38; Mary C. 38; O. 134; Orren 4, 5, 27, 38; R. 7, 40, 140, 152; Richard 38, 107; Richard LeRoy 107; Susan 38, 107; Thomas 94
Patterson A.H. 36; Billy 73; Eliza Jane 36; Geo. 61; R. Noble 67
Patton A.M. 188; Martha 99; Robert 99
Paxson 53
Paxton 78; W.F. 78
Payne Angeline 70; Charlotte 16; David J. 185; Emeline 144; Sarah Marenda 185; William T. 34
Peak J.D. 101
Pearce 47; Henry F. 44; Isaiah 44
Peckenpaugh Grafton M. 191; M.E.G. 191; S. 144, 175, 191
Pentash Augustus 160
Peters 73; Corilla A. 44; E. 73,134, 152, 154, 186, 196; Eben. 73; Ebenezer 16, 43, 151; Edward 50; Elizabeth L. 43; Ella Margaret 43; H. 44, 119, 153; Harvey 198; Henry 7; Kate Elvira 73; N. 134, 154; Nathan 7; P.H. 44; S. 50
Peterson J. 167; Kate 31; Lewis 31
Petri John 51
Pettet Vincent D. 44

Pettit Benjamin D. 171; D. 154, 193; David 151, 171; J.N. 107; Patsy 171; V.D. 193
Petty Hugh B. 125; John 35
Phelps 179
Phillips 179; P. 189
Piel Caroline 21
Pierce 65, 100, 192; Andrew 159; Asa 74; Elder Asa 74; Filander 162; Phil 185; Philander 174; Simon 174
Pigman 9, 13; Nathaniel 29
Pilcher H.E. 177
Pitman Solomon 42
Pixley Eliza P. 62; M. 184; M.O. 184, 185; Mary P. 36; Olive L. 95
Plumb M.L. 5
Plummer 166
Ponser 166
Pool Eliza 177; J.B. 103; J.D. 50
Porter Charles 18; Eli 77; Jane 192
Postle Eliza J. 96; M.E. 122
Postles George 93
Potter Wm. 125
Powell Henry 182; J. 95; Jane 45; Joseph 4; Martha J. 95; Samuel 50; Thomas W. 4
Powers A. 167
Pratt Hiram 14; Parley P. 104
Prettyman George W. 35
Price Dorliska S. 28
Priest James L. 21; Laura T. 4
Purdy James 3
Purvis Alexander A. 23

Q

Quay James F. 175
Quigley 51

R

Raichley Christopher 85; Elizabeth A. 16; L.F. 190; Louis F. 145; Margaret 183
Railroad 7, 12, 27, 31, 50, 64, 65, 67, 70, 113
Rainey 176
Rammonar 50
Randall Ann 168; Keziah J. 34; Levi H. 56; Lizzie 194; Mattie T. 188; Samantha 46; Sarah A. 165; Sarah J. 60
Ranney A. 112
Rarey W.H. 24

Rawles Oscar 94
Rayle Samuel L. 191
Raymond W.B. 179
Red 44
Redd Jacob G. 37; Nathaniel 180
Redding Elizabeth 53
Redman Michael 19; Priscilla 155
Reed 17, 74, 121, 149; Alfred A. 49; David 71; Franklin L. 18; J.S. 56, 114, 120, 152, 154, 179; James 16, 70; M.C. 85; Maria 184; Samuel 49; Sarah H. 16; Sophronia 71; Zepheriah 49
Reeding Amilla 138
Reese Mary Ann 4; William 188
Reheis 96; John 95, 96
Rehies John 95
Reily Elias 2
Renick Abel 2
Revival 125, 156, 157
Reynolds William 50
Rhoades Geo. 167
Rhoads James C. 196
Rhodes Mary E. 195
Rice Dan 136; John 16; R.S. 169
Richardson Eliza J. 68
Richey 50
Richy Lavina 67
Ridgway Clegget C. 155
Riggle George H. 194
Riley Amanda 74; Benjamin 125; Elias 39; George W. 178; Hiram W. 173; I.N. 191; Lovey Jane 190; W. 82
Ripley Thomas 50
Ritner Racheal S. 77
Roach James E. 190
Road, Plank 50, 68
Roakley John 194
Robbins Edward 118, 122, 125, 126, 130, 133, 135, 136, 137, 138, 146; William 5
Roberts Jane E. 24; Thomson W. 93; Truman H. 86
Robinson Ann 56; James B. 32; Madison 81; Mary 56; Thomas 56; Thomas A. 20
Robison John D. 31; Mary Louisa 31; Susanna 31
Rogers 39
Rollston Joseph 43
Romoser Elizabeth 33
Rosa Willard 31
Rose George W. 60
Rosencrance 189

Rosencrancon Ellen 197
Ross Hugh W. 114
Rouse 184
Rowan T.M. 50
Rowe 39; Elizabeth 43; Geo. 39; George 7, 43
Rubins Helen 5
Ruehrmund 117; F.C. 117; Ferdinand C. 126
Ruhermund F.C. 55; Henry L. 55; Mary 55
Rumbaugh John 68
Rundle A.S. 59; Minerva 57; Niram 57; Nirum C. 14; Princess M. 57
Runyan Alexander C. 38; N.M. 88, 89
Rupely 55
Ruple Jane 50
Rupp George 173; George W. 122
Rush Elijah 130; John B. 2; Rachael 38
Russel Eliza 125
Russell Joseph B. 50; Rosilla 80
Ryan Michael 193; Patrick 193
Ryne Patrick 50

S

Saiter F. 184; Mattie Lee 196; Samuel 60
Salmon Camelia 5
Sanford Elmira 37; Henrietta 37
Santa Anna 22
Sapington Narcissa 76
Sargeant Deborah 5; James 5; Ruth 5
Sargent Francis M. 142
Saylor Henry 77
Scheble Joseph 16
Schneider John 185
School 61, 83, 116, 123, 132, 134, 140, 165, 167, 179, 181
Schooner Maglier 50
Schultz Mary 80
Scofield William 114
Scott 65; D. 196; Dred 108; Mary E. 34
Scribner Artamissa 5; Eliza 71; Elmira 192; H.H. 38; Martha 48; S. 2; Samuel 38, 192; Wm. H. 150
Search 5, 77, 142; Hannah 45; T., Jr. 116; Thomas 45; Thomas, Jr. 15; Thos., Sen. 7

Sears Adam 40; Julia Ann 40; Rebecca 40
Seater Margaret 144
Sefner 161, 196
Seibert Cy. 113; John 2, 7
Seibold 151
Seiples Lucetta 156
Seitz A. 10
Selman J. 7
Sexton Mary Ann 91
Seymour 188; Ann 84; Geo. 84; Hanford 188
Shaffer Barney 74
Sharitt Joe 100
Sharp Alexander 101, 102; Mary 199
Sharpless Ann 33, 34; Benjamin 66; Corilla P. 33; E. 154; Edward 33, 34; Marietta E. 34; Matilda C. 15; P.O. 115; Paul 34, 36
Sharrock Benjamin 133
Shaw Margaret 10
Shawn N.A. 192
Shefts G.H. 34
Shepherd I.N. 91
Sherford J.M. 192
Sherman Adam 41, 44; C.M. 182; Mary 50
Sherwood 194
Shewey Caroline 100
Shields 179
Shipley Carrie 167
Shoots B.F. 166; Eleanor 23; Landy 154
Shorn Alexander 175
Short M.E. 77; Martha A. 71
Shoub 151
Showers Helen 188; Susan 188
Shrigley Samuel 157
Shriner Emily Jane 28
Shrock Adam 25
Shrung A. 152; G. 152
Shunk Jane L. 10; John 23; Margaret Ellen 23; Rebecca 23; William 10
Sickle Columbus 185
Siebert John 159
Siler Jacob 12, 64
Silverthorn Thomas 36
Simms Alcinda 37
Simpson William 156
Sims A. 188
Sinclair 58
Sinderman Martha J. 25
Skinner Henry 40; Mary Ann 40
Slavery 2, 4, 82, 93, 108, 152

Slick 176
Sligerman M. 50
Sloan 90; Amanda S. 28; T.M. 8, 62; William 58
Slyter Polly 23
Smith 36, 163; Abby 69; Abraham 154; C. 151; C.B. 98, 159; Catherine J. 110; Charles 2, 58, 69; Charles W. 110; Fanny 110; G.B. 173; Geo. B. 8; George 73; Hannah 29; Henry 187; Hugh V. 5; Hyrum 4; J.L. 168; Jo 4; John 39, 85, 86, 87, 89, 93, 122; Jonathan 152; Lewis 37; Magdalena 155; Martha A. 70; Martha C. 115; Mary Ann 5; Mary C. 197, 199; Mary Elizabeth 110; Mary Florence 69; Noah 67; Robert 50, 73; Samuel 48; Samuel C. 155; Sarah 50; Thomas W. 41; W. 106
Snell Betsy 18
Snider 187
Snyder 114; Christian J. 50; Elizabeth 166; Hannah 96; Jacob 50; John 22; Samuel 161
Sordon John 125
Sorrick David 65
Sosey Emeline C. 34; J. 167; Joseph 34; Laura Ann 34
Southwick Araminta 60; Arnold 94; Electa 20; Pernina J. 142; Russell 197
Spalding Luella Helen 31; Princess 31; Rodney 31, 60
Spangler Nancy 35
Sparks 169; John 141
Spaulding Lyman 67
Spencer Calvin 113
Spirit Rappers 61
Spooner 185
Sprague Elisha D. 35; Mary Maria 91; Satina 18; Thos. J. 9
Sprung George W. 14
Squibb Mariah 178
St. John Dubois 53
Stafford 50
Stagg Abraham 150
Stailey Nancy 88
Staly Caroline E. 73
Stanton George R. 99
Staulding Helen May 32
Stayner John W. 157
Stecher Magdalina 51
Stephens Henry R. 50
Stephenson Eliza 104

Stepman Mary Jane 35
Stevenson William 21
Steverson Elizabeth 21
Stiverson Mariah 10
Stockton 123; William K. 121
Stokes 149; J. 179
Stone O.R. 24, 38, 59, 67
Stoneberger Sarah 69
Storner Helena 55
Story Nehemiah 133
Stout Martha P. 57
Stratton Issac 27
Straw 50; Robert 182
Strawbridge Jos. M. 26; Susannah R. 26
Strawser John 124; Sarah Ann 41
Strelitz J. 182
Strine Catharine 195; Jacob 108
Stroble Rebeca Jane 65
Strode 162, 164, 169, 182; George 163
Stroub Andrew 125
Strowbridge J.M. 73
Stull Matthew 69
Sturges G.B. 124; George B. 57
Sturgis George B. 113
Suicide 31, 33, 87, 115
Sullivan Eliza J. 70; Phama 178
Sult Daniel 28; Susan 180
Sumerkott John 43
Summerlot John 39
Sutherland R. 50
Sutly Angeline 45
Sutton D.D. 82
Swan Joseph R. 137
Sweeney 154, 160
Sweitzer Maria 190
Sweney 63, 118; R.L. 66
Swigart John 28
Swinerton Wm. B. 133
Swisheim 56
Swisher A.R. 188
Swordon Clarissa J. 91

T

Taney 108
Taverner 78; Noble R. 91
Taylor Amanda 67; Amos 174; Davis 115; James 132, 133, 134; Victor J. 144; William 18; Zachary 32
Tehl Anna M. 80
Telegraph 26
Temperance 4, 12, 61, 77, 83, 101

Terpany Phebe 39; Samuel 39, 46
Terrill Forrilla 16; Hiram 2
Terry Mary P. 66
Tharp 118; Jane 153; Maranda A. 125
Thatcher Cyntha Ann 182; Jane 115
Thew Ellen Mary 32; Joseph 32; Mary S. 32; Parkinson B. 53; Timothy T. 35; W.P. 77; William 151
Thomas 185; B.C. 2; Barbara R. 30; Elizabeth 81; W.H. 175
Thomhson Jane 47
Thompkins Thomas 153
Thompson 65, 151, 194; Edmon 62; Elija W. 175; Franklin W. 62; Isabella 66; J.M.C. 194; Lydia 62; Sarah Jane 37; Tabitha Jane 28; Thomas W. 192; William M. 157
Thumb Tom 65
Thurlow Ruth 57
Tillotson 8
Toben Willaim T. 25
Tooly Hannah 3
Topping Benj. R. 39
Townsend Lydia 18
Travenner A. 151
Travis Mary 34
Trimble 45, 63; J.B. 176; L.M. 63; Lewis 121, 173; W.C. 63, 79; William C. 41, 67; Wm. C. iv, 63
True H.A. 16, 28; Henry A. 3, 57
Tuck A.M. 157
Tunis Josiah 50; Mary J. 153
Turner J.N. 50
Turney Gertrude Jane 143; Joseph 190; Margaret 190; W.A. 20, 103, 107
Tweddle John 91
Tyler 66, 186

U

Uhl Wm. J. 50
Ullman J. 196; Joseph 19
Ulsh Isaac 44, 47; Isaac W. 99; Jacob 20, 99; John 60; Samuel 33
Uncapher 168; Geo. 162; George 65; John 65; Joseph 161; Mary 56; Priscilla 191; Solomon 26
Underwood 167, 179; Joseph 41; Mary M. 190; Sarah 71; William 100
Ush John 35